CW01022002

GEORGE HARRISON
SOUL MAN

GEORGE HARRISON
SOUL MAN

John Blaney

Paper Jukebox

CONTENTS

ACKNOWLEDGEMENTS

I would like to thank all the journalists, broadcasters and disc jockeys who were privileged enough to interview George Harrison. Without them much of the original source material used in this book would not exist. I would also like to thank all the fans who have collected audio and video material and shared it with such impunity and enthusiasm via the world wide web. In particular, I would like to thank Peter Black, who very kindly shared some naughty recordings from his collection with me.

I would also like to thank Andrew Marshall for the loan of his eyes and for proofreading the first draft of this book.

The enthusiasm and support shown by family and friends has, as ever, been much appreciated.

In particular, I would like to thank George Harrison for the music and for guiding me to a more enlightened place. His words of wisdom were always there, but it took the process of writing this book to bring them into focus.

Om shanti shanti shanti

INTRODUCTION

George Harrison; the Quiet One. This oft quoted piece of journalistic shorthand stuck fast and hard and is the default stereotype that's still used to describe him to this day. It's an image that's been perpetrated and disseminated as much by The Beatles' own marketing machine as by the press that first coined it. But he was never the quiet one. Listen to the early radio interviews, watch the television appearances, the press conferences, he always had something clever, witty, cutting and insightful to say.

George Harrison; the Thinker might have been a better epithet. He did a great deal of thinking, sometimes he'd think about thinking, and that's philosophy, isn't it? He was a seeker after truth. He spent his entire life searching for the Truth; pondering questions that have occupied mankind for millennia. The big questions. What is life? What is love? What is God? He was also a teacher who liked to share his knowledge with the world. He did it one on one and he did it through his songs, planting seeds in the minds of those willing to listen and think for themselves.

In a way this book is about what he thought. Or rather it's about what I think he thought. I have no way of knowing what he really thought. Only he knew that, and thankfully he shared his thoughts in interviews and in his book *I Me Mine*. But gaps remain. Hopefully this book goes some way to filling them. But nobody knows how many holes it takes to fill the Albert Hall, and even if that wasn't written by Harrison, it could have been.

When I started this book, I thought I knew quite a lot about George Harrison. I'd heard his songs, but never really listened to what it was he was saying. To do that, I had to immerse myself in his music. Until I did that, I was, not to put too fine a point on it, ignorant. I should have known better because Harrison wanted to enlighten me, he wanted to enlighten everyone. All anybody had to do was listen. I mean really listen. Is that so hard?

In the three years I've spent researching and writing this book, I've learnt a lot. Hopefully, like Harrison, I'll pass on some of the knowledge I've acquired. I'm not making any claims or promises and I'm certainly not saying I'm right. I've done my best to decode his songs and uncover what they may or may not mean. What you're about to read is only my opinion. You're more than welcome to disagree. After all, I'd rather you think for yourself than slavishly agree with me just because it's in a book. We all need a little help sometimes, particularly when what was thought and said was reliant on metaphors, tropes and deliberately obtuse language. Harrison didn't make it easy, partly because he wanted to make us think, to question and to discover the answer (it's at the end), for ourselves.

This book, the first of two volumes, covers the first eleven years of Harrison's solo recording career. Eleven years in which he recorded and released nine albums, two of them three-record boxed sets. Eleven years in which he produced eleven albums for other artists, including Jackie Lomax, Ravi Shankar and Splinter, to name but three. Eleven years in which he played on records by Cream, Leon

Russell and John Lennon and many, many more. George Harrison; the Quiet One. Yeah, right. In the first half of his solo career, he was by far the most prolific ex-Beatle. He was the first Fab to have a number 1 single. He staged the first all star charity concert. He was the first to promote what we now call 'world music'. He was the first Beatle to tour America. Not bad for somebody as quiet as he was supposed to be.

A good number of songs recorded during this period were written while he was still a Beatle. If he wasn't contributing songs from the very start of Beatlemania, he quickly realized the importance of song writing as a communications medium and potential source of income. In the space of three years he went from having only one song on an album ('Don't Bother Me' on *With The Beatles*) to having three songs on what is arguably The Beatles' finest album, *Revolver*. He managed to get four songs on the sprawling *The Beatles* double album. But still the backlog of songs kept growing. His misfortune, if you can call it that, was being in a band with Lennon and McCartney. With competition like that, it was never going to be easy getting songs onto long-players.

The backlog would form the bulk of *All Things Must Pass*, but even then he had plenty to spare. He'd dip into his cache of songs each time he recorded a new album. And even then he didn't get round to recording everything he'd written while he was Fab. I haven't touched on the unreleased songs that have crept out on bootlegs over the years. There simply wasn't the room. Now I know how he felt when yet another song was added to the pile because there wasn't room on The Beatles' new LP.

Harrison was many things, but above all he was a musician and songwriter. Music and songs flowed out of him like water from a tap. This book examines Harrison's song writing and record making in an attempt to shine a light on a small part of this complex and contradictory individual. I don't make any claims for this being the definitive discography. It isn't. Its focus is on his official releases, and while I have included a full British and American discography, there simply wasn't space to feature every release variation from around the world. There are plenty of places to look online if you're looking for obscure releases to complete your collection. This discography is more concerned with what he said than trying to catalogue every version of 'My Sweet Lord' that has ever been issued. And there are quite a few.

Neither is it any kind of biography, there are already plenty of those available. What I've tried to do is place his recordings in a historical and cultural setting and to shed new light on a remarkable body of work. I don't just confine myself to his solo recordings, I've also included records that he produced for others. These alone tell us much about Harrison, his tastes and beliefs. They are, for the most part, recordings that can be broadly classified as devotional or spiritual in nature – soul music. Music for the soul, music that made him feel nice. Nice is a word he used time and again to describe the kind of music he enjoyed making and listening to. If it made him feel nice, the chances were that it made the listener feel nice too. That's why we listen to music, isn't it? I don't know about you, but I don't listen to music that makes me feel uptight or angry. That's why they invented the off switch and channel changer.

Harrison grew up at a time when songs were 'nice'. Before rock'n'roll made a big noise, melody was king and beat was something you did to eggs. Records swung; singers crooned and the combination was pleasing to the ear. The popular music he grew up listening to was deliberately anodyne. Although like many of his generation he'd rebel and play rock'n'roll, those early experiences of listening to Slim Whitman, Bing Crosby, Hoagy Carmichael and George Formby never left him.

He was a fan of Motown and soul music. While most Western pop music had little to connect it to the devotional music that it evolved from, soul music was still rooted in the gospel tradition. If he had a favourite soul singer it was Smokey Robinson. His high, delicate voice that glided from tenor to heartbreaking falsetto, when combined with a sweet musical setting, captivated Harrison. Robinson's music made him feel 'nice', it was music that took him higher and a little bit closer to God. Harrison was so captivated by Robinson's 'quiet storm' aesthetic that he applied it to his own recordings and those he produced for his Dark Horse record label. There were, of course, records that gave it a twist, but from 1975's *Extra Texture (Read All About It)* to 1982's *Gone Troppo* the feel of a George Harrison record was of mellow equanimity.

Having lived life in the eye of a hurricane for eight years, he was looking for calm and balance. In 1965 he stumbled upon the very thing that would deliver it to him. A chance encounter with some Indian musicians whilst filming *Help!* set him on a path of Self discovery that would rebalance his life. India is a nation of seekers and in it he saw potential solutions that could put his life, and the lives of others, back into balance.

Indian classical music fascinated him, just as the music of Slim Whitman and Carl Perkins had fascinated him when he was a child. No longer the Quite One, he became the Mystical One. He wanted to share his knowledge with the world, but the world wasn't always receptive to his message. Consequently, he found increasingly subtle ways to convey his ideas and beliefs. This was partly to avoid criticism and partly because he delighted in slipping profound ideas into what appeared to be profane pop songs. Harrison's songs were rarely as vacuous as those they rubbed shoulders with in the charts. One thing that became patently clear while writing this book was just how many of his songs are about becoming and being God-conscious. If you're uncomfortable with that think of it instead as being at one with the world, feeling part of the world and everything in it, being everywhere and nowhere, being a part of everything and nothing simultaneously. For those who can decode the clues his songs are guideposts in a spiritual journey that are as instructive as they are enjoyable.

Indian classical music, and in particular the music of Ravi Shankar, became a lifelong passion. Indian classical music is devotional music, and when combined with Yoga, it has the potential to elevate one to a state of awareness where the true meaning of the universe – its eternal and unchanging essence – can be experienced. Not only did he enjoy listening to Indian classical music, but under Shankar's tutelage he became a devoted student of the sitar. Although he abandoned his attempts to master the instrument, it had a significant influence on this guitar playing. The microtones he heard in Indian classical music were absorbed and added another colour to his sonic palate. His choice of notes and the way he played them, his tone and touch, created a style and sound that was instantly recognizable.

It was a nice sound, a warm sound, a commercial sound. It was his sound and there were plenty who liked it. Whenever somebody wanted a slide solo on their record they called Harrison. Everyone from Jim Capaldi to Belinda Carlisle made records graced by his playing. As with so many things, he was always generous with his time and talent.

George Harrison; the Quiet One? He was never the Quiet One. The very idea does him an injustice. He had so much to say, important things to say, and he communicated his ideas in insipring, thought provoking and entertaining ways. That takes some doing. The kind of people who can do that are few and far between. That's what made in special. His music and spirit is here and there, everywhere and nowhere, flowing, ever flowing within you and without you.

1968 to 1970 : New Horizons In Sound

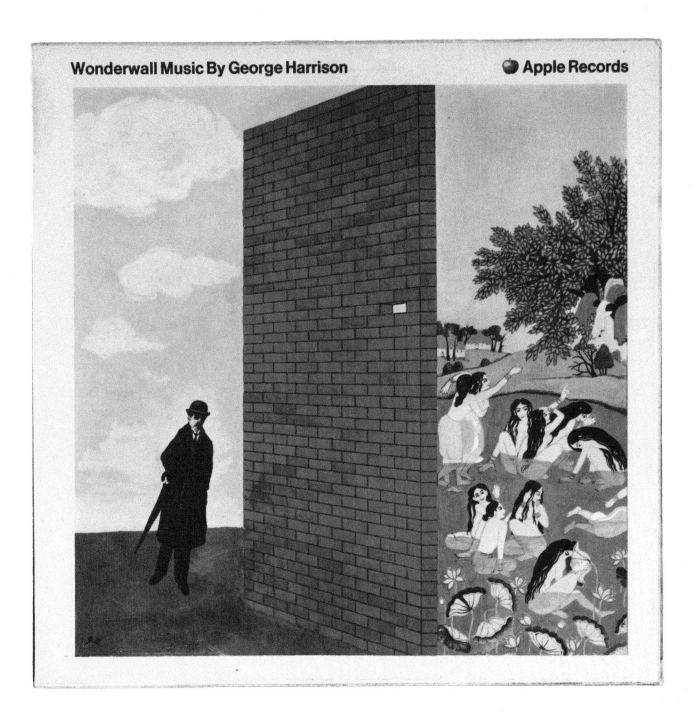

Wonderwall Music By George Harrison

Apple Records

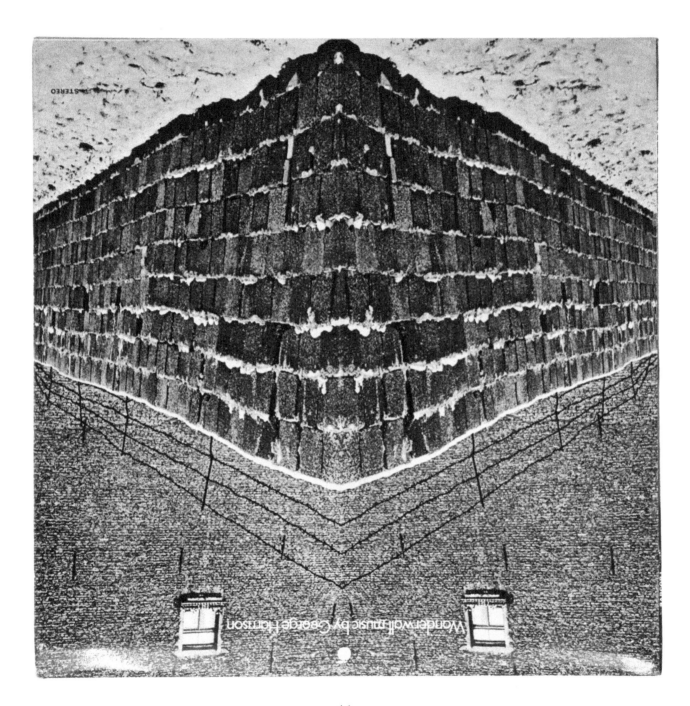

the music:

published by Northern Songs
written, arranged and produced by
George Harrison for Apple Records
Recorded: December 1967

the film:

Wonderwall
starring Jack MacGowran, Jane Birkin
directed by Joe Massot
produced by Andrew Bronsberg

photo by Astrid Kemp
sleeve designs by Bob Gill
John Kelly Alan Aldridge from a
photograph by Camera Press

APCOR 1 Mono   SAPCOR 1 Stereo
Wonderwall Music By George Harrison

side one

1 Microbes   3.39
2 Red Lady Too   1.58
3 Tabla And Pakavaj   1.04
4 In The Park   4.05
5 Drilling a Home   3.08
6 Guru Vandana   1.02
7 Greasy Legs   1.27
8 Ski-ing   1.37
9 Gat Kirwani   1.15
10 Dream scene   5.33

side two

1 Party Seacombe   4.20
2 Love Scene   4.15
3 Crying   1.12
4 Cowboy Music   1.22
5 Fantasy Sequins   1.43
6 On the Bed   1.03
7 Glass Box   2.15
8 Wonderwall To Be Here 1.23
9 Singing Om   1.53

the musicians:

Ashish Kahn, sarod

Mahapurush Misra, tabla & pakavaj

Sharad & Hanuman Jadev, shanhais
Shambu-Das, sitar
Indril Bhattacharya, sitar
Shankar Ghosh, sitar
Chandra Shakher, sur-bahar
Shiv Kumar Shermar, santoor

S.R. Kenkare, flute
Vinaik Vora, thar-shanhai
Rij Ram Desad, harmonium & tabla-tarang
John Barham, piano & flugel horn
Tommy Reilly, harmonica
Colin Manley, guitar & steel guitar
Edward Antony Ashton, jangle piano & organ
Philip Rogers, bass
Roy Dyke, drums

Special thanks to friends loops and
all the staff at EMI Bombay

15

Apple Records Ltd 3 Savile Row London W1

16

WONDERWALL MUSIC
by GEORGE HARRISON

33⅓
Mfd. in U.K.
SIDE 1

APCOR 1
(APCOR 1A)
℗ 1968

Sold in U.K. subject to resale price conditions, see price lists

1. Microbes   2. Red Lady Too   3. Tabla and Pakavaj
4. In The Park   5. Drilling a Home   6. Guru Vandana
7. Greasy Legs   8. Ski-ing   9. Gat Kirwani
10. Dream Scene

All numbers composed by: Harrison
Published by: Apple Publishing Ltd

WONDERWALL MUSIC
by GEORGE HARRISON

33⅓
Mfd. in U.K.
SIDE 2

APCOR 1
(APCOR 1B)
℗ 1968

Sold in U.K. subject to resale price conditions, see price lists

1. Party Seacombe   2. Love Scene   3. Crying
4. Cowboy Music   5. Fantasy Sequins   6. On The Bed
7. Glass Box   8. Wonderwall To Be Here
9. Singing Om

All numbers composed by: Harrison
Published by: Apple Publishing Ltd.

WONDERWALL MUSIC
by GEORGE HARRISON

33⅓
Mfd. in U.K
SIDE 1

STEREO
SAPCOR 1
(SAPCOR 1A)
℗ 1968

1. Microbes   2. Red Lady Too   3. Tabla and Pakavaj
4. In The Park   5. Drilling a Home   6. Guru Vandana
7. Greasy Legs   8. Ski-ing   9. Gat Kirwani
10. Dream Scene

All numbers composed by: Harrison
Published by: Northern Songs Ltd.

WONDERWALL MUSIC
by GEORGE HARRISON

33⅓
Mfd. in U.K
SIDE 2

STEREO
SAPCOR 1
(SAPCOR 1B)
℗ 1968

1. Party Seacombe   2. Love Scene   3. Crying
4. Cowboy Music   5. Fantasy Sequins   6. On The Bed
7. Glass Box   8. Wonderwall To Be Here
9. Singing Om

All numbers composed by: Harrison
Published by: Northern Songs Ltd.

WONDERWALL MUSIC
GEORGE HARRISON

UK release: 1 November 1968; Apple APCOR 1 / SAPCOR 1; failed to chart.
US release: 2 December 1968; Apple ST-3350; chart high; number 49.
Side one: Microbes / Red Lady Too / Tabla and Pakavaj / In the Park / Drilling a Home / Guru Vandana / Greasy Legs / Ski-ing / Gat Kirwani / Dream Scene
Side two: Party Seacombe / Love Scene / Crying / Cowboy Music / Fantasy Sequins / On the Bed / Glass Box / Wonderwall to Be Here / Singing Om
Produced by George Harrison.

England (December 1967)
George Harrison (piano, Mellotron, electric and acoustic guitars, musical arrangements), John Barham (piano, flugelhorn, harmonium, orchestral arrangement), Colin Manley (electric and acoustic guitars, steel guitar), Tony Ashton (tack piano, organ, Mellotron, piano), Philip Rogers (bass), Roy Dyke (drums), Tommy Reilly (harmonica), Eric Clapton (electric guitar), Ringo Starr (drums), Big Jim Sullivan (bass), Peter Tork (banjo), The Fool (flutes, reed instruments).

India (January 1968)
Aashish Khan (sarod), Mahapurush Misra (tabla and pakavaj), Sharad Jadev (shehnai), Hanuman Jadev (shehnai), Shambu-Das (sitar), Indril Bhattacharya (sitar), Shankar Ghosh (sitar), Chandra Shekhar (surbahar), Shivkumar Sharma (santoor), S. R. Kenkare (flute), Vinaik Vora (thar-shehnai), Rijram Desad (harmonium, tabla-tarang).

Harrison wasn't the first Beatle to issue a solo record, nor was he the first to compose music for a film soundtrack, that distinction belongs to Paul McCartney. But his soundtrack for the Joe Massot film *Wonderwall* was the first solo album issued by a member of The Beatles on their new Apple Records label. Like McCartney's soundtrack to the Boulting Brothers' film *The Family Way*, Harrison's soundtrack was performed by session musicians, and as McCartney's score reflected his musical tastes, so did Harrison's. While McCartney's score reeked of brass bands, tradition and a deeply rooted sense of place – the North Country – Harrison's score mixed rock 'n' roll and classical Indian music with wild sonic experimentation.

Joe Massot was an up-and-coming film director whose 1966 film *Space Riders and Reflections On Love* had been nominated as the best short film at the Cannes Film Festival. Part of a select creative scene based in London, and the kind of savvy American who wasn't backward in coming forward, he said: "The thing about then, which is difficult now to understand, was we were all together, we'd see each other in clubs. You'd see the Beatles and Stones, and various music groups and artists like Peter Blake converged into a small circle. There were writers and painters, that was what attracted me to it. But it was a candle you knew was burning at a short end."[1]

Working at a time when anything seemed possible, and mindful that he had to move fast and seize the moment, Massot felt no apprehension when he sidled up to Harrison and asked him to score his latest film. Harrison wasn't convinced that he was the right person for the job, but once the director gave him carte blanche to do as he pleased, he was in. "Joe Massot, the director, asked me would I do the music for his film and I said, 'I don't know how to do music for film,' and he said, 'Anything you do I will have in the film,' and those were the terms on which I agreed to do the work."[2]

Writing music for a film gave him space to express himself outside of The Beatles, and the opportunity to promote his new passion, Indian classical music. Roy Dyke, a member of the Remo Four, performed on the soundtrack recording and suggests it was a time of great change for The Beatles, both emotionally and creatively. "It was a wild time, what with Brian dying, and Apple starting, and all the parties. But George – like all The Beatles – was more grown up and serious now. There was this confidence about them because they had the money to execute ideas – ideas that had nothing to do with The Beatles. They could all go their own way. And George wanted to promote Indian music."[3]

Harrison had immersed himself in Indian music, culture and religion since picking up a sitar while filming The Beatles' second film, *Help!*. The following year he was introduced to the virtuoso Indian musician Ravi Shankar, who became his teacher, inspiration and life-long friend. Harrison wasn't the only British musician interested in Indian music, but he certainly became its biggest champion. He introduced fans of pop music to the sitar when he employed it on 'Norwegian Wood (This Bird Has Flown)', and used Indian musicians exclusively to record his contribution to *Sgt. Pepper*, 'Within You Without You'.

Indian classical music was more than a passing fad, it would remain his passion for the rest of his life. When, in 1984, he was asked what his favourite kind of music was, he said: "If I was only allowed one kind of music to listen to, I would have to say north Indian classical music. That is to say Ravi Shankar [and] Ali Akbar Khan. That kind of stuff."[4] Given the chance to record an entire long-player of his own music, rather than the one or two songs per album he'd been given thus far, Harrison jumped at the chance to indulge his new passion and educate people too. "I decided to do it as a mini-anthology of Indian music because I wanted to help turn the public on to Indian music," he said.[5]

It wasn't simply all about promoting Indian classical music, it was an opportunity to introduce his audience to alternative ways of thinking that focused on the spiritual rather than the material. As Ravi Shankar notes, Indian classical music is deeply spiritual: "To us, music can be a spiritual discipline on the path to self-realisation, for we follow the traditional teaching that sound is God – Nada Brahma: By this process individual consciousness can be elevated to a realm of awareness where the revelation

19

of the true meaning of the universe – its eternal and unchanging essence – can be joyfully experienced. Our ragas are the vehicles by which this essence can be perceived."[6]

To disseminate these ideas, Harrison needed a collaborator. Luckily for him, John Barham, a former student of the Royal College of Music, had learnt from and worked with the great Indian virtuoso and could write notation. "I met Ravi Shankar and started working with him on the *Alice In Wonderland* film in late 1966," explained Barham. "I met Ravi because I had been writing some music that used Indian scales and that's why Ravi took an interest in me. George came down to some of the sessions at the BBC and Ravi introduced me to him. From my work with Ravi, George knew that I could compose and arrange music, so he asked me to do *Wonderwall*."[7]

To prepare for the task, Harrison did what every composer of film music does, he watched the film and timed the scenes that needed music. "I had a regular wind-up stopwatch and I watched the film to 'spot-in' the music with the watch,' he said 'I wrote the timings down in my book, then I'd go into Abbey Road, make up a piece, record it and then we'd synch it up at Twickenham it always worked. It was always right."[8] Before he entered EMI Studios, Harrison composed a number of musical themes which he had Barham write out for him. "I would go up to George's house in Esher and he would play things on guitar and sing them to me and I would write them down," he explained. "[But] most of the *Wonderwall* music was composed when we went into the studio. It was really improvised. We recorded it at EMI with Tony Ashton and the Remo Four. We also did overdubs on some of the Indian tracks. It was very much a collaboration with all the musicians. Obviously George knew what he wanted and he was guiding it the whole time."[9]

Prior to recording in London, Harrison flew to Bombay to record the Indian music. He wanted his music played by the best musicians available, and the place to find them was India. Recording took place at EMI's studios, Bombay on 9 January and ended on 12 January. The studio was basic with only a mono tape machine and mediocre sound-proofing. However, because he was a Beatle, EMI India bent over backwards to accommodate him and had a two-track stereo tape recorder shipped in specially. "I worked with Indian musicians at the EMI/HMV studios in Bombay," recalled Harrison. "Mr. Bhaskar Menon brought a two-track stereo machine all the way from Calcutta on the train for me, because all they had in Bombay was a mono machine."[10]

Because the studio didn't have adequate sound-proofing, recording had to stop every time EMI office staff finished work. "The studio is on top of the offices but there's no sound-proofing. So if you listen closely to some of the Indian tracks on the LP you can hear taxis going by. Every time the offices knocked off at 5.30 we had to stop recording because you could just hear everybody stomping down the steps."[11] Despite this, Harrison recorded more than enough Indian music for the soundtrack as well as the backing track for the b-side of The Beatles next single, *The Inner Light*.

Harrison returned to England on 16 January and continued working on the music at EMI Studios with session musicians and friends. Throughout 1967, The Beatles had honed their studio practice by spending hours improvising and searching for new sounds. No longer content to merely perform their songs, they now created complex and lavish settings that were as sophisticated as their early recordings had been startlingly simple. The quintessence of their avant-garde music making is the still unreleased 'Carnival Of Light', a 14 minute 'freak-out' recorded for a happening held at the Roundhouse in Camden Town, North London.

The Beatles absorbed avant-garde theories and techniques and employed them with remarkable panache. Everyone from Stockhausen to Cage influenced their work and Harrison was the first within the group to harness the full power of avant-garde music making for a piece of solo music. Although his real interest was Indian classical music, he learnt fast and put the group's sonic experiments to good use for his own work. Recorded months before Lennon's 'Revolution 9', his 'Dream Scene' is every bit as fractured, mesmeric and haunting as Lennon's later recording. Its juxtapositions and incongruities takes the listener on an acid-fuelled journey that begins with an intimate love duet and ends five minutes later with the harsh, discordant pierce of a police siren.

It was in this spirit of good humoured experimentation that Harrison began work at EMI Studios with a select group of musicians that included Ringo Starr, Eric Clapton and Peter Tork. The basic ideas he'd mapped out with Barham were developed by the musicians in the studio. Roy Dyke: "George didn't have any arrangements, just little ideas. He'd say, 'I want a jangle piano here, like a cowboy film,' so Tony Ashton would play something, and George would say, 'That's great. Now I don't want full drumming, just a snare on certain beats.' We made it all up together Colin [bassist], Philip Rogers and Tony. George would demonstrate a guitar line to give us a framework, but Colin played all the parts. We were jamming, which felt a little bit like how The Beatles did things, experimenting, always looking for new sounds."[12]

Harrison delivered more music for the film soundtrack than could be accommodated on a long-playing record. Consequently, the film soundtrack and LP differ considerably. Not only are there differences in mixes used for the film and record, but several pieces of music feature in the film that were not used for the soundtrack album. When Massot decided to compile a director's cut of the film in 1998, he asked Harrison to trawl his personal archives for the multi-tracks he'd recorded. While reviewing the tapes an unreleased recording by the Remo Four, 'In the First Place', was discovered. Harrison hadn't used it because he thought Massot only wanted instrumental music. 'In the First Place' was used for the new director's cut and released as a single. Two versions, 'Abbey Road' mix and 'movie mix', were issued as a 7-inch single (PILAR02V) and CD (PILAR01CD) by Pilar Records in 1999. Harrison produced the song and may have played on it, but despite claims that he sings lead vocals, he does not.

Wonderwall Music data

The first long-playing record issued by Apple Records, *Wonderwall Music* was issued in the UK in mono (APCOR 1) and stereo (SAPCOR 1) with a printed insert on 1 November 1968. The America edition also came with an insert, but was issued in stereo only (ST-3350) on 2 December 1968. The album did not chart in the UK, but because of The Beatles' massive popularity in America, it made a respectable number 49 on the US charts. Harrison's soundtrack was the first Apple album to be deleted, although, like many Apple albums, American pressings were available well into the 1970s. Out of print for years, it was eventually re-issued on vinyl and CD on 29 June 1992. The album was remastered again and reissued in September 2014, as part of the Harrison box set *The Apple Years 1968–75*. The reissue adds the previously unreleased Indian piece 'Almost Shankara', an alternate instrumental take of 'The Inner Light', and 'In the First Place' by the Remo Four.

George Harrison's Wonderwall Music.

An Apple LP. (Apcor 1 Mono   Sapcor 1 Stereo)

U.K. SAPCOR 6
164 7 97784 1
564-7 97581 2
264-7 97581 4
1074

Sold in U.K. subject to resale price conditions, see price lists

IS THIS WHAT YOU WANT

JACKIE LOMAX

33⅓
Mfd. in U.K.
SIDE 1

STEREO
SAPCOR 6
(SAPCOR 6A)
℗ 1969

1. Speak To Me   2. Is This What You Want
3. How Can You Say Goodbye   4. Sunset
5. Sour Milk Sea (Composed: George Harrison)
6. Fall Inside Your Eyes
All numbers (with the exception of Track 5)
composed: Jackie Lomax
All numbers published: Apple Publishing Ltd.
Produced by: George Harrison

Sold in U.K. subject to resale price conditions, see price lists

IS THIS WHAT YOU WANT

JACKIE LOMAX

33⅓
Mfd. in U.K.
SIDE 2

STEREO
SAPCOR 6
(SAPCOR 6B)
℗ 1969

1. Little Yellow Pills   2. Take My Word
3. The Eagle Laughs At You   4. Baby You're A
Lover   5. You've Got Me Thinking
6. I Just Don't Know
All numbers composed: Jackie Lomax
All numbers published: Apple Publishing Ltd.
Produced by: George Harrison

IS THIS WHAT
YOU WANT?

JACKIE LOMAX

STEREO

ST-3354
(ST1-3354)
SIDE 1

1. SPEAK TO ME (ASCAP 3:06) (Jackie Lomax)
2. IS THIS WHAT YOU WANT? (ASCAP 2:44)
(Jackie Lomax)
3. NEW DAY (ASCAP 3:16) (Jackie Lomax)
Recorded in England
4. SUNSET (ASCAP 3:54) (Jackie Lomax)
5. SOUR MILK SEA (George Harrison) (ASCAP 3:51)
6. FALL INSIDE YOUR EYES (ASCAP 3:08)
(Jackie Lomax)
Arranged and Produced by George Harrison
except Track 3.
Produced by Jackie & Mal
Manufactured by Apple Records, Inc.

IS THIS WHAT
YOU WANT?

JACKIE LOMAX

STEREO

ST-3354
(ST2-3354)
SIDE 2

1. LITTLE YELLOW PILLS (ASCAP 4:01)
2. TAKE MY WORD (ASCAP 3:55)
3. THE EAGLE LAUGHS AT YOU (ASCAP 2:22)
4. BABY YOU'RE A LOVER (ASCAP 3:01)
5. YOU'VE GOT ME THINKING (ASCAP 2:53)
6. I JUST DON'T KNOW (ASCAP 2:53)
All songs composed by Jackie Lomax
Arranged and
Produced by
Manufactured by
George Harrison
Apple Records, Inc.
MFD. BY APPLE RECORDS, INC.

'Sour Milk Sea' / 'The Eagle Laughs At You'
JACKIE LOMAX
Produced by George Harrison.
UK release: 6 September 1968; Apple 3; failed to chart.
US release: 26 August 1968; Apple 1802; failed to chart.

'Sour Milk Sea' (George Harrison)
Jackie Lomax (double-tracked lead vocals), George Harrison (lead and rhythm guitars), Eric Clapton (lead and rhythm guitars), Nicky Hopkins (piano, Hammond organ), Paul McCartney (bass), Ringo Starr (drums).
Recorded at Abbey Road Studios London, England. Both produced by George Harrison.

IS THIS WHAT YOU WANT?
JACKIE LOMAX
UK release: 21 March 1969; Apple APCOR 6 / SAPCOR 6; failed to chart.
US release: 19 May 1969; Apple ST-3354; failed to chart.

Side one: Speak To Me / Is This What You Want? / How Can You Say Goodbye / Sunset / Sour Milk Sea / Fall Inside Your Eyes
Side two: Little Yellow Pills / Take My Word / The Eagle Laughs At You / Baby You're A Lover / You've Got Me Thinking / I Just Don't Know
Produced by George Harrison.

Recorded 1968-1969.
Engineered by Barry Sheffield & Pete Bown at Trident Studios, London, Ken Scott & Geoff Emerick at EMI Studios, London and Armin Steiner at Sound Recorders Studios, Los Angeles.

Jackie Lomax (vocals, rhythm guitar, percussion), George Harrison (lead & rhythm guitars), Paul McCartney (bass), Bishop O'Brien (drums), Tony Newman (guitar), Joe Osborn (bass), Ringo Starr (drums), Paul Beaver, Mal Evans, Bernie Krause, Alan Pariser (special effects), John Barham (horn & string arrangements), Hal Blaine (drums), Alan Branscombe (tenor sax), Eric Clapton (lead and rhythm guitar), Pete Clark (drums), Chris Hatfield (piano), Spike Heatley (stand-up bass), Nicky Hopkins (piano), Billy Kinsley (bass), Larry Knechtel (keyboards).

When The Beatles formed Apple Corps in the summer of 1967, one of the first things they did was start a music publishing company. If they had learnt anything since becoming pop stars, it was the value of copyrights. Lennon and McCartney had benefited the most from song writing because they wrote most of the group's material. While George and Ringo weren't as prolific, there was no reason why they shouldn't profit from publishing, too. By forming Apple Publishing, all four would benefit financially from the income it generated.

Apple Publishing opened for business in a one-room office in Curzon Street, London, with Terry Doran appointed to oversee its day-to-day running. The office soon moved to 94 Baker Street, which The Beatles had purchased as part of an investment portfolio. It would, in due course, become the ever so hip Apple Boutique, but in September 1967 its upper floors were occupied by Apple Publishing.

It wasn't long before a steady stream of would-be songwriters climbed the stairs to Doran's office in the hope of securing a contract with the hippest publishers on the planet. Dave Lambert fronted a happening new band, Fire, and recalls visiting Apple Publishing for the first time. "It was so exciting. I was shaking the first time I went up there, shaking with excitement. It was an absolute thrill just to be there, the pinnacle of the business in those days, the epicentre. Everything revolved around The Beatles, the whole business. And just to be there was enough for me. I was so excited and everybody was so nice, it was a lovely company to be with."[13]

Jackie Lomax also headed to Baker Street by way of NEMS offices on Argyll Street. Lomax, a former member of the Liverpool beat group The Undertakers, knew The Beatles from their Cavern days and decided to reacquaint himself with them with a view to them funding a band he was putting together. Lomax: "Well now, before there was Apple Records, there was two Beatles in an office called NEMS and I went to see them about would they back a band I was in. John Lennon pulled me aside and said 'Look, I hear you're writing songs. Is that right?' I said 'Yeah, I got a few. I'm working on some more.' He said 'Well, go and see this guy at Apple Publishing, Terry Doran.' I went to see him and he signed me as a writer and put me to work upstairs on a tape recorder."[14]

Harrison got to hear Lomax's demo tape and was so impressed he offered to sign him to the newly formed Apple Records and produce him. As Lomax recalled, early on Apple was rather chaotic but there was also freedom and optimism. "People really could come off the street and be listened to. Not just musicians, but film-makers and artists as well. I was especially lucky that George took such a strong personal interest. He had a lot of time on his hands, because even on a big project like the *White Album* he only had four songs. I think he was feeling held back."[15]

Harrison had a huge backlog of his own songs to record, but those would have to wait. In February 1968 The Beatles departed to Rishikesh in India to attend an advanced Transcendental Meditation training session at the ashram of Maharishi Mahesh Yogi. Harrison's interest in Indian culture, music and religion had been deepening for some time. His desire to learn was insatiable. However, as he immersed himself in the teachings of Hinduism his personality changed. According to his then wife Pattie Boyd: "He became so very serious about meditating that the lightness did disappear. I don't know… I felt maybe he was unhappy. He meditated for so long, for hours. It seemed to me as if he preferred to be in a meditate state than in a waking, conscious state. He liked the peace and calm. There was a lot going on. We weren't even 30."[16]

Harrison was unhappy with his role in The Beatles and was seeking something beyond the fame and wealth the group had brought him. He desired something lasting, something spiritual; India offered that alternative. "You can be a multi-millionaire and have everything you can think of in life, but it's shit – you're still going to die. You can go through life, go through millions of lives, and still not even catch on to what the purpose is, and try to relate back to Lime Street, Liverpool, just being a Scouse kid. That's what I thought: "Well, this step from one to the other isn't really that difficult; it's just a change of attitude and a shift in perception," Harrison explained.[17]

'Sour Milk Sea' was about taking the first step towards changing attitudes and shifting perceptions, even if it did mean becoming a little po-faced in the process. Rather than using a musical setting borrowed from Indian classical music, Harrison related his experience back to the rock 'n' roll he heard as a teenager growing up in Liverpool. "I wrote [*Sour Milk Sea*] in Rishikesh in ten minutes. I didn't have a guitar in India, and John had a guitar, but he was always playing it and there was only about ten minutes or half-an-hour say, of an evening when I could borrow this guitar and write this song. Even though I was in India, I always imagined the song as rock 'n' roll. That was the intention."[18] Speaking to the *New Musical Express* in 1968, he said: "I'm back to being a rocker now… for a bit, at least. You go through so many changes and realizations, and sometimes you come right back to where you started."[19]

If the music was inspired by rock 'n' roll, the song's subject was inspired by a picture called 'Sour Milk Sea' – Kalladadi Samudra in Sanskrit. Harrison's up beat number has a fairly unadventurous melody, but its spirited tempo nevertheless matches its theme of positive change. "I used 'Sour Milk Sea' as the idea of – if you're in the shit, don't go around moaning about it: do something about it," Harrison explained.[20]

Recording began at EMI Studios on 24 June during sessions for what would become the *White Album*. Although it could have been a contender for inclusion on The Beatles forthcoming long player, Harrison generously gave the song to Lomax for his debut Apple single. Although the recording features Paul McCartney on bass, his contribution must have been overdubbed later because he was in America and didn't return to Britain until 26 June, when he joined the group to record 'Everybody's Got Something To Hide Except Me And My Monkey'.

The first recording to feature Harrison playing guitar alongside his friend Eric Clapton, who plays the first guitar solo, it foreshadows The Beatles' second Apple Records 45, 'Get Back'. It not only closes with the repeated refrain 'get back', missing from The Beatles' demo of 'Sour Milk Sea' recorded at Harrison's house in May 1968, but also has a similar guitar figure that Lennon, absent from this recording, would employ himself only a few months later for 'Get Back'.

Released simultaneously with The Beatles' 'Hey Jude', Mary Hopkin's 'Those Were The Days' – both hits – and the Black Dyke Mills Band's 'Thingumybob', 'Sour Milk Sea' wasn't a hit. As Lomax recalls there simply wasn't enough airtime to promote his single as well as the others. "'Hey Jude'. The first seven minute single. Tell me how much it was played. Tell me how much it was saturating the airwaves. It was unbelievable. I couldn't get a [look in] for six months. I couldn't even get it played. Mary Hopkin was another one that was taking up all the airwaves. They couldn't play more than two songs from the same label without Warner Brothers and Capitol all raising a fuss. So, I got put back on the shelf, if you like. Then they started playing me after all that excitement died down and it was too late."[21]

Even Harrison had his doubts about the song's appeal: "I don't think it's an obvious hit," he said, "but I think it's a very good record. I think that in a way it goes over the heads of some people. It's not the type of record all the mums and dads and all those types of people would buy – like a Mary Hopkin record."[22] Despite the lack of success, Harrison wasn't disappointed. "When we started Apple, we thought even if we don't have a hit, as long as every record is good, that's all that matters," he told *Melody Maker.*[23]

Far from being disheartened, Harrison kept to his word and continued work on Lomax's album. A few sessions were held in London during August and September, but the bulk of the album was completed at Sound Recorders Studios, Los Angeles in October and November. Harrison delighted in his new role as producer, telling the *Melody Maker,* "I'm getting more and more into it now. It's another side to the music. It's the idea of getting it all together, trying to get everybody to do their best. Also it makes you aware of the musicians around the scene. You get to know who is best in their field, whether it's guitar, organ, bass or drums."[24]

On 16 October Harrison flew to Los Angeles to finish recording the album with Lomax. During his almost seven weeks stay, he employed the best session musicians available. The likes of Hal Blaine, Larry Knechtel and Joe Osborn were part of a select pool of musicians know as the Wrecking Crew. Employed by legendary producer Phil Spector, they had played on some of the biggest hits of the day. Harrison's goal was to make the best record he could, success would be measured in the quality of the music rather than in the quantity of records sold.

While recording in Los Angeles, Harrison met Bernie Krause, who introduced him to the Moog synthesizer. Harrison bought one of the newfangled keyboards and had it shipped back to England and installed at his home. It would later feature on The Beatles' *Abbey Road* album and on Harrison's second solo album, *Electronic Sound.* Returning to London in November, Harrison completed the Lomax album with the addition of backing vocals, strings and brass arrangements.

Is This What You Want? data

Apple Records issued *Is This What You Want?* in Britain in mono (APCOR 6) and stereo (SAPCOR 6) on 21 March 1969. The album was issued in America in stereo only (ST-3354) on 19 May 1969. The album sold steadily, but like many albums issued by Apple its commercial success was limited. According to a report in *Rolling Stone* magazine, the album sold 50,000 copies. It would have sold considerably fewer copies in Britain and Europe simply because the market was smaller. American copies of the original LP are still relatively easy to acquire, but the British pressing is becoming difficult to locate, particularly in mint condition. *Is This What You Want?* was eventually reissued on vinyl and CD with bonus tracks in 1991. It was only then that Lomax received any royalties. "I never got much out of it actually. When they re-released it, I got money out of it on CD. But that was only '93. How many years have gone by?"[25]

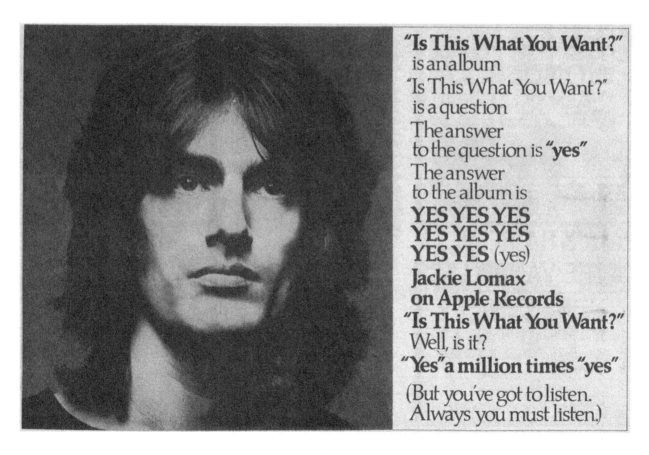

'Badge' / 'What A Bringdown'
CREAM
UK release: April 1969; Polydor 56315; chart high; number 18.
US release: April 1969; Atco 45-6668; chart high; number 60.

'Badge' (Eric Clapton-George Harrison)
Eric Clapton (lead guitar and vocals), Jack Bruce (bass guitar and backing vocals), Ginger Baker (drums), Felix Pappalardi (piano and mellotron), George Harrison [credited, for contractual reasons, as L'Angelo Misterioso] (rhythm guitar).

Recorded at Wally Heider Studios, Los Angeles (basic track early November 1968) and IBC Studios, London 21 November 1968 (overdubs).

By late 1968, Eric Clapton had added his guitar to several Harrison recording projects and songs, the most famous being 'While My Guitar Gently Weeps'. It was now Harrison's turn to help his friend by writing and recording a song for Cream's farewell album, *Goodbye*.

Cream had become one of the biggest rock bands in the world, but were on the verge of breaking up. Their farewell album was planned as a two-record set comprising live and studio recordings, but it was decided to condense it to a single album featuring three live recordings and one new song from each member of the band.

Jack Bruce wrote most of the band's material with poet and performance artist Pete Brown. Although Clapton had tried writing with Brown, the chemistry wasn't right, so he turned to Harrison for help. "I helped Eric Clapton write 'Badge'. Each of them had to come up with a song for the *Goodbye* album and Eric didn't have his written. We were working across from each other and I was writing the lyrics down and we came to the middle part, so I wrote down 'bridge'. Eric read it upside down, and cracked up laughing. 'What's badge?' he asked. After that Ringo walked in and gave us the line about the swans in the park."[26]

Cream's farewell tour took them to the West Coast of America at precisely the time that Harrison was in Los Angeles recording with Jackie Lomax. Cream hit town to perform at The Forum on 19 October, from where the three live recordings on *Goodbye* were taken. The tour over, Cream entered Wally Heider Studios with Harrison, who played rhythm guitar on the song he'd written with Clapton. Muting the strings with the heel of his right hand, Harrison laid down a solid rhythm that becomes increasingly choppy and energetic as the song reaches its climax. The Leslie guitar part may or may not be Harrison, but it does incorporate the tone and style he'd employed when recording with The Beatles. Recalling the session, Harrison said: "We recorded the track in L.A.: it was Eric, plus Ginger Baker and Jack Bruce, and I think the producer, Felix Pappalardi, played the piano part. I was just playing chops on the guitar chords and we went right through the second verse and into the bridge, which is where Eric comes in. Again, it sounds Beatles-ish because we ran it through a Leslie speaker."[27] The song was finished back in London with an overdub on 21 November at IBC Studios. Harrison was not present at his session.

Badge data

Issued by Polydor in Britain and Atco in America, 'Badge' hit the top twenty in Britain but only managed number 60 in America.

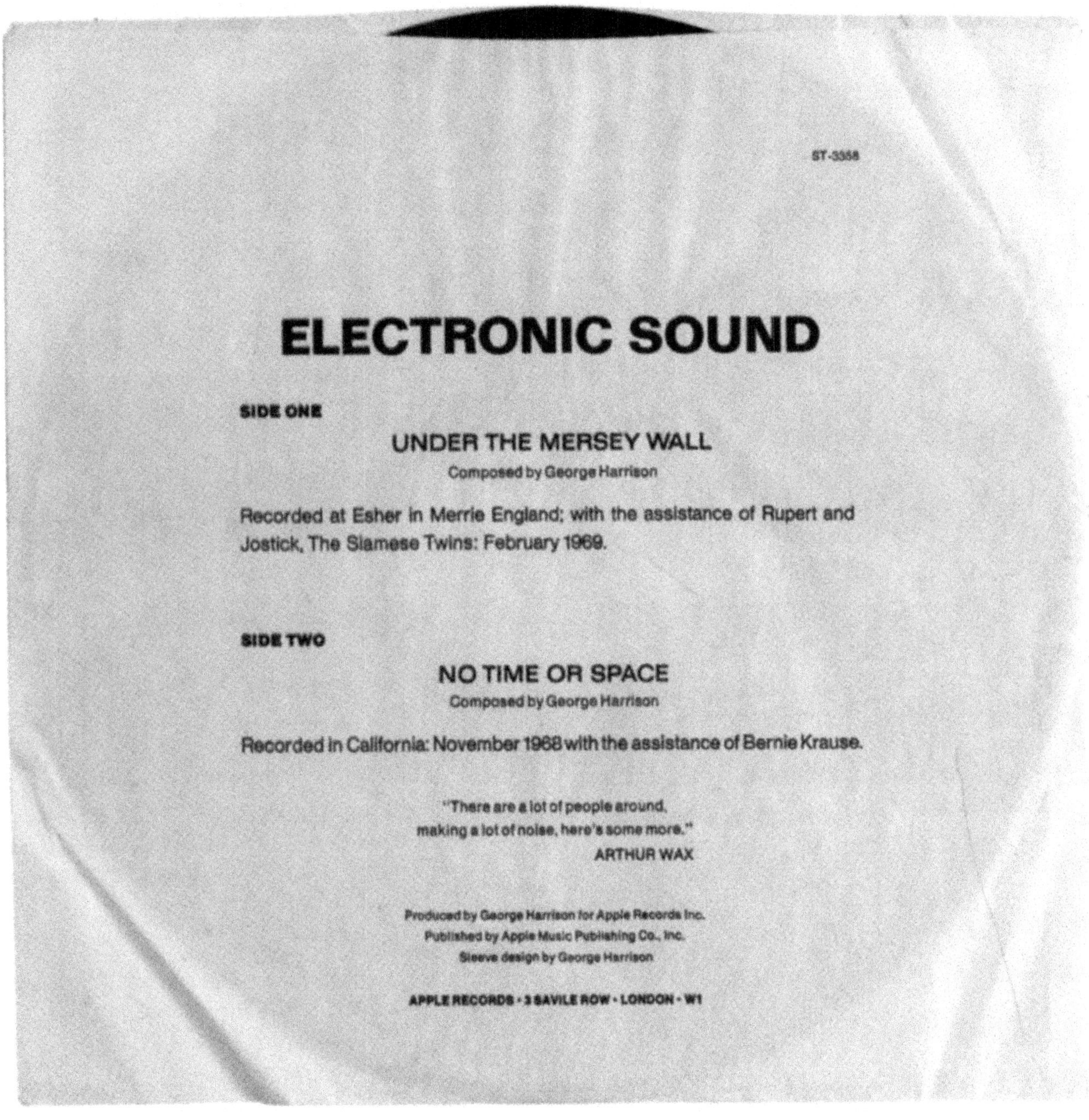

ST-3358

ELECTRONIC SOUND

SIDE ONE

UNDER THE MERSEY WALL

Composed by George Harrison

Recorded at Esher in Merrie England; with the assistance of Rupert and
Jostick, The Siamese Twins: February 1969.

SIDE TWO

NO TIME OR SPACE

Composed by George Harrison

Recorded in California: November 1968 with the assistance of Bernie Krause.

"There are a lot of people around,
making a lot of noise, here's some more."

ARTHUR WAX

Produced by George Harrison for Apple Records Inc.
Published by Apple Music Publishing Co., Inc.
Sleeve design by George Harrison

APPLE RECORDS · 3 SAVILE ROW · LONDON · W1

ELECTRONIC SOUND
GEORGE HARRISON

33⅓
Mfd. in U.K.
SIDE 1

ZAPPLE 02
(ZAPPLE 02A)
℗ 1969

UNDER THE MERSEY WALL
Composed: George Harrison
Published: Apple Publishing Ltd

Produced by George Harrison

ELECTRONIC SOUND
GEORGE HARRISON

33⅓
Mfd. in U.K.
SIDE 2

ZAPPLE 02
(ZAPPLE 02B)
℗ 1969

NO TIME OR SPACE
Composed: George Harrison
Published: Apple Publishing Ltd.

Produced by George Harrison

ELECTRONIC SOUND
GEORGE HARRISON

STEREO

ST-3358
(ST 1-3358)
SIDE 1

1. UNDER THE MERSEY WALL   ASCAP 25:10

Composed and Produced by George Harrison
Recorded in England

ELECTRONIC SOUND   GEORGE HARRISON

STEREO

ST-3358
(ST 2-3358)
SIDE 2

1. NO TIME OR SPACE   ASCAP 18:41

Composed and Produced by George Harrison

MFD. BY APPLE RECORDS, INC.

ELECTRONIC SOUND
GEORGE HARRISON
Side one: Under The Mersey Wall
Side two: No Time Or Space
UK release: 9 May 1969; Zapple ZAPPLE 02; failed to chart.
US release: 26 May 1969; Zapple ST-3358; failed to chart.
Produced by George Harrison.

Los Angeles (November 1968)
Bernie Krause and George Harrison (Moog Synthesiser).
Esher (February 1969)
George Harrison (Moog Synthesiser).

Recorded at Sound Recorders Studios, Los Angeles and Kinfauns, Esher.

Sessions for what became known as the *White Album* were tense affairs that often saw individual Beatles working in isolation. When they did come together, either to record or for business meetings, they invariably rubbed each other up the wrong way. The Beatles weren't getting along and as 1968 rolled over into 1969, Harrison felt increasingly stifled by his role in the group. Speaking to David Wigg in October the same year, he said: "All I'm doing, I'm acting out the part of Beatle George and, you know, we're all acting out our own parts. The world is a stage and the people are the players. Shakespeare said that. And he's right."[28] The trouble was Beatle George didn't like his part and wanted out of the production.

Harrison was so disillusioned that he didn't even bother hanging around to see the *White Album* finished, that was done by Lennon and McCartney. Instead, he flew to Los Angeles to produce an album with Jackie Lomax and guest on a recording by Cream. For the first time in years Harrison felt free to play what he wanted, how he wanted, with whomsoever the wanted. And he was loving it. On his way back to England, he spent Thanksgiving with the Dylans at their family home in Woodstock. While he was there he hung out with The Band and co-wrote a couple of songs with Dylan, one of which, 'If Not For You', would find its way onto *All Things Must Pass*.

His American odyssey was a liberating revelation. His first tentative steps outside of The Beatles showed that not only was he a promising producer, but that he was quite capable of playing and writing with rock's elite as an equal. But more importantly, he discovered that he didn't need The Beatles to do what he enjoyed doing most – making music. The world was his oyster. But his heart must have sank when he received a call from Paul McCartney telling him that The Beatles were returning to work on 2 January 1969 to rehearse new material for a concert, television special and album.

Twickenham Film Studios wasn't the most comfortable place to make music, particularly at the hours they were forced to adopt thanks to the unionized film crew. The presence of cameras only made things worse because it put them under a cold, microscopic gaze that made them all the more petulant. "They were filming us having a row," Harrison recalled. "It never came to blows, but I thought, 'What's the point of this? I'm quite capable of being relatively happy on my own and I'm not able to be happy in this situation. I'm getting out of here.' Everybody had gone through that. Ringo had left at one point. I know John wanted out. It was a very, very difficult, stressful time, and being filmed having a row as well was terrible. I got up and I thought, 'I'm not doing this any more. I'm out of here.'"[29] Harrison was persuaded back and drafted in Billy Preston to play on the sessions which dragged on until 31 January. With some free time on his hands, Harrison plugged in his newly acquired Moog synthesizer and made a recording like no other.

The music he made, although unconventional, wasn't all that radical. People had been making music with electronic equipment for well over a decade. Most of it was made on war surplus equipment by amateurs, but some of it found its way into the public domain. The 1950 film *The Man In The White Suit* used sound effects created by the director Alexander Mackendrick and sound editor Mary Habberfield using musique concrète techniques. These very same sounds were incorporated into *The White Suit Samba* by Jack Parnell and His Rhythm which was produced for record by none other than George Martin. In early 1962, the same year in which he produced The Beatles debut single, Martin issued an early electronic dance single *Time Beat* under the pseudonym Ray Cathode. It had been recorded at the BBC Radiophonic Workshop, a hotbed of musical experimentation that in 1963 produced the theme music to the science fiction programme *Doctor Who*.

The kind of electronic music that was being made by amateurs and professionals alike was different. It completely redefined music and the process of making music. Music didn't have to be made using conventional instruments, it didn't rely on conventional scales and tempos. It was free of all the conventions and rules that governed established music making. All of The Beatles were intrigued by sound and the ways in which it could be manipulated. They all made tape loops, some of which featured on recordings like 'Tomorrow Never Knows'.

When Harrison visited a Capitol Records pressing plant to see his *All Things Must Pass* album being pressed, he was so captivated by the sound of the machines that he recorded it. Why couldn't the sound of a room full of presses be music? It could if that was what rocked your boat. This must have appealed to Harrison at the time. He was, after all, engaging with a broad spectrum of music that encompassed everything from rock to ragas. To somebody as open to ideas as Harrison, electronic music was just another genre.

The machine he used to made his electronic sound was a Moog III. The instrument was designed by Dr. Robert Moog in the 1950s, but Harrison didn't become aware of it until he booked Bernie

Krause to play his Moog III on the Jackie Lomax sessions in late 1968. Harrison asked for a demonstration and left the tape rolling as Krause played. The resulting music was edited down to 25 minutes to form 'No Time Or Space' and issued on *Electronic Sound*. Its release led Krause to sue because, he claimed, the recording had been made without his knowledge or consent, and issued without due acknowledgement. Look carefully at the sleeve and you can see where Krause's name was painted over. However, copies of the album that came with a printed inner sleeve did carry the legend "Assisted by Bernie Krause".

The inner sleeve also states that 'Under The Mersey Wall' was recorded in February 1969. As Harrison was hospitalized from 7 to 15 February the recording has to have been made in either the first or last week of that month. On 25 February, his 26th birthday, Harrison headed to EMI Studios, Abbey Road, to record demos of three songs, 'All Things Must Pass', 'Old Brown Shoe' and 'Something'. It is most likely, then, that 'Under The Mersey Wall' was recorded in the first week of February, not simply because of the calendar of events, but more importantly because it is the most free form piece of music he ever created. Coming off the back of creatively stifling sessions for The Beatles, it's as if Harrison set about expressing his pent up anger and frustration by making the biggest racket he could. It's the sonic equivalent of uncontrolled, visceral action painting. This is pure, raw expression.

Unfortunately, Harrison and his chums at Apple thought it had artistic merit and gave its release the green light. It's as if he was telling the hordes of fans who still saw him as Beatle George to "FUCK OFF". This is the kind of record disgruntled rock stars from Lou Reed (*Metal Machine Music*) to David Bowie (*Low*) have insisted on making when they want to piss off their audience and record company. Perhaps this was Harrison's way of purging himself of Beatle George, a process that started with the infamous *Yesterday… And Today* 'butcher' cover and ended with his 1974 tour of America. Whatever his reasons for releasing this album, it's almost unlistenable. One can only imagine the look of horror and disappointment on the faces of fans when they played it for the first and possibly last time.

Electronic Sound data

Electronic Sound was issued on the short-live Apple imprint Zapple Records in May 1969. The album was issued with a printed inner sleeve, although it can also be found with plain white inner sleeve. An error in the manufacturing process meant that the American edition had 'A' and 'B' sides reversed. While the 'A' side label reads 'Under The Mersey Wall', it actually plays 'No Time Or Space'. Not that anybody noticed or cared. Harrison painted the cover, the rear of which depicts Derek Taylor's press office at Apple Records H.Q..

Remarkably, the album was re-issued on vinyl and CD in 1996 at the tail end of Apple's re-issue campaign which was intended to re-establish itself as a bona fide record company. It worked in the short term, but in a remarkable twist Apple Computers eventually won ownership of The Beatles long held Apple trademark, which it now licences back to them.

'Z' is for Zapple.

Introducing Zapple, a new label from Apple Records.

John Lennon/Yoko Ono: 'Life with the Lions:
(Zapple 01)   Unfinished Music No. 2.'

George Harrison: 'Electronic Sounds.'
(Zapple 02)

I'm interested in 'Zapple'. I'd like to know
where my nearest stockist is. Also, could
you please let me know what you'll be up
to next before you get up to it.

Name

Address

**Send this coupon to JACK OLIVER
(ZAPPLE) APPLE RECORDS
3 SAVILE ROW, LONDON W.1.**

42

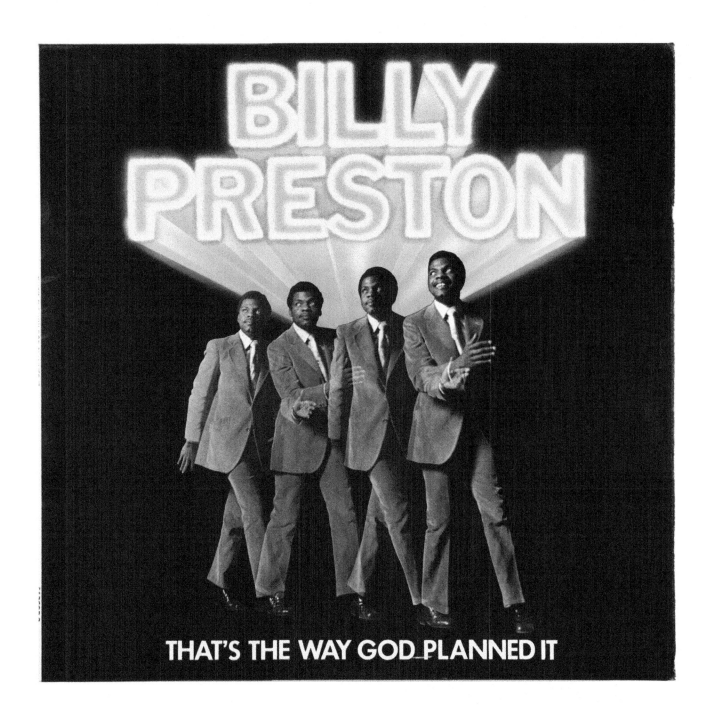

BILLY PRESTON

THAT'S THE WAY GOD PLANNED IT

BILLY PRESTON THAT'S THE WAY GOD PLANNED IT

Billy Preston is the best thing to happen to Apple this year. He's young and beautiful and kind and he sings and plays like the son of God.

Born in Houston, Texas and raised in Los Angeles, Billy discovered the piano at three and started playing organ at six. His mother played in the church choir, and this gospel background influenced him until much later in life. At ten, Billy made his film debut. "I played in a movie with Nat 'King' Cole, Ella Fitzgerald and Pearl Bailey. Nat was playing W. G. Handy the New Orleans Musician and I played him as a little boy. The movie was called 'St. Louis Blues'."

"When I did a tour in 1962 with Little Richard – we kicked off in England doing shows with Sam Cooke – that was the first time I'd played rock 'n' roll. Up to then, I'd been playing only gospel music, and Richard thought it was to be a gospel tour. But everyone wanted the old rock 'n' roll bit and so we played it," he says. "I joined James Cleveland who works with choirs and groups. He's sort of the Ray Charles of gospel."

"Later I formed my own group and we did mostly Ray Charles numbers. Then I met him at the 'Shindig' T.V. Show in California where I was standing in for him during rehearsals. After the actual performance, I sang 'Georgia' for him and a couple of days later he called me and we joined up."

Preston played on many Ray Charles singles including 'Let's Go Get Stoned', 'In the Heat of the Night' and the LP 'Cryin' Time' adding a new lead to his recording career that produced three solo Billy Preston albums"

'Sixteen Year Old Soul'. 'The Wildest Organ Ever' and 'The Most Electrifying Organ Ever'.

Touring with the Ray Charles band, Billy had his own solo spot and Ray Charles would introduce him as 'The Young man that anytime I leave this business I want him to take over what I started'.

With Charles Billy toured America, Europe, and Australia and he finally brought him to England for a Television show with the band.

It was then he decided to telephone Apple.

And that was the beginning of some mammoth recording sessions with the Beatles which included his playing on their new album, as well as on 'Get Back'.

"One day the Beatles said they'd like me on Apple".

Doodling on a typewriter, Billy wrote:

"Music is my life and everyday I live it, and it's a good life to everything I want to say through music it gets to you. I may not be the best around but I'm surely not the worst. I learned to play and sing since the age of three, you don't know how glad I am God laid his hands on me. Apple is the Company for all people that know where it s at and love peace love joy and all mankind. I am very grateful to be a part of it. It won't be long before we change the whole system that holds and keeps the artist's mind messed up. All thanks must be given to the fab Beatles. People should realize that what they have gone through has not been in vain and they are using it to the best of their ability."

That's all. Just fill your heads with sounds.

Derek Taylor

APPLE RECORDS
SAPCOR 9

SIDE ONE
Do what you want *(Preston)*
I want to thank you * *(Preston)*
Everything's all right *(Preston/Troy)*
She belongs to me *(Dylan)* **
It doesn't matter *(Preston)*
Morning Star *(W C Handy/David)* ***

SIDE TWO
Hey brother * *(Preston)*
What about you? *(Preston)*
Let us all get together now *(Preston/Troy)*
This is it *(Preston/Troy)*
Keep it to yourself * *(Preston)*
That's the way God planned it
(parts 1 & 2) *(Preston)*

"Morning Star" strings by John Barham
All numbers published by Apple Publishing Ltd
except: ** Warner Brothers Seven Arts Music.
*** Francis Day & Hunter
Remix Engineer: Glyn Johns
Recording first published 1969

Produced by George Harrison
* Produced by Wayne Schuler

supplied by
peter russell ltd.
24, market avenue,
plymouth, england
phone 60256 & 69611

This Stereo record can be played on mono reproducers provided either a compatible or stereo cartridge wired for mono is fitted. Recent equipment may already be fitted with a suitable cartridge. If in doubt consult your dealer.

THAT'S THE WAY GOD PLANNED IT
BILLY PRESTON

STEREO

33⅓
Mfd. in U.K.
SIDE 1

SAPCOR 9
(SAPCOR 9A)

℗ 1969

DO WHAT YOU WANT (Billy Preston) Apple Publishing Ltd. **I
WANT TO THANK YOU (Billy Preston) Apple Publishing Ltd.
EVERYTHING'S ALL RIGHT (Billy Preston/Doris Troy)
Apple Publishing Ltd. SHE BELONGS TO ME (Dylan)
Warner Bros. Seven Arts Music. IT DOESN'T MATTER
(Billy Preston) Apple Publishing Ltd. MORNING
STAR (W. C. Handy/David) Francis Day & Hunter.

Produced: GEORGE HARRISON
**Produced: WAYNE SCHULER

THAT'S THE WAY GOD PLANNED IT
BILLY PRESTON

STEREO

33⅓
Mfd. in U.K.
SIDE 2

SAPCOR 9
(SAPCOR 9B)

℗ 1969

**HEY BROTHER (Billy Preston) Apple Publishing Ltd. WHAT
ABOUT YOU (Billy Preston) Apple Publishing Ltd. LET US
ALL GET TOGETHER RIGHT NOW (Billy Preston/Doris
Troy) Apple Publishing Ltd. THIS IS IT (Billy Preston/
Doris Troy) Apple Publishing Ltd. **KEEP IT TO
YOURSELF (Billy Preston) Apple Publishing Ltd.
THAT'S THE WAY GOD PLANNED IT (Parts 1 & 2)
(Billy Preston) Apple Publishing Ltd.

Produced: GEORGE HARRISON
**Produced: WAYNE SCHULER

THAT'S THE WAY GOD PLANNED IT
BILLY PRESTON

STEREO

ST-3359
(ST 1-3359)
SIDE 1

1. DO WHAT YOU WANT (Billy Preston) ASCAP 3:40
*2. I WANT TO THANK YOU (Billy Preston) ASCAP 3:10
3. EVERYTHING'S ALL RIGHT ASCAP 2:41
(Billy Preston-Doris Troy)
4. SHE BELONGS TO ME (Bob Dylan) ASCAP 4:06
5. IT DOESN'T MATTER (Billy Preston) ASCAP 2:39
6. MORNING STAR (W.C. Handy-David) ASCAP 3:19

PRODUCED BY GEORGE HARRISON
*Produced by Wayne Shuler
Recorded in England

THAT'S THE WAY
GOD PLANNED IT

BILLY PRESTON

STEREO

ST-3359
(ST 2-3359)
SIDE 2

*1. HEY BROTHER BMI 2:30
(Billy Preston-Jesse J. Kirkland)
2. WHAT ABOUT YOU (Billy Preston) ASCAP 2:07
3. LET US ALL GET TOGETHER RIGHT NOW ASCAP 3:05
(Billy Preston-Doris Troy)
4. THIS IS IT (Billy Preston-Doris Troy) ASCAP 2:38
*5. KEEP IT TO YOURSELF (Billy Preston) ASCAP 2:35
6. THAT'S THE WAY GOD PLANNED IT (Parts 1 & 2)
(Billy Preston) ASCAP 5:34

PRODUCED BY
GEORGE HARRISON

Produced by
Wayne Shuler
Recorded in
England

'That's The Way God Planned It' / 'What About You?'
BILLY PRESTON
Produced by George Harrison.
UK release: 29 August 1969; Apple 12; chart high; number 11.
US release: 14 July 1969; Apple 1808; failed to chart.

THAT'S THE WAY GOD PLANNED IT
BILLY PRESTON
Side one: Do What You Want / I Want To Thank You / Everything's Alright / She Belongs to Me / It Doesn't Matter / Morning Star
Side two: Hey Brother / What About You / Let Us All Get Together (Right Now) / This Is it / Keep It To Yourself / That's The Way God Planned It (Parts 1 & 2)
UK release 22 August 1969; SAPCOR 9; failed to chart.
US release 10 September 1969; ST-3359; failed to chart.
Produced by George Harrison (Except I Want To Thank You, Hey Brother, Keep It To Yourself produced by Wayne Schuler).

London sessions
Billy Preston (vocals, piano, organ, tack piano, backing vocals; electric piano), George Harrison (electric and acoustic guitars, Moog synthesiser, sitar), Eric Clapton (electric guitar), Keith Richards (bass), Ginger Baker (drums, tambourine), Richie Havens (guitar), Doris Troy (backing vocals), Madeline Bell (backing vocals), John Barham (string arrangements).

Billy Preston was a remarkable, gifted musician, singer and songwriter. A child prodigy, at the age of 10 he backed Mahalia Jackson, at 11 he sang with Nat 'King' Cole and by the time he was 15 he was playing the organ for Sam Cooke, Little Richard and Ray Charles. A year later at the age of 16, he recorded his debut album.

Billy Preston was touring with Little Richard when he first met The Beatles. In late 1962 the Georgia Peach had a residency at the Star Club, Germany, and the Fab Four were the opening act. Harrison, who wasn't much older than Preston, introduced himself to the young musical whiz-kid between sets. "He was a bit in awe when he said hello but the feeling was mutual. We were the youngest two there and that drew us together," Preston recalled.[30] The friendship had barely started when it was cut short. The Beatles returned to Liverpool and became the most successful band on the planet. Preston went on to join Ray Charles' band, tour the world and release a string of solo albums.

Their paths didn't cross again until 1969 when Harrison and Eric Clapton went to see Ray Charles at the Festival Hall on London's South Bank. At first Harrison didn't recognize the young man performing 'Double-O-Soul'. It was only when Ray Charles introduced his organist that the penny dropped. "So I put a message out to find out if Billy was in town, and told him to come to Savile Row, which he did,"[31] Harrison recalled. Preston was reacquainted with The Beatles and invited to help record their *Get Back/Let It Be* album. Preston became such an integral part of the group that he was credited on their next single, 'Get Back'. The first and only time an outsider received such recognition. Not even Eric Clapton was awarded that accolade.

At the time, Preston was contracted to Capitol Records and had already begun recording an album with Wayne Schuler in Los Angeles. Harrison pushed for Apple to sign Preston because he was a fan and because they shared the same beliefs. Preston came from a gospel background which dovetailed nicely with Harrison's own spiritual values. Speaking in 1975, Preston said: "I've never asked anybody to help me or give me a break. Whatever I don't have now I believe will eventually come. Why? I have to say it's God... the God in me."[32] Delighted to be signed to Apple, Preston later said: "Apple was a fantastic place. It was full of life and yet homely at the same time."[33]

The Beatles' *Get Back/Let It Be* sessions ended on 31 January 1969, whereupon Harrison was hospitalized for two weeks in February. Consequently, sessions for the Preston album couldn't have started until March at the earliest. One of the first songs they recorded at Olympic Studios was an early version of 'That's The Way God Planned It', issued as a bonus track in 1991 when the album was re-issued. The album sessions were star studded affairs with Eric Clapton, Keith Richards and Ginger Baker joining Harrison and Preston in the studio. Working together they created a hybrid of rock, soul and gospel that became Preston's signature sound.

Harrison's production is again flawless, partly because he treated Preston as an equal. "We work together and it's a beautiful combination," Preston explained. "Usually he just wants to be out there playing all the time."[34] Harrison ensured there was space for Preston's talent to shine, which it does on songs like 'What About You', 'It Doesn't Matter', and the opener 'Do What You Want'. Another highlight was 'That's The Way God Planned It', an uplifting gospel song that reached number 11 in the UK charts in July 1969. However, the single wasn't anywhere near as successful in America. These were early days and according to Preston the label was still trying to figure out how to market and sell non-Beatle records. "It didn't happen for me in the States. At that time, the company didn't really know how to promote – because you didn't have to promote a Beatle record! They had other artists – like James Taylor, Mary Hopkin and Doris Troy. But they didn't know how to physically promote a record."[35]

That's The Way God Planned It data

Apple issued 'That's The Way God Planned It' with generic labels and paper sleeve in Britain and America. Some European countries issued the single in a picture sleeve. The LP was also issued with generic Apple labels but British and America covers differ. The British edition has multiple images of Preston beneath his name in large lime green letters. The American sleeve featured a close up of Preston and the album title in large blue letters. The album was reissued on CD and vinyl in 1991. The vinyl edition has a gatefold sleeve and a bonus 12-inch disc featuring B-sides. These additional tracks were also issued on the CD. The CD was re-issued in 2010 with an additional bonus track the previously un-issued 'Something's Got To Change'.

Apple 15

Radha Krishna Temple (London)

Side One
HARE KRISHNA MANTRA

HARE KRISHNA, HARE KRISHNA, KRISHNA, KRISHNA, HARE HARE
HARE RAMA, HARE RAMA, RAMA RAMA, HARE, HARE

Side Two
PRAYER TO THE SPIRITUAL MASTERS

NAMAH OM VISHNUPADAYA KRISHNA PRESTHAYA BHUTALE
SRIMATE BHAKTIVEDANTA SWAMIN ITI NAMINE.

SRI KRISHNA CHAITANYA PRABHU NITYANANDA SRI ADWAITA GADADHAR
SRI VASADI GOUR BHAKTAVRINDAM.

BANDE RUPA SANATANA RAGHUNATH SRI JIVA GOPALA KO.

ON CHANTING THE HARE KRISHNA MANTRA

by A. C. Bhaktivedanta Swami

The transcendental vibration established by the chanting of HARE KRISHNA, HARE KRISHNA, KRISHNA KRISHNA, HARE HARE/HARE RAMA, HARE RAMA, RAMA RAMA, HARA HARE is the sublime method for reviving our transcendental consciousness. As living spiritual souls, we are all originally Krishna conscious entities, but due to our association with matter from time immemorial, our consciousness is now adulterated by the material atmosphere. The material atmosphere, in which we are now living, is called Maya, or Illusion. Maya means that which is not. And what is this Illusion? The illusion is that we are all trying to be lords of material Nature, while actually we are under the grip of her stringent laws. When a servant artificially tries to imitate the all-powerful master, it is called illusion. We are trying to exploit the resources of material Nature, but actually we are becoming more and more entangled in her complexities. Therefore, although we are engaged in a hard struggle to conquer Nature, we are ever more dependent on her. This illusory struggle against material Nature can be stopped at once by revival of our eternal Krishna consciousness.

Hare Krishna, Hare Krishna, Krishna Krishna, Hare Hare is the transcendental process for reviving this original pure consciousness. By chanting this transcendental vibration, we can cleanse away all misgivings within our hearts. The basic principle of all such misgivings is the false consciousness that I am the lord of all I survey.

Krishna consciousness is not an artificial imposition on the mind. This consciousness is the original natural energy of the living entity. When we hear the transcendental vibration, this consciousness is revived. This simplest method is recommended for this age. By practical experience also, one can perceive that by the chanting of this Maha Mantra, or the Great Chanting for Deliverance, one can at once feel a transcendental ecstasy coming through from the spiritual stratum. In the material concept of life we are busy in the matter of sense gratification as if we were in the lower animal stage. A little elevated from this status of sense gratification, one is engaged in mental speculation for the purpose of getting out of the material clutches. A little elevated from this speculative status, when one is intelligent enough, one tries to find out the Supreme Cause of all causes—within and without. And when one is factually on the plane of spiritual understanding, surpassing the stages of sense, mind and intelligence, he is then on the transcendental plane. This chanting of the Hare Krishna Mantra is enacted from the spiritual platform, and thus this sound vibration surpasses all lower strata of consciousness—namely sensual, mental, and intellectual. *There is no need, therefore, to understand the language of the Mantra, nor is there any need for mental speculation, nor any intellectual adjustment for chanting this Maha Mantra.* It is automatic, from the spiritual platform, and as such anyone can take part in vibrating this transcendental sound without any previous qualifications. In a more advanced stage, of course, one is not expected to commit offences on grounds of spiritual understandings.

In the beginning, there may not be the presence of all transcendental ecstasies, which are eight in number. These are: 1) Being stopped as though dumb; 2) perspiration; 3) standing up of the hairs on the body; 4) dislocation of voice; 5) trembling; 6) fading of the body; 7) crying in ecstasy; and 8) trance. But there is no doubt that chanting for a while takes one immediately to the spiritual platform, and one shows the first symptom of this in the urge to dance along with the chanting of the Mantra. We have seen this practically. Even a child can take part in the chanting and dancing. Of course, for one who is too entangled in material life, it takes a little more time to come to the spiritual platform very quickly. When it is chanted by a pure devotee of the Lord in love, it has the greatest efficacy on hearers, and as such this chanting should be heard from the lips of a pure devotee of the Lord, so that immediate effects can be achieved. As far as possible, chanting from the lips of non-devotees should be avoided. Milk touched by the lips of a serpent has poisonous effects.

The word "Hare" is the form of addressing the energy of the Lord, and the words "Krishna" and "Rama" are forms of addressing the Lord Himself. Both Krishna and Rama mean the Supreme Pleasure, and Hara is the Supreme Pleasure-Energy of the Lord. The Supreme Pleasure Energy of the Lord helps us to reach the Lord.

The material energy, called Maya, is also one of the multi-energies of the Lord. And we the living entities are also the energy—marginal energy—of the Lord. The living entities are described as superior to material energy. When the superior energy is in contact with the inferior energy, an incompatible situation arises; but when the superior marginal energy is in contact with the Superior Energy, called Hara, it is established in its happy, normal condition.

These three words, namely Hara, Krishna and Rama, are the transcendental seeds of the Maha Mantra. The chanting is a spiritual call for the Lord and His Energy, to give protection to the conditioned soul. This chanting is exactly like the genuine cry of a child for its mother's presence. Mother Hara helps the devotee to achieve the Lord Father's Grace, and the Lord reveals Himself to the devotee who chants this Mantra sincerely.

No other means of spiritual realization is as effective in this age of quarrel and hypocrisy as is the Maha Mantra.

Hare Krishna, Hare Krishna, Krishna Krishna, Hare Hare
Hare Rama, Hare Rama, Rama Rama, Hare Hare.

'Hare Krishna Mantra' / 'Prayer To The Spiritual Masters'
RADHA KRSNA TEMPLE [LONDON]
Produced by George Harrison.
UK release: 29 August 1969; Apple 15; chart high; number 12.
US release: 22 August 1969; Apple 1810; failed to chart.

George Harrison (harmonium, guitar and bass), Tamal Krishna Go swami (flute), Harivilas, Yamuna, Jivananda, Lilavati and Yogesvara (lead vocals) assembled Hare Krishna devotees (backing vocals, mridanga and kartals). Alan White (Indian drums on Hare Krishna Mantra). John Barham orchestral arrangement Govinda. Mukunda Goswami (as Makunda Das Adhikary) (arrangements).

One week after it issued Billy Preston's gospel-styled single 'That's The Way God Planned It', Apple issued another single with spiritual overtones, 'Hare Krishna Mantra' by the Radha Krsna Temple [London]. Harrison produced both records and each shows how keen he was to explore different musical styles. "I've realized another thing, that you can write a melody and it can be absolutely anything you like. It can be a jazz song, a folk song, a rock 'n' roll song – it can be anything. It just depends how you treat it," he said.[36] As far as he was concerned, 'Hare Krishna Mantra' was as soulful as the music he'd produced with Preston. It also let him promote and help finance the fledgling International Society For Krishna Consciousness (ISKCON). Speaking to Howard Smith in May 1970, he said: "I wanted to try and help them [Radha Krsna Temple], and at the same time help a few other people who'll be able to hear the music. There are people out in the world who this music means something to. I know maybe it's not going to crash into the top ten, or maybe you're not going to play it on soul stations, but it's more soulful than any soul music."[37]

Harrison first heard this kind of devotional music when he bought a record of mantras by Srila Prabhupada while in America. Harrison may have been introduced to the teachings of Srila Prabhupada by Allen Ginsberg. On 9 May 1965, The Beatles visited Bob Dylan at the Savoy hotel where they were introduced to the hirsute Beat poet. Ginsberg was already well acquainted with the teachings of Srila Prabhupada and would chant 'Hare Krishna Mantra' to whomsoever he thought needed enlightenment. Two years after meeting Ginsberg, Harrison and Lennon were infatuated with the mantra. "I remember we sang it ['Hare Krishna Mantra'] for days, John and I, with ukulele banjos, sailing through the Greek Islands chanting Hare Krishna. Like six hours we sang, because we couldn't stop once we got going. As soon as we stopped, it was like the lights went out. It went on to the point where our jaws were aching, singing the mantra over and over and over and over and over. We felt exalted; it was a very happy time for us."[38]

ISKCON was formed by Srila Prabhupada in America in 1966. The British mission was established when three devotees moved to a warehouse in Betterton Street, London, in 1968. They were later given houseroom at John Lennon's Tittenhurst Park estate, (only a Beatle would have a religious order living in the garden) before relocating to Bloomsbury in central London. In 1973 Harrison donated what became the movement's permanent British home Bhaktivedanta Manor, in the village of Aldenham.

A meeting was arranged by Peter Asher (head of A&R at Apple) who introduced the devotees to Harrison. "The people from the Radha Krishna Temple were over here since about a year," Harrison told David Wigg. "And I got to know a couple of them, because they were in and out of Apple office. And I've known about Hare Krishna Mantra anyway for a number of years. Originally, the Spiritual Master made a record in America, which didn't really sell well. And apparently the people ran off with the money."[39]

It made perfect sense for Harrison to produce a record of devotional music by the newly arrived devotees. As Harrison said: "After all, the sound is God."[40] Besides promoting ISKCON, he was simply doing God's work. "Well, it's just all a part of service, isn't it? Spiritual service, in order to try to spread the mantra all over the world. Also, to try and give the devotees a wider base and a bigger foothold in England and everywhere else."[41] "There was less commercial potential in it, but it was much more satisfying to do, knowing the possibilities that it was going to create, the connotations it would have just by doing a three-and-a-half-minute mantra. That was more fun really than trying to make a pop hit record. It was the feeling of trying to utilize your skills or job to make it into some spiritual service to Krishna," he said.[42]

The basic track for 'Hare Krishna Mantra' was recorded at EMI Studios by Harrison prior to a Beatles session. "First, I played the entire song on a pedal harmonium and then I played my guitar through a Leslie speaker and had someone beat time with a pair of kartals and Indian drums. All the devotees came in later to overdub the 'answering' singing. There were so many of them banging drums and singing that it was very difficult to keep any kind of separation so the feeling of the recording is very 'live'," he explained.[43]

Hare Krishna Mantra data

Apple Records issued 'Hare Krishna Mantra' with a picture sleeve and double-sided insert that featured an essay *On Chanting The Hare Krishna Mantra* by A. C. Bhaktivedanta Swami. The American single was issued in a generic Apple Records sleeve. A picture sleeve identical to the British issue was prepared for release in America, but withdrawn before release.

Produced by George Harrison.
UK release: 17 October 1969; Apple 19; failed to chart.
US release: 10 November 1969; Apple 1814; failed to chart.

Billy Preston (vocals, piano, organ), Doris Troy (backing vocals), George Harrison (electric guitar), Carl Radle (bass), Jim Gordon or Ginger Baker (drums).

Issued four months after Preston's debut single for Apple Records, 'Everything's All Right' was the second track lifted from the album *That's The Way God Planned It*. Co-written with Doris Troy, it's another gospel-style song that bounces along rather merrily thanks to a prominent bass line. Preston had performed both sides of the single while recording with The Beatles in January 1969, they were recorded not long after with Harrison producing.

The single failed to repeat the success of 'That's The Way God Planned It' on either side of the Atlantic. While Preston would score a further two minor hits for Apple in America, like many artistes signed to the label he would have to wait until he signed to another label, in his case A&M, before scoring another hit.

BILLY PRESTON
'Everything's all right'
b/w 'I want to thank you'
OUT NOW Apple 19

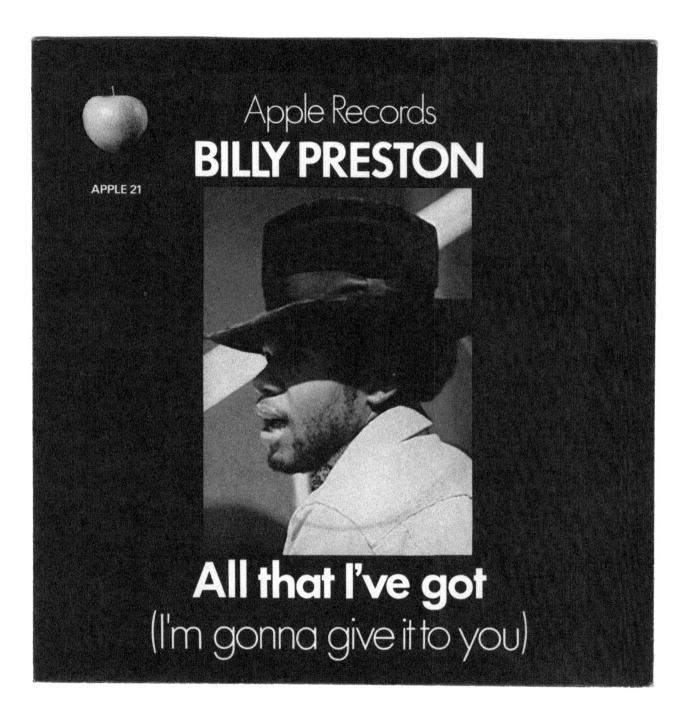

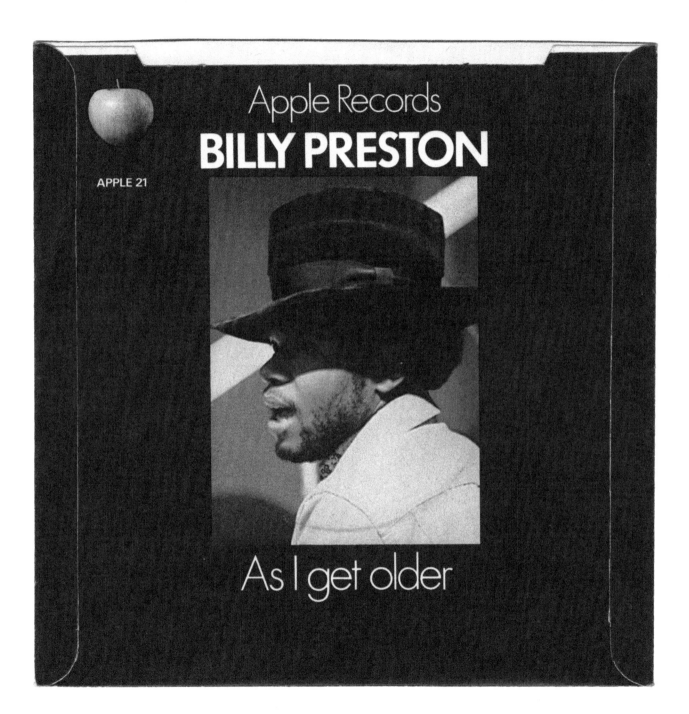

'All That I Got (I'm Going To Give It To You)' / 'As I Get Older'
BILLY PRESTON
Produced by George Harrison.
UK release: 30 January 1970; Apple 21; failed to chart.
US release: 2 March 1970; Apple 1817; failed to chart.

Billy Preston (vocals, piano, organ), George Harrison (electric guitar), Eric Clapton (electric guitar), Delaney Bramlett (electric guitar, backing vocals), Carl Radle (bass), Jim Gordon (drums), Bobby Keys (saxophones), Jim Price (trumpet, trombone, horn arrangements).

Despite being preoccupied with recording The Beatles' *Abbey Road* album, Harrison still managed to find time to produce several records for Apple. To the outside world, it looked as if The Beatles would keep on trucking forever. But Harrison, like his bandmates, was thinking ahead and of life outside the group. On 31 October, Apple issued Harrison's 'Something' as the new Beatles single, the first time he'd been given an 'A' side. Speaking some time later, Harrison explained what influenced it. "When I wrote it, I imagined someone like Ray Charles doing it. I could hear Ray Charles singing it."[44] Ray Charles did record it, although probably not in the way Harrison imagined. Perhaps a more contemporary and equally soulful choice might have been Bonnie Bramlett. Indeed, Bramlett would perform the song many years later, but in 1969 she had yet to establish a reputation in Britain. However, as 1969 slid into 1970 that changed.

On 1 December, Harrison went to see his best mate perform with Delaney & Bonnie and Friends at the Albert Hall, London. Like the time he'd seen Billy Preston perform with Ray Charles it turned out to be another important musical milestone. Clapton had been hanging out with the group of friends since they supported Blind Faith on an American tour. "I first heard them when I went to the States with Cream for the last time, I came back and didn't really think much about them. Then I heard George [Harrison] was going after them. We asked them to be on the Blind Faith tour," Clapton recalled.[45]

Blind Faith was about to crash and burn and Clapton found that hanging out with Delaney & Bonnie and Friends was a much more enjoyable experience. Bobby Whitlock played keyboards with the band and recalls the impact the band had on the guitarist. "We were a tough act to follow – we opened up for Blind Faith in America, and we were shuttin' 'em down. We were getting front-page reviews, and that's where we met Eric. See, we befriended Eric – he couldn't believe our camaraderie – we always hung out in hotel rooms and stayed up all night, playin' guitars and singin' and raising hell, telling people to go to sleep and quit bangin' on the walls (laughs)."[46]

Delaney & Bonnie and Friends had its roots in The Shindogs, a group of session musicians that provided musical support for the American TV pop music show *Shindig!*. Bramlett met his wife and musical partner Bonnie Lynn O'Farrell in 1967 while she was a member of Ike & Tina Turner's backup group the Ikettes. The couple had a whirlwind romance, married within five days and formed a duo Delaney & Bonnie. The couple recorded an album for Stax Records with Booker T. & the MG's, William Bell and Isaac Hayes. Unfortunately, Stax didn't know what to do with the record and did what all record companies do in similar situations, nothing.

Their next move was to expand the line-up to include players like Leon Russell, Bobby Whitlock, Carl Radle, and Jim Keltner. Delaney & Bonnie were now Delaney & Bonnie and Friends, and the band kept growing. Such was the nature of the band that any musician with the right chops could join them. So it was that the guitarist known as 'God' joined them to have some fun and forget the vicissitudes of playing with Blind Faith. "I just wanted to play with a band. I don't have to play more than one part now – I'm just laying in and laying out whenever I want, and it makes me feel a lot more at ease," Clapton told Lenny Kaye.[47] Clapton enjoyed himself so much he put up the money to take the group to Europe for a short tour.

Naturally, he invited Harrison to see them when they played in London. Harrison was equally smitten with their big, tight, gospel sound and when they suggested he join them for the rest of the tour he jumped at the chance. "So they were playing on the stage at the Albert Hall. And I remember two occasions being at the Albert Hall thinking, That's a great band, I'd love to be playing with them. One was The Band when they played with Bob Dylan and he other was the Delaney And Bonnie show with Eric! After the Albert Hall they played The Speakeasy and I went down there, and then they said, 'OK, are you coming on the road with us?' And the next morning this big bus pulled up outside my house with all these musicians on their way to Bristol to start this British and European tour. And I thought, 'Why not?' And I just grabbed my guitar and an amplifier and went with them. That was fun for a while because I could just be at the back – you know, long hair and a guitar – and join in with the band. And I was supposed to be producing a Billy Preston album so I took Billy with us to Sweden and Denmark. It was good fun."[48]

Harrison later professed that he preferred playing sideman to standing in the spotlight; here was the ideal opportunity to do just that. Joining the band on 2 December for its appearance at the Colston Hall, Bristol, he played rhythm to Clapton's lead. (A composite of this performance was issued in 2010 as part of a 4 CD boxed set.) As the tour progressed, Delaney and Bonnie picked up people as they went along, expanding the Friends into a kind of all star travelling circus. "Why, I'll bet one night we must've had twenty people on the stage. We had four guitarists, lots of keyboards, all sorts of singers and road managers… everybody was up there," recalled Delaney.[49]

Returning to London, Delaney & Bonnie and Friends joined forces with the Plastic Ono Band for a performance of Lennon's *Cold Turkey* and Ono's *Don't Worry Kyoko (Mummy's Only Looking For Her Hand In The Snow)* at the Lyceum Ballroom, London. (This performance was also recorded and eventually formed part of the Lennons *Some Time In New York City* album.) The band then moved to the studio to record Preston's next single 'All That I Got'. Written by Preston and Doris Troy, who was letting him crash at her pad until he found somewhere of his own, it's a soulful, up tempo song with a strong pop feel.

'All That I Got (I'm Going To Give It To You)' was recorded with what was in effect Delaney & Bonnie's band, which would soon morph into Derek And The Dominos. It was the perfect band to back Preston; its soul-gospel sensibility and tight, driving rhythm was augmented with a small brass section that complemented Preston's soulful style perfectly. Once again, Harrison's production is faultless. His ability to create an atmosphere in which people could perform to the best of their abilities paid dividends. A joyous soul-gospel confection with a driving rhythm section and brass stabs, it should have been a hit. Yet, despite an appearance on the BBC flagship pop music programme *Top Of The Pops,* where Preston performed solo to a backing track, it didn't perform as well as his previous single.

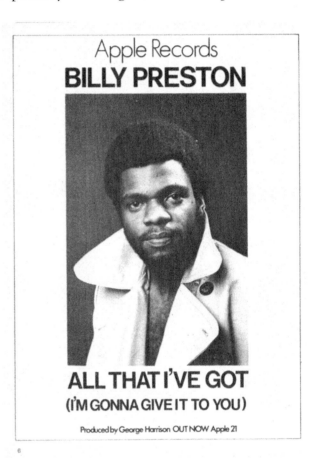

All That I Got data

Apple issued the single with generic labels similar to those used for Lennon's 'Instant Karma' single – the words PLAY LOUD printed above and below the centre hole– with a picture sleeve. The 'B' side was produced by Preston's old band leader, Ray Charles.

Apple Records

JACKIE LOMAX

APPLE 23

How the web was woven

Apple Records
JACKIE LOMAX

APPLE 23

Thumbing a ride

(APPLE.23A)
APPLE 23

Fluke Music
Ltd./Enquiry
Music/Carlin
℗ 1970

Produced:
GEORGE
HARRISON

Mfd. in U.K.

HOW THE WEB WAS WOVEN
(Clive Westlake/David Most)
JACKIE LOMAX

(APPLE.23B)
APPLE 23

Carlin Music
℗ 1970

Produced:
PAUL
McCARTNEY

Mfd. in U.K.

THUMBIN' A RIDE
(Leiber-Stoller)
JACKIE LOMAX

**JACKIE
LOMAX**

STEREO

Recorded in
England

Noma
Music, Inc.
Inquiry
Music, Inc.
BMI
Intro.–:15
Total–3:52

1819
(S45-X47131)
PRODUCED BY
GEORGE
HARRISON

**HOW THE WEB
WAS WOVEN**
(Clive Westlake-David Most)

**(I) FALL
INSIDE
YOUR
EYES**
(Jackie
Lomax)

STEREO

Apple Music
Publishing
Co., Inc.-ASCAP
Intro.–:11
Total–3:12

1819
(S45-X47132)
PRODUCED BY
GEORGE
HARRISON

**JACKIE
LOMAX**

Recorded in
England

MFD. BY APPLE RECORDS, INC.

'How The Web Was Woven' / 'Thumbin' A Ride'*
JACKIE LOMAX
Produced by George Harrison and Paul McCartney*.
UK release: 6 February 1970; Apple 23; failed to chart.
US release: 8 March 1970; Apple 1819; failed to chart.

Jackie Lomax (vocals, guitar), Leon Russell (piano, organ. slide guitar, drums).

Jackie Lomax (vocals, guitar), Paul McCartney (drums), George Harrison (guitar), Billy Preston (piano and organ), Klaus Voormann (bass)*.

With *Is This What You Want?* in the shops, Lomax's thoughts turned to its follow up. He persuaded Apple to let him produce himself, and in April 1969 he recorded 'New Day' with the assistance of Mal Evans and the musical arranger John Barham. "It was after the album was finished and out, they were trying desperately to find a single for old, little Jackie Lomax. So that's why we did 'Thumbin' A Ride', 'How The Web Was Woven' I did 'New Day' on my own. Kind of slunk off and did it with Mal Evans. And I still like it. I noticed the horns are kind of like R&B horns," Lomax explained. 'New Day' was recorded with his touring band of the time: Tim Renwick, Chris Hatfield, Billy Kinsley and Pete Clark.

Although Apple afforded its artistes some creative freedom, it would, on occasion, insist that artistes record specific songs with specific producers. Lomax was none too keen on 'How The Web Was Woven' and he told *ZigZag* magazine that he had to be "pretty well talked into [doing] it." An early version of the song was recorded by Lomax with some friends from Spooky Tooth, but somebody at Apple didn't like it and Lomax was sent back to the studio to try again, this time with Harrison producing. Lomax recalled: "I remember we tried a couple of versions of that, had to do it with some other musicians. But it ended up not being right and we just redid the whole thing with Leon [Russell]." A German language version of the song later surfaced on an Apple acetate. Whether or not this version was recorded at this Harrison produced session is not known.

Harrison booked the session for October and asked Nicky Hopkins to play on it but it had to be postponed because Hopkins was unable to return from Los Angeles in time. Then Harrison's mother became ill and it was postponed again. By the time everything could be reorganised, Leon Russell had agreed to take part and it's he who plays piano, organ, drums and slide guitar on the track. When asked who it was playing slide on the song Lomax said: "Leon Russell. He played everything on that. Including the drums. He's a monster. He's like a mad genius but like great, you know? Great musician. And that slide, he just asked to borrow my lighter, sat down and played it lap steel and my lighter as a slide. Pretty good, huh? Real casual but pretty good."

How The Web Was Woven data

Apple issued 'How The Web Was Woven' with generic labels and a picture sleeve. An identical sleeve design was used for British and American editions of the single. The British pressing was manufactured with solid or push-out centres. American copies were manufactured by Capitol in two different factories resulting in slight differences to the label text layout.

Apple Records
DORIS TROY

APPLE 24

Photograph by Richard Polak

Ain't that cute

Apple Records

DORIS TROY

Photograph by Richard Polak

APPLE 24

Ain't that cute

(APPLE.24A)
APPLE 24

Harrisongs/
Apple
Pub. Ltd.
℗ 1970

Produced
by:
GEORGE
HARRISON

Mfd. in U.K.

AIN'T THAT CUTE
(Harrison/Troy)
DORIS TROY

(APPLE.24B)
APPLE 24

E. H. Morris
Publishing
℗ 1970

Mfd. in U.K.

VAYA CON DIOS
(Russell/James/Pepper)
DORIS TROY

DORIS
TROY

STEREO

Recorded
In England

Harrisongs
Music, Inc.
BMI
Intro.—:28
Total—3:50

1820

(S45-X47133)
Produced by
GEORGE
HARRISON

AIN'T THAT CUTE
(Harrison-Troy)

VAYA
CON
DIOS
(Russell-
James-
Pepper)

STEREO

DORIS
TROY

Morley Music
Co., Inc.
ASCAP
Intro.—:02
Total—3:27

1820

(S45-X47134)

Recorded
in England

MFD. BY APPLE RECORDS, INC.

'Ain't That Cute' / 'Vaya Con Dios'*
DORIS TROY
Produced by George Harrison* and Doris Troy.
UK release: 13 February 1970; Apple 24; failed to chart.
US release: 16 March 1970; Apple 1820; failed to chart.

Doris Troy (vocals, piano), Billy Preston (keyboards, backing vocals), George Harrison (electric guitar), Peter Frampton (electric guitar), Daryl Runswick (bass), Bobby Keys (saxophones), Jim Price (trumpet, trombone, horn arrangements), Bill Moody (drums) or Berry Morgan (drums), Madeline Bell (backing vocals), Eliza Strike (backing vocals), Nanette Workman (backing vocals).

Doris Troy moved to London in the mid-1960s to further her career, which, until then, was based on just two hit singles – 'Just One Look' and 'What'cha Gonna Do About It?'. The former had been an American top ten hit that reached number 2 on the British charts when recorded by The Hollies. The following year 'What'cha Gonna Do About It?' was re-issued and became her first British top 40 hit in her own right.

On arrival in London, Troy slipped into session work and one day got a call from Madeline Bell. "George was producing Billy Preston's album (*That's The Way God Planned It*) and my girl friend Madeline Bell called me up and said, 'Come on, Doris, you want to work?'. And that's how I met Billy Preston and George."[50] Harrison asked if she was a free agent or under contract to another record label. "I said, 'Yeah, man, I'm free.' He said 'Do you want to sign to Apple?' I said 'Sure! Are you serious?' He said, 'Yeah'. I said, 'Well, I want to be a writer, producer and artist, OK?'. He said 'OK'."[51]

Things were obviously simpler in those days; particularly if a Beatle was involved. No sooner had Harrison offered her a deal than Troy was signed to Apple and given her own office on the top floor at 3 Savile Row. Harrison and Troy began work on her album at Trident Studios, London, in the summer of '69. Although Harrison and Troy shared production duties, only Troy was credited as producer when the album was issued.

Besides co-producing, Harrison and Troy wrote 'Ain't That Cute', 'Give Me Back My Dynamite' and arranged the traditional 'Jacob's Ladder'. Although Troy had a few finished songs, most of the material was written in the studio. Troy had written the lyric for 'Ain't That Cute' but was struggling with the tune. Harrison had recently played on some Leon Russell sessions, and with the infections 'Delta Lady' still fresh in his memory, he borrowed from it to finish Troy's song. "We did her single, 'Ain't That Cute', which we wrote in the studio, actually. This is a good exercise because… I wouldn't consider going in there and just making it up on the spot, which is what we did with 'Ain't That Cute'.

76

We didn't have a song, so we made it up, and I just pinched the chords from Leon Russell's 'Delta Lady' and away I went. We wrote that, and it's very nice, with Pete Frampton playing guitar."[52]

Ever generous, Harrison gave Frampton the opening guitar motif to play, as he recalled: "He [Harrison] gave me a Les Paul guitar and I started playing rhythm on 'Ain't That Cute'. George stopped me and said, 'Pete, you don't understand; I play rhythm, you play lead!' That's when I developed the lead riff for that; that's not Clapton, that's me! Eric wasn't there when I was."[53]

Harrison contributed rhythm guitar and a brief slide guitar passage to the bridge. Unlike some of his contemporaries, who were extending their solos to the limits of human endurance, his soloing is stylish and to the point. It may only be a few seconds of playing, but even at this early stage, he'd developed an unmistakable slide guitar style that moved effortlessly between Eastern and Western motifs with remarkable inventiveness and expression. Speaking in 1988 about what influenced his slide playing he said: "I never really played slide until the Delaney & Bonnie tour, and then I thought that's sort of interesting. I bought a lot of Ry Cooder records and Robert Johnson. I feel like Ry Cooder's the guy who plays the good stuff and he's what inspires me to try and play better. And at the same time I'm into this Indian music, and there a guy called Brij Bhushan Kabra who plays a guitar. But he plays it like a lap steel and plays all the groovy Indian stuff on it. So that inspires me too. Maybe my style has got a little touch of stuff that got into me when I was spending all that time with the Indian musicians."[54]

Ain't That Cute data

Issued as a single by Apple with generic labels and a picture sleeve, 'Ain't That Cute' / 'Vaya Con Dios' failed to perform as well as Harrison and Apple had hoped. While Preston was of the impression that Apple had yet to learn how to promote non-Beatles records, Troy suggested that her lack of success was entirely Harrison's fault. "People ask me what went wrong at Apple and I think part of the problem may have been that George Harrison was trying to experiment with soul," she told David Nathan. "Look at Billy [Preston]: He had to go back to the States to get a hit and now he's had two million sellers!"[55] Troy's criticism was a little harsh and no doubt soured by Apple's marketing and business problems. Speaking in 1971 she reported that "it was a nightmare and the split in the Beatles' ranks led to bad vibes".[56] Without Harrison she would never have been signed to Apple; nor experienced the kind of freedom it offered. Harrison may have been 'experimenting' with soul in the same way he was 'experimenting' with Indian classical music, but his aim was always to produce the best music of its kind, which he did.

Apple Records

RADHA KRISHNA TEMPLE

Side One Govinda
Side Two Govinda Jai Jai

APPLE 25

Chorus. GOVINDA ADI PURUSHAM TAMAHAM BHAJAMI

Verse 1. VENUM KANVANTA MARAVINDA DALAYATAKSHAM
BARHAVATAM SAMASITAMBUDA SUNDARANGAM
KANDAR PAKOTIKAMANI YAVISESHASOBHAM

Chorus.

Verse 2. ANGANI YASYA SAKALENDRIYA VRITTIMANTI
PASYANTI PANTI KALAYANTI
CHIRAM JAGANTI
ANANDACHINMAYA SADUJJALA VIGRAHASYA

Chorus.

Translations :
Verse 1.

I worship Govinda the primeval Lord, who is adept in playing on his flute with blooming eyes
like lotus petals with head decked with peacocks feathers with the figure of beauty tinged with
the hue of blue clouds, and his unique loveliness charming millions of cupids.

Verse 2.

I worship Govinda, the primeval Lord, whose transcendental form is full of bliss, truth,sub-
stantiality and is thus full of the most dazzling splendour. Each of the limbs of the transcendental
figure possesses in himself, the full fledged functions of all the organs, and eternally sees,
maintaining and manifests the infinite universes, both spiritual and mundane.

You are heartily invited to
THE RADHA KRISHNA TEMPLE, 7 BURY PLACE, LONDON W.C.1. ENGLAND.

"Spiritual Master of the Hare Krishna Movement :
PRABHUPAD A.C. BHAKTIVEDANTA SWAMI"

(APPLE.25A)
APPLE 25
Apple
Publishing
Ltd.
℗ 1970

Produced
by:
GEORGE
HARRISON

Mfd. in U.K.

GOVINDA
(Trad. arr. by
MUKUNDA DAS ADHIKARY)
RADHA KRISHNA TEMPLE

(APPLE.25B)
APPLE 25
Apple
Publishing
Ltd.
℗ 1970

Produced
by:
GEORGE
HARRISON

Mfd. in U.K.

GOVINDA JAI JAI
(Trad. arr. by
MUKUNDA DAS ADHIKARY)
RADHA KRISHNA TEMPLE

GOVINDA
(Makunda Das
Adhikary)

STEREO

RADHA KRISHNA TEMPLE
(LONDON)

Apple Music
Publishing
Co., Inc.
ASCAP
Intro.—:10
Total-4:45

1821
(S45-X47135)
Produced by
GEORGE
HARRISON

Recorded
in England

GOVINDA
JAI JAI
(Makunda Das
Adhikary)

STEREO

RADHA
KRISHNA
TEMPLE
(LONDON)

Apple Music
Publishing
Co., Inc.
ASCAP
Intro.—:08
Total-5:58

1821
(S45-X47136)
Produced by
GEORGE
HARRISON

Recorded
in England

80

'Govinda' / 'Govinda Jai Jai'
RADHA KRSNA TEMPLE [LONDON]
Produced by George Harrison.
UK release: 6 March 1970; Apple 25; number 23.
US release: 24 March 1970; Apple 1821; failed to chart.

George Harrison (harmonium, guitar and bass), Tamal Krishna Go swami (flute), Harivilas, Yamuna, Jivananda, Lilavati and Yogesvara (lead vocals) assembled Hare Krishna devotees (backing vocals, mridanga and kartals). Alan White (Indian drums on Hare Krishna Mantra).

The second Harrison produced single from the Radha Krsna Temple, and another unexpected hit. Something about these devotional songs clicked with radio programmers and the British record buying public in the late '60s and early '70s. Had the records not been given airplay by BBC Radio there would have been little hope of them becoming hits. That neither song performed well in America shows just how important national airplay was. The BBC dominated British broadcasting at the time, and somebody at the corporation obviously liked both records. That the first Radha Krsna Temple single had been a hit helped, as 'Govinda' shares similarities with the earlier hit single. Like 'Hare Krishna Mantra', it builds to a spirited crescendo, this time aided by an orchestral arrangement by John Barham.

Govinda data

Apple Records issued 'Govinda' with generic labels and a picture sleeve. The American single was issued in a generic labels and picture sleeve identical to the British edition.

(APPLE.28A)
APPLE 28

Harrisongs/
Apple
Publishing
℗ 1970

Produced
by:
DORIS TROY

Mfd. in U.K.

JACOB'S LADDER
(Trad. arr. by George Harrison & Doris Troy)

DORIS TROY

(APPLE.28B)
APPLE 28

Northern
Songs
℗ 1970

Produced
by:
DORIS TROY

Mfd. in U.K.

GET BACK
(Lennon-McCartney)

DORIS TROY

Harrisongs
Music, Inc.
BMI
Intro.—:06
Total—3:02

STEREO

1824
(S45-X47309)

Recorded
in England

Produced By
DORIS TROY

JACOB'S LADDER
(Trad.—arr/G. Harrison-D. Troy)
DORIS TROY

**GET
BACK**
(J. Lennon-
P. McCartney)

STEREO

Maclen
Music, Inc.
BMI
Intro.—:02
Total—3:04

1824
(S45-X47310)

Produced By
DORIS TROY

**DORIS
TROY**

Recorded
in England

MFD. BY APPLE RECORDS, INC.

83

'Jacob's Ladder'* / 'Get Back'
DORIS TROY
Arranged by George Harrison and Doris Troy* and by Doris Troy.
UK release: 28 August 1970; Apple 28; failed to chart.
US release: 21 September 1970; Apple 1824; failed to chart.

Doris Troy (vocals, piano), Billy Preston (keyboards), Delaney Bramlett (electric guitar), Klaus Voorman or Carl Radle (bass guitar), Jim Gordon (drums), Bobby Keys (saxophones), Madeline Bell (backing vocals), Eliza Strike (backing vocals), Nanette Workman (backing vocals).

Troy's second single for Apple Records was a reworking of 'Jacob's Ladder', a traditional gospel song that draws parallels with the exile of the Jews and the oppression of American slavery. Arranged by Harrison and Troy, it extends the theme of spiritual and personal emancipation that lies at the heart of Harrison's music. The music he made with Troy and Preston satisfied his soul. Like the ladder in the song, music has the potential to elevate an individual's consciousness to a level where they become aware of the true meaning of the universe. That's what Harrison was aiming for.

Unlike Troy's previous single, which was good-time R&B, 'Jacob's Ladder' was deep soul music. Combining elements of secular and devotional music, it encompassed many of Harrison's beliefs, values and aspirations – perfectly. Harrison often said that one should be in the world – physically present – but not of it. Many people find this aspect of his life difficult to square, but just because he could afford a luxurious lifestyle doesn't mean it was any more important than his spiritual life. Being in the world meant he could enjoy the beautiful things that God provided without necessarily being worldly. As Troy noted: "He was into his spiritual life – that was who he was, he wasn't a partying person."[57]

Most of his life was spent trying to experience soul; the music he made early in his solo career was no more or less soulful than the music that came later. However, because he was working with artists who were rooted in the gospel tradition, these early records appear more overtly soulful. If, as Troy suggests, he was experimenting with soul music he was simply practicing what he preached. For 'Jacob's Ladder' is a joyous celebration of the spiritual and the secular. The trick is to get the balance right, and one has to assume that Harrison did.

The arrangement he wrote with Troy employs call and response vocals to emphasize the song's gospel feel and employed the kind of harmonies he'd utilize for 'My Sweet Lord'. As Harrison is credited with co-arranging the song, one would assume he played on it. But the rather thin sounding guitar solo doesn't sound like him, and it's not confident enough to be Clapton either. Bramlett thinks it might be him because "it's too sloppy to be Eric Clapton".[58]

The B-side is a cover of Lennon and McCartney's 'Get Back'. A version with Harrison on vocals and acoustic guitar exists with a similar piano and horn arrangement. It has been argued that his recording may have been intended as a demo for Troy. However, as the song was released a year before Troy recorded it, Harrison's 'demo' would have been superfluous. There's also speculation that it was recorded while making *All Things Must Pass*. But by then the Troy sessions were over. It's more likely that Harrison's version was recorded at the same session that produced Troy's version. As un-credited producer it would have been his job to rehearse the band before recording a take with Troy on vocals.

Jacob's Ladder data

Apple Records issued 'Jacob's Ladder' in Britain and America with generic labels and sleeve. As with Troy's previous Apple single it did not chart on either side of the Atlantic, possibly because of the upheavals taking place within Apple at the time. When the album from which it was taken also failed to sell, Troy terminated her relationship with the company.

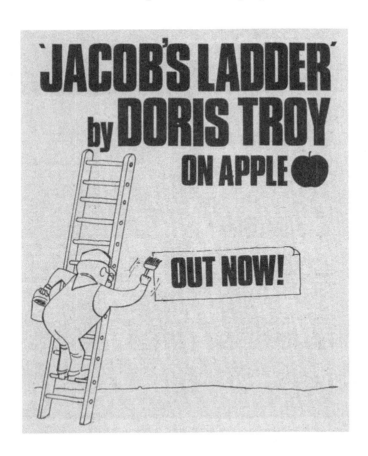

DORIS TROY

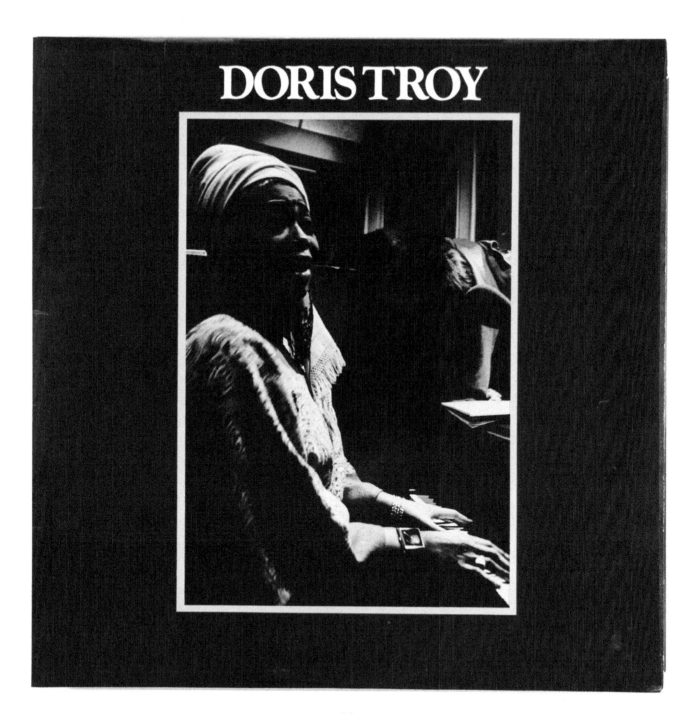

Thanks You All Love Doris

Apple Records 3 Savile Row, London W.1.

Side One	Side Two
Ain't that cute	Hurry
Special care	So far
Give me back my dynamite	Exactly like you
You tore me up inside	You give me joy joy
Games people play	Don't call me no more
Gonna get my baby back	Jacob's ladder
I've got to be strong	

Produced by Doris Troy
Photograph by Mal Evans
Designed by John Kosh

Printed and made by Garrod & Lofthouse Ltd.

DORIS TROY
DORIS TROY
Side one: Ain't That Cute / Special Care / Give Me Back My Dynamite / You Tore Me Up Inside / Games People Play / Gonna Get My Baby Back / I've Got To Be Strong
Side two: Hurry / So Far / Exactly Like You / You Give Me Joy Joy / Don't Call Me No More / Jacob's Ladder
UK release: 4 September 1970, SAPCOR 13; failed to chart.
US release: 11 September 1970, ST-3371; failed to chart.
Produced by Doris Troy.

Doris Troy (vocals, piano) Billy Preston (keyboards, backing vocals), Reg Powell (piano), Leon Russell (keyboards), Gary Wright (keyboards), George Harrison (electric guitar), Eric Clapton (electric guitar), Peter Frampton (electric guitar), Delaney Bramlett (electric guitar), Stephen Stills (guitar), Daryl Runswick (bass), Klaus Voormann (bass), Carl Radle (bass), Bobby Keys (saxophones), Jim Price (trumpet, trombone, horn arrangements), Ringo Starr (drums), Alan White (drums), Jim Gordon (Drums), Bill Moody (drums), Berry Morgan (drums), Ray Schinnery (backing vocals), Madeline Bell (backing vocals), Eliza Strike (backing vocals), Nanette Workman (backing vocals), John Barham (orchestral arrangements).

The culmination of many months hard work, Doris Troy's self-titled album for Apple finally reached the public in the early autumn of 1970. Beside featuring both of her Apple 45s, it featured three new Harrison-Troy compositions 'Give Me Back My Dynamite', 'You Give Me Joy Joy' and 'Gonna Get My Baby Back'.

'Give Me Back My Dynamite' is the kind of down home blues shuffle that Harrison would have knocked out night after night on the Delaney & Bonnie and Friends tour. Their influence here is unmistakable. Although the British blues boom was at its height with bands like Fleetwood Mac, Chicken Shack and Savoy Brown, this Harrison-Troy composition bears more than a passing resemblance to the southern rock performed by Delaney & Bonnie. Harrison had obviously been paying attention and learnt a lot from his brief time with the band. His playing is considerably more bluesy than usual and at times sounds remarkably similar to that of Eric Clapton.

'You Give Me Joy Joy' is another song that would have sat comfortably in Delaney & Bonnie and Friends set. Its tight rhythm section pushes the song along like molasses rolling off the back of a spoon. Another fine example of Harrison's soulful side, if you didn't know better you might think that it came straight out of Muscle Shoals. It's unclear how much Harrison contributed to the lyrics, but there's an ambiguity to them that suggests Harrison's hand. What is it that gives Troy and Harrison joy? Is it their baby or is it God?

If 'You Give Me Joy Joy' had an ambiguity to it, then 'Gonna Get My Baby Back' is crystal clear. A good time, up-tempo song about lost love, it's the kind of pop song that's been endlessly recycled by generations of lovelorn teenagers.

Doris Troy data

Issued by Apple in September 1970, *Doris Troy* was not the success either Harrison or Troy had hoped for. Original copies of the album were issued in a very plain cover with no mention of the all-star cast that helped record it. Had this information featured prominently on the cover it might have encouraged more people to purchase the LP. As it was, Apple's promotion of non-Beatle albums wasn't good at this time, and consequently the album did not register with the record buying public. The album was reissued on CD and vinyl in 1991. The vinyl edition has a gatefold sleeve and a bonus 12-inch disc featuring B-sides and outtakes. These additional tracks were also issued on the CD. The CD was reissued in 2010 with an additional bonus track a previously un-issued version of Billy Preston's 'All That I've Got (I'm Gonna Give It To You)'.

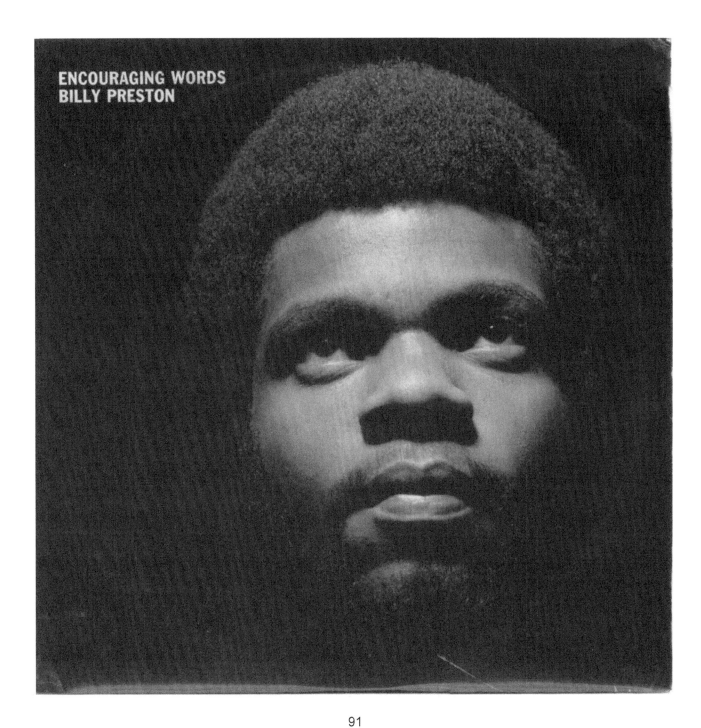

ENCOURAGING WORDS
BILLY PRESTON

Side One
Right Now
Little Girl
Use What You've Got
My Sweet Lord
Let the Music Play
The Same Thing Again

Side Two
I've Got a Feeling
Sing One for the Lord
When You Are Mine
I Don't Want You to Pretend
Encouraging Words
All Things Must Pass
You've Been Acting Strange

Produced by George Harrison
and Billy Preston
Photograph by Richard Polak

Apple Records 3, Savile Row, London W.1

Printed and made by Garrod & Lofthouse Ltd.

92

ENCOURAGING WORDS
BILLY PRESTON
Side one: Right Now / Little Girl / Use What You Got / My Sweet Lord (George Harrison) / Let the Music Play / The Same Thing Again
Side two: I've Got a Feeling / Sing One for the Lord (Harrison–Preston) / When You Are Mine / I Don't Want You to Pretend / Encouraging Words / All Things Must Pass (Harrison) / You've Been Acting Strange
UK release: 11 September 1970, SAPCOR 14; failed to chart.
US release: 1970, ST-3370; failed to chart.
Produced by George Harrison.

Billy Preston (vocals, organ, piano, electric piano, harmonica, backing vocals), George Harrison (electric guitar, Moog synthesizer, backing vocals), Eric Clapton (electric guitar), Delaney Bramlett (electric guitar, backing vocals), Carl Radle (bass), Jim Gordon (drums), Klaus Voormann (bass), Ringo Starr (drums), Bobby Keys (saxophones), Jim Price (trumpet, trombone, horn arrangements), The Edwin Hawkins Singers (backing vocals), members of The Temptations' tour band (electric guitar, bass, drums), members of Sam & Dave's tour band (bass, drums).

Harrison's soul experiments continued with the release of Billy Preston's second album for Apple, *Encouraging Words*. Their partnership was obviously sparking because between them they managed to take Preston's music to a whole other level. Preston's gospel-soul aesthetic and Harrison's natural talent as a producer created a powerful soul record that rates among Preston's best.

Harrison continued to use many of the musicians who comprised the Delaney & Bonnie and Friends/Derek and The Dominos nexus. The band of southern rockers was fast becoming Harrison's very own Wrecking Crew. Besides playing on Doris Troy's and Billy Preston's sessions, many would go on to assist with the recording of Harrison's own *All Things Must Pass*. Perhaps, as Troy suggested, Harrison was using these sessions as experiments to develop a sonic signature of his own. Had he not employed Phil Spector to produce *All Things Must Pass,* it may well have sounded something like this. As it was he went for a bigger, heavier, rockier sound which he later considered too bombastic.

Harrison and Preston also used a number Afro-American musicians who were passing through London to record with. Speaking in a BBC interview in March 1970, Harrison said: "On the Doris Troy album and (the second) Billy Preston, we've been using all sorts of people, whoever comes to town comes and plays on the sessions. We had the Temptations' rhythm section – bass player, guitarist and drummer – which is really nice. Also, Sam & Dave's… I think it was the drummer and the saxophonist playing bass. They played on a couple of Billy Preston's."[59]

Besides experimenting with new sounds and combinations of players, it's possible that Harrison was trying out songs for his forthcoming solo album. *Encouraging Words* features not one, but three Harrison compositions, and could have featured more. He certainly had no shortage of songs, and not everything recorded for *All Things Must Pass* made it onto the sprawling three record set. No more than six months earlier, he thought about offering Preston 'What Is Life' but kept it for himself. "'What Is Life' was written for Billy Preston in 1969… when I was producing one of his albums…," Harrison recalled, "it seemed too difficult to go in there and say 'Hey, I wrote this catchy pop song' while Billy was playing his funky stuff."[60] Of the two songs he gave to Preston, both would feature on *All Things Must Pass*, and one, 'My Sweet Lord', would become his best known and most controversial song.

The collaboration that had started with *That's The Way God Planned It* continued with Harrison and Preston singing, playing and writing together. 'Sing One For The Lord' was written in early 1969 while Preston was recording with The Beatles. It was recorded on 12 February 1969, perhaps with the intention of including it on Preston's debut Apple long-player. For whatever reason, it didn't make the cut and had to wait a further year before being selected for *Encouraging Words*.

A gospel-style hymn in praise of God, it's intended to take the singer and listener to another emotional state; a state of grace, if you will. Gospel music, like its Eastern counterpart, a Bhagwan Bhajan – a devotional song, sung with Bhakti (loving devotion), has the power to take us to another level emotionally, and, if you're a believer, spiritually. Perhaps these states of being are one and the same. How many times have you heard the phrase 'take me higher' in soul music? They're not always singing about altered states induced by pharmaceutical stimulants or their baby's love.

According to Hindu teachings, because every human being is different, everyone should be allowed to connect to God in their own way. It doesn't matter what route you take, the destination is the same. As Harrison sang in a later song "any road will take you there". In this respect Harrison and Preston were in perfect harmony. "The names change," explained Preston. "His is Krishna; mine is Christ. The spiritual promotion – praising God, chanting, spreading it, turning people onto it – these are the things we have in common."[61]

'All Things Must Pass' dates from 1968 and had been looking for a home for some time before Preston recorded his version. Harrison offered it to The Beatles on the first day of filming for *Let It Be*. Although it would never make it onto a Beatles record the group put considerable time and effort into working on its arrangement. On day two of filming, they ran though no fewer than thirty-seven takes of the song before drifting off to perform some rambling oldies.

Undeterred by The Beatles lack of interest, Harrison recorded a solo guitar based demo at EMI Studios on 25 February 1969, but the song remained dormant for the best part of a year. Having failed to get it on either The Beatles' *Let It Be* or *Abbey Road* albums, he gave the song to Preston. Preston instills it with warmth and light. There's a feeling of passion and joy in his voice which is echoed by a bright and lively string arrangement that gives the song the sense of chiaroscuro it needs. Preston's reading conveys a feeling that all things will pass, and for the better. Harrison's interpretation doesn't.

Preston's performance of another Harrison song destined for *All Things Must Pass*, 'My Sweet Lord', is again markedly different from Harrison's version. Harrison had his doubts about releasing the song himself because of public perceptions. "I was inspired to write 'My Sweet Lord' by the Edwin Hawkins Singers' version of 'Oh Happy Day'," he explained. "I thought a lot about whether to do 'My Sweet Lord' or not, because I would be committing myself publicly and I anticipated that a lot of people might get weird about it."[62] He appears to have forgotten that he'd already put his name to several religious records and people hadn't got 'weird' about those. Why should they? It wasn't as if he was the first pop star to come out of the closet and proclaim his belief in God. Little Richard, Al Green, Elvis Presley, Cat Stevens and Pete Townshend had all recorded music praising the Lord. People didn't get 'weird' when they came out of the spiritual closet, so why should they think any less of Harrison?

Harrison invited the Edwin Hawkins Singers to record with Preston at Olympic Studio in January 1970. Combined with the Temptations rhythm section they gave the song an uplifting gospel groove that swings and sways like a congregation in full effect. Preston's version of 'My Sweet Lord' was scheduled as his fourth Apple single in September 1970. It's British release was scrapped but it was issued in France, the Netherlands and America where it achieved modest success.

Encouraging Words data

Issued in September 1970, original copies of the album were issued with Apple labels and a standard single pocket sleeve. The album was reissued on CD and vinyl in 1991. The vinyl edition has a gatefold sleeve and a bonus 12-inch disc featuring 'All That I Got (I'm Going To Give It To You)' and the previously unreleased 'As Long As I Got My Baby'. These additional tracks were also issued on the CD. The CD was reissued in 2010 with an additional bonus track 'How Long Has The Train Been Gone'.

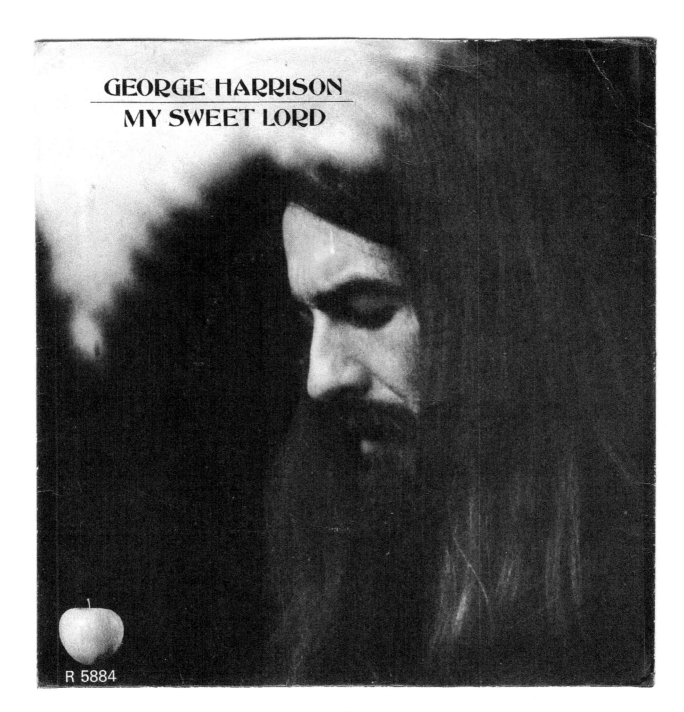

GEORGE HARRISON
MY SWEET LORD

R 5884

GEORGE HARRISON
MY SWEET LORD

'My Sweet Lord' / 'Isn't It a Pity' (US)
'My Sweet Lord' / 'What Is Life' (UK)
GEORGE HARRISON
Produced by George Harrison and Phil Spector.
US release: 23 November 1970; Apple 2995; chart high; number 1.
UK release: 15 January 1971; Apple R5884; chart high; number 1.

George Harrison (vocals, acoustic guitars, electric slide guitar, backing vocals), Eric Clapton (guitar, backing vocals), Billy Preston (piano), Gary Wright (electric piano), Bobby Whitlock (pump organ or harmonium), Badfinger (acoustic guitars), Klaus Voormann (bass), Ringo Starr (drums), Mike Gibbins (tambourine).

The Beatles were never keen on lifting singles from albums, although there were exceptions. This attitude stayed with them when they became solo artists. Harrison did not want any singles released from *All Things Must Pass* in case it lessened the impart of his colossal debut album. However, pressure from his manager, producer and record company ensured that he relented, and 'My Sweet Lord' was issued as the album's lead single.

'My Sweet Lord' was issued as a single in America four days ahead of the *All Things Must Pass* album. Radio loved it. Both sides of the single received almost equal airtime which meant that *Billboard* magazine had to chart the two songs as a single entry. The single entered the American charts at number 72 and reached number 1 on 26 December.

In Britain, 'My Sweet Lord' entered the charts at number 7, before reaching number 1 on 30 January 1971 and staying there for five weeks. It became the biggest-selling single of 1971 in Britain and performed similarly well in France and Germany, where it was number 1 for nine and ten weeks, respectively.

My Sweet Lord data

'My Sweet Lord' was re-mixed for single release with less echo and slightly different backing-vocals. In America, 'My Sweet Lord'/'Isn't It A Pity' was officially released as a double A-side. American pressings have the full Apple label on each side of the record and were issued in a picture sleeve featuring a photograph of Harrison taken by Barry Feinstein. This configuration was also used for most other territories. When the single was issued in Britain, 'Isn't It A Pity' was replaced with 'What Is Life', which was already scheduled as the follow up to 'My Sweet Lord' for the rest of the world.

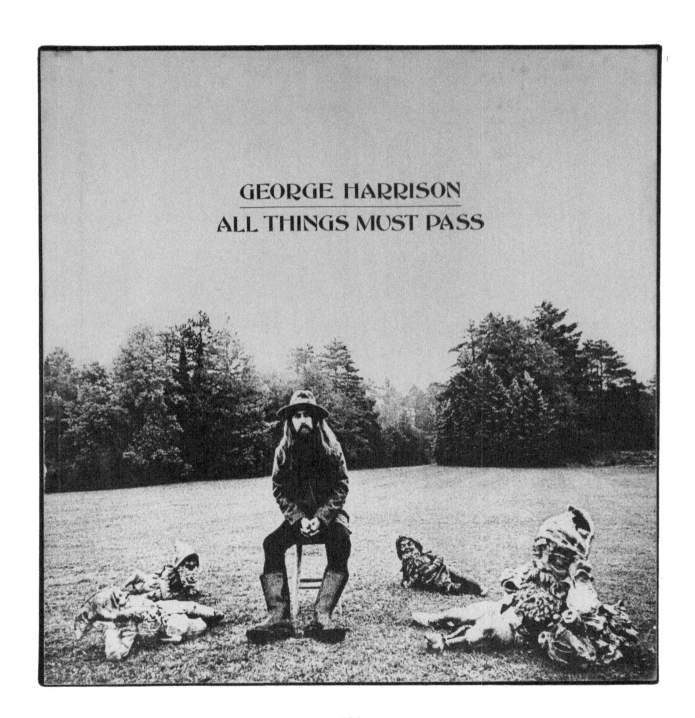

SIDE 1
I'd Have You Anytime
My Sweet Lord
Wah-Wah
Isn't It A Pity (version one)

SIDE 2
What Is Life
If Not For You
Behind That Locked Door
Let It Down
Run Of The Mill

SIDE 3
Beware Of Darkness
Apple Scruffs
Ballad of Sir Frankie Crisp
Let It Roll
Awaiting On You All
All Things Must Pass

SIDE 4
I Dig Love
Art Of Dying
Isn't It A Pity (version two)
Hear Me Lord

SIDE 5
Out Of The Blue
It's Johnny's Birthday
Plug Me In

SIDE 6
I Remember Jeep
Thanks For The Pepperoni

**THE FOLLOWING MUSICIANS
CONTRIBUTED TO THIS ALBUM:**

Drums and Percussion:
 Ringo Starr
 Jim Gordon
 Alan White

Bass Guitar:
 Klaus Voormann
 Carl Radle

Keyboard:
 Gary Wright
 Bobby Whitlock
 Billy Preston
 Gary Brooker

Pedal Steel Guitar:
 Pete Drake

Guitar:
 George Harrison
 Dave Mason

Tenor Saxophone:
 Bobby Keys

Trumpet
 Jim Price

Rhythm Guitars & Percussion:
 Badfinger

Mal Evans: Tea; Sympathy;
and Tambourine
and introducing the
George O'Hara-Smith Singers

Orchestral arrangements by
John Barham

Recording Engineers:
Ken Scott and Philip McDonald

Package design & Photography:
Tom Wilkes and Barry Feinstein
for Camouflage Productions

Produced by George Harrison
and Phil Spector for APPLE RECORDS.

MADE AND PRINTED IN GREAT BRITAIN

ALL THINGS MUST PASS

33⅓
Mfd. in U.K.
STEREO

STCH 2-639
(YEX 819)
SIDE THREE
℗1970

BEWARE OF DARKNESS
APPLE SCRUFFS
BALLAD OF SIR FRANKIE CRISP (LET IT ROLL)
AWAITING ON YOU ALL
ALL THINGS MUST PASS
All composed by GEORGE HARRISON
All published by HARRISONGS ESSEX INT.
MECOLICO BIEM NCB

Produced by HARRISON/SPECTOR

GEORGE HARRISON

An E.M.I. Recording

ALL THINGS MUST PASS

33⅓
Mfd. in U.K.
STEREO

STCH 2-639
(YEX 820)
SIDE FOUR
℗1970

I DIG LOVE
ART OF DYING
ISN'T IT A PITY (Version Two)
HEAR ME LORD
All composed by GEORGE HARRISON
All published by HARRISONGS ESSEX INT.
MECOLICO BIEM NCB
Produced by HARRISON/SPECTOR

GEORGE HARRISON

An E.M.I. Recording

Apple Jam

ALL THINGS MUST PASS

33⅓
Mfd. in U.K.
An E.M.I. Recording
℗1970

Side Five

OUT OF THE BLUE
IT'S JOHNNY'S BIRTHDAY
(based upon Congratulations by Martin & Coulter)
PLUG ME IN
All published by HARRISONGS
Essex Int. except track 2
Peter Maurice. World Music
Mecolico. BIEM. NCB.
Produced by HARRISON/SPECTOR
GEORGE HARRISON

Apple Jam

ALL THINGS MUST PASS

33⅓
Mfd. in U.K.
An E.M.I. Recording
℗1970

STEREO
STCH 3-639
(YEX 822)
Side Six

I REMEMBER JEEP
THANKS FOR THE PEPPERONI
All published by HARRISONGS
Essex Int. Mecolico. BIEM. NCB.
Produced by HARRISON/SPECTOR
GEORGE HARRISON

106

ALL THINGS MUST PASS
GEORGE HARRISON

Side one: I'd Have You Anytime (Harrison–Dylan) / My Sweet Lord / Wah-Wah / Isn't It A Pity (Version One)

Side two: What Is Life / If Not for You (Dylan) / Behind That Locked Door / Let It Down / Run Of The Mill

Side three: Beware of Darkness / Apple Scruffs / Ballad Of Sir Frankie Crisp (Let It Roll) /Awaiting On You All / All Things Must Pass

Side four: I Dig Love / Art Of Dying / Isn't It A Pity (Version Two) / Hear Me Lord

Side five: Out of the Blue / It's Johnny's Birthday (Bill Martin, Phil Coulter, Harrison) / Plug Me In

Side six: I Remember Jeep / Thanks For The Pepperoni

UK release: November 30 1970; STCH 639; chart high; number 1.

US release: November 27 1970; STCH 639; chart high; number 1.

Produced by George Harrison and Phil Spector.

George Harrison (vocals, electric and acoustic guitars, dobro, harmonica, Moog synthesizer, backing vocals), Eric Clapton (electric and acoustic guitars, backing vocals), Gary Wright (piano, organ, electric piano), Bobby Whitlock (piano, organ, backing vocals), Klaus Voormann (bass, electric guitar), Carl Radle (bass), Jim Gordon (drums), Ringo Starr (drums, percussion), Billy Preston (organ, piano), Alan White (drums, vibraphone), Jim Price (trumpet, trombone, horn arrangements), Bobby Keys (saxophones), Pete Drake (pedal steel), Dave Mason (electric and acoustic guitars), Pete Ham (acoustic guitar), Tom Evans (acoustic guitar), Joey Molland (acoustic guitar), Mike Gibbins (percussion), John Barham (orchestral arrangements, choral arrangement, harmonium, vibraphone), Tony Ashton (piano), Gary Brooker (piano), Mal Evans (percussion, backing vocals), Phil Collins (percussion), Ginger Baker (drums), Al Abramowitz (unspecified), Eddie Klein (backing vocals).

On 26 May 1970, George Harrison began work on his third solo album, *All Things Must Pass*. It was to be his defining statement, personally, musically and spiritually. This was pop music on a grand scale, a Phil Spector scale, a scale befitting an ex-Beatle. Everything about it was immense; from Spector's wall of sound, to the army of musicians involved in its recording, from the quantity and variety of music to the weighty three LP boxed set itself; *All Things Must Pass* was a statement of imposing grandure. Its sonic superstructure towered over his contemporaries, dwarfing everything in its path. All they could do was look on in admiration as the quite one stepped out of the shadows and into the spotlight.

The last song The Beatles recorded as a group, albeit without Lennon, was by George Harrison. On 3 January 1970, one year and one day after Harrison proffered 'All Things Must Pass' to the group while filming *Let It Be* at Twickenham film studios, Harrison, McCartney and Starr recorded 'I Me Mine' at EMI Studios for inclusion on their swan song album. The following day they added overdubs to McCartney's 'Let It Be'. And with that The Beatles were no more.

Twenty-five days later, Harrison returned to EMI Studios to assist John Lennon with the recording of 'Instant Karma (We All Shine On)'. The recording was produced by Phil Spector, who was in town to try and salvage The Beatles' *Let It Be* album. Spector was typically twitchy and insisted that sound engineer Geoff Emerick be removed from the session because he was freaking him out. Despite this, the producer worked his magic on Lennon's song and transformed it into a sonic sledgehammer that hit you right between the ears. It couldn't have been more different from the subtle, unprocessed sound Harrison had been developing with Billy Preston and Doris Troy. But something about Spector impressed Harrison, and before he knew it the legendary producer was not only 'reproducing' The Beatles, but co-producing records for Lennon and Harrison, too.

In the months that followed, Harrison produced albums by Billy Preston and Doris Troy, and jammed with Bob Dylan at Columbia Studios, New York. In April, he entered EMI Studios to showcase fifteen songs he'd provisionally earmarked for his new album. "I had to go over the songs I had with Phil Spector, 'cause he was the co-producer, and we were in, I think, Studio 2 at Abbey Road, and the engineer had a microphone and taped it," Harrison recalled.[63] Speaking to Howard Smith on 3 May 1970 he said: "I sang him [Spector] a couple of the songs... I sang him a lot of songs that I had, but umm, at that time I hadn't decided really that I was doing an album. You know, I knew I'd do one eventually but I hadn't decided to do it this soon. And it was only after that I decided that I'd do it straight away. So now I've got to meet with Phil and decide really which tunes, you know. I've got an idea which ones I'd like to use."[64]

Of the songs Harrison performed for Spector only seven made the finished album; 'Run Of The Mill', 'Art Of Dying', 'Wah-Wah', 'Beware Of Darkness', 'Let It Down', 'Hear Me Lord' and 'If Not For You'. A version of 'Let It Down' from this session was later overdubbed and issued on the 2001 edition of *All Things Must Pass*. Eight songs performed this day didn't appear on the album: 'Window, Window', 'Tell Me What Has Happened To You', 'Nowhere To Go', 'Cosmic Empire', 'Beautiful Girl', 'I Don't Wanna Do It', 'Everybody, Nobody' and 'Mother Divine'. Some of the songs were reworked, the 'Sir Frankie Crisp' refrain from 'Everybody, Nobody' was incorporated into 'The Ballad Of Sir Frankie Crisp'. Others, 'Beautiful Girl' and 'I Don't Wanna Do It', were saved for later albums.

Harrison recorded several other songs during the sessions for *All Things Must Pass*, which also failed to make the final cut. 'I Live for You', 'Dehra Dun', 'Gopala Krishna', 'Down To The River', 'Whenever' and 'Going Down to Golders Green' were recorded but not used. 'I Live for You' appeared in 2001 on the re-mastered version of the album. 'Down To The River' was re-recorded for Harrison's last album *Brainwashed*. 'Whenever', later re-titled 'When Every Song Is Sung', was given to Cilla Black before it was successfully recorded by Ringo Starr on his album *Ringo's Rotogravure*.

The sessions kicked off on 26 May 1970 with Eric Clapton, Carl Radle, Jim Gordon, and Bobby Whitlock. However, when Harrison heard the results he was shocked. "The first track we ever did was this song 'Wah-Wah', and it sounded really nice in the studio, all this nice acoustic [guitars] and piano and no echo on anything," he explained. "We did it for hours, until he [Spector] had it right in the control room. Then we went in to listen to it, and I listened to it, and I thought, 'I hate it. It's horrible.' I said [to Spector], 'It's horrible, I hate it.' And Eric [Clapton] said, 'Oh, I love it.' So I said, 'Well you can have it on your album, then.' But I grew to like it."[65]

Spector's wall of sound obviously wasn't what Harrison was expecting, or what he wanted. Although Harrison wasn't sure how he wanted the album to sound, he did know he wanted a "production album". Speaking to Howard Smith in May 1970, he said: "So the songs – it depends really on how I see the arrangements. Some songs maybe I'll do just one or two just with acoustic guitars or something, but it's really down to how I see the songs should be interpreted. But I really want to use as much instrumentation as I think the songs need. You know, some will have orchestras, and some will have rock 'n' roll, and some will have trumpets. You know, whatever. It'll be a production album."[66]

Although he'd be recording a solo record, he wasn't going to play all the instruments himself like McCartney did. This record was going to be recorded with friends. "I'd much rather play with other people, you know, because... united we stand, divided we fall. I think, musically it can sound much more together if you have a bass player, a drummer, and you know, a few friends. A little help from your friends," he said.[67] Naturally, he asked Eric Clapton to help. Clapton was putting a new band together that would become Derek and the Dominoes. "George was working on his first album *All Things Must Pass*, and one day asked if the Tulsa guys and me would play on it," Clapton explained. "I knew he had Spector producing him, so we made a deal whereby he would get Spector to produce a couple of tracks for us, in return for having the use of our band for his album."[68]

Although he'd recorded two solo albums and written several hits for others, he still wasn't sure that his songs were good enough, or if he had what it took to be a solo performer. Surrounding himself with friends gave him the confidence to step out of the long shadow cast by The Beatles and stand alone. "Derek and the Dominoes played on most of the tracks and it was a really nice experience making that album – because I was really a bit paranoid, musically. Having this whole thing with the Beatles had left me really paranoid. I remember having those people in the studio and thinking, 'God, these songs are so fruity! I can't think of which song to do.' Slowly I realized, 'We can do this one,' and I'd play it to them and they'd say, 'Wow, yeah! Great song!' And I'd say, 'Really? Do you really like it?' I realized that it was okay... that they were sick of playing all that other stuff."[69]

While Derek and the Dominoes provided the musical backbone, many other musicians were employed to flesh out the sound. Spector recorded this album as he had recorded everything else he'd ever produced. A large group of musicians was assembled that would run through each song until Spector was satisfied that he'd captured his trademark wall of sound on tape. A young Phil Collins was among the small army of musicians and he recalls the lengthy recording process: "I was asked to play percussion on this track. I had never played congas or anything like that before. Anyway, the way Phil Spector used to work would be to say, 'OK, let's hear the keyboards, the drums and the guitars play through the track.' And every time he said 'Drums' I played, figuring he meant me. Since I'd never played congas, my hands were getting pretty bad blisters by the time half an hour had gone past. And then he said, 'OK, let's hear the bass, the acoustic guitars, the guitar and the drums.' And he'd go through all these combinations from the control room. About two and a half hours later, he says, 'Right – congas, you play this time!' My hands were bleeding by then. He hadn't been listening to me at all."[70] Collin's is supposed to have played on 'The Art Of Dying', a song devoid of congas. A more likely candidate is 'Wah-Wah', which does feature some 'adventurous' conga playing.

While Spector was in the control room, turning engineers into nervous wrecks, the band jammed away on long, meandering instrumentals, some of which would appear on disc three of the album. According to Bobby Whitlock it was Spector's habit to capture everything on tape: "Phil Spector was so funny in the control room; man, they really needed to have the whole thing running in the control room. And, plus, we did the 'Apple Jams'. When we got to Miami, I told Ronnie and Howie Albert, and Tom Dowd, 'If anybody walks in, it's just tape; just turn it on!' – whether it's Eric by himself, or me and Carl (Radle), or whomever it may be, just turn the tape on. So that's how we wound up with all those jams and everything."[71] Derek and The Dominoes developed their jamming habit at Clapton's house. It was a great way of developing a musical intuitiveness, if somewhat annoying for the neighbours. "When we were doing the band, we would play in 'E,' – just 'E' – for hours and hours and hours down at Eric's house, and we had a complaint from a neighbour: Can you guys change the chord? Just change keys, please!," recalled Whitlock.[72]

Spector's habit of constantly running expensive multi-track tape added to the cost of the album, which, when combined with the expense of hiring session musicians, rankled with the ever parsimonious EMI. "George was pissed off with EMI, you know. 'What are they saying that I'm taking too much studio time?' EMI was on his back because he'd been in the studio so long and it was so expensive," recalled Klaus Voormann.[73] It wasn't only expensive studio time that worried EMI. When Harrison and Spector decided to add pedal steel to some tracks they flew Pete Drake in from America. Drake claimed: "It cost them $10,000 just to fly me to London to play on it and about $80,000 or so for the whole album."[74] $10,000 to fly one man and his guitar to London seems a little expensive, particularly as in 1970 a return flight from New York to San Francisco cost about $300. Drake appears to have been exaggerating, which calls into question the $80,000 he claimed it cost to record the album. Harrison certainly didn't scrimp on production costs and besides recording at EMI and Trident studios, he flew to America to finish mixing the album and to have it mastered. When you factor in the additional costs $80,000 might not be so far off the mark.

Not only did Harrison have EMI to contend with, he also had to deal with an increasingly unstable producer. "He [Spector] used to have 18 cherry brandies before he could get himself down to the studio," Harrison said in 1987. "I got so tired of that because I needed someone to help. I was ending up with more work than if I'd just been doing it on my own."[75] According to Klaus Voormann that's exactly what happened. "Sometimes it became too much," he confirms. "In the end, I think George was getting fed up with him, so he did some of it himself. He was getting very drunk. He just didn't stick to one thing – he'd suddenly be off on something that had nothing to do with the record."[76]

It's fairly easy to tell who produced what. Listen to 'Run Of The Mill', a song with a big production comprising acoustic guitars, keyboards and a prominent brass arrangement. The one thing you don't hear is Spector's over-the-top use of echo. Compare it with 'Wah-Wah', a production so sodden in echo it's an audio quagmire. It's big and intimidating and the sonic equivalent of a headache, which is what the song is about. But it's so drenched in echo it's difficult to distinguish one instrument from another. That can't be said of 'Run Of The Mill'. It still has the big sound associated with the album, but each instrument is clearly defined. It has a clarity to it, it's clean and crisp while Spector's work is muddy, squelchy and impressionistic. That's not to say that Spector wasn't the right man for the job, when he was kept in check he helped Harrison create some beautiful music. But left to his own devices he didn't know when to stop, consequently some of Harrison's personality is lost in the thick production.

Ironically, this was something Spector picked up on when he was sent early mixes of the album. In a letter dated 19 August the mercurial producer passed judgement on the work completed thus far. Besides noting that Harrison's vocals were too low in the mix, Spector suggested revisiting some performances because: "I really feel that your voice has got to be heard throughout the album so that the greatness of the songs can really come through."[77] He also suggested adding additional instruments to some tracks; he thought 'Let It Down' could be improved with some "wailing saxophone". But his main concern was with the mixing. It was here that he would work his magic. "I'm sure the album will be able to be remixed excellently. I also feel that therein lies much of the album because many of the tracks are really quite good and will reproduce on record very well."[78]

EMI Studios only had eight-track facilities, so it was decided to mix the album at Trident Studios because it had sixteen-track machines. This allowed for further overdubbing without the need to bounce down tracks with resulting loss of sound quality. In October, Harrison flew with the master tapes to New York for further mixing at Mediasound Studios. With work on the album almost complete, Harrison had reference acetates cut with the result that at least one song, 'What Is Life', was remixed before the finished master was readied for production. To ensure the highest quality control, Harrison even went as far as to visit one of Capitol's pressing plants to check on the production of records.

With so many songs to choose from, some artists would have selected a single album's worth of songs and kept the rest back for future use. But not Harrison. Having finally purged himself of the Lennon – McCartney imposed backlog, he decided to include almost everything, including a disc of spontaneous jams. "I did *All Things Must Pass*, the basic tracks, seventeen of them, just one after another.

I suddenly thought, 'I had better check out and see what I have got here,' and I found out that I had seventeen tracks, some dating back to '66 and '67. Then I had to decide which ones to use. In the end, I thought, 'Use them all,' because a lot of them were a backlog and, in order to clear the way for what I was writing, at that time and in the future, I used all of them. Even before I started, I knew I was gonna make a good album because I had so many songs and I had so much energy," he explained.[79]

The critics agreed with Harrison. What he'd produced was good, very good. Reviewing the album for the *New Musical Express,* Alan Smith wrote: "George Harrison's three-album set *All Things Must Pass,* which finds its way into the shops this week, will prove that it's a long time since so much love and care and work have been wrapped into one package by one specific artist. Like the McCartney album, all I can say is that *All Things Must Pass* stands head and shoulders above just about any other solo album released this year."[80]

Ben Gerson's review for *Rolling Stone* was equally fulsome in its praise. "It is both an intensely personal statement and a grandiose gesture, a triumph over artistic modesty, even frustration. In this extravaganza of piety and sacrifice and joy, whose sheer magnitude and ambition may dub it the War and Peace of rock and roll, the music itself is no longer the only message."[81]

The public agreed and sent the album to the top of the charts on both sides of the Atlantic, well almost. In Britain the album fell foul of a strike by postal workers. Shops providing sales figures for the pop charts did so by post. A two-month postal strike over the winter of 1970-71 meant that sales data didn't reach the chart compilers in time, consequently *All Things Must Pass* was originally listed as having reached number 4. (During the eight weeks between February 6 and March 27, 1971, Simon and Garfunkel remained at the top of the charts with *Bridge Over Troubled.*) However, in 2006 the Official UK Charts Company changed its records to show that *All Things Must Pass* did top the charts throughout that time.

All Things Must Pass data

The finished album was issued as a three-record boxed set with printed inner sleeves, colour poster and in some cases an orange separator board. Discs one and two were issued with orange tinted Apple labels, the third disc with a bespoke green label with an apple jam jar logo. The cover slicks were printed in America and shipped to Britain and assembled at EMI's factory in Hayes, Middlesex. Having the cover slicks produced centrally may have saved money, but it caused problems in Britain. A batch of slicks was held up by British Customs officials, which resulted in EMI running dangerously low of stock just as sales were peaking. An Apple spokesperson said: "The triple LPs are pressed here, along with the presentation package; but all the inner sleeves and colour posters of George are printed in the States. We sold out of initial supplies and couldn't get any more through because around 250,000 altogether were stuck in freight at London's Heathrow Airport. As a result, nearly 100,000 *All Things Must Pass* albums could not be sent to retailers around the country between December 18 and January 15, 1971."[82]

I'd Have You Anytime (Harrison – Dylan)

George Harrison (vocals, acoustic guitars), Eric Clapton (electric guitar), Carl Radle or Klaus Voormann (bass), Jim Gordon or Alan White (drums), Bobby Whitlock (pump organ), John Barham (possible vibrophone), Badfinger (possible acoustic guitars)

All Things Must Pass slides into life with a song Harrison co-wrote with Bob Dylan while staying at his Woodstock home in late 1968. Dylan wasn't in a particularly responsive mood and didn't warm to his houseguest until the guitars came out. With the ice broken, the two musicians began communicating and sharing their skills. "I was saying to him, 'You write incredible lyrics,' and he was saying, 'How do you write those tunes?' So I was just showing him chords like crazy, and I was saying, 'Come on, write me some words,' and he was scribbling words down and it just killed me because he had been doing all these sensational lyrics. And he wrote, 'All I have is yours, All you see is mine, And I'm glad to hold you in my arms, I'd have you anytime.' The idea of Dylan writing something, like, so very simple, was amazing to me," recalled Harrison.[83]

Harrison took Dylan's simple lyric and, empathizing with the singer's fragile sensibility, crafted a melody with an autumnal feel that matched Dylan's state of mind perfectly. Harrison: "I had felt strongly about Bob when I had been in India years before, the only record I took with me along with all my Indian records was *Blonde On Blonde*. I somehow got very close to him, you know, because he was so great, so heavy and so observant about everything. And yet, to find him later very nervous and with no confidence. But the thing he said on *Blonde On Blonde* about what price you have to pay to get out of going through all these things twice, 'Oh mama, can this really be the end.' And I thought, 'Isn't it great?' because I know people are going to think, 'Shit, what's Dylan doing?' But as far as I was concerned, it was great for him to realize his own peace and it meant something."[84]

Harrison and Dylan recorded a rough demo of the song in which Harrison takes the lead both as guitarist and singer. It's clear that they have yet to finish the lyrics with Dylan struggling to follow what he's only recently put down on paper. The briefest of sketches, it stops abruptly after two passes of the verse and chorus. An early take recorded during sessions for *All Things Must Pass* was issued on the *George Harrison: Living In The Material World* album that companioned the Martin Scorsese documentary.

My Sweet Lord

George Harrison (vocals, acoustic guitars, electric slide guitar, backing vocals), Eric Clapton (guitar, backing vocals), Billy Preston (piano), Gary Wright (electric piano), Bobby Whitlock (pump organ or harmonium), Badfinger (acoustic guitars), Klaus Voormann (bass), Ringo Starr (drums), Mike Gibbins (tambourine)

Harrison's greatest hit and biggest headache was born when Delaney & Bonnie and Friends played in Copenhagen. With time on his hands, he began work on a new song that he hoped would take 'Oh

Happy Day' to another level. "I remember Eric and Delaney & Bonnie were doing interviews with somebody in either Copenhagen or Gothenburg, somewhere in Sweden and I was so thrilled with 'Oh Happy Day', by The Edwin Hawkins Singers. It really just knocked me out, the idea of that song and I just felt a great feeling of the Lord. So I thought, 'I'll write another 'Oh Happy Day',' which became 'My Sweet Lord', he explained.[85]

A gospel group from California, The Edwin Hawkins Singers took the 18th century hymn high into the charts on both sides of the Atlantic. The song's surprise success brought them to Britain to promote the record at the same time as Delaney & Bonnie and Friends toured the country – the gospel group appeared on *The Val Doonican Show* in November and sang on the Billy Preston version of 'My Sweet Lord', which suggests that his version was recorded in late 1969 as the group didn't return to Britain again until December 1970, by which time both Preston's and Harrison's versions had been released.

Like 'Oh Happy Day', 'My Sweet Lord' is a prayer, but with a twist. In Harrison's version, East meets West without the barriers of sectarianism. The product of his investigations into religion and spiritual music, it combines elements drawn from pop, gospel, choral music and Indian classical music with not a hint of incongruity. Harrison's slide guitar playing is a model of perfection. Melodic and inventive, it references the Indian classical music he loved, lifts the song and praises the Lord. "If anything any good comes out of my life or out of my music or out of my mouth, then let the glories be to the Lord," Harrison explained.[86]

Harrison kept the lyrics deliberately simple and added a clever twist by incorporating both Hallelujah and Hare Krishna. "My idea in 'My Sweet Lord', because it sounded like a 'pop song', was to sneak up on them a bit. The point was to have the people not offended by 'Hallelujah', and by the time it gets to 'Hare Krishna', they're already hooked, and their foot's tapping, and they're already singing along 'Hallelujah', to kind of lull them into a sense of false security. And then suddenly it turns into 'Hare Krishna', and they will all be singing that before they know what's happened, and they will think, 'Hey, I thought I wasn't supposed to like Hare Krishna!'"[87]

Having cleverly incorporated Hallelujah and Hare Krishna into the song, Harrison also introduced a Vedic Sanskrit prayer into the song's coda. "Gururbrahmaa Guru visnuh, Gururdevo Mahesvarah / Gurussaakshaat Param Brahma / Tasmai Shri Gurave Namhah" which translates as: "The teacher is Brahma, the teacher is Visnu, the teacher is the Lord Mahesvarah. Verily the teacher is the supreme Brahman, to that respected teacher I bow down." It was a neat way of praising the Lord, spreading the message and breaking down barriers. How many people have found themselves singing along to this part of the song without realizing what it is they are doing? Every time it was played on the radio it did the Lord's work and turned Harrison into the world's most popular evangelist.

As with everything else on *All Things Must Pass*, the song was recorded live in the studio with a large group of well rehearsed musicians. Harrison and Spector planned its recording meticulously. With so many musicians involved, it was vital that everybody knew what they were doing. Particular attention was paid to the acoustic guitars which give the song its distinctive sound. "The sound of that record, it sounds like one huge guitar," Harrison enthused. "The way Phil Spector and I put that down was we had two drummers, a bass player, two pianos and about five acoustic guitars, a tambourine player and we sequenced it in order. Everybody plays live in the studio. I spent a lot of time with the other rhythm guitar players to get them all to play exactly the same rhythm so it just sounded perfectly in synch. The way we spread the stereo in the recording, the spread of five guitars across the stereo, made it sound like one big record. The other things, I overdubbed, like I overdubbed the voices, which I sang all the back-up parts as well and overdubbed the slide guitars, but everything else on it was live."[88]

The song sounded great on the radio and when issued as a single, 'My Sweet Lord' topped the charts on both sides of the Atlantic. Two weeks after Apple issued Harrison's version of 'My Sweet Lord' in America, it issued Billy Preston's version as a single too. Preston's recording of the song had already been issued on his *Encouraging Words* album without a hint of the trouble that was to dog Harrison's recording. Once Harrison's version hit the airwaves it wasn't long before people picked up on the similarities between his version of 'My Sweet Lord' and 'He's So Fine'. And that included Harrison. "I guess I finally realized that the songs sounded similar when the song came out on the radio in 1970 and a few disc jockeys got off on the idea. But you can listen to a number of records and hear other songs in them. I don't consider it a lift because in my mind I was trying to do 'Oh Happy Day'," he said.[89]

Bright Tunes, the publishers of 'He's So Fine', didn't see it that way. On 27 February 1971 the *New Musical Express* reported that Bright Tunes was suing Harrison for copyright infringement. "A lot of people sue people like us because it's aggravation for us; they think we'll settle. The guy who wrote 'He's So Fine' actually died in 1967 or 1968 – he never even heard 'My Sweet Lord'. And I'm sure if he was a musician, he wouldn't have flinched. But the guy who was his accountant... he saw this as money pouring out of the sky. There are different mentalities. People who go out of their way to do something like that, to copy something, and then there are musicians who realize that all music is in some way related to something else," Harrison explained.[90]

While Harrison may have convinced himself that "all music is in some way related to something else", the lawyers for Bright Tunes thought otherwise. They argued that 'My Sweet Lord' was cloned from 'He's So Fine'. In a rather crass attempt to drive the point home, Bright Tunes had Jodie Miller record a version of 'He's So Fine' in the style of 'My Sweet Lord'. "The first thing I knew was Klein said something to me about it. He said: 'Somebody has made a recording.' And it was like the company Bright Tunes; they had got this version recorded by Jodie Miller of 'He's So Fine', which was really like, you know, putting the screws in. What they did was to change the chords of 'He's So Fine', and make them completely into the same chords as 'My Sweet Lord' because there is actually a slight difference, and then also put on top of it the slide guitar part. So it was really trying to rub it in. That was the first thing I heard about it, and I thought: 'God!' So then all the people started hustling each other, and the guy from Bright Tunes was demanding money and various things. I really didn't hear anything about it for years. The attorneys were supposedly settling the thing, and in the end, I said:

'Look, it is just a lot of aggravation. Just give the guy some money.' And so they were going to give him two hundred thousand dollars. I found out, last week, after it has been to court, and been a big scene, now the guy only gets fifty thousand: And the judge made a slip after the court case. He just said to my attorney: "Actually, I like both of the songs," Harrison recalled.[91]

Before the case was settled, Bright Tunes sold the rights of 'He's So Fine' to Allen Klein's ABKCO company. In effect this meant that Harrison was now being sued by his own manager! The court eventually found that Klein's insider knowledge meant that he had acted improperly and ordered him to hold the rights to 'He's So Fine' in trust for Harrison. Harrison was ordered to pay $587,000 which meant that Klein broke even on the deal and the rights to 'He's So Fine' were transferred to Harrison. "After 20 years, eventually the judge awarded the song to me... and the money that had been taken for 'My Sweet Lord'. So I suddenly end up with 'He's So Fine'!," recalled an exasperated Harrison.[92]

Thanks to Klein's intervention, an already unpleasant experience turned into a farce. It was something Harrison could have done without. "It was a heavy emotional thing to go to court and play the guitar. All the secretaries from the other court came along. It was like, 'Oh, let's go see George Harrison doin' a concert in court.' Personally, I don't feel it damaged me. If it was the only song I'd ever written I'd feel bad, you know? But I just feel annoyed, because of the motives behind," Harrison explained.[93]

Long after the litigation was resolved, Delaney Bramlett bragged that it was he, not Harrison, who originated 'My Sweet Lord'. According to Bramlett, Harrison asked him to show him some gospel chord changes and he improvised a melody around the Chiffons song 'He's So Fine'. "So we used the melody for a quickie lesson. And I started singing (sings) 'My sweet Lord. I just want to feel you Lord.' And I said we'll throw these backing singers in there singing 'Hallelujah'," he claimed. "George's eyes were getting bigger and bigger. The next thing I knew I was hearing that record out on the radio. And George called me up and told me 'Your name's not on it as a writer but it will be on the next pressing.' But I knew it wouldn't be because they'd have to change the whole cover and everything. But he didn't mean to leave my name off and it didn't matter anyway, I was just happy to help him out. He told me 'That song got me to where I've been looking to go.' And I said 'Well, it was worth it.'"[94] Harrison may well have disagreed with Bramlett on that last point because the song became a headache that he could well have done without.

A 'demo' version of 'My Sweet Lord', possibly recorded at the same session Harrison used to showcase his songs for Phil Spector, was issued in 2012. Featuring Harrison on vocals and acoustic guitar, Klaus Voormann on bass and Ringo Starr on drums, it is the simplest of sketches that would be fleshed out once recording proper started. A rough mix with guide vocals was issued on the bootleg *Songs For Pattie*. Backing vocals and Harrison's slide guitar solo were overdubbed later at Trident Studios. Harrison re-worked the song in 2000 for the re-mastered *All Things Must Pass* album. Adding sitar and a new slide guitar part, Harrison also re-recorded his vocal, had his son Dhani overdub acoustic guitar and Sam Brown add new lead and backing vocals. 'My Sweet Lord (2000)' was issued as 7-inch promo single (7PRO 15930) backed with the original mix in January 2001 by Capitol in America to promote the re-mastered *All Things Must Pass*.

Wah-Wah

George Harrison (electric guitar, vocals, backing vocals), Eric Clapton (electric guitar), Carl Radle (bass), Bobby Whitlock (electric piano), Jim Gordon (drums), Jim Price (trumpet), Bobby Keys (saxophone), Phil Collins (congas), Mike Gibbins (tambourine)

Dating from January 1969, 'Wah-Wah' was written by Harrison to vent the anger and frustration he was experiencing while filming *Let It Be*. "We [The Beatles] had been away from each other after having a very difficult time recording the *White Album*, which went on so long," he recalled. "It went on forever. When we came back from holiday, we went straight back into the old routine. I remember Paul and I were trying to have an argument and the crew carried on filming and recording us. I couldn't stand it and I decided, 'This is it! Thank you, I'm leaving!' 'Wah-Wah' was a headache as well as a foot pedal. It was written during the time in the film where John and Yoko were freaking out and screaming. I wrote this tune at home."[95]

It wasn't just Lennon and McCartney who were causing Harrison grief. It was celebrity and life itself. Harrison dismissed his celebrity status has being 'cheaper than a dime'. What he longed for was a time when he would be free of such distractions. Meditation brought temporary relief, but ultimately he would only be free of worldly concerns once he'd achieved God consciousness and perfected the art of dying – a subject he'd address later in the album.

Written around a growling guitar riff, doubled by Clapton, who uses a wah-wah effect pedal, the song was given a spectacularly echo-drenched production by Spector that captures the feeling of a headache perfectly. There is so much echo used that at times it's difficult to distinguish individual instruments. Listen carefully and you can hear congas drifting in and out of the echo-y soundscape. Phil Collins is usually credited with playing this instrument but on 'The Art Of Dying', a song that doesn't feature congas. It's more likely that he played on 'Wah-Wah', which does feature some fairly 'adventurous' conga playing.

Badfinger and Peter Frampton are also usually credited with playing acoustic guitars on the track, which is odd because I can't hear a single acoustic guitar on it. Take three of the song was issued on the bootleg CD *Songs For Pattie*. This version has considerably less echo applied to it and therefore it's easier to distinguish individual instruments. Close examination reveals that there are no acoustic guitars present. Neither are there any organ parts, which means that Billy Preston and Gary Wright don't appear on the track either. The song does feature an electric piano, played by Bobby Whitlock.

However, his recollection of the session appears hazy at best. On one occasion he suggested that Preston and Wright were present, while on another that they were not. "I was the last one to show up at the session – I was running late and my car went down on me. It was getting started, I walked in and Phil Spector said, 'Phase those drums! Phase those guitars!' He's standing there looking out like he's the captain of a ship, and he says, 'Phase everything!' A guy had to operate this phase shifter by hand, his name was Eddie Albert, and he had to work it by twisting this knob to the left, to the right, to the left, to the right. You had to do it manually then. He's saying, 'Phase this, phase that,' I come in, I'm late and Billy Preston's sitting down at the organ, Gary Brooker is on the piano, where's my spot? Everything was on the downbeat. I said, 'I've got it, give me that little piano over there, I've got my part. I played everything that nobody was playing – I played on the upbeat. That's me on the electric piano playing the exact opposite."[96]

About the only thing Whitlock got right was the fact that he plays electric piano on the track. There is no phasing. Echo, yes. Phasing, no. Drugs and time have taken their toll on memories. He did correct himself when he published his book *Bobby Whitlock: A rock 'n' roll Autobiography*, and all the evidence points to the fact that that time he got it right. Overdubs were recorded at Trident Studios, which is where Pete Drake overdubbed a pedal steel guitar part using a Talk Box effect pedal similar to that later used by Peter Frampton on his hit 'Show Me The Way'. A rough mix featuring Pete Drake's talking steel guitar appeared on the bootleg *Songs For Pattie*.

Isn't It A Pity (version one)
George Harrison (slide guitar, vocals, backing vocals), Tony Ashton (piano), Gary Wright (keyboards), Billy Preston (keyboards), Klaus Voormann (bass), Badfinger (acoustic guitars), Ringo Starr (drums), Mike Gibbins (tambourine), John Barham (orchestral arrangement)

'Isn't It A Pity' brings together two themes that had occupied Harrison for sometime – hope and despair. The break up of The Beatles, a disintegrating marriage and difficult friendship, Clapton was infatuated with Pattie Harrison, meant his personal relationships were in tatters. In an attempt to relieve some of the stress he was experiencing, Harrison wrote 'Isn't It A Pity'. As he later explained: "'Isn't It A Pity' is about whenever a relationship hit's a down point – instead of whatever other people do (like break the other's jaws) I wrote a song."[97]

The song's stately tempo and descending chord progression elicits a sense of relentless emotional pressure bearing down on Harrison as he makes his way through the song like a modern day Jacob Marley. His ascending vocal melody offers the merest glimpse of hope and suggests that despite the difficulties everything will change for the better. But the song remains rooted in stoic resignation. The lengthy, repeated coda, borrowed from 'Hey Jude', becomes a pseudo mantra reinforcing the suggestion that it will take many lifetimes for things to improve.

Harrison recorded two versions of 'Isn't It A Pity'. The version that closes side one has an uncompromising down beat that gives it its sombre tone; punctuated by Harrison's bright slide guitar it never quite resolves the sense of impending gloom established in the opening bars. The shorter second version, which appears as the penultimate track on side four, is lighter and consequently more suggestive of the enlightenment Harrison was seeking.

What Is Life

George Harrison (guitar, bass guitar, vocals), Eric Clapton (guitar), Carl Radle (bass), Bobby Whitlock (piano), Badfinger (acoustic rhythm guitars), Jim Gordon (drums), Jim Price (trumpet), Bobby Keys (saxophone), John Barham (string arrangement), Mike Gibbins (tambourine)

Harrison wrote 'What Is Life' for Billy Preston in 1969, but decided to keep it for himself. Unlike some songs that take weeks, months or years to finish, according to Harrison 'What Is Life' came to him in less than an hour. "I wrote it very quickly, maybe in fifteen or thirty minutes, on the way to the Olympic Studios in London when I was producing one of his [Billy Preston] albums. Although Billy was such a great artist, I didn't think his songs were potential hits. Before the session, I just suddenly thought, 'Let's see if I can write a sort of up-tempo song for Billy,' and I wrote 'What Is Life' in about half an hour. And as it happened, we got to the session and Billy and the musicians had arrived and had already started rehearsing for some of the songs and that's the reason why we never got round to recording it. So I did it myself and recorded it."[98]

Harrison drew on his love and knowledge of soul and R&B to fashion an up-tempo love song that did indeed become a hit. Issued as the B-side of 'My Sweet Lord' in Britain, it was issued as an A-side in America and Europe. The single became Harrison's second top ten solo hit in America, making him the first ex-Beatle to score two top 10 hits in the United States. It performed even better in Europe, where it went top five in most countries and topped the charts in Switzerland.

On the surface 'What Is Life' appears to be a carefree, up-tempo love song. But as Harrison was found of pointing out, the world is full of illusion. Look beyond its glitzy façade and you'll discover a darker truth. Harrison not only questions the validity of personal relationships, but the existence of God and the meaning of life itself. The frothy, up-beat musical setting negates an otherwise dark, brooding lyric that is riddled with ontological doubt. 'What Is Life' consolidates Harrison's quest for certitude in his personal and spiritual relationships. But this is no dark existential crisis. Harrison's buoyant vocal suggests that there is light at the end of the tunnel and he will discover the Truth.

Harrison produced 'What Is Life' without Spector. By the time it was recorded, the legendary producer had returned to America to recover from his 'illness'. Harrison tried recording the song with Spector, but didn't like the results so decided to produce it himself. "It was one of those tracks that Phil wasn't there for, because Phil was coming and going during the sessions," he explained. "In fact, we did most of the basic tracks with Phil and then he disappeared and I finished the recording. I recorded 'What Is Life' one way and didn't like it. I decided it wasn't right. Then we worked on it a second time and then I came up with the bass line, which I play on my bass guitar, and then I got the feel to it, then it was okay and we re-recorded it and it came out much better."[99]

Three mixes of the backing track that highlight different instruments were issued on the bootleg *The Making Of All Things Must Pass*. A rough mix with bass, but without a lead vocal, was issued on the bootleg *Songs For Patti*. When *All Things Must Pass* was re-issued in 2001, Harrison included an alternative version that featured additional piccolo, trumpet and oboe parts.

If Not For You (Dylan)
George Harrison (guitar, dobro, harmonica, vocals), Klaus Voormann (bass), Gary Wright (piano), Billy Preston (organ), Alan White (drums) and Ringo Starr (tambourine)

As mentioned earlier, in May 1970 Harrison joined Bob Dylan at Columbia's Studio B in New York City for an impromptu jam session. Joined by Charlie Daniels and Russ Kunkel they spent most of the session jamming on a bunch of oldies. Charlie Daniels recalled: "I remember Dylan got very loose and in a good mood that day and sang song after song, almost anything that we'd ask him to sing. I don't know what happened to those tapes, and I don't remember what the songs were, only that there were several of them."[100]

Some of the tapes escaped the studio and were bootlegged, and they do indeed reveal that both Dylan and Harrison were having fun. Dylan indulged Harrison's Carl Perkins fixation by leading the band through 'Matchbox' to which Harrison's replied with 'True Love'. The assembled musicians even managed to get Dylan to warble his way through Lennon and McCartney's evergreen 'Yesterday', much to Harrison's delight. They also spent some time perfecting a new Dylan song, 'If Not For You'. (This version was issued on the Bob Dylan boxed set *The Bootleg Series Volumes 1 – 3 (Rare & Unreleased)*).

Unlike the other songs recorded that day, 'If Not For You' sounds quite polished. Harrison played lead guitar double-tracked in places. Consequently, the second guitar part must have been overdubbed, because Dylan was playing acoustic rhythm guitar and harmonica. Dylan re-recorded 'If Not For You' for his *New Morning* album at a later session. Issued as a single, it made the top ten in Britain and America.

Harrison performed the song for Phil Spector at the pre-production session in May (issued on the bootleg *Beware Of ABCKO!*). Recorded with a band for *All Things Must Pass*, it was given a light swing arrangement that emphasized the song's swaying melody. A tight, polished production, it is more structured than Dylan's earlier take, which is considerably more visceral. Harrison's pop sensibility shines through and for once Spector didn't smother it in reverb.

Harrison's arrangement may well have inspired the version produced by Bruce Welch and John Farrar for Olivia Newton John – their version has very similar slide guitar and drum parts, although it doesn't swing as easily as Harrison's recording. Issued as a single it went to number 7 in the British pop charts.

Behind That Locked Door

George Harrison (guitar, vocals), Pete Drake (pedal steel guitar), Billy Preston (piano), Bobby Whitlock (Hammond organ) Klaus Voormann (bass), Ringo Starr (drums) Peter Frampton (possible second acoustic guitar)

A song inspired by his friendship with Bob Dylan, 'Behind That Locked Door' was influenced by Dylan's *Nashville Skyline* album and written the night before the Isle of Wight Festival in August 1970. Like many of the songs destined for *All Things Must Pass* it deals with life's vicissitudes. In this instance, Harrison plays a pastoral role, acting both spirituality and altruistically in an attempt to coax Dylan out of his self-imposed exile. "I wrote this song for him [Dylan]. It was a good excuse to do a country tune with a pedal steel guitar," Harrison recalled.[101]

While 'All Things Must Pass' had been an attempt to write a "Robbie Robertson – Band sort of tune", 'Behind That Locked Door' more successfully captures The Band's lazy country vibe. The choice of instruments and arrangement not only evoke the spirit of The Band but emphasize the soulful nature of the dialogue Harrison hoped to engage his friend in. Bobby Whitlock's playing is exquisite and recalls that of The Band's Garth Hudson, but it is Pete Drake's pedal steel playing which evokes the spirit of Dylan's recent past.

Drake had played on Dylan's *Nashville Skyline* album and was invited to play on *All Things Must Pass*. There is some dispute about who suggested Drake for the job. Some sources suggest it was Dylan, while Bobby Whitlock suggests that he was responsible for getting Drake the gig. "It [the melody] came from a whistle I was doing on the playback of the song 'All Things Must Pass'", he explained. "I was whistling the part while we were listening back and Phil [Spector] said, 'Who's that?' I thought that I was in trouble but I said, 'It's me'. He asked me to whistle it on tape and I did. It just didn't sound right the first go-around, so I told both George and Phil when we were listening back that they should call Pete Drake in Nashville. He was there two days later, and there were two special Pete Drake sessions. The part that Pete plays is from the old gospel song 'Hallelujah Thine The Glory'. Pete recognized the organ part because of his church background and capitalized on it. I'm playing the Hammond and it's Klaus on bass and Ringo on drums with Billy on Piano."[102]

There is also speculation that Peter Frampton played on the session. An early 'demo' version of 'Behind That Locked Door' issued on the *Living In The Material World* soundtrack features two guitars, Harrison's vocal and Drake's pedal steel. The second guitarist may or may not be Frampton. If it is him, then there's a good chance that he played on the tracking session too. Two alternative takes of 'Behind That Locked Door' were issued on the bootleg *Songs For Pattie*. Each has a guide vocal from Harrison and each has a slightly different mix. One mix features the organ prominently, as does the master mix, while the second mix gives prominence to the piano.

Let It Down
George Harrison (guitar, vocals, backup vocal), Eric Clapton (guitar, backing vocal), Bobby Whitlock (Hammond organ, backup vocal), Carl Radle (bass), Jim Gordon (drums), Jim Price (trumpet), Bobby Keys (saxophone), John Barham (string arrangement)

'Let It Down' finds Harrison afflicted with ambivalence. Whoever he's addressing, Pattie Harrison, perhaps?, he finds himself unable to express his true feelings. Intoxicated by his love, he can't stop thinking about her – even when he's supposed to be meditating on more spiritual matters she creeps into his mind. Musically, this tension is conveyed by the dynamic shift between the sweet, mellifluous verses and the hard, visceral choruses. For somebody as pious as Harrison, his lyrics are overtly lascivious. He longs to be engulfed by his lover's hair. Long hair often symbolizes sexual power, but it can also represent a trap, a web in which the lover may be ensnared. Unable to reconcile his sexual and spiritual desires, he finds himself caught in the horns of a dilemma.

'Let It Down' began life as a simple but poignant ballad. Harrison recorded a version accompanying himself on acoustic guitar for Phil Spector prior to recording the album. He obviously liked this treatment because, when he reissued *All Things Must Pass* in 2001, he included this recording, albeit re-worked with additional guitar and keyboard. However, when he recorded the song with Derek and The Dominos at EMI Studios in 1970, the song received a hard rock treatment. Bobby Whitlock says: "We rehearsed this in the little room next to the tea room [at EMI] where they keep the pump organ, and it was strictly a ballad. Right away when I heard it, I told him that we ought to rock it right there when it says 'Let It Down'. George was completely open to everything that we had to say because he knew we were all about the music."[103]

Take 8, the master take, was issued on the bootleg *The Making of All Things Must Pass* with various elements from the multi-track tape isolated to illustrate the song's development. Harrison continued to work on the song replacing the trombone and saxophone parts with a slide guitar overdub.

Run Of The Mill
George Harrison (guitar, vocals), Bobby Whitlock (organ), Gary Wright (piano), Carl Radle (bass), Ringo Starr (drums), Jim Gordon (drums), Jim Price (trumpet), Bobby Keys (saxophone)

As The Beatles empire crumbled all four Fabs turned to song writing to tell their side of the story. Lennon and McCartney engaged in a war of words, expressing themselves in song and the pages if the music weeklies. Starr sat on the fence and Harrison addressed the situation with elegant resignation. Commenting on the choices, actions and values that he and his friends had made and were making, he concludes that each must carry the weight of their own decisions. It's as potent a break-up song as Lennon's 'God' (I don't believe in Beatles) but more universal. The dream was well and truly over. It was time for them to accept individual responsibility and stop placing the burden of culpability on the group. 'Run Of The Mill' attempts to draw a line under The Beatles as a group and friends. Although the partnership (Apple Corps) would go on forever.

'Run Of The Mill' is both a lecture and a wry put down addressed to one individual in particular – Paul McCartney. The phrase 'run of the mill' often refers to something ordinary; perhaps Harrison was suggesting that McCartney was less extraordinary than people thought. He may have also intended it as a droll reference to McCartney's bossy nature. After all it was McCartney who thought he knew how best to run the mill. It was McCartney who wanted the mill run his way or not at all. As Harrison explained in his autobiography, "It's like the North of England thing – you know – 'Trouble at t'mill': it was when Apple was getting crazy – Ringo wanted it blue, John wanted it white, Paul wanted it green and I wanted it orange. Paul was falling out with us all and going around Apple offices saying 'You're no good' – everybody was just incompetent."[104]

'Run Of The Mill' was one of fifteen songs he routined for Phil Spector before recording began at EMI Studios in the early summer of 1970. His acoustic guitar and vocal demo was eventually issued on the soundtrack to the documentary *Living In The Material World*. It's possible that the master take of 'Run Of The Mill' was recorded after Spector returned to America. It's a comparatively dry recording compared to Spector's usual echo drenched productions. Three mixes of the finished master appeared on the bootleg *The Making Of All Things Must Pass*. Listening to these mixes it is obvious that there are two drummers on the recording, one of whom sounds very much like Ringo Starr. Bobby Whitlock has suggested that Starr was joined by Jim Gordon on drums and also claims that Billy Preston played piano. However, it just doesn't sound like Preston. The playing isn't quite fluid enough and it doesn't feature the kind of gospel licks or feel you would expect from him. I would suggest that it's Gary Wright on piano and Bobby Whitlock on organ.

Beware of Darkness
George Harrison (guitar, vocals), Eric Clapton (guitar), Dave Mason (guitar), Bobby Whitlock (piano), Gary Wright (organ), Carl Radle (bass), Ringo Starr (drums), John Barham (string arrangement and possible vibrophone)

When Harrison sat down to play Phil Spector the songs he planned to record for what would become *All Things Must Pass*, he announced 'Beware Of Darkness' with the words, "This one is the last one I wrote the other day, and [there's] a few words needed yet". The only changes he needed to make was to remove a reference to Allen Klein's company, ABKCO, and change a line about being 'pushed into puddles' to one about 'unconscious suffers'. Even in its unfinished state Harrison thought enough of it to include it as a 'bonus' track on the 2001 re-issue of *All Things Must Pass*.

He later said that the lyric was self-explanatory and about Maya – the cosmic illusion. Ironically, the lyric is full of illusions and allusions, and far from self-explanatory. Could the 'falling swingers' be a reference to The Beatles? Weren't they symbolic of the swinging sixties and the cause of the pain

Harrison was experiencing? Then there is the explicit reference in his demo to "beware of ABKCO". Klein and his management company played a significant part in The Beatles downfall and Harrison's unhappiness. It's not until the middle eight that Harrison realizes that he must rise above his suffering because that is not what he was put here for. His goal was to attain enlightenment and God consciousness. If he could only see Maya for what it was, an illusion, then in the fullness of time his troubles and pain would fade away.

When he came to record 'Beware Of Darkness' at EMI Studios, Harrison once again called on a familiar group of musicians to realize his song. The basic track of bass, drums, acoustic guitar, piano, organ and vibraphone was augmented by guitar and orchestral overdubs. Eric Clapton added a lead guitar part played through a Leslie speaker, while Harrison added a second lead guitar part to complement that played by his friend. Finally, John Barham's orchestration was added to the multi-track to complete the recording.

Apple Scruffs
George Harrison (guitar, vocals, harmonica)

The Apple scruffs were a group of female fans who used to hang around The Beatles' London offices in the hope of spotting a real live Beatle. Harrison wrote this ode to his fans and recorded it solo at EMI Studios. He didn't make the job easy for himself. He elected to record acoustic guitar, vocals and harmonica, an instrument he'd rarely played before, all in one go. Before take one, he remarked: "It's really hell this mouth organ, especially with the beard and moustache, it just keeps ripping it out". That's the kind of torture artistes put themselves through for the sake of their art. He also tapped his foot, rather erratically, as percussion.

Harrison attempted some twenty takes of the song in this fashion before a satisfactory take was captured. If Spector had his wits about him, if indeed he was present when the song was recorded, it would have made better sense to have Harrison record his vocal and guitar live and overdub the harmonica and percussion later. As it was, Harrison struggled through take after take, which more often than not broke down because of his inability to play the harmonica.

Once he'd recorded a successful take, Harrison added layers of harmony vocals and a slide guitar solo which he doubled tracked. Harrison's toe tapping had some slap-back delay added in an attempt to give it a little consistency, although it drops out at the points where he lost concentration. The song was remixed by Spector, the echo is subtle but much in evidence, and edited. Take eighteen was marked best and edited by repeating the first and only chorus, which was then faded out at the end.

Ballad of Sir Frankie Crisp (Let It Roll)
George Harrison (guitars, vocals), Pete Drake (pedal steel guitar), Billy Preston (piano), Gary Wright (organ), Klaus Voormann (bass), Alan White (drums)

Sir Frank Crisp was a successful commercial lawyer who owned Friar Park, Henley-on-Thames, from 1895 until his death in 1919. By the late '60s the estate was in a state of disrepair and about to be demolished until it was saved by Harrison. Crisp fascinated and inspired Harrison for years. Described by Harrison as "a piece of personal indulgence", 'Ballad of Sir Frankie Crisp (Let It Roll)' began as a song about his other great passion, motoring. Titled 'Everybody, Nobody' the song employed a string of driving related metaphors to convey a sense of aimless drifting. In its draft form the solitary reference to Sir Frankie Crisp made no sense whatsoever. Neither did the song have a strong musical structure. Lacking a conventional verse/chorus construction, it was still very much a work in progress.

Harrison obviously wasn't satisfied with the song and reworked both the melody and lyrics. The song still didn't have a chorus as such, but a bridge in which Harrison intones the Victorian lawyer's moniker links the verses. In its finished state, and with Pete Drake's pedal steel to the fore, it has a filmy, fin de siecle atmosphere that captures perfectly the feeling of a slightly decaying stately home on a warm summer day. In the last verse Harrison once again addresses himself and his situation ('fools illusions everywhere') and his Radha Krsna Temple house guests ('eyes that shining full of inner light'). 'Ballad of Sir Frankie Crisp (Let It Roll)' is a song inspired by the previous tenant of Friar Park, a song about Harrison's home and a song about spiritual rejuvenation.

Awaiting On You All
George Harrison (guitar, vocal), Eric Clapton (guitar, backing vocals), Carl Radle or Klaus Voormann (bass), Bobby Whitlock (backing vocals), Ringo Starr (drums), Jim Price (trumpet), Bobby Keys (saxophone)

'Awaiting On You All' was another song that pretty much wrote itself. As Harrison explained: "I was just going to bed and I was cleaning my teeth, strumming my teeth and suddenly, in my head, came this, 'You don't want a ...' And all I had to do was pick up a guitar, find what key I was in and fill in the missing words."[105] He went on to say that the finished song was about Japa Yoga, a repetition of mantras using beads not dissimilar to the Roman Catholic rosary. "A mantra is mystical energy encased in a sound structure, and each mantra contains within its vibrations, a certain power," he explained. "Most mantras for Japa utilize the many names of God, and the maha-mantra has been prescribed as the easiest and surest way of attaining God-Realization in this present age."[106] "If you say the mantra enough, you build up an identification with God. God's all happiness, all bliss, and by chanting His names we connect with Him. So it's really a process of actually having a realization of God, which all becomes clear with the expanded state of consciousness that develops when you chant. Like I said in the introduction I wrote for Prabhupada's Krsna book some years ago, 'If there's a God, I want to see Him.' It's pointless to believe in something without proof, and Krishna consciousness and meditation are methods where you can actually obtain God perception."[107]

Harrison took his beads with him everywhere and relied on them so much that after years of use he'd worn them smooth. "I remember when I first got them, they were just big knobby globs of wood, but now I'm very glad to say that they're smooth from chanting a lot."[108] However, he soon grew tired of telling people what he was doing and took to saying he'd hurt his hand rather than explain himself. "You know, the frustrating thing about it was in the beginning there was a period when I was heavy into chanting and I had my hand in my bead bag all the time. And I got so tired of people asking me, 'Did you hurt your hand, break it or something?' In the end I used to say, 'Yeah. Yeah. I had an accident,' because it was easier than explaining everything."[109]

The song features a litany of things to be avoided. Harrison had no time for love-ins – peaceful public gatherings focused on meditation, love and music, possibly because they were also associated with psychedelic drugs. But surely, any form of meditation is better than no meditation at all? Obviously, Harrison preferred to chant without the distraction of others. Perhaps love-ins were too much like attending church or the temple, which he also suggests are best avoided.

Simon Leng suggests the opening lines are also a dig at John and Yoko's bed-ins (you don't need a bedpan). If so, John and Yoko got off lightly compared to the tongue lashing Harrison reserved for the Pope. Symbolic of a religious system that he had long outgrown, according to him all the head of the Catholic church was good for was quoting prices on the stock exchange. It's a stinging attack on Western religion and capitalism. Such was its ferocity that the offending lyrics were not printed on the album's inner sleeve. But for all his protesting he chose to ignore the similarities the two faiths shared rather than embrace them. He states "You don't need no rosary beads or them books to read", but couldn't the same be said of those big knobby globs of wood he spent hours fingering?

Harrison recorded a demo of 'Awaiting On You All' with Ringo Starr on drums and a un-named bassist, possibly Klaus Vormann, before recording the song at EMI Studios with a bigger band. Take 1 of Harrison's demo was issued on the soundtrack album *Living In The Material World*. Several mixes of the master take were issued on the bootleg *The Making Of All Things Must Pass*. These mixes were later used to create the 'isolated' tracks that appeared on the ten CD bootleg *All Things Must Pass Isolated Tracks Edition* in 2012. A mono mix without vocals was issued on the bootleg *Songs For Pattie*.

All Things Must Pass

George Harrison (acoustic guitar, vocals), Eric Clapton (electric guitar, backup vocals), Bobby Whitlock (organ, backup vocals), Billy Preston (piano), Pete Drake (pedal steel guitar), Klaus Voormann (bass), Ringo Starr (drums), Jim Price (trombone), Bobby Keys (saxophone), John Barham (string arrangement)

Dating from Harrison's visit to Woodstock in the winter of 1968, when he hung out with Dylan and The Band, 'All Things Must Pass' was originally offered to The Beatles in January 1969. "I wrote it after [the Band's 1968] *Music From Big Pink* album; when I heard that song in my head I always heard Levon Helm singing it!," he told Timothy White in 1999.[110] *Music From Big Pink*, had a huge influence on musicians in the late '60s and early '70s. The Band possessed an earthy authenticity that appealed to those seeking an alternative to the increasingly turgid rock music being produced by certain bands at that time. Their blend of American roots music harked back to simpler times and Harrison was smitten.

Leading the Fabs through the song, he had definite ideas as to how it should be arranged and played. Attempting to explain how he heard the song, he told Lennon, who was playing organ: "The thing I feel about the emotion [of it] is very, you know, very Band-y."[111] Despite his best efforts to explain how he thought the song should feel, The Beatles weren't The Band and he was fighting a loosing battle. Although Lennon didn't contribute much to the song musically, he did suggest changing the line "A wind can blow those clouds away" to "A mind can blow those clouds away". Harrison also changed "It's not always been this grey" to "it's not always gonna be this grey". The Beatles being unable or unwilling to do the song justice, it was put to one side for later use.

A few weeks after attempting the song with The Beatles, Harrison booked into EMI Studios to celebrate his 26th birthday by recording demos of 'Something', 'Old Brown Shoe' and 'All Things Must Pass'. Accompanying himself on electric guitar, he recorded a simple but affecting demo of what became his signature song. Of the three songs he recorded that day two made it onto Beatles records. 'All Things Must Pass', however, remained unused by The Beatles and would remain idle until Harrison gave it to Billy Preston to record for his *Encouraging Words* album. Although he now had two recordings of the song, in April 1970 he recorded another demo with support from Ringo Starr and Klaus Vorrmann. This version, issued on the soundtrack album *Living In The Material World*, is closer to the master take.

If Harrison took his musical inspiration from the down-home musings of The Band, his lyrics were inspired by the heady world of psychedelics and spirituality. Speaking in 1999, he thought he got the title from the spiritual teacher Ram Dass: "I think I got it from Richard Alpert/Baba Ram Dass, but I'm not sure. When you read of philosophy or spiritual things, it's a pretty widely used phrase."[112] The phrase is indeed widely used. Baba Ram Dass wasn't the only one to use it. When Harrison played the song to The Beatles at Twickenham Film Studios, Lennon asked what had inspired him, and it wasn't Baba Ram Dass. "Timothy Leary, I suppose," he replied. "In his psychedelic prayers he had one I remember just from years ago. That is sunrise doesn't last all morning. That gave me the idea, apart from life."[113] The first verse of 'All Things Must Pass' is pretty much lifted straight from Leary's 'Prayers for preparation – Homage to Lao Tse'.

All things pass
A sunrise does not last all morning
All things pass
A cloudburst does not last all day
All things pass
Nor a sunset all night

All Harrison did was add 'must' to make the line fit his melody and add a couple of new lines of his own. It wasn't the first time he'd 'borrowed' an idea to kick start a song. He'd appropriated lines from a religious anthology *Lamps Of Fire* to write 'The Inner Light'. He did the same with 'All Things Must Pass' developing Leary's original idea as an extended metaphor for life itself.

'All Things Must Pass' is a song of hope that explores the transitory nature of human existence and rebirth. While Leary wanted to prepare the individual for an experience, an acid trip, that could be mystical, but which was by its very nature transitory, Harrison wanted to prepare the listener for something far more lasting – something eternal. Interviewed by *International Times* in 1967 he said: "There's this Indian fellow who worked out a cycle like the idea of stone-age, bronze-age, only he did it on an Indian one. The cycle goes from nothing until now the 20th century and then on and right round the cycle until the people are really grooving and then it just sinks back into ignorance until it gets back into the beginning again. So the 20th century is a fraction of that cycle, and how many of those cycles has it done yet? It's done as many as you think and all these times its been through exactly the same things, and it'll be this again. Only be a few million years and it'll be exactly the same thing going on, only with other people doing it... I am part of the cycle, rebirth death, rebirth death, rebirth death."[114]

Besides exploring the cosmic cycle of birth, death and rebirth it's also concerned with the vicissitudes of personal relationships. These too are transitory and fleeting and further complicate one's life journey. They are the knots in the string that is life. Writing in *I Me Mine*, Harrison said: "When you are born, your life (past karma) is like a piece of string with knots in it and you've got to try, before you die, to undo all the knots: but you tie another twenty knots trying to get one undone."[115] What Harrison longs for is a time of blissful consistency, a state of being that will only be gained through knowledge and awareness. "They say ignorance is bliss, but bliss is not ignorance – it's the opposite of that, which is knowledge," Harrison told Mick Brown in 1979. "And there's a lot of people who have fear. And the fear of failure is a bad thing in life; it stops people from gaining more knowledge or just understanding deeper things. Basically, I feel fortunate to have realized what the goal is in life. There's no point in dying, having gone through your life without knowing who you are, what you are or what the purpose of life is. And that's all it is."[116] A few years earlier, he told Howard Smith: "The only purpose for being alive is to get yourself straight. Each soul is potentially divine. The goal is to manifest that divinity. What I want to do is liberate myself from this chaos and of this body. I want to be free of this body. I want to be God conscious. That really is my only ambition."[117]

I Dig Love
George Harrison (guitar, vocals), Eric Clapton (guitar), Gary Wright (electric piano), Billy Preston (piano), Bobby Whitlock (Hammond organ), Klaus Voormann or Carl Radle (bass), Ringo Starr (drums), Jim Gordon (drums)

On the surface 'I Dig Love' sounds like little more than a piece of frothy pop. If previous songs had dense or unfamiliar themes, that is to say the kind of themes alien to most popular music, then 'I Dig Love' seems to be little more than pop for pop's sake. Based on a simple descending and rising four note riff, its simplistic word play suggests that it's little more than a frivolous interlude in what is an otherwise serious album. But let us not forget that it was written by George Harrison, and the love he digs is God's love.

Harrison repeats the title no fewer than 28 times. It's no less a mantra than 'Hare Krishna' or 'Govinda'. He couldn't drive the point home any more if he wanted to. It doesn't matter what kind of love you experience or where you experience it, it is all good because love is God and God is love. But it's not enough to simply repeat the phrase. One has to experience God for oneself, that's a rare love indeed. Harrison clarifies his message towards the end of the song. "Make love, take love, but you should give love. And try to live love, come on that's where you should be" he sings. Don't just dig love, live love. If you can do that, you've go it made.

Art Of Dying
George Harrison (guitar, vocals), Eric Clapton (guitar), Bobby Whitlock (tubular bells), Gary Wright (electric piano), Billy Preston (organ), Carl Radle (bass), Jim Gordon (drums), Jim Price (trumpet), Bobby Keys (saxophone)

'Art Of Dying' opens with the kind of killer riff that was turning pop into rock. The likes of the Jimi Hendrix Experience ('Purple Haze'), The Rolling Stones ('Satisfaction') and Cream (Sunshine Of Your Love') had turned these simple melodic phrases into the stuff of rock legend. It's fitting then that Harrison should ask no less a person than god to play his newly composed riff. Eric Clapton, for it is he, employs his trusty wah-wah pedal to set the tone for this blistering rocker. However, the finished take couldn't differ more from Harrison's simple acoustic demo. Neither the lyrics nor its distinctive riff were finished when he first recorded the song. He still hadn't finished it when he took the song to EMI Studios to record it with a band. Early takes don't have any of the dramatic light and shade he employed later, and without Clapton's riffing the song simply doesn't pack a punch. (Take 9 which doesn't have Clapton's guitar or the horn section was issued on the bootleg *Songs For Pattie*.)

If the song was to be saved, it required a dramatic rethink. The tempo was increased, honking saxophone and trumpet stabs were added to the arrangement and Clapton added his stinging lead guitar. Bobby Whitlock moved to tubular bells which, combined with Harrison's scratchy rhythm guitar, create a piercing, distorted banshee howl. But the most starting part of the new arrangement was the use of dynamics that let Clapton's searing guitar riff smash through the enveloping silence. It is, perhaps, the best piece of ensemble playing on the album, with each musician playing an integral part to create the whole.

If 'All Things Must Pass' is about the inevitability of rebirth, 'Art Of Dying' is about how to avoid it. Of all the songs discussed in Harrison's book *I Me Mine*, 'Art Of Dying' has the longest explanation, which suggests just how strongly he felt about it. "The 'art of dying' is when somebody can consciously leave the body at death, as opposed to falling down dying without knowing what's going on," he said. "The Yogi who does that (Maha-Samadhi) doesn't have to reincarnate again."[118] There was nothing Harrison cared about more. He longed for, and one hopes achieved, a liberated death. Talking about his death, his wife, Olivia Harrison, said: "George was at peace and ready. There was a great light in the room when he passed."[119] Make of that what you will.

Isn't It A Pity (Version 2)
George Harrison (guitar, vocals), Eric Clapton (guitar), Billy Preston (piano), Bobby Whitlock (organ), Carl Radle (bass), Ringo Starr (drums), Badfinger (acoustic guitars), Mike Gibbins (tambourine)

Harrison must have considered 'Isn't It A Pity' one of the foundation stones upon which *All Things Must Pass* was built. It's not unusual for musicians to record different arrangements of songs – 'Art Of Dying', for example, was recorded twice – before they are satisfied with the results. It is, however, unusual to release different versions of the same song on an album, albeit an album as sprawling as this.

The second version of Harrison's magnum opus has a stately swagger and cinematic quality that evokes images of grand processions and ceremonies. This arrangement transforms the song from something personal into something universal. Despite the sense of elation at the end of the second verse, when the band enters there is no resolution to the sense of sorrow established in the opening bars.

An alternate mix of this version, take thirty, appeared on the bootleg *Songs For Pattie* with a guide vocal. This version is without strings and has a slightly more prominent organ part played by Bobby Whitlock.

Hear Me Lord

George Harrison (vocals, electric guitar, slide guitar, backing vocals), Eric Clapton, (guitar) Carl Radle (bass), Bobby Whitlock (organ), Billy Preston (piano), Jim Gordon (drums), Jim Price (trumpet), Bobby Keys (saxophone)

'Hear Me Lord' was written over the weekend of 4/5 January 1969. When Harrison returned to work at Twickenham Film Studios on Monday 6 January, he offered the song to The Beatles, announcing that he had written it over the weekend. His attempt to sell the song to his band mates fell on deaf ears. The Beatles played through the song a few times, but if Lennon's attempts at formulating a guitar part were anything to go by, he couldn't have cared less. Such was his indifference that at one point he suggested they try a song on which he'd played organ (probably 'All Things Must Pass') rather than attempt 'Hear Me Lord' again. Harrison had to admit defeat and put the song to bed.

A little over a year later, Harrison recorded a demo for Phil Spector. Little more than the roughest of sketches, it does, however, feature a bassist (perhaps Klaus Voormann) trying to figure out the chord changes, without much success. The hapless bassist would have faired better had he been given a chord sheet, which Harrison obviously hadn't bothered to prepare. By now Harrison had added the 'above and below us' refrain which he hadn't written when he offered the song to The Beatles in January 1969.

The basic track was recorded with the usual crew of The Dominos and Billy Preston. Gary Wright is usually credited with keyboards, but if one listens to the different versions available on bootlegs it's clear that there are only two keyboard players on the track. Bobby Whitlock has said that he plays the organ, which leaves Billy Preston on piano. A couple of different mixes of the basic track were issued on *The Making Of All Things Must Pass* bootleg, which were subsequently used for *The Making Of All Things Must Pass Isolated Tracks* bootleg.

'Hear Me Lord' is one of the most honest and open songs on *All Things Must Pass*. Part confession, part prayer, it's as revealing as anything Lennon recorded for his *John Lennon Plastic Ono Band* album. Indeed, while Lennon was disavowing his beliefs, Harrison was in the very same studio complex doing the exact opposite. Harrison not only believed in God, he wanted God to hear him. There's no attempt to hide behind metaphors or allusions, this is a very public expression of faith. Harrison stands before God and us completely unprotected. His desire to be possessed by God is made transparent and proffered to the world. The very act of writing and recording this music could be considered an act of prayer. Perhaps it's not the deepest form of prayer in which Harrison engaged, but it is a sincere attempt to direct the heart and mind to God and to encourage others to do the same.

Out Of The Blue

George Harrison (guitar), Klaus Voormann (guitar), Carl Radle (bass), Jim Gordon (drums), Bobby Keys (saxophone), Gary Wright (organ), Bobby Whitlock (Hammond organ), Billy Preston (piano), Jim Price (trumpet), Al Abramowitz (unspecified instrument)

Sides five and six of *All Things Must Pass* comprise informal jams complied by Harrison and issued as a bonus disc *Apple Jam*. "[On] the *Apple Jam*, where as we were recording tracks, inevitably in between – I mean, we used to do that ourselves you know, the Fabs, back in the early days. So you'd have a break, somebody'd go to the toilet, they have a cigarette, and the next minute you'd break into a jam session, and the engineer taped it on a 2-track. When we were mixing the album and getting toward the end of it, I listened to that stuff, and I thought, 'It's got some fire in it,' particularly Eric. He plays some hot stuff on there!," Harrison told Timothy White in 1999.[120]

Unlike some of the improvised instrumentals Harrison decided to release, 'Out Of The Blue' swings. Carl Radle and Jim Gordon lay down a tight groove over which the rest of the musicians trade licks. It's the rhythm section that leads the band through this jam, determining mood, dynamics, tempo and ultimately its crescendo. Without Clapton's guitar pyrotechnics to enliven things, it's Bobby Keys and Bobby Whitlock textural washes of sound that save this lengthy, monolithic piece from tedium.

It's Johnny's Birthday
George Harrison (vocal), Mal Evans (vocal), Eddie Klein (vocal)

To celebrate John Lennon's 30th birthday several musicians were asked to record a piece of music as a gift. Janis Joplin, Donovan, Ringo Starr and Harrison were among those to wish Lennon a happy birthday in song. Harrison was the only one to issue his on record. Loosely based on 'Congratulations', the 1968 British entry in the Eurovision Song Contest, it appears to have been constructed from multi-tracking tape loops of the song played on various mechanical organs and then treated with vari-speed (pitch control). It's all great fun and injects a little party atmosphere to lift the spirits as we near journey's end.

Plug Me In
George Harrison (guitar), Eric Clapton (guitar), Dave Mason (guitar), Bobby Whitlock (piano), Carl Radle (bass), Jim Gordon (drums)

'Plug Me In' was recorded at the end of a session that produced Derek and the Dominos debut single 'Roll It Over'/'Tell The Truth'. In return for having Derek and the Dominos play on the album, Harrison had Spector produce their debut single. 'Roll It Over' was issued by Atco Records in America in September 1970, but quickly withdrawn because the band was unhappy with Spector's production. The session itself must have gone well because there was time at the end for some jamming. Clapton battles it out with Harrison on this up-tempo rocker and comes out on top, again. Dave Mason must have been hanging out at the studio because he appears on 'Plug Me In', but does not play on 'Roll It Over'/'Tell The Truth'.

I Remember Jeep

George Harrison (guitar), Eric Clapton (guitar), Billy Preston (piano), Klaus Voormann (bass), Ginger Baker (drums), Jim Gordon (drums)

This is what musicians do for fun. Somebody comes up with a riff, the rest of the band jump on it and jam away until it falls apart or somebody gets bored and brings it to a sloppy end. The song features two thirds of Cream, a band that delighted in improvising. Although this was Harrison's album, 'I Remember Jeep' is a showcase for Clapton's playing. Listen to the way he picks up on another players motifs, responds to them for a few bars and then improvises something of his own, which in turn is picked up and developed by somebody else. The basic track was overdubbed with handclaps and cheering and elements from Harrison's *Electronic Sound*. Bobby Whitlock claims to have played Hammond organ on the track. But try as I might, I can't hear him. The track was named after Clapton's dog: "Jeep was actually Eric's dog – a funny kind of orangy-brown dog with pink eyes [laughs]. I think he might have kicked it – I'm sure he has by now – but I know it was his dog," Harrison recalled.[121]

Thanks For The Pepperoni

George Harrison (guitar), Eric Clapton (guitar), Dave Mason (guitar), Bobby Whitlock (piano), Carl Radle (bass), Jim Gordon (drums)

'Thanks For The Pepperoni' was improvised between takes and is the kind of thing The Beatles used to jam on when they were schoolboys. Based on a slack handful of Chuck Berry riffs, this 12-bar rocks at a fair pace but drags a bit towards the end. Once again, it's Clapton who shines. Harrison and Dave Mason handle themselves proficiently, but can't match Clapton. Indeed, it's Clapton who lifts this otherwise workman like rocker from the rock 'n' roll sludge it could have easily descended into. The title was inspired by one of Lenny Bruce's satirical sketches. Speaking to Timothy White in 1999, Harrison said: "If you listen to Lenny Bruce's 'Religions, Inc.,' he goes on about the Pope and things, and then he goes, 'And thanks for the pepperoni' [laughs]. I mean, you got random tracks, so it's like, 'What can we call it?' For the jams, I didn't want to just throw it in the cupboard, and yet at the same time it wasn't part of the record; that's why I put it on a separate label to go in the package as a kind of bonus."[122]

George Harrison's Album

'All Things Must Pass'

Out Now
on
Apple Records

1971 to 1972 : We've got to relieve Bangla Desh

GEORGE HARRISON
what is life / apple scruffs

APPLE 1828

Recorded in England

STEREO

Harrisongs Music, Inc. BMI 4:18

1828

(S45-X47407) Produced by GEORGE HARRISON & PHIL SPECTOR

(From the LP "All Things Must Pass" STCH-639)

WHAT IS LIFE
(George Harrison)
GEORGE HARRISON

MFD. BY APPLE RECORDS, INC.

APPLE SCRUFFS
(George Harrison)

STEREO

Harrisongs Music, Inc. BMI 3:03

1828

(S45-X47413) Produced by GEORGE HARRISON & PHIL SPECTOR

(From the LP "All Things Must Pass" STCH-639)

GEORGE HARRISON

Recorded in England

STEREO

Startling Music, Inc. BMI 3:00

1831

(S45-X47507) Produced: GEORGE HARRISON

Recorded in England

IT DON'T COME EASY
(Richard Starkey)
RINGO STARR

MFD. BY APPLE RECORDS, INC.

EARLY 1970
(Richard Starkey)

STEREO

Startling Music, Inc. BMI 2:19

1831

(S45-X47508) Produced: RINGO STARR

RINGO STARR

Recorded in England

'What Is Life' / 'Apple Scruffs'
GEORGE HARRISON
Produced by George Harrison and Phil Spector
US release: 27 February 1971; Apple 1821; chart high; number 10.

The second single from *All Things Must Pass* was issued worldwide, except in Britain, where no follow up was issued. Apple Records issued the single in a picture sleeve and, in the days before globalization, the individual territories produced their own designs. The American sleeve used a photo of Harrison playing guitar at one of the many windows in his new house in Henley-on-Thames. Most European sleeves were based on the *All Things Must Pass* album cover. Because Apple Records still hadn't got round to registering its trademark in South Africa, 'What Is Life', like 'My Sweet Lord', was issued there by Parlophone.

Having released her version of 'If Not For You', Olivia Newton John followed it with 'What Is Life'. Such was the popularity of the song that Newton John took her version to number 34 and 16 in the American and British charts respectively.

'It Don't Come Easy' / 'Early 1970'
RINGO STARR
Produced by George Harrison
UK release: 9 April 1971 ; Apple R 5898; chart high; number 4.
US release: 16 April 1971; Apple 1831; chart high; number 4.
Ringo Starr (vocals and drums), George Harrison (guitar), Klaus Voormann (bass), Stephen Stills (guitar), Gary Wright (piano), Ron Cattermole (saxophone and trumpet), Pete Ham (backing vocals), Tom Evans (backing vocals)

Before Harrison began work on *All Things Must Pass*, he helped his old buddy Ringo Starr record his second solo single, 'It Don't Come Easy'. ('Beaucoups of Blues' was issued in most countries as a single, but not in Britain.) The rift between ex-members of The Beatles is no better illustrated than in their early solo recordings. Harrison, Starr and Lennon continued to work closely together, while McCartney eschewed their services entirely. Harrison and Starr played on each others records and on several by Lennon. While Lennon would go on to write songs for and record with Starr, his move to New York in 1971 meant that he never did get round to playing on any of Harrison's records. It wasn't until after Lennon's death that Harrison, Starr and McCartney appeared together on record ('All Those Years Ago'), and even then McCartney added his parts after Harrison and Starr had recorded theirs.

George Martin was initially employed to produce what became 'It Don't Come Easy' with Harrison

acting as musical director and guitarist. Recording began on the evening of 18 February 1970 at EMI's Studio 2, Abbey Road, London. Starr was recording his *Sentimental Journey* album and earlier that day had added vocals to 'Have I Told You Lately That I Love You' and 'Let the Rest of the World Go By'. At the end of the session Starr, Harrison, Klaus Voormann and Stephen Stills recorded 20 takes of 'You've Gotta Pay Your Dues'.

The following day, Starr recorded a new vocal, but decided to remake the song, taping takes 21-30 between 7 and 11 p.m. However, Starr still wasn't satisfied with the recording and decided to start again from scratch. On 8 March he began recording the third version of what was now titled 'It Don't Come Easy', this time with Harrison producing and playing guitar. However, because Harrison was busy planning *All Things Must Pass*, the song wasn't completed until October, when further overdubs were added.

To help Starr with his vocal performance, Harrison recorded a guide vocal for the drummer to sing along with. Rough mixes of this early version featuring Harrison's guide vocal have appeared on bootlegs. Almost identical to the finished master recording, the rough mix does not feature horns and has Pete Ham and Tom Evans backing vocals placed much higher in the mix.

It Don't Come Easy data

When news of 'It Don't Come Easy' leaked to the press, Apple said there were "absolutely no plans for the record to be released as a single at the present time". 'It Don't Come Easy' was eventually issued on 9 April 1971 (UK) and 16 April (US) with Apple labels and a picture sleeve. It reached number 4 in both America and Britain. Initial copies of the single issued in Britain stated that Harrison had produced the B-side. He hadn't, it was produced by Ringo. Later pressings corrected the mistake.

Ronnie
Spector

TRY SOME,
BUY SOME

Apple
33

143

RONNIE SPECTOR
'Try Some ~ Buy Some'

Her first single on Apple. Composed by George Harrison.
Produced by Phil Spector & George Harrison. APPLE 33

'Try Some, Buy Some' / 'Tandoori Chicken'
RONNIE SPECTOR
Produced by George Harrison and Phil Spector
UK release: 16 April 1971; Apple 33; chart high; failed to chart.
US release: 19 April 1971; Apple 1832; chart high; number 77.
Ronnie Spector (vocals), George Harrison (guitar), Carl Radle (bass), Jim Gordon (drums), Leon Russell (piano), Pete Ham (acoustic guitar, backing vocals)

Following their successful collaboration with *All Things Must Pass*, the Harrison/Spector partnership continued, albeit falteringly, to work on a proposed Ronnie Spector album. Ronnie's solo career had been put on ice by her domineering husband. "I stopped singing when I married Phil because he retired and being his wife, I had to do the same," she said. "Phil didn't want to carry on in the business because he didn't respect it any more."[1] However, with his respect for the music business now fully restored, and his career back on track, Spector allowed his wife to resume her career too. "Phil knew how much I loved the business, so when he got involved with it again the first thing he thought of was recording his wife. George Harrison told him he had a song for me to do," Ronnie recalled.[2]

It's alleged that Ronnie Spector was signed to Apple Records as part of her husband's deal with the company. Others have suggested that this was never the case. As Spector licensed his Christmas album to Apple he obviously had a good relationship with the company and it wouldn't have been too difficult to persuade them to sign his wife too. There were also reports that Apple planned to reissue more Spector produced albums by the like of The Ronettes, The Crystals and even Bob B Soxx and The Blue Jeans. As it was, Apple Records only licensed *A Christmas Gift for You* from Phil Spector. Re-titled *Phil Spector's Christmas Album* (APCOR 24) it went to No. 6 on *Billboard's* special Christmas Albums chart in December 1972, its highest chart ranking.

Despite having recently issued a sprawling solo album, Harrison still had plenty of songs floating around. The plan was to produce Ronnie Spector's comeback album with Harrison providing the bulk of the songs. Work began in early February 1971. Over two days Harrison and Spector produced backing tracks for 'You', 'Try Some, Buy Some', 'When Every Song Is Sung' (originally titled 'Whenever'), 'Loverly Laddy Day' and 'Tandoori Chicken'. However, Ronnie only managed to record vocals for 'Try Some, Buy Some', 'Loverly Laddy Day', 'You' and 'Tandoori Chicken'. Writing in *I, Me, Mine*, Harrison explained: "[We] only did four or five tracks before Phil fell over."[3] Drinking heavily, Spector was incapable of finishing the sessions, which ground to a halt not long after they'd started.

Spector was also having problems producing his wife, who didn't understand what it was she was singing about. Ronnie Spector: "Phil said it was difficult getting back into it at first because my voice had changed a little bit and it took me a long time to learn the song as it was hard to understand."[4]

Writing in her autobiography, she said that the song was "terrible" and admitted that its meaning was totally beyond her – "Religion? Drugs? Sex? I was mystified. And the more George sang, the more mystified I got."[5]

Harrison wrote 'Try Some, Buy Some' on an organ. Fascinated by the possibilities it offered the composer, he discovered that he could write a descending bass line to accompany an ascending melody, which wasn't possible when writing with the guitar. "This tune was based on the weird chords that I got. I couldn't play both parts (left and right hand) at the same time and I had a friend write it down for me."[6] The friend was Klaus Voormann who recalled: "He couldn't play with five fingers and he couldn't play the whole song with two hands on the piano. I had to play the left hand part so he could hear how the whole song sounded."[7]

Harrison's autobiographical lyric encapsulates a spiritual and physical dichotomy in very simple language. Harrison said: "Even though the words are mundane if the attitude is directed back towards the source, then it becomes more spiritual for me and has more meaning, even though it can still be regarded as a simple tune."[8] The physical temptations Harrison alludes to are ephemeral, inherently corrupt and dismissed in favour of the spiritual. Harrison is redeemed by God's love which was absent from his former hedonistic lifestyle. Spector's grandiose production emphasizes the spiritual element of the song. The scale of his production is breathtaking. John Barham's orchestration and choir help make this the aural equivalent of Michelangelo's painting of the Sistine Chapel. The only difference is that Spector's monumental vision was completed somewhat quicker.

The B-side, 'Tandoori Chicken' was written by Harrison and Spector. Before Spector 'fell over' he joined Harrison in the studio to play a batch of rock 'n' roll oldies that included 'The Great Pretender', 'Baby Let's Play House', recent Lennon compositions 'God' and 'Remember' and Harrison's 'Let It Down'. 'Tandoori Chicken' may well have been the product of jamming because its chord structure and arrangement has more than a passing resemblance to 'Baby Let's Play House'. A good time rock 'n' roll song about a takeaway Indian meal, it is the very antithesis of the record's finger-pointing A-side.

Try Some, Buy Some data

Apple issued 'Try Some, Buy Some' in a picture sleeve on 16 April 1971 in Britain and three days later in America. The song made its début on the *Billboard* Hot 100 on 8 May and reached number 77, remaining on the chart for four weeks. 'Try Some, Buy Some' did not chart in Britain. This was, possibly, due to lack of airplay. A report in *Record Mirror* suggested that the BBC was reluctant to play the song and urged readers to listen to it at their local record shop.

The Radha Kṛṣṇa Temple

Kṛṣṇa consciousness is not merely for renunciates. Kṛṣṇa realisation is practiced as actively by 'working' men and women as by full-time devotees. Kṛṣṇa says in the *Bhagavad Gita* (ch. III, 4, 7), 'Not by merely abstaining from work can one achieve freedom from reaction, nor by renunciation alone can one attain perfection. On the other hand, he who controls the senses by the mind and engages his active organs in works of devotion, without attachment, is by far superior.' All connections with Kṛṣṇa, although from apparently different angles, occur in the Absolute realm and are therefore equal. Persons of any occupation, nationality, age, religion, etc. can, by Kṛṣṇa consciousness, easily award themselves and those around them the highest benefit.

All this is possible because Kṛṣṇa consciousness is a very potent system of yoga called *bhakti-yoga*. Yoga means 'link' or 'linking' with God'. Bhakti is the topmost process in the yoga system and includes hatha, raja, karma, jnana, samkya, mantra, kriya, and all other yogic methods. Bhakti means devotion and provides the most direct contact between us, finite living entities, and the infinite energy of the Lord.

Throughout the world massive amounts of capital are disbursed every year on education in an attempt to improve the quality of human beings. But it is uncertain as to whether the desired result is being achieved. Kṛṣṇa consciousness is a process of plain living and high thinking which is producing men and women of character. These people show by example that a world, as well as a society, based on highest religious principles and with God at the centre, is the way to real peace and happiness.

We humbly request you to chant HARE KṚṢṆA HARE KṚṢṆA KṚṢṆA KṚṢṆA HARE HARE, HARE RĀMA HARE RĀMA RĀMA RĀMA HARE HARE . . . and your life will be sublime!

Side One

Govinda
Sri Guruvastak
Bhaja Bhakata Arotrika
Hare Kṛṣṇa Mantra

Side Two

Sri Isopanisad
Bhaja Hure Mana
Govinda Jai Jai

Produced by George Harrison

Balance Engineer: Ken Scott
Recorded in London, England

Orchestral arrangements on Govinda by John Barham

All titles trad. arr. Mukunda Das Adhikary, Radha Kṛṣṇa Temple, London

All titles published by Apple Publishing Ltd.

Front cover photograph: Altar Deities at the Radha Kṛṣṇa Temple, London

Inside liner photographs: Rathayatra Festival 1970 and Lord Chaitanya Mahaprabhu, India circa 1500

Back cover photograph: His Divine Grace Shri Shrimad 108 Tridandi Goswami A.C. Bhaktivedanta Swami Prabhupada

Designed by John Kosh

Apple Records, 3 Savile Row, London W1

Printed in England by West Brothers · Printers · Limited

THE RADHA KRSNA TEMPLE

STEREO
SAPCOR 18
(SAPCOR.18A)

$33\frac{1}{3}$
Mfd. in U.K.
SIDE 1

℗ 1971

GOVINDA SRI GURUVASTRK
BHAJA BHAKATA—ARATRIKA HARE KRSHA MANTRA
All titles traditional arranged by MUKUNDA DAS ADHIKARY
All titles published by APPLE PUBLISHING LTD.
Produced by GEORGE HARRISON
Recorded in LONDON, England

THE RADHA KRSNA TEMPLE

THE RADHA KRSNA TEMPLE

STEREO
SAPCOR 18
(SAPCOR.18B)

$33\frac{1}{3}$
Mfd. in U.K.
SIDE 2

℗ 1971

SRI ISOPANISAD BHAJA HURE MANA
GOVINDA JAI JAI
All titles traditional arranged by MUKUNDA DAS ADHIKARY
All titles published by APPLE PUBLISHING LTD.
Produced by GEORGE HARRISON
Recorded in LONDON, England

THE RADHA KRSNA TEMPLE

KRSNA
The Supreme Personality of Godhead

A. C. Bhaktivedanta Swami

KRSNA
The Supreme
Personality of Godhead
by
His Divine Grace
A.C.Bhaktivedanta Swami
Prabhupada

introduction by George Harrison
383 pp. Vol I   370 pp. Vol II

112 full colour plates

NOW in words and pictures... the most intimate and confidential world of Shri Krsna, the Supreme Personality of Godhead, unfolds before your eyes in two gorgeously illustrated volumes rendered by His Divine Grace Shri Shrimad Tridandi Goswami A.C. Bhaktivedanta Swami Prabhupad Maharaj (Vol. I, 400 pages; Vol. II, 369 pages; 122 full-colour plates).

Introduced by George Harrison, these books communicate with humour, love, laughter, chivalry, anger, shock... the most confidential pastimes of Shri Krsna, as contained within the Tenth Canto of the Shrimad Bhagwatam, written by the great saint Vyasadev. The Shrimad Bhagwatam is known as the cream of the Vedic literature, the oldest and most extensive Scriptures in existence. Although Vyasadev compiled the Bhagwatam over 5,000 years ago, he is recognised as an incarnation of Lord Krsna, and it is sometimes said that he still lives in the Himalayas.

This may appear to be a mixture of fact and fiction, but actually there is no fiction involved. It is scientific, realistic and authorised. Through bhaktiyoga (devotional service) one can come to know of the infinite spiritual sky filled with innumerable planets on which there are people, trees, rivers, lakes, animals and, of course, Krsna Himself.

Through the medium of A.C. Bhaktivedanta Swami, anyone can relish the miraculous and inconceivable pastimes of Krsna as revealed in these volumes. You do not have to be a mystic, a yogi or a scholar to love and understand Him... ANYONE can. Hare Krsna.

AVAILABLE THROUGH
BOOKSHOPS
AND
THE LONDON RADHA KRSNA TEMPLE
7, Bury Place, W.C.1.
Tel: 242-0394

RADHA KRSNA TEMPLE
RADHA KRSNA TEMPLE
Side one: Govinda / Sri Guruvastakam / Bhaja Bhakata-Arati / Hare Krishna Mantra
Side two: Sri Ishopanishad / Bhajahu Re Mana / Govinda Jai Jai
UK release: 21 May 1971; SAPCOR 18; chart high; failed to chart.
US release: 28 May 1971; ST3359; chart high; failed to chart.
Produced by George Harrison.

George Harrison (harmonium, guitar and bass), Tamal Krishna Go swami (flute), Harivilas, Yamuna, Jivananda, Lilavati and Yogesvara (lead vocals) assembled Hare Krishna devotees (backing vocals, mridanga and kartals). Alan White (drums on Hare Krishna Mantra). John Barham orchestral arrangement Govinda. Mukunda Goswami (as Makunda Das Adhikary) (arrangements).

The Radha Krsna Temple album features seven Sanskrit hymns to Krishna and the movement's spiritual masters. 'Bhaja Hure Mana' was written especially for the album as a reminder to the listener that physical life is an illusion and that the origin and meaning of existence is not to be found on this earthly plane, but in the spiritual realm.

Although 'Bhaja Hure Mana' wasn't written by Harrison, it perfectly encapsulates his beliefs and philosophy. Harrison was far more interested in the spiritual realm than he was with the physical world of illusions. As far as he was concerned, Hinduism offered the best possible path to enlightenment and God consciousness. "I'm interested in this because the Krishna scene is the same as several others, a lot of branches on the same tree, and I'm involved in a lot of them," he said. "The thing they have in common is to get back to God, and to get consciousness. With the Krishna consciousness people, there are probably more people I can identify with, because there are younger people, and they've been through different scenes like we all have. They've been drunkards at one time or another."[9]

As far as Harrison was concerned, there was little to distinguish between himself and the devotees of ISKCON. There was also, he reasoned, little difference between this album of hymns and the pop songs he'd written and recorded himself. It was all music made with God in mind. Speaking to David Wigg, he said: "It's just another process. It's really the same sort of thing as meditation, but this is the thing – it has more effect, I think. Or quicker effect, because music is such a powerful force. And it's like God likes me when I work, but loves me when I sing."[10]

Harrison's close association with Krishna consciousness and his willingness to share his beliefs helped introduce ISKCON to the public. "I figured this is the space age, with airplanes and everything. If everyone can go around the world on their holidays, there's no reason why a mantra can't go a few miles as well. So the idea was to try to spiritually infiltrate society, so to speak," he explained.[11] As an ex-Beatle and one of the bosses of Apple Records he had the power to do just that. While other record companies were promoting progressive rock, heavy metal, glam rock and pop, Apple released an album of Sanskrit hymns.

Work on the album started at EMI Studios, Abbey Road before moving to Trident Studios, were Harrison added harmonium, bass guitar and slide guitar to the mix of traditional Indian instruments. His slide playing can be heard on *Sri Guruvastak* and *Sri Ishopanishad*.

Radha Krsna Temple data

Apple Records issued the album in a gatefold sleeve with lyrics, a biography of the Spiritual Master, a history of KRSNA Consciousness and a leaflet advertising the Harrison endorsed and financed book *KRSNA The Supreme Personality of Godhead*.

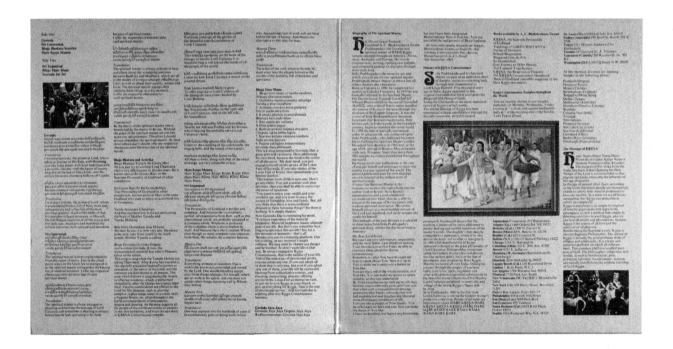

COURTESY POLAROID

154

R 5912

BANGLA DESH
george harrison

'Bangla-Desh' / 'Deep Blue'*
GEORGE HARRISON
Produced by George Harrison and Phil Spector
UK release: 30 July 1971 ; Apple R5912; chart high; number 10.
US release: 28 July 1971; Apple 1836; chart high; number 23.

George Harrison (vocals, guitar, dobro*), Leon Russell (piano), Klaus Voormann (bass)*, Jesse Ed Davis (guitar), Ringo Starr (drums), Jim Horn (saxophone), Jim Keltner (drums)*

In April 1971, Harrison flew to Los Angeles to discuss finance and distribution for the film *Raga* with its director Howard Worth and its star and producer Ravi Shankar. Production had ground to a halt because the project had run out of money. Harrison intervened and secured financial backing and distribution by Apple Films. At some point he found time to compile the soundtrack album that Apple would issue to coincide with the release of the film later in the year. He also learnt of the full scale of the humanitarian crisis taking place in Bangladesh from Shankar.

East Pakistan had been hit by a tropical cyclone in November 1970. 500,000 people died as a result. The situation worsened in early 1971 when the Awami League, one of the main political parties in the region, demanded autonomy for East Pakistan, and an end to military rule that was responsible for a widespread genocide against the Bengali population. How many civilians died in the conflict is unclear, however, ten million refugees fled to India, overwhelming the country's resources and galvanizing the Indian government to military intervention.

Shankar wanted to perform a concert to raise money for the refugees. "Originally, Ravi was going to do the concert, and he was telling me, and he was saying that he wanted to do something which would make a little bit more money than he normally made. He can only make a thousand, two thousand dollars at a concert, playing sitar. And he said he would like to do something, maybe I could help, think of some ideas, in order to make something like twenty or thirty five thousand dollars. He gave me all this information and articles on what was going on in Bangladesh, and I slowly got pulled into it."[12]

Harrison took Shankar's idea and made it bigger, much bigger. They would stage a star studded concert in New York City, produce a film and record of the concert and record two charity singles to raise awareness of the crisis and money for the refugees.

Bangla-Desh

George Harrison (vocals, guitar), Leon Russell (piano), Jesse Ed Davis (guitar), Ringo Starr (drums), Jim Horn (saxophone), Jim Keltner (drums)

One of the best ways to raise awareness and money was by releasing a single. As John Lennon had demonstrated with 'Give Peace A Chance', it was the perfect medium when you wanted to get your message across to an audience in a hurry. Not only would a single by an ex-Beatle attract attention to the crisis, it would raise a substantial sum of money. Better still would have been to put the income into a trust that could help with future aid projects as well as the immediate crisis. Unfortunately, that didn't happen. Leon Russell: "I told him that rather than raising money just one time, that we should start a foundation, because that type of thing was happening around the world continually. We could put the money into the foundation and do 2-3 of those shows a year, and only use the interest from the foundation for the relief effort. But they didn't do that I'm afraid it was turned over to the United Nations and I heard that a lot of the supplies got to the docks and there wasn't any way to get them to the needed areas. So there wasn't as much good done at the time as there could have been."[13]

Harrison was well aware of the issues surrounding the distribution of aid to refugees. Raising money to purchase aid was important, but only part of his plan. As important was the need to raise awareness of the crisis. The Western media had been somewhat ambivalent in its reporting of the genocide and mass exodus, to the extent that in Britain the BBC even went as far as to initially ban Harrison's single from radio play-lists. "The reluctance of the press to report the full details created the need to bring attention to it," Harrison explained. "So the song 'Bangla-Desh' was written specifically to get attention to the war prior to the concert."[14]

Writing about the genocide taking place in a post-colonial country wasn't the stuff of pop songs. Few, if any, songwriters had tackled such a troubling subject, and few would have been able to write about it to order. Turning cold, impersonal facts into an emotive plea for help, Harrison turned something political into something personal. Drawing on his friendship with Shankar, his lyric is empathetic and imploring. "I really wanted to tell people about Bangladesh and I wrote this song in ten minutes. I sat at the piano and that was the idea I had. That came out and I made a record of it. I didn't expect it to be a big hit, but I hoped it would because all the money was going to the refugees."[15]

Although Harrison had been inspired by his friendship with Shankar, the first draft was missing the all important introduction. Luckily, Leon Russell was on hand and suggested a slow, gospel-tinged preamble to draw the listener in. "Leon Russell was the one who suggested that I do something in the beginning of the song to try and explain: a slow introduction. So I took his idea and shortened it," Harrison explained.[16]

Harrison asked Phil Spector to co-produce the record, but compared to their work on *All Things Must Pass*, the results were disappointing. While there is no doubting the conviction of Harrison's performance, the musical support is too pedestrian. 'Bangla-Desh' simply doesn't have any of the

Spector magic that he usually created in the studio. The live version has a drive and urgency that knocks the socks of the studio recording. Harrison sounds more confident performing the song in concert. His vocal has a depth of conviction and warmth that he didn't capture in the studio. Not that it mattered much. Harrison was at the top of his game and could have issued pretty much anything and it would have been a hit.

Deep Blue
George Harrison (vocals, dobro), Klaus Voormann (bass), Jim Keltner (drums)

'Deep Blue' was written while recording *All Things Must Pass*. It should have been a joyous album to make, but illness and despair haunted the sessions like a grievous angel. Harrison's mother was dying; writing 'Deep Blue' was his way of dealing with his emotions and confronting his fears. In doing so he takes us into his confidence in a startlingly open and honest way. Death is rarely dealt with in pop songs, except, perhaps, as a macabre fascination with songs like 'Dead Man's Curve' or 'Leader Of The Pack'. As a subject it's more often left to poets and artists to ponder, rather than pop stars.

Having to confront his mother's mortality brought about a realization that all life is transitory. Nothing we can do alters the fact that we are mortal and helpless beings; 'Deep Blue' is a symbolic reminder of the inevitability of death. Like the memento mori of old, it is a contemplation of mortality, divine judgement and salvation. Set to a beautifully crafted folk-blues shuffle performed by Harrison, Voormann and Keltner, it has an honesty and intimacy that makes it all the more intense and powerful. By stripping away the layers of bombastic production that were a feature of *All Things Must Pass*, Harrison reveals his true self, exposing the reality that had been masked by Spector's wall of sound to let us glimpse the truth, albeit fleetingly.

Bangla-Desh data

In America, Apple issued 'Bangla-Desh'/'Deep Blue' with Apple labels and a picture sleeve with press cuttings on one side and a photograph of a starving mother and child on the other. In a rush to get the song aired on the radio, Capitol Records issued one-sided white label copies of the A-side to radio stations. While American radio stations were fully supportive and played the record, in Britain the BBC initially banned it from its play-lists. "Plays were erased from six shows, including the Stuart Henry, Rosko and John Peel slots last Saturday. It was something about the song persuading people to recognize Bangladesh, but the record's only trying to persuade people to think about children... Now it's to be played without mentioning the title or the charity concerned," explained head of Apple Films, Tony Bramwell.[17]

Despite the fact that BBC disc jockeys couldn't mention the record by name, it managed a respectable number 10 in Britain. It didn't fair as well in America where the initial rush of interest soon faded. The record only made it to number 23 on the *Billboard* charts for seven weeks. As Harrison's well intentioned single slipped down the charts, Paul and Linda McCartney's pop confection 'Uncle Albert/Admiral Halsey' was on its way to the top.

In Britain, Apple issued a picture sleeve with the photograph of a starving child and mother on one side and 'Bangla Desh' above 'George Harrison' top centre. The sleeve was made from thick card, typical of Apple's British picture sleeves of the time, in very small numbers and has become one of Apple's rarest 7-inch picture sleeves. Promotional copies of the single issued in Britain have a large 'A' at ten o'clock with the date 30.7.71 at four o'clock. Both EMI and Decca manufactured copies of the single. The Decca pressings have a wider space between the centre and the rest of the label and the pressing ring or indentation is smaller and deeper on Decca pressings compared to EMI pressings. The single was re-issued in America in 1976 with an orange Capitol Records label

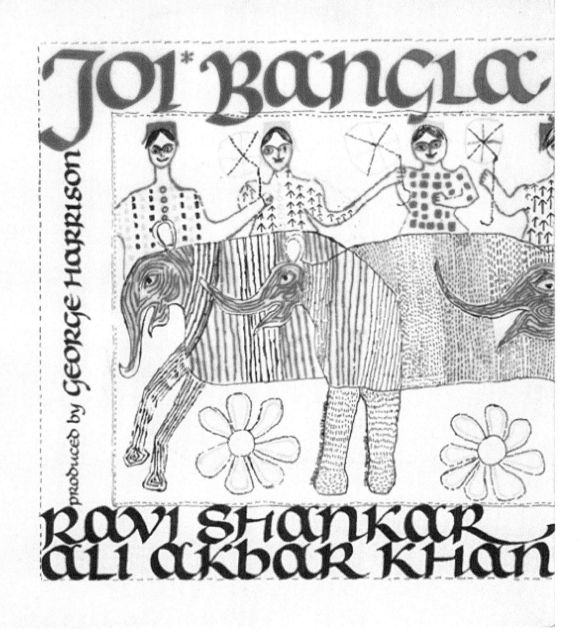

RAGA MISHRA JHINJHOTI (DADRA TAL)

THIS PIECE EVOLVED DURING THE RECORDING SESSION AND IS INSPIRED BY THE FOLK MELODIES OF BENGAL

(RAVI SHANKAR, ALI AKBAR KHAN, ALLA RAKHA)

SING OF UNDYING
BANGLA DESH
JOI
BANGALA JOI
LAND OF BEAUTY
GRACEFUL GREEN
SWEET TO NOSTRILS
AND HEART
THE LANGUAGE SWEET
UPON TONGUES OF
PEOPLE POSSESSED
OF THE LAND
DYING
BY THE LAND
RIPPED
FROM THE BOWELS
OF THE LAND
SWEET EARTH
MAKING
US ONE
BEYOND CONSCIENCE
OR CREED
JOI

✳ BE TRIUMPHANT

O BHAUGOWAN

O GOD
WHERE
HAVE YOU GONE
DESERTING US
SICKNESS
CYCLONES
FLOODS
ARE UPON US
DO YOU NOT
CARE
FOR US
O GOD
WHO COUNTS
HOW MANY
DIE
WHO HEARS
OUR CRY
TELL US
WHAT MORE
BURDENS
ARE WE
TO BEAR
O GOD

ALLA RAKHA

Contributions for the benefit of the homeless children of Bangla Desh (East Pakistan) can be sent to: THE GEORGE HARRISON-RAVI SHANKAR SPECIAL EMERGENCY RELIEF FUND c/o UNICEF, UNITED NATIONS, N.Y. City

APPLE 37

RAVI SHANKAR APPEARS BY PERMISSION OF GRAMOPHONE CO. OF INDIA LTD.

162

'Joi Bangla' / 'Oh Bhaugowan' / 'Raga Mishra-Jhinjhoti'*
**RAVI SHANKAR / RAVI SHANKAR (Sitar) and ALIAKBAR KHAN (Sarod) with ALLA
RAKAH (Tabla).***
Produced by George Harrison.
UK release: 27 August 1971; Apple 37; chart high; failed to chart.
US release: 28 August 1971; Apple 1838; chart high; failed to chart.

Ravi Shankar (sitar and vocals), Ali Akbar Khan (sarod), Alla Rakah (tabla), Shubho Shankar*
(vocals), Sanjukta Ghosh* (vocals), G. Sachdev* (flute), Harihar Rao* (ek tara)

At roughly the same time as Harrison recorded his 'Bangla-Desh' single, he produced a companion
single by Ravi Shankar. Shankar had written some songs in Bengali, the mother tongue of what is now
Bangladesh, among them 'Joi Bangla'. Influenced by the events taking place in East Pakistan, it was
born of sympathy, pain and unity. "Before the show (The Concert For Bangla-Desh) I was so inspired,
or in so much pain, over what was happening, that I wrote two songs. One was 'Joi Bangla'–that is 'Joy
Bangla', a short name for Bangladesh," Shankar told *Yoga Journal*.[18]

A popular slogan of the time, 'Joi Bangla' roughly translates into English as "long live Bangladesh".
At the time it was a politically loaded statement that attacked the Pakistani regime and sided with the
oppressed Bengali people. Today its meaning has changed to become an expression of love for the
mother country, rather than a victory cry.

'Oh Bhaugowan' is a lament for Bangladesh. "'Oh Bhaugowan' is 'Oh God' as the Hindus would
say. 'Khodatala' is as the Muslims would say. The whole song was a lament, 'Oh God, why are you
punishing us? Why all these calamities, these floods, these droughts, these terrible things happening?'
A very short song. It was a lamentation for all the Bangladesh people, which is predominantly a Muslim
country, but there are millions of Hindus still there," Shankar explained.[19] By incorporating both
languages, Shankar was attempting to bring people together. It was a plea not only to God, but to the
people of East Pakistan to understand their differences, tolerate one another and to live together in
peace and harmony

The third piece of music on the record, 'Raga Mishra-Jhinjhoti', was improvised in the studio.
Shankar often entered the studio with only a rough idea of what he wanted to record, which he would
then develop into a finished piece of music. A slow raga that increases in intensity and tempo, it features
Ali Akbar Khan and Alla Rakah. Shankar and Khan engage in a call and response dialogue that displays
their musical virtuosity, particularly as the tempo builds to a frantic climax.

Joi Bangla data

Apple Records issued 'Joi Bangla' with Apple labels and a picture sleeve. Advertisements were placed in music papers in Britain and America, but the single did not enter the charts. No doubt Harrison and Apple hoped that 'Joi Bangla' would become as popular as 'Hare Krishna Mantra' and 'Govinda', but it wasn't to be. Then, as now, classical Indian music was rarely played on mainstream radio. Furthermore, the BBC was keen to appear impartial, and Shankar's plea for independence for Bangladesh, even if it wasn't understood by the majority of English speaking listeners, was too partisan and therefore ignored.

RAGA
RAVI SHANKAR
Side one: Dawn To Dusk / Vedic Hymns / Baba Teaching / Birth To Death / Vinus House / Gurur Bramha / United Nations
Side two: Raga Parameshwari / Rangeswhari / Banaras Ghat / Bombay Studio / Kinnara School / Frenzy And Distortion / Raga Desh
US release: 7 December 1971, Apple SWAO 3384; chart high; failed to chart.
Re-Produced for disc by George Harrison.

With the music for *Raga* having been recorded in the two years prior to the film's release, Harrison's task as producer was to compile a soundtrack album from the available material. Few studio recordings were available, and no new recordings were made. Thus Harrison had no other choice than to lift large sections directly from the mono recordings made on battery-operated portable professional tape recorders. These recordings were made in various locations in India and America and were augmented with professionally recorded concert performances – 'United Nations' is a excerpt from a recording with Yehudi Menuhim previously available on *East Meets West Vol. 2.*

Raga data

Apple Records issued the soundtrack album in America with a gatefold sleeve. The album was not issued in Britain. Harrison appeared on the Dick Cavett Show to promote both *Raga* and the *Concert for Bangladesh* album. But as Cavett spent most of the show discussing other topics there was little time to plug either album. Even when Shankar appeared in the second half of the show, Cavett failed to discuss the *Raga* album or film with him, preferring to talk about the perceived connection Indian classical music had with drugs, which must have irked Shankar greatly.

SWAO 3384

167

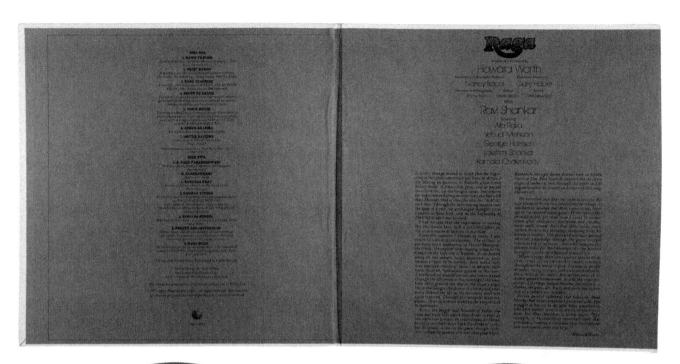

RAGA
Original Soundtrack

Stereo

SWAO—3384
(SWAO 1-3384)

Side 1

1. DAWN TO DUSK   3:38   BMI
2. VEDIC HYMNS   1:30   NONE
3. BABA TEACHING   1:08   NONE
4. BIRTH TO DEATH   3:10   BMI
5. VINUS HOUSE   2:37   BMI
6. GURUR BRAMHA   1:10   BMI
7. UNITED NATIONS   4:33   BMI

Ravi Shankar performs courtesy
Gramophone Co. of India, Ltd.
Re-Produced for disc by
GEORGE HARRISON

MFG. BY APPLE RECORDS, INC.

RAGA
Original Soundtrack

Stereo

SWAO—3384
(SWAO 2-3384)

Side 2

1. Medley:
   a. RAGA PARAMESHWARI   2:51   BMI
   b. RANGESWHART   1:40   BMI
2. BANARAS GHAT   2:45   BMI
3. BOMBAY STUDIO   1:28   BMI
4. KINNARA SCHOOL   1:51   BMI
5. FRENZY AND DISTORTION 1:06   BMI
6. RAGA DESH   8:50   BMI

Ravi Shankar performs
courtesy Gramophone
Co. of India, Ltd.

Re-Produced for
disc by GEORGE
HARRISON

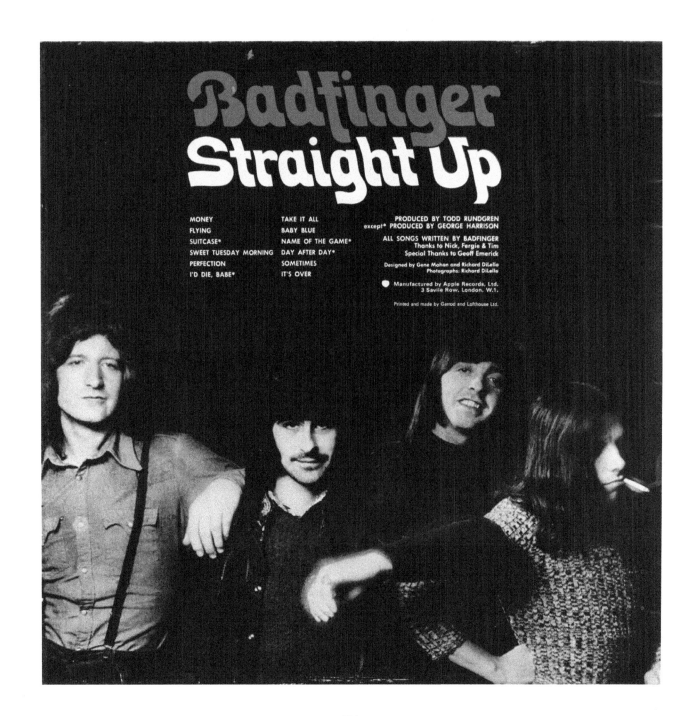

STRAIGHT UP

33⅓
Mfd. in U.K.
SIDE 1

STEREO
SAPCOR 19

(SAPCOR 19A)
℗ 1972

TAKE IT ALL (Peter Ham)
BABY BLUE (Peter Ham)
MONEY (Tom Evans)
FLYING (Tom Evans—Joey Molland)
*I'D DIE BABE (Joey Molland)
*NAME OF THE GAME (Peter Ham)
Apple Publishing Ltd.
BADFINGER
Produced by Todd Rundgren
except * Produced by George Harrison

STRAIGHT UP

33⅓
Mfd. in U.K.
SIDE 2

STEREO
SAPCOR 19

(SAPCOR 19B)
℗ 1972

*SUITCASE (Joey Molland)
SWEET TUESDAY MORNING (Joey Molland)
*DAY AFTER DAY (Peter Ham)
SOMETIMES (Joey Molland)
PERFECTION (Peter Ham)
IT'S OVER (Tom Evans)
Apple Publishing Ltd.
BADFINGER
Produced by Todd Rundgren
except * Produced by George Harrison

BADFINGER
"DAY AFTER DAY"

● APPLE 40
Produced by George Harrison

(APPLE.40A)
APPLE 40

Apple
Publishing
Ltd.
℗ 1972

Produced by:
GEORGE
HARRISON

Mfd. in U.K.

DAY AFTER DAY
(Pete Ham)
BADFINGER
(From their forthcoming album
"STRAIGHT UP" SAPCOR 19)

STRAIGHT UP
BADFINGER
Side one: Take It All / Baby Blue / Money / Flying / I'd Die Babe* / Name of the Game*
Side two: Suitcase*Δ / Sweet Tuesday Morning** / Day After Day* / Sometimes / Perfection / It's Over
UK release: 13 December 1971; Apple SAPCOR 19; chart high; failed to chart.
US release: 11 February 1972, Apple ST3387; chart high; number 31.
Produced by George Harrison*
Produced by Todd Rundgren

Pete Ham (guitar, piano, vocals), Tom Evans (bass, vocals) Joey Molland (guitar, vocals), Mike Gibbins (drums), George Harrison (slide guitar*), Leon Russell (piano*, guitar**) Bobby Diebold (bass**), Klaus Voormann (electric pianoΔ), Bill Collins (accordion**)

Badfinger's third album for Apple Records, *Straight Up*, was the victim of record company interference and the fickle hand of fate. Badfinger began work on the album in early January 1971 with Geoff Emerick producing. The album took two months to record, but was mixed in just one day because the band had been booked into a hastily arranged tour of America. When they returned in May they were surprised to learn that the album had been rejected. Al Steckler, the head of Apple Records American division, rejected the album because he felt Emerick "didn't have the ears to hear something commercial. I felt the group didn't have a real producer."[20] It wasn't all bad news because Steckler asked Harrison if he'd like to have a go at producing the band.

With Harrison now engaged as producer, Badfinger returned to EMI Studios, Abbey Road, in late May to begin again. Harrison took the band's music and began to refine it. "Pete and George were already working out new arrangements," recalled Joey Molland, "I think George wanted to make our music more sophisticated."[21] Making their music more sophisticated involved spending hours perfecting arrangements and solos. Ever the hands on producer, Harrison asked if he could play the slide solo on the Pete Ham song 'Day After Day'. Joining Pete Ham in the studio, Harrison set about recording the solo the way he'd always done, live. Doing it this way achieved the result he was after, but as studio engineer Richard Lush recalled, this was the hard way of doing it. "They were playing their slide parts simultaneously. I remember thinking, 'There's an easier way to do this,' but George really wanted to do it that way."[22]

Harrison's way of recording was to capture a performance, but he wanted it to be perfect. Capturing a perfect live performance involving two or more musicians is never easy, particularly when one is in awe of the other, as Ham was of Harrison. He also had a habit of finding fault in the smallest detail and would re-record parts until they matched his exacting standards, even if that meant sacrificing feel for perfection. It was a foible some found frustrating. "Did you know that George wanted to redo his guitar solos on 'Gimme Some Truth' and 'How Do You Sleep?'," remarked an incredulous Lennon. "That's the best he's ever fucking played in his life! He'd never get that feeling again. He'd go on forever if you let him."[23]

Whichever way you looked at it, Harrison's perfectionism paid off. 'Day After Day' proved once again that he had the ears to produce hit records. When issued as a single, the song became Badfinger's biggest hit, peaking at number four on the *Billboard* Pop Singles chart. The single performed just as well in Britain, where it peaked at number 10 on the UK Singles Chart.

Harrison would have gone on forever if he'd been allowed. Having spent just over a month in the studio with the band, he'd produced only four songs, 'I'd Die Babe', 'Name of the Game', 'Suitcase' and 'Day After Day'. In mid-July he informed the band that he was going to have to put the album on hold while he organized the Concert for Bangladesh.

Sessions for the album had already dragged on for six months and all Apple Records had to show for it was four songs. Time was running out and Apple Records wanted it finished. Enter Todd Rundgren, who was hired to complete the job. Rundgren had the band re-record some songs and remixed others originally produced by Emerick and Harrison. Badfinger, however, were far from happy with either his production or attitude. "First off, he wanted four times the money he deserved," recalled Pete Ham. "He even wanted credit for the things George had already produced. It was ridiculous. And his ideas restricted the band's own ideas and creativity. He certainly won't be producing our next LP."[24] (Actually Rundgren did begin producing their follow up, but was sacked after just four days.)

As far as Rundgren was concerned, because he was responsible for the final mix, he had every right to claim production credit for the songs produced by Harrison. "The songs I revamped had been credited to George Harrison, including the big hit single, 'Day After Day'. George had originally said, 'Take these tapes, do anything you want.' I should have credit and be paid for those tracks," he reckoned.[25] Rundgren might not have endeared himself to Badfinger, but he did what had been asked of him, he brought the project to a swift conclusion and produced a commercial record. But even though it featured a hit single, *Straight Up* fared no better than the band's previous album. *Straight Up* peaked at 31 on the *Billboard* charts, three places lower than *No Dice*.

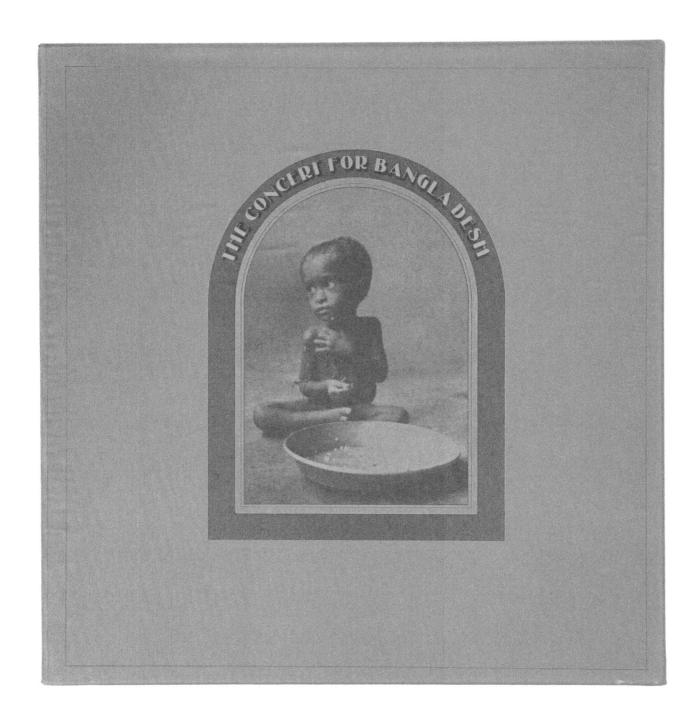

174

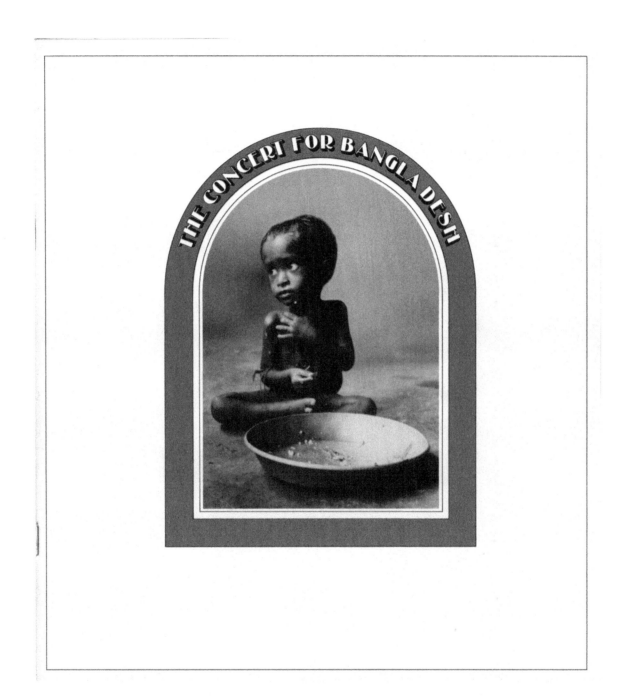

THE CONCERT FOR BANGLA DESH

SIDE ONE
STCX 3385
(STCX-1-3385)

1. GEORGE HARRISON/RAVI SHANKAR INTRODUCTION Harrisongs Ltd. 6:16
2. BANGLA DHUN 16:19

RAVI SHANKAR, Sitar
ALIAKBAR KHAN, Sarod
ALLA RAKAH, Tabla
KAMALA CHAKRAVARTY, Tamboura

APPLE
℗1971

Produced by George Harrison
and Phil Spector

MADE IN ENGLAND

THE CONCERT FOR BANGLA DESH

SIDE SIX
STCX 3385
(STCX-6-3385)

1. SOMETHING (George Harrison) Harrisongs Ltd. 3:05
2. BANGLA DESH (George Harrison) Harrisongs Ltd. 4:14

APPLE
℗1971

Produced by George Harrison
and Phil Spector

MADE IN ENGLAND

THE CONCERT FOR BANGLA DESH

SIDE TWO
STCX 3385
(STCX-2-3385)

1. WAH-WAH (George Harrison) Harrisongs Ltd. 3:15
2. MY SWEET LORD (George Harrison) Harrisongs Ltd. 4:16
3. AWAITING ON YOU ALL (George Harrison) Harrisongs Ltd. 2:37
4. THAT'S THE WAY GOD PLANNED IT (Billy Preston) Apple Pub. Ltd. 4:05

APPLE
℗1971

Produced by George Harrison
and Phil Spector

MADE IN ENGLAND

THE CONCERT FOR BANGLA DESH

SIDE FIVE
STCX 3385
(STCX-5-3385)

1. A HARD RAIN'S GONNA FALL (Bob Dylan) Kinney Music Ltd. 5:04
2. IT TAKES A LOT TO LAUGH, IT TAKES A TRAIN TO CRY (Bob Dylan) Kinney Music Ltd. 2:54
3. BLOWIN' IN THE WIND (Bob Dylan) Kinney Music Ltd. 3:34
4. MR. TAMBOURINE MAN (Bob Dylan) Kinney Music Ltd. 4:06
5. JUST LIKE A WOMAN (Bob Dylan) B. Feldman Ltd. 4:14

APPLE
℗1971

Produced by George Harrison
and Phil Spector

MADE IN ENGLAND

THE CONCERT FOR BANGLA DESH

SIDE THREE
STCX 3385

(STCX-3-3385)

1. IT DON'T COME EASY (Richard Starkey)
   Startling Music Ltd.   2:38
2. BEWARE OF DARKNESS (George Harrison)
   Harrisongs Ltd.   3:26
3. INTRODUCTION OF THE BAND   3:00
4. WHILE MY GUITAR GENTLY WEEPS
   (George Harrison) Harrisongs Ltd.   4:39

APPLE
℗ 1971

Produced by George Harrison
and Phil Spector

MADE IN ENGLAND

THE CONCERT FOR BANGLA DESH

SIDE FOUR
STCX 3385

(STCX-4-3385)

1. MEDLEY
   JUMPING JACK FLASH (Mick Jagger –
   Keith Richard) Essex International Ltd
   YOUNGBLOOD (Jerry Lieber – Mike Stoller –
   Doc Pomus) Carlin Music Corp.   9:11
2. HERE COMES THE SUN (George Harrison)
   Harrisongs Ltd.   2:51

APPLE
℗ 1971

Produced by George Harrison
and Phil Spector

MADE IN ENGLAND

THE CONCERT FOR BANGLA DESH

Apple

Available Now STCX3385

THE CONCERT FOR BANGLADESH
VARIOUS ARTISTS

Side one: Introduction (Harrison and Shankar) / Bangla Dhun (Shankar)

Side two: Wah-Wah (Harrison) / My Sweet Lord (Harrison) / Awaiting On You All (Harrison) / That's The Way God Planned It (Billy Preston)

Side three: It Don't Come Easy (Ringo Starr) / Beware of Darkness (Harrison and Russell) / Band Introduction (Harrison) / While My Guitar Gently Weeps (Harrison)

Side four: Medley: Jumpin' Jack Flash/Youngblood (Russell and Don Preston) / Here Comes The Sun (Harrison)

Side five: A Hard Rain's A-Gonna Fall (Dylan) / It Takes A Lot To Laugh, It Takes A Train To Cry (Dylan) / Blowin' In The Wind (Dylan) / Mr. Tambourine Man (Dylan) / Just Like A Woman (Dylan)

Side six: Something (Harrison) / Bangla-Desh

UK release: 10 January 1972; Apple; chart high; number 1.

US release: 20 December 1971, Apple; chart high; number 2.

Produced by George Harrison and Phil Spector.

The Artists: George Harrison (vocals, electric and acoustic guitars, backing vocals), Ravi Shankar (sitar), Bob Dylan (vocals, acoustic guitar, harmonica), Leon Russell (piano, vocals, bass, backing vocals), Ringo Starr (drums, vocals, tambourine), Billy Preston (Hammond organ, vocals), Eric Clapton (electric guitar), Ali Akbar Khan (sarod), Alla Rakha (tabla), Kamala Chakravarty (tambura).

The Band: Jesse Ed Davis (electric guitar), Klaus Voormann (bass), Jim Keltner (drums), Pete Ham (acoustic guitar), Tom Evans (twelve-string acoustic guitar), Joey Molland (acoustic guitar), Mike Gibbins (tambourine, maracas), Don Preston (electric guitar, vocals (on 'Jumpin' Jack Flash/Young Blood' and 'Bangla-Desh' only), Carl Radle (bass (on 'Jumpin' Jack Flash/Young Blood' only).

The Hollywood Horns: Jim Horn (saxophones, horn arrangements), Chuck Findley (trumpet), Jackie Kelso (saxophones), Allan Beutler (saxophones), Lou McCreary (trombone), Ollie Mitchell (trumpet).

The Backing Vocalists/Soul Choir: Claudia Linnear, Jo Green, Jeanie Greene, Marlin Greene, Dolores Hall, Don Nix, Don Preston (backing vocals, percussion)

Although Harrison hadn't intended it as such, the Concert For Bangladesh was the crowning accomplishment of eighteen months hard work. The seeds he'd planted since becoming a solo performer germinated and blossomed at this one-off concert. Calling on many of the friends and musicians he worked with recently, Harrison formed the first ever superstar band to perform at the first ever superstar charity concert. "I decided to do the concert myself, and pull in a lot of people, whoever I could recruit, and I thought would make a good show," Harrison explained. "Try to film and record it, in case it worked, came off good. Because, at that time, there was a chance it could have been the biggest disaster in the world."[26]

While he'd been happy to tread the boards as a sideman, where he could hide in the shadows, now he'd have to step into the full glare of the spotlight. For the first time in his career, he was the star. That was something he wasn't used to or comfortable with. But he wasn't going to be alone. He surrounded himself with friends who would not only perform but advise. Harrison spoke with all the artistes, most of whom he'd previously worked with, to ask if they'd appear. The only exception being the soul choir, which was assembled by Don Nix. Klaus Voormann: "While in L.A. George had met Don Nix. We went on a boat trip to Catalina Island and suddenly Don had the job of putting the soul choir together..." [27] In return for their help with the concert, Harrison wrote personal thank you letters to all the artists who performed at the concert, and in some cases donated songs or his guitar playing skills to their records. Jesse Ed Davis was gifted 'Sue Me, Sue You Blues' and Harrison played guitar on albums by Billy Preston and Don Nix.

Rehearsals took place the week before the concert in a large rehearsal room at Carnegie Hall. However, most of the key players didn't arrive in New York City until days before the concert. Eric Clapton was absent for most of the week because he'd developed a heroin habit and was in no fit state to travel, let alone perform. "Eric was in a bit of a state," recalled Harrison. "He was on heroin, at the time. We had him booked on every flight out of London to New York for about seven days. Finally, he came in about the night before, and nobody saw him. He just checked into his hotel, went up to his room, and he was just there, sick as a dog."[28] Clapton: "I was laid up sick for a week while all the rehearsals were going on, you see. Everyone got there a week early for the gig and I got very ill and couldn't move. I was literally in a very bad way. So I missed all the rehearsals, I just got there in time for the first show. So, I mean, just being in tune was enough of a problem for me. I really felt they were carrying my weight, in a way."[29]

Harrison didn't give up on his friend, and Clapton did attend the sound-check, but he did hire Jesse Ed Davis to deputize for the guitarist should he be to 'ill' to perform. According to a report in the *L.A. Free Press*, Davis had played on the 'Bangla-Desh' recording sessions where he'd learnt about Harrison's plans for the concert. Davis asked if he could attend the concert, perhaps with an eye to performing. "We flew up to New York expecting to be spectators," Davis explained. "And Eric Clapton pulled up sick and recommended me to take over, so George called me and asked and of course I said 'Yes'. And we had a big rehearsal the night before and all day Saturday. Klaus Voormann was drilling the songs into me. The next day at the concert it was just magic and fortunately Eric recovered in time and he came and played his ass off, but they still let me go ahead and play, which I thought was real nice."[30]

Unlike Clapton, Bob Dylan was fit, but hadn't played for a couple of years and was nervous. "Dylan was very difficult to get, because had been laid up for years, and he [had] just done the one show, in the Isle Of Wight. He was not feeling that strong about it because he had been out of it for so long," Harrison recalled.[31] However, Dylan did rehearse with Harrison, and promised to perform at both shows. At this point Dylan got cold feet and had to be persuaded by Harrison to make good his promise. After all, it was for the greater good. "I found that the musicians were great," Harrison said. "They completely put down their own egos, to a large extent, to play together and do something. Because the whole vibe of that concert was that it was something bigger than the lot of us."[32]

The concert was recorded by the Record Plant sixteen-track mobile recording studio and filmed by technicians supplied by Madison Square Garden, who were more familiar with filming sporting events than rock concerts. Consequently, some of the footage was unusable (one camera was out of focus for the duration of the concert and another had cables obscuring part of its view). Luckily, the audio recording didn't suffer from the same glitches, and Harrison and Spector began mixing the album the day after the concert. Little was done to sweeten the recordings, the only exception being a double-tracked vocal on 'While My Guitar Gently Weeps' and an edit of 'Wah-Wah' made from the afternoon and evening shows. Mixing was completed at A&M Studios in L.A.. But before he moved to the west coast, Harrison made good a promise he'd made to the star performers, and provided them with recordings of their performances to approve. "One thing I wanted to do, to cover everybody, like Leon and Bob and Eric, [I said]: 'Look, we are recording and filming it, but if it turns out lousy, I promise you we are not going to put it out'. I sent them copies of their parts of the show. In some cases, we remixed them differently, for Leon."[33]

Harrison wanted to keep his friends sweet and make a professional sounding album. After all, everything rested on the album selling in its millions. Although everybody performed free of charge, expenses for staging the concert, which were met by Apple, came to an estimated $300,000. (Apple would recoup its expenses from distributing the film of the concert.) The concert made $243,418, ten times what Shankar had originally hoped for, but it didn't even cover costs. Nobody would have bought an album that sounded like a badly recorded bootleg. Harrison had to get it right and his attention to detail paid dividends. The album topped the British charts, reached number two in America and made millions of dollars for the charity. "Then, with the album, we started making money. We gave about one million, two hundred thousand dollars, and then the money got frozen, and is still there," recalled an exasperated Harrison.[34]

Because nobody had done anything like it before, those organizing the finances made a disastrous error. "It was uncharted territory, the scale of it," recalled Jonathan Clyde, of Apple. "The money did eventually reach Bangladesh, although perhaps not in time to help the refugees at that point. The big mistake was that UNICEF wasn't chosen beforehand, and so the IRS [the US tax service] took the view that because the charity wasn't involved in the mounting of the concert, they'd take their cut. This distressed George hugely, it really angered him. There was an ongoing tussle for years, but I'm afraid even now the IRS still take their slice."[35]

It was the same story in Britain; the Treasury insisted it keep all tax revenues from the sale of the album. Harrison took it upon himself to negotiate an exemption, but without success. "It's with this in mind that I went to see Patrick Jenkin. He's the Chief Financial Under-Secretary to the Chancellor Of The Exchequer and I asked him if it would be possible to reduce, or even scrub completely, the purchase tax on the record. Unfortunately, he seemed to think it was more important for this country to get the tax than for extra money to go to starving kids in Bangla Desh and, I'm afraid, he refused. They seemed to think that I was asking too much, but I don't think that anything is too much when you're trying to help millions of starving people," Harrison recalled.[36]

Beside having to battle the IRS, Harrison also had to fight corporate greed. Because Dylan was signed to CBS it wanted compensation in the form of distribution rights. "There was a little trouble with Bob's [Dylan] contribution because at first it looked like his record company wouldn't allow us [Apple] to release his part on records, but that, along with all the other contributions, has been resolved," Harrison told the *New Musical Express*.[37] CBS eventually got the right to distribute the eight-track and cassette tape versions of the album for America and vinyl and tapes for the rest of the world.

Capitol was awarded the right to distribute the vinyl edition in America, but wanted to profit from it. However, Harrison was adamant that the album should sell for a reasonable price and that all of the profits should go to UNICEF. "I don't want to ask people to pay over £6 for the set and I don't want to make any money for myself out of it," he explained. "At that price we'll probably sell 100,000 albums, but if the price were reduced we'd probably sell more like half a million and, as the profit remains constant, that's a lot more money for the relief and refugees.[38] Such was his disgust with Bhaskar Menon, the head of Capitol, who'd previously bent over backwards to help when he recorded part of the *Wonderwall Music* soundtrack in India, that when he appeared on the Dick Cavett show he threatened to give exclusive distribution right to rivals CBS. "We'll get it out. I'll even put it out with CBS," he said. "Bhaskar will then have to sue me! We're going to play the sue me, sue you blues. Sue me Bhaskar!"[39]

The Concert For Bangladesh data

The Concert For Bangladesh was issued by Apple Records on 20 December 1971 (US) and 10 January 1972 (UK). Apple issued the album as a three-record set with the records pressed in 1/6/2/5/3/4 parings. Side one was paired with side six, side two with side five and side three with side four. This meant that if you still had a stacking record player you could play three sides without interruption. The records were issued with bespoke labels based on the concert logo and came with custom inner sleeves. CBS did not manufacture copies of the album in the UK, instead it imported albums manufactured by Capitol in America.

The album was beautifully packaged with a 64 page full-colour book of photographs taken at the concert. Once Apple had paid manufacturing and distribution costs, and donated $5 from each album sold to UNICEF, Klein claimed that Apple would lose between $1 and 0.031 cents per album depending on the quantity sold. That was a lot of money to lose. At least one publication, *New York Magazine*, suggested that Klein was working a scam. Klein countered by suing the magazine and placing an advertisement in *Billboard* with a breakdown of costs, which included the cost of putting on the concert. Apple only stood to lose money if the album failed to sell. It did sell. It sold in its millions. With receipts from the film adding to the pot, Apple could cover its costs and still donate millions of dollars to charity.

On 5 June 1972, George Harrison, Ravi Shankar and Allen Klein were jointly honoured by UNICEF with its "Child Is the Father of the Man" award in recognition of their 'pioneering' fund-raising efforts for the refugees of Bangladesh. In March 1973, the album won the Grammy Award for Album of the Year.

The album was issued on CD on 30 July 1991 in America and 19 August in Britain, as a two-disc set. On 24 October 2005, a re-mastered *The Concert For Bangladesh* was released, with revised album packaging, and the addition of Dylan's afternoon-show performance of 'Love Minus Zero/No Limit'.

The film was released on VHS and later DVD. The release of the DVD was accompanied by the *Concert For Bangladesh Revisited with George Harrison and Friends* making-of documentary and the deluxe edition included a revamped version of the book, a reproduction concert poster, hand-written lyrics for 'Bangla-Desh', sticker and postcards.

DAVID BROMBERG
DAVID BROMBERG
Side one: (Introduction) Last Song for Shelby Jean / Suffer to Sing the Blues / The Boggy Road to Milledgeville (Arkansas Traveler) / Dehlia
Side two: Pine Tree Woman / Lonesome Dave's Lovesick Blues #3 / Mississippi Blues /The Holdup* (George Harrison, David Bromberg) / Sammy's Song
UK release: 16 February 1972; CBS 64906; chart high; failed to chart.
US release: 2 June 1972; Columbia 31104; chart high; failed to chart.
Produced by David Bromberg

David Bromberg (guitar and vocals), George Harrison (slide guitar*), David Nichtene (piano), Jody Stecher (mandolin), David Amram (French horn), Willow Scarlett (harmonica), Steve Burgh (bass), Steve Mosley (drums)

Late in 1970, Harrison once again found himself in America at Thanksgiving. Invited to dinner by Al Aronowitz, he was introduced to the then up and coming guitarist David Bromberg. A session guitarist who'd played with Jerry Jeff Walker, Tom Paxton and Bob Dylan, Bromberg was working on his début album, but had no idea that he'd end the night by writing a song with Harrison. His manager, Al Aronowitz, just happened to have a guitar lying around and after dinner Bromberg picked it up and began strumming some chords. Harrison couldn't stop himself and before long he'd suggested a few pivotal lines in the song. Within half an hour they'd written 'The Hold Up'.

Harrison had previously explored the song's theme, taxation, with 'Taxman'. This time he's more oblique, but no less cutting. The lyric employs metaphors and a jokey turn of phrase to critique the tax system Harrison resented. By the time the song was released in 1972, he had even more reason to despise the money grabbing authorities who would rather tax income from the *Concert For Bangladesh* than use it to feed starving people.

Because Lennon had been labelled the 'witty' Beatle and Harrison the 'quiet one', people tend to forget just how much Harrison loved jokes and word play. 'The Hold Up' oozes with Harrison's dry humour; his piercing lyrics and sense of the absurd driving the narrative forward and the point home. On first hearing it sounds like a fun song about bandits, but the real message is made all the more powerful because of Harrison's humour.

The song was recorded live in Philadelphia without Harrison. His slide guitar was added at CBS 30th Street Studio, New York City at a later date. Ever the perfectionist, Harrison spent hours developing and perfecting his guitar parts to complement Bromberg's melody. "He could develop a simple little melodic idea that would be repeated in the course of the song, so that you would never be able to hear the song, without hearing the hook," Bromberg explained.[40] 'The Hold Up' was issued on Bromberg's eponymous début album and as a single by Columbia (4-45612) in 1972.

"back off boogaloo"

Ringo Starr

'Back Off Boogaloo' / 'Blindman'
RINGO STARR
Produced by George Harrison
UK release: 17 March 1972 ; Apple R 5944; chart high; number 2.
US release: 20 March 1972; Apple 1849; chart high; number 9.
Ringo Starr (vocals and drums), George Harrison (slide guitar), Klaus Voormann (bass), Gary Wright (piano), Madeline Bell (background vocals), Lesley Duncan (backing vocals)

The follow-up to Ringo Starr's first hit record, 'It Don't Come Easy', was again produced by Harrison. 'Back Off Boogaloo' was inspired by a phrase Starr heard fellow musician and friend Marc Bolan use one night at dinner. "He came over to dinner one night and he had this infectious laugh, and 'Back off', in a friendly way, was one of his lines. 'Back off, Boogaloo!' I was in bed later and in that twilight zone the whole song just came: [sings] 'Back off Boogaloo, ah said, Back off Boogaloo' – this won't look great in black and white, folks – 'Back off Boogaloo-hoo'. I just jumped out of bed, I got a song going. And I couldn't find a tape that wasn't broken, then I found batteries in the kids' toys, and got it down. So I went over to George's, because I'm a limited guitar player, I can only play three chords. I'd got the melody down with my three chords and took it over to George's: 'Would you put in a few more chords? It makes me sound like a genius.'"[41]

There wasn't much Harrison could do with Starr's song to make him sound like a genius, because it wasn't much of a song. Far from adding chords, he left the simple two chord vamp untouched. What's more likely is that he helped Starr finish the lyrics and arrangement. "I started to write a bit, and I did 'It Don't Come Easy', 'Back Off Boogaloo', tracks that George Harrison co-wrote with me. Because I'm great at two verses and a chorus, but ending songs is difficult for me," explained Starr.[42] Besides helping complete the song, Harrison tailored his production to match its simplicity. The record is introduced with Starr's trademark drumming, establishing both the groove and the fact that this was a record by the world's favourite drummer. "So I did the single with George. It came about, the riff we had – and I still think it's one of the strongest tracks I ever did – we were doing it and it wasn't working. And anyone who works in a studio knows that feeling. So George [suggested] a bass drum riff. Then I started doing it on the snare drum and the whole track just fell together. Before that it was a bit too light."[43] The other notable instrument on the record is Harrison's slide guitar. It's his slide guitar licks that provide the song's melodic interest and hooks. Take away the guitar and there's little more than a plodding bass and pounding pub piano.

Back Off Boogaloo data

Released as a single by Apple in the UK on 17 March 1972 and in the US on 20 March, 'Back Off Boogaloo' was a hit on both sides of the Atlantic. The single reached number 9 on the US charts and soared to number 2 on the UK charts, Starr's highest position on the UK singles chart. Starr remade the song in 1981 for his album *Stop and Smell the Roses*. Although Harrison produced two songs on the album he had nothing to do with the remake, which was produced by Harry Nilsson.

1973 : Standing At The Crossroads

'Give Me Love (Give Me Peace On Earth)' / 'Miss O'Dell'*
GEORGE HARRISON
Produced by George Harrison
UK release: 25 May 1973; Apple R 5988; chart high; number 8.
US release: 7 May 1973; Apple 1862; chart high; number 1.

George Harrison (vocals, acoustic guitar, slide guitars, backing vocals, harmonica*), Nicky Hopkins (piano), Gary Wright (organ), Klaus Voormann (bass*), Jim Keltner (drums*)

The early 1970s were troubled times. The Vietnam war was at its most ferrous and East Pakistan was ravaged by bloody conflict. Terrorist groups pursued bombing campaigns in mainland Britain and Germany. Corruption stalked the Nixon administration. With so much turmoil in the world, it was perhaps inevitable that Harrison should manifest his prayers in song. 'Give Me Love (Give Me Peace On Earth)' is an appeal for personal and universal love that came to him as easily as a mantra. "Sometimes you open your mouth and you don't know what you are going to say, and whatever comes out is the starting point. If that happens and you are lucky, it can usually be turned into a song. This song ['Give Me Love (Give Me Peace On Earth)'] is a prayer and personal statement between me, the Lord, and whoever likes it," he explained.[1]

Give Me Love (Give Me Peace On Earth)
George Harrison (vocals, acoustic guitar, slide guitars, backing vocals), Nicky Hopkins (piano), Gary Wright (organ), Jim Keltner (drums*)

Like the best of his work 'Give Me Love (Give Me Peace On Earth)' transcends the spiritual-secular divide. A song of hope and faith for all mankind, it was a beacon of light in a world overcast with doubt and despair. Harrison offers a positive message, but there's a world weary acceptance that not all who hear it will heed it. This stemmed from the aftershocks that followed the Concert For Bangladesh. Despite his best intentions, Harrison couldn't beat a corrupt, greedy and ambivalent system. "I felt slightly enraged because, let's face it, the whole problem and how to solve it lies within the power of the governments and world leaders," he said. "They have enough resources, food, money and wealth enough for twice our world's population, yet they choose to squander it on weapons and other objects that destroy mankind. It seems to me to be a poor state of affairs when 'pop stars' are required to set an example in order to solve this type of problem."[2]

Unlike the world's leaders, Harrison did set an example. Not only did he provide food for the starving, he provided food for thought too. Like Lennon, he suggested that the revolution starts with oneself. "It's like to give peace a chance, or all you need is love. The thing is, you can't just stand there and say, love, love, love or peace, peace, peace and get it. You have to have a direct process of attaining that. Like Christ said, 'Put your own house in order.' Maharishi said, 'For a forest to be green, each tree must be green.' So the same for the world to have peace, each individual must have peace."[3]

If only the message could reach critical mass, then real and lasting change would take place. The problem was how to engage an audience that didn't understand or felt troubled by it? "They [the audience] feel threatened, when you talk about something that isn't just: 'Be-Bop-A-Lula'. Not all of them, but a lot of them. They don't want to hear anything. And if you say something that is not just trivia, then their only way out of that is to say: 'You're lecturing us,' or, 'you're preaching,' which it isn't either. It is just another point of view on certain things. But they don't like the idea of talking about some things. And if you say the words 'God' or 'Lord', it makes some people's-hair curl. They just can't come to terms with the word, or with the idea that there may just be something else going on apart from their individual egos."[4]

Harrison had to find a way to get his message across to as many people as possible. Even if some of them didn't want to hear it, the important thing was to get the process started. The opening lines could be interpreted as a plea for romantic love. It's only once the listener has been hooked that it becomes clear he's singing about spiritual love; a love that would bring one closer to God. "It's a process of actually having that realization and direct God perception, which is the thing you can attain through chanting and through meditation. And then you don't have any questions. You don't have to ask the vicar about this, because it all becomes clear with the expanded state of consciousness."[5]

As with 'My Sweet Lord', Harrison employed both Christian and Hindu names for God. He cleverly created a homophone by singing 'Om' in such a way as to make it sound like 'Oh my'. Harrison was broadcasting "the sacred sound, the Yes!, the Vedas, the Udgitha (song of the universe), the infinite, the all encompassing, the whole world, the truth, the ultimate reality, the finest essence, the cause of the Universe, the essence of life, the Brahman, the Atman, the vehicle of deepest knowledge, and Self-knowledge" around the world and his audience were joining in without them even noticing.

Recorded at Apple Studios and Harrison's newly finished F.P.S.H.O.T. (Friar Park Studio Henley-on-Thames), 'Give Me Love (Give Me Peace On Earth)' was stripped of Spector's bombast and excessive echo drenched production. Harrison's production is light and open, a breath of fresh air after the dense, claustrophobic sounding *All Things Must Pass*. It's as if a great weight had been lifted from his shoulders. This feeling is exemplified by his trademark slide guitar playing which shimmers in the mix. His tone is pure and silky but with enough bite to cut through crisp and clean. His solos play a key part in the song and it's only when you hear the track without them that you realize how much they enhance the melody. An alternative rough mix without any slide guitar overdubs was issued on the bootleg *Living In The Alternative Material World*. Without Harrison's inventive melodic hooks it sounds lifeless and spiritless.

Miss O'Dell
George Harrison (vocals, acoustic guitar, harmonica), Klaus Voormann (bass), Jim Keltner (drums)

'Miss O'Dell' was written in Malibu, California, while Harrison was working on the soundtrack to *Raga*. Inspired by Chris O'Dell, a former Apple employee, it deals with the growing crisis in East Pakistan and the consequences of fame.

The song begins with Harrison contemplating Ravi Shankar's revelations about the war in East Pakistan. International donations of rice intended for refugees had somehow become the property of the Indian Government and failed to reach those most in need. The situation didn't improve once Harrison and Shankar got involved with UNICEF. But there was little either could do to rectify the situation other than make it public. "Unless you physically go there yourself, and buy big bags of rice with the money, and give it out yourself. Then it would have taken me a lifetime," Harrison explained.[6]

The remainder of the song finds Harrison dealing with the trappings and consequences of fame. Holed up in a luxury beachfront house he cogitates on the business that had rewarded him with fame and wealth, but left him alone, bored and far from home. Despite the melancholy nature of the lyrics, 'Miss O'Dell' has a bubbly melody and its stripped down arrangement, similar to that used for 'Deep Blue', lets Harrison's self-deprecating humour shine through.

Harrison's vocal is equally blithe, if a little self-conscious. As light-hearted as the A-side is earnest, it finds Harrison attempting to burst the pimple of pomposity that had infected 'serious' rock and offset the downbeat lyric with some much needed fun. An alternative vocal without the giggling was issued on the deluxe reissue if *Living In The Material World* album in 2006. The song ends with Harrison giving out Paul McCartney's old home telephone number. Relations between the two were still tense and further digs would appear on Harrison's next album *Living In The Material World*.

Give Me Love (Give me Peace On Earth) data

Apple issued 'Give Me Love (Give Me Peace On Earth)' with generic Apple labels and a generic black paper sleeve. Promotional copies of the single issued in Britain have a large 'A' at two o'clock with the date 25.2.73 below. EMI subcontracted manufacturing of the single to Decca, whose pressings having a wider gap of approximately 2.5 mm between the push-out centre and the body of the disc. In America, Apple issued mono/stereo promotional copies of the single (P-1862) to radio stations and the media. It issued the single with generic Apple labels and plain black paper sleeve. Picture sleeves were issued in Europe, Japan and other countries. In Angola, the single was issued in a picture sleeve and with the same dissolving heads label design that had been used for John Lennon's single 'Happy Xmas (War Is Over)'.

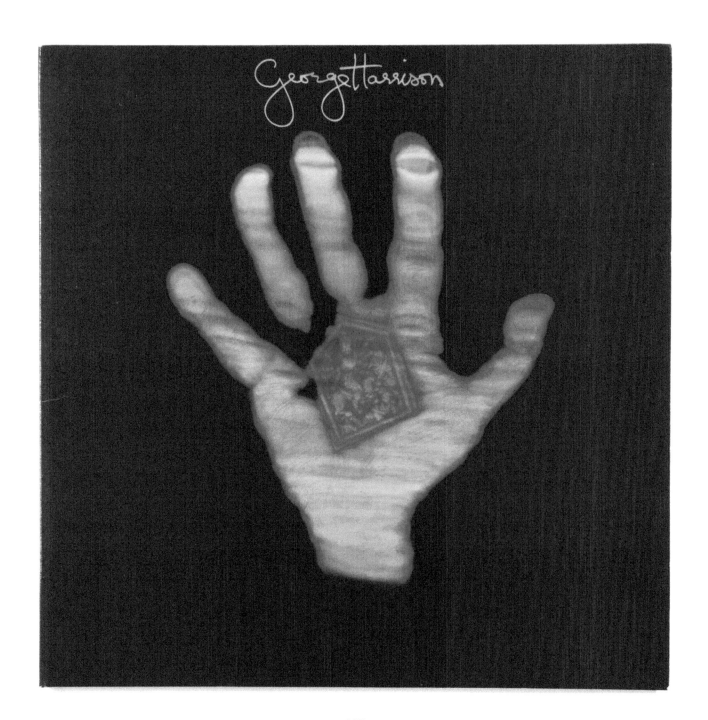

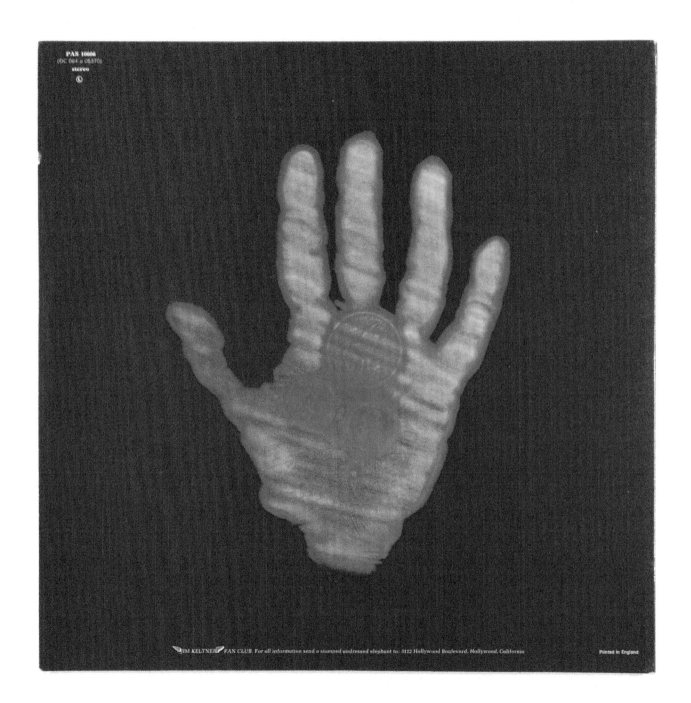

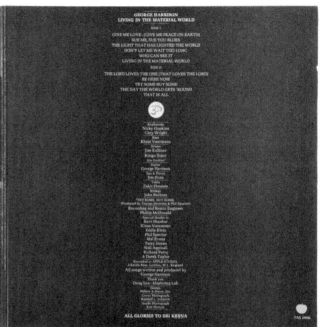

GEORGE HARRISON
LIVING IN THE MATERIAL WORLD

SIDE I

GIVE ME LOVE -(GIVE ME PEACE ON EARTH)
SUE ME, SUE YOU BLUES
THE LIGHT THAT HAS LIGHTED THE WORLD
DON'T LET ME WAIT TOO LONG
WHO CAN SEE IT
LIVING IN THE MATERIAL WORLD

SIDE II

THE LORD LOVES THE ONE (THAT LOVES THE LORD)
BE HERE NOW
TRY SOME BUY SOME
THE DAY THE WORLD GETS 'ROUND
THAT IS ALL

Keyboards
Nicky Hopkins
Gary Wright
Bass
Klaus Voormann
Drums
Jim Keltner
Ringo Starr
(Jim Gordon)
Guitar
George Harrison
Sax & Flutes
Jim Horn
Tabla
Zakir Hussein
Strings
John Barham
"TRY SOME, BUY SOME"
(Produced by George Harrison & Phil Spector)
Recording and Remix Engineer
Phillip McDonald
Special thanks to
Ravi Shankar
Klaus Voormann
Eddie Klein
Phil Spector
Mal Evans
Terry Doran
Neil Aspinall
Richard Perry
& Derek Taylor
Recorded at APPLE STUDIO,
3 Savile Row, London, W.1, England
All songs written and produced by
George Harrison
Thank you
Doug Sax - Mastering Lab
Design
Wilkes & Braun, Inc.
Cover Photography
Kendall L. Johnson
Studio Photography
Ken Marcus

ALL GLORIES TO SRI KṚṢṆA

PAS 10006

Krishna and Arjuna Paintings from Bhagavad-Gita as it is by A.C. Bhaktivedanta Swami Prabhupada (Macmillan)

PAS 10006

200

An Apple Record
An EMI Recording
APPLE
THE GRAMOPHONE CO.LTD. ALL RIGHTS OF THE MANUFACTURER AND OF THE OWNER OF THE RECORDED WORK RESERVED. UNAUTHORISED PUBLIC PERFORMANCE, BROADCASTING, AND COPYING OF THIS RECORD PROHIBITED.

STEREO
PAS10006
YEX 917

GEORGE HARRISON
LIVING IN THE MATERIAL WORLD
Side One
1. GIVE ME LOVE (GIVE ME PEACE ON EARTH)*
2. SUE ME, SUE YOU BLUES‡
3. THE LIGHT THAT HAS LIGHTED THE WORLD*
4. DON'T LET ME WAIT TOO LONG*
5. WHO CAN SEE IT*
6. LIVING IN THE MATERIAL WORLD*
Written and Produced by George Harrison
*The "Material World" Charitable Foundation
‡Harrisongs
℗ 1973 EMI Records Limited

An Apple Record
An EMI Recording
APPLE
THE GRAMOPHONE CO.LTD. ALL RIGHTS OF THE MANUFACTURER AND OF THE OWNER OF THE RECORDED WORK RESERVED. UNAUTHORISED PUBLIC PERFORMANCE, BROADCASTING, AND COPYING OF THIS RECORD PROHIBITED.

STEREO
PAS10006
YEX 918

GEORGE HARRISON
LIVING IN THE MATERIAL WORLD
Side Two
1. THE LORD LOVES THE ONE
(THAT LOVES THE LORD)*
2. BE HERE NOW*
3. TRY SOME BUY SOME†‡
4. THE DAY THE WORLD GETS 'ROUND*
5. THAT IS ALL*
Written and Produced by George Harrison except
†Produced by George Harrison and Phil Spector
*The "Material World" Charitable Foundation
‡Harrisongs
℗ 1973 EMI Records Limited

APPLE
℗ 1973 The Gramophone Company Limited. Manufactured by Apple Records, Inc., 1370 Avenue of the Americas, New York, N.Y.

SMAS-3410

GEORGE HARRISON
LIVING IN THE MATERIAL WORLD
Side One
1. GIVE ME LOVE—(GIVE ME PEACE ON EARTH) 3:32
2. SUE ME, SUE YOU BLUES 4:43
3. THE LIGHT THAT HAS LIGHTED THE WORLD 3:28
4. DON'T LET ME WAIT TOO LONG 2:54
5. WHO CAN SEE IT 3:49
6. LIVING IN THE MATERIAL WORLD 5:27
All Songs Written and Produced by George Harrison
All Songs BMI
Recorded in England

APPLE
℗ 1973 The Gramophone Company Limited. Manufactured by Apple Records, Inc., 1370 Avenue of the Americas, New York, N.Y.

SMAS-3410

GEORGE HARRISON
LIVING IN THE MATERIAL WORLD
Side Two
1. THE LORD LOVES THE ONE (THAT LOVES THE LORD) 4:32
2. BE HERE NOW 4:07
3. TRY SOME BUY SOME* 4:06
4. THE DAY THE WORLD GETS 'ROUND 2:50
5. THAT IS ALL 3:40
All Songs Written and Produced by George Harrison
*Produced by George Harrison and Phil Spector
All Songs BMI
Recorded in England

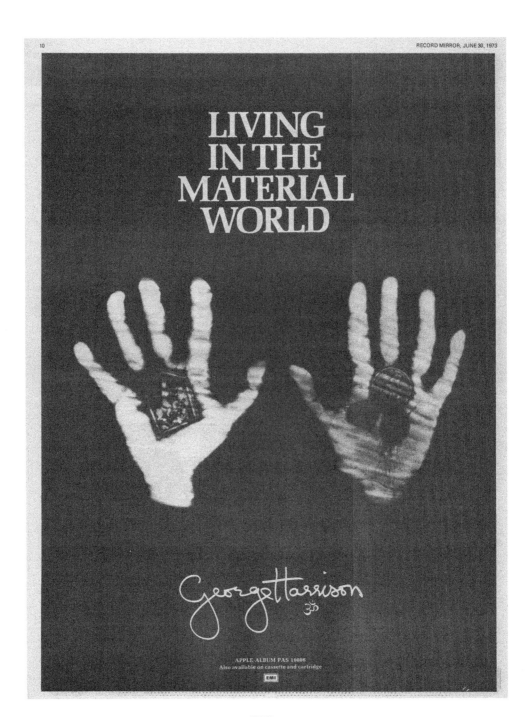

LIVING IN THE MATERIAL WORLD
GEORGE HARRISON
Side one: Give Me Love (Give Me Peace On Earth) / Sue Me, Sue You Blues / The Light That
Has Lighted The World / Don't Let Me Wait Too Long / Who Can See It / Living In The
Material World
Side two: The Lord Loves The One (That Loves The Lord) / Be Here Now / Try Some, Buy
Some / The Day The World Gets 'Round / That Is All
UK release: 22 June 1973; Apple PAS 10006; chart high; number 2.
US release: 30 May 1973; Apple SMAS 3410; chart high; number 1.
Produced by George Harrison.

George Harrison (vocals, electric and acoustic guitars, dobro, sitar, backing vocals), Nicky
Hopkins (piano, electric piano), Gary Wright (organ, harmonium, electric piano, harpsichord),
Klaus Voormann (bass, upright bass, tenor saxophone), Jim Keltner (drums, percussion), Ringo
Starr (drums, percussion), Jim Horn (saxophones, flute, horn arrangements), Zakir Hussain
(tabla), John Barham (orchestral and choral arrangements), Leon Russell (piano on 'Try Some,
Buy Some'), Jim Gordon (drums, tambourine on 'Try Some, Buy Some'), Pete Ham (acoustic
guitar on 'Try Some, Buy Some')

The follow up to Harrison's colossal *All Thing Must Pass* was delayed by more than a year because
of the commitment he'd given Ravi Shankar to raise money for the people of Bangladesh. Beside
arranging and performing at the all-star fund raising concert, he produced the *Concert For Bangla Desh*
live album, helped edit the film of the concert and became embroiled with tax issues surrounding the
money it raised. He also found time to play on several of his friends records, produce another hit
single for Ringo Starr ('Back Off Boogaloo'), produce a song for Apple protégés Lon & Derrek Van
Eaton ('Sweet Music') and write enough songs for a new album. Speaking in the British music weekly
Disc and Music Echo, pianist Nicky Hopkins explained that while he was in New York recording John
Lennon's 'Happy Xmas (War Is Over)', Harrison had played them his new songs. "George was in
New York when we went there to do Lennon's new single. He played some new songs for us for
about two or three hours. They were really incredible. So he has plenty of material for an album."[7]
Previous to that, Harrison had alluded to another new song, 'Sue Me, Sue You Blues', when he
appeared on the Dick Cavett show on 23 November.

Although Apple had recently opened its new state-of-the-art recording studio in London, which
was launched by Harrison with a playback of the *Concert For Bangla Desh* album, Harrison intended to
record his new album at his own recently installed studio at his house in Henley-on-Thames.

Although the sleeve notes claim the album was recorded at Apple, Klaus Voormann has stated that it was recorded almost entirely in Harrison's home studio F.P.S.H.O.T.. Weekdays were spent recording Harrison's album, while at weekends the musicians worked on Nicky Hopkins' solo album, *The Tin Man Was a Dreamer*. "I wanted to record it at Apple, but George [Harrison] started doing his album, which I think turned out great. So we'd record George during the week, and I'd do my album on the weekends," Hopkins explained.[8] The basic backing tracks were finished by December '72. These were made into an acetate disc that later surfaced as the bootleg *Living In The Alternative World*.

Taking a break from his own album, Harrison co-produced Ravi Shankar's and Ali Akbar Khan's live album *In Concert 1972*, released by Apple Records in January 1973 (US) and April (UK). Work on *Living In The Material World* resumed in January '73 with overdubs, namely vocals, lead guitar parts, Jim Horn's contributions and percussion. The Indian classical instruments sitar, flute and tabla were also added to the 'spiritual sky' sections of 'Living In The Material World'. The final elements to be recorded were John Barham's orchestral and choir arrangements for 'The Day The World Gets 'Round', 'Who Can See It' and 'That Is All'. The album finished, Harrison flew to Los Angeles to attend Beatles/Apple-related business talks and to begin work on Ravi Shankar's *Shankar Family & Friends* and Ringo Starr's *Ringo*.

By the time Harrison came to make *Living In The Material World*, he found himself in the exact same situation that had led him to Hinduism in the first place. He was, if anything, an even bigger star now than he had been as a Beatle. He had more money, more possessions and more worries. Fame and adulation had brought him many things, but had left him feeling unfulfilled, and it sat uncomfortably with his avowed spirituality. The album became a confessional and cathartic exploration of the personal doubt and spiritual crisis affecting him. The spiritual songs were among the most powerful manifestations of faith he wrote. As his friend and devotee Shyamasundar Das noted: "*All Things Must Pass* that was the first album [he made] that reflects Prabhupada's philosophy. And then, later in '73, *Living In The Material World*, which is all Krishna Consciousness philosophy."[9]

While some took exception to what they viewed as the album's "preachy overtones" and "relentlessly pious nature", *Rolling Stone* recognized it for what it is "the most concise, universally conceived work by a former Beatle since *John Lennon/Plastic Ono Band*." Unlike Lennon, Harrison didn't need revolutionary psychotherapy to discover his inner truth, he had his faith. Harrison presents the listener with a classic dialectic narrative that explores the spiritual and secular nature of human existence. What comes across most potently is his desire to become God conscious. But the distractions of the physical world remained ever present. Never claiming to be the perfect devotee, he simply could not relinquish the temptations of the material world. Pattie Harrison later suggested that: "George seemed torn between the deep beneath us and the glitter on the surface."[10] His main concern was how to be in the world but not of it. He makes an explicit visual reference to this thorny issue with the album's dramatic cover. The front depicts his right hand holding a Hindu medallion, the back shows him holding three coins. Harrison is somewhere in the middle, a typical Piscean seeking enlightenment in the unseen realm, but rooted in the physical world.

Living In The Material World data

Apple issued *Living In The Material World* with bespoke labels that mirror the album's spiritual/secular theme. Side one has a detail from a painting of Krishna and Arjuna in a carriage pulled by Uchchairsrava, the enchanted seven-headed horse. Side two use a detail from the inner sleeve photograph of a chauffeur standing by a limousine. The records were packed in kraft paper sleeves. The laminated gatefold sleeve featured photographs of Harrison's hands created by Tom Wilkes using a process know as Kirlian photography that captures the aura of an individual. The inner sleeve featured a photograph of Harrison and some of the musicians who helped record the album taken at attorney Abe Sommer's house. A four page insert was included with the album. The first page reproduced the painting of Krishna used for the labels in-full. The inner pages reproduced the lyrics to the songs. The back features a large yellow circle with the 'Om' symbol in red. In America, *Living In The Material World* reached number one in the *Cash Box* and *Record World* charts, replacing Paul McCartney & Wings *Red Rose Speedway* album. The album reached number two in the British charts.

Sue Me, Sue You Blues
George Harrison (vocals, guitar and dobro), Nicky Hopkins (piano), Gary Wright (electric piano), Klaus Voormann (bass), Jim Keltner (drums)

The album opens with 'Give Me Love (Give Me Peace On Earth)', discussed earlier, and is followed by 'Sue Me, Sue You Blues'. A somewhat jaded take on The Beatles' break-up and subsequent legal fallout, 'Sue Me, Sue You Blues' is as much an attack on the lawyers and the legal system as it is a scathing commentary on the sad demise of a great band and long-standing friendships. Based on the conventions found in square dancing, in which two dancers approach each other and circle back to back, then return to their original positions, it's both bitter observation and metaphor for eternal return. As Harrison put it, all that was left was to find yourself and new band and start all over again.

Harrison wasn't the only Beatle to comment on the group's demise, all four expressed their ire in song. But while Lennon and McCartney got nasty and railed at one another in both the press and in song, Harrison did it without pointing the finger at any one Beatle and with dry, cutting wit. The good times were well and truly over, they had been for some time. Harrison's song underscores the sense of resentment that each ex-Beatle experienced as the group spun out of control and the euphoria turned to discontent. Harrison's guitar conveys as much meaning as the song's lyrics. His opening slide guitar lick is the very antithesis of the mellifluous motifs he wrote for 'My Sweet Lord'. Its descending slide down the fretboard and pithy, stinging turnaround express his annoyance, frustration and bitterness with self assured confidence. Like the best of Harrison's playing, it's simple, but remarkably expressive. Nicky Hopkins' playing is of equal measure. Complementing the melody and intensifying the emotional content of the song, his contribution is as central to the arrangement as Harrison's.

'Sue Me, Sue You Blues' may well have been one of the songs Harrison played to Hopkins in December 1971. Only months earlier he'd given it to Jesse Ed Davis, who had worked with him on the 'Bangla-Desh' single. "When he [Harrison] was in L.A., just before the Bangla-Desh concert, in the summer of '71, recording a single 'Bangla-Desh', I said 'George, I've got a new album coming out pretty soon and I need one more really dynamite song just to make it come off right'," Davis explained. "And he says, 'Well, I'll come over and play you what I've got'. So he came over to my house and played 'Sue Me, Sue You Blues' for me, which is really a kind of personal song, you know, but it was the only thing that was really funky enough to fit my blues bag."[11]

Davis recorded Harrison playing the song and the resulting recording eventually found its way onto the bootleg CD *Pirate Songs*. At this stage the song lacked the half-verse beginning "Hold the block on money flow / Move it into joint escrow". Consequently, it's also missing from Davis' recording. Released as a single on 25 January 1972, it also featured on Davis' second solo album *Ululu*.

The Light That Has Lighted The World
George Harrison (vocals and guitars), Nicky Hopkins (piano), Gary Wright (organ), Klaus Voormann (bass), Jim Keltner (drums)

In early August 1972, Harrison began working on a single for Cilla Black. The plan was to record 'When Every Song is Sung', a song he'd played for Phil Spector in the spring of 1970. Harrison had attempted to record the song with Ronnie Spector in 1971 but without success. Eventually he gave the song to Ringo Starr, who recorded it for his 1976 album *Ringo's Rotogravure*. While Harrison had the record's top side mapped out, he needed a B-side. In trying to write a song for Black, Harrison began to think about how he could best connect with her. "I thought 'How do I relate to Cilla?' Well, she was from Liverpool and had left Liverpool the same way I had, and that experience you have when you first make it, everyone is pleased – 'Local boy/girl makes good' – but once you *leave*, they say 'He's changed – he's not what he used to be!' So I started with that idea," Harrison explained.[12]

'The Light That Has Lighted The World' is an appeal for greater tolerance and understanding based on the teachings of Krishna. Although it has been suggested that Harrison took his title from the Bible (John 8:12): "I am the light of the world. Whoever follows me will never walk in darkness, but will have the light of life", it is more likely that he was thinking of a line from the Bhagavad Gita: "Just to bless them, I, residing in their intellect, destroy the darkness born of ignorance by the resplendent light of knowledge." This is what Harrison was seeking, and what he hoped others would also find. Harrison didn't want to merely chastise those who judged him, he wanted to enlighten them. The way to enlightenment is through a better understanding that the material things surrounding us are unimportant because they can never satisfy us the way God can. By his own admission, Harrison was still searching for the light, but he drew comfort from those who shared his beliefs and aspiration to see the light, or in other words to become God conscious.

Harrison recorded a simple demo accompanying himself on 12-string acoustic guitar. Issued on the soundtrack album *Living In The Material World*, it doesn't feature any solos or indeed space for solos, but does have a double tracked vocal at the very end of the song. An early studio version of the song was issued on the *Living in the Alternate World* bootleg. Featuring a more prominent and melodic harmonium part from Wright, it does not feature Harrison's overdubbed guitar parts or his slide guitar solo. It does, however, conclude with an improvised vocal falsetto that was replaced by a more considered slide guitar embellishment. Once again, Hopkins' piano playing features prominently. Supported by Wright's harmonium, at times it's a delicate crucible supporting Harrison's world-weary vocal. Harrison's acoustic guitars underpin Hopkins' playing, extending the arrangement's dynamics, while his exquisite slide playing provides subtle ornamentation to the melody.

Don't Let Me Wait Too Long
George Harrison (vocals and guitars), Nicky Hopkins (piano and harpsichord), Gary Wright (organ), Klaus Voormann (bass), Ringo Starr (drums), Jim Keltner (drums)

Scheduled to be released as a single on 24 September 1973 (Apple 1866), 'Don't Let Me Wait Too Long' was withdrawn from the release schedules before it could go into production. As good a pop song as you are likely to hear, it was a near perfect turntable hit that would have been a considerable chart smash had it been issued as a 45.

Placed in the context of the album, it finds Harrison contemplating earthly desires rather than spiritual fulfillment. 'Don't Let Me Wait Too Long' is a musing on physical love, he's clearly singing to his 'baby'. But whoever he's singing to it's unlikely to have been written for Pattie Harrison, their relationship having failed long before the song was recorded. Perhaps he was considering idealized love, or unrequited love. Whatever kind of love it was that he was contemplating it had yet to happen or had been temporarily taken from him.

Harrison's early musical influences resonate throughout the song. A fan of girl groups like the The Shirelles, The Marvelettes and the The Ronettes, he drew on them to fashion 'Don't Let Me Wait Too Long'. An elegantly simple pop song that could have been penned by the likes of Ellie Greenwich and Jeff Barry or Gerry Goffin and Carole King. Had Harrison ever finished the album he intended to make with Ronnie Spector, 'Don't Let Me Wait Too Long' would have surely been a contender. It comes from the same musical melting pot as songs like 'You' and 'Try Some, Buy Some', which also appears on the album with a new Harrison vocal. Its lyrical simplicity, Spectoresque production and Harrison's vocal delivery add up to one big girl group infatuation.

Harrison had obviously been paying attention whist Spector twiddled the knobs for *All Things Must Pass*. The producer's influence is evident, both in the arrangement and the feel of the song. But

Harrison employed Spector's techniques with subtlety. The drum sound isn't too big, the guitars aren't over layered, and the use of reverb, while noticeable, isn't deafening. The basic track was recorded in late 1972 in between Ringo Starr's acting duties on *That'll Be the Day* and was issued on the bootleg album *Living In The Alternative World*. Listening to the song in its naked form reveals just how meticulously it was arranged and produced. Starr's and Keltner's drumming is a master-class in the use of drums and percussion to develop depth, light and shade in an arrangement. The drummers leave yawning gaps for the lead vocal to sit in. Harrison laid a bed of acoustic guitars, piano and harpsichord over the rhythm section creating a richly textured support for his vocal and slide guitar to rest on.

Ravi Shankar's influence on Harrison's guitar playing makes itself felt at the beginning of the second chorus. Using microtones, infinitesimal harmonic steps, Harrison plays a brief but sophisticated slide guitar motif that mirrors the upward movement of the melody. Technically simple, it was nevertheless incredibly difficult to perfect. His playing reveals a level of harmonic sophistication that was rarely matched by his peers. No longer was he improvising simple guitar breaks as he had on The Beatles' early recordings, these were carefully considered and performed solos that took hours to perfect in the studio.

Who Can See It
George Harrison (vocals and Leslie guitars), Nicky Hopkins (piano), Gary Wright (organ), Klaus Voormann (bass), Jim Keltner (drums), John Barham – string, brass and choral arrangements

Like Robert Johnson, The Beatles made a deal with the devil. (The devil being the music business and the rewards, fame and wealth it gave them in return for their souls.) Unlike Johnson, who died tragically young, The Beatles got to enjoy their wealth but not the fame. Like all The Beatles, Harrison felt that he had given himself totally and the rewards, no mater how great, didn't justify the sacrifice he'd made. It was something that had been eating away at him for years. Speaking in 1969 about the constant stress of Beatlemania, he told *Disc*: 'I was fed up. I couldn't take it anymore, but I resigned myself to suffering for another year.'

Harrison had been troubled by Beatlemania long before the group imploded. The first in the group to seriously think through the consequences of his actions, he didn't like what he found. The suffering got worse after the break-up. It was painful and the scars itched like crazy. One way to cope was to disavow the recent past. Lennon dismissed the '60s and The Beatles with the line 'I don't believe in Beatles, I just believe in me'. Harrison's disavow was less succinct but just as fervent.

By the time he wrote 'Who Can See It', he had it all worked out. Speaking to Dave Herman in 1975, he said: "What we are now is the effect of whatever we're been in the past. I do, through Hinduism, believe in reincarnation. So what I believe is we all live from birth to death, we all create a lot of action, which is action / reaction that they call karma, it's like credit and debit."[13] With The Beatles he'd created a lot of action. The reaction had been immense. It was a reaction that showed few signs to abating and now he wanted to kick against it.

With the help of Hinduism, he'd seen the consequences of his actions and wanted to re-balance the books. The key phrase in Harrison's lyric is 'my life belongs to me'. He was not public property and would not be treated as such. By disavowing his past and by re-balancing his spiritual ledger, he could step out of the Beatles' shadow, be himself and deal with his karma. "Everyone fell into the Beatle trip. We didn't encourage it. The problem was that people got into the 'trip'… The record business is all based on getting into the trip; that's how it is. Making the trip all big, you know, 'BIG'. The business side is trying to take something and then talk about it so much so as to spread more and more ripples until they become waves, whereas my own personal life, having been all waves, has to change to a normality where I try to stop the waves, quieten them down to make myself a calm little pool. It is hard work trying to do that with your life. One is trying however, while at the same time the people you are involved with are sometimes trying to stir it up. There is such a collision."[14]

He wasn't alone in feeling this way. Speaking in 1980, John Lennon reacted with similar disdain to being questioned about a possible Beatles reunion: "Why should the Beatles give more? Didn't they give everything on God's earth for ten years? Didn't they give themselves? You're like the typical sort of love-hate fan who says, 'Thank you for everything you did for us in the Sixties... would you just give me another shot? Just one more miracle?'"[15] Writing in his autobiography, Harrison framed his response with succinct, offhand wit: "It is a true story meaning 'Give us a break, squire'".[16]

However, the song is anything but light-hearted. Its stately, measured tempo gives it gravitas and Barham's arrangement piles on the drama. The Leslie-toned guitar not only references late period recordings by The Beatles, it conveys a sense of brooding melancholy that's countered by the swelling orchestration and Harrison's soaring, defiant vocal. Combined, they create a striking musical tension that dovetails opposing emotions that lie at the very heart of the album.

The basic track was issued on the *Living in the Alternate World* bootleg and has a guide vocal from Harrison and Gary Wright's harmonium placed slightly higher in the mix. Harrison added his lead vocal in January or February '73, and Barham's strings and brass were added in March.

Living In The Material World

George Harrison (vocals, guitars and sitar), Nicky Hopkins (piano), Gary Wright (organ), Klaus Voormann (bass), Ringo Starr (drums), Jim Keltner (drums), Zakir Hussain (tabla), Jim Horn (saxophones)

Having disavowed his former existence as a Beatle and bemoaned the vicissitudes of fame ('Who Can See It'), Harrison offered a more balanced view of his current state of being with the song 'Living In The Material World'. Part biography, part confession, part prayer and part roadmap, it's an attempt to reconcile opposing aspects of human existence, materialism and spiritualism, set to a rollicking rock 'n' roll song.

The song was inspired, in part, by an interest in scansion. "It was written because it sounded good," Harrison said, "MA-TE-RIAL WORLD–LI-VING IN THE MA-TE-RIAL WORLD."[17] But the main inspiration came from the teachings of Abhay Charanaravinda Bhaktivedanta Swami Prabhupada, the founder-acharya of the International Society for Krishna Consciousness. "Material World is the influence of A. C. Bhaktivedanta Swami and the realizing 'we are not these bodies', we are *in* these bodies in the physical world," Harrison wrote in *I Me Mine*.[18] Hinduism teaches that we are all potentially divine but as we journey through life we become tainted by aspects of the world around us. As Harrison had said many times before, the goal is to decontaminate oneself and depart the world with a pure soul.

The message was serious, but Harrison later claimed that: "It's also a comedy song with a few jokes in case you didn't notice!".[19] Perhaps he felt compelled to mention this because 'Living In The Material World' isn't an obviously funny song. Nor is it a tongue in cheek review of the pre-fab four. It's another treatise based on Krishna consciousness dogma set to a rock 'n' roll back beat. Once again, Harrison resists the temptation of going for a full on 'Wall of Sound' production and reigns in the more excessive aspects of his former producer's style for a leaner, cleaner sound. The song's rock 'n' roll sections representing the 'Material World' are contrasted with refrains representing the 'Spiritual World', identified by the use of Indian instruments. Harrison's singing during the Indian interludes is among the best he recorded. It's obvious that while rock 'n' roll was fun, what he really longed for was spiritual bliss. The Indian classical instruments were overdubbed onto the basic track along with Harrison's vocal in early 1973. The basic track without Indian instrumentation was issued on the bootleg *Living In The Alternative World*.

The Lord Loves The One (That Loves The Lord)
George Harrison (vocals and guitars), Nicky Hopkins (electric piano), Klaus Voormann (bass), Jim Keltner (drums), Jim Horn (saxophones)

There's a line from the Old Testament Book of Isaiah, "All flesh is grass", that's been much-quoted by artists and poets through the ages. It's a form of memento mori – a reminder that all life is transitory. These Christian symbols of mortality were intended to show that material pleasures, luxuries, and status are empty and fleeting and that death is a great leveller. Memento mori don't feature much in Hinduism, but that's not to say the two religions don't share common ground. The answers they proffer don't differ much, but the problems they consider relevant do.

A Westerner may see insignificance in a problem that a Hindu considers significant. Many in the West think that they can overcome personal problems by acquiring money, possessions and status. Harrison knew from experience and the teachings of the International Society for Krishna Consciousness that that wasn't the case. 'The Lord Loves The One (That Loves The Lord)' is a spiritual reminder inspired by A. C. Bhaktivedanta set to pop music.

Writing in his biography, Harrison said he wrote the song: "in order to make myself remember".[20] Like the phrase "All flesh is grass", it's a reminder that the possessions and drives that tempt us away from the spiritual world are inconsequential. Professor Satya Pal Sharma: "The temptations come and occupy. And, if the mind is caught in the passions – the temptations – it becomes a slave itself and it enslaves our emotions and senses. People call this enslavement 'Maya'. Often Maya is defined as illusion. But, really, Maya is not illusion. Maya is not an illusion. Don't think God is a cheat to create this Maya. It is only you, you are cheating yourself. The mind is so mighty that once it discards the passions, it can easily make the soul its master."[21]

Harrison desperately wanted to make his soul its master, but he knew it was never going to be easy. Speaking to Nicky Horne in 1974, he said: "In life Jesus taught the law of karma, which means action reaction. Whatever we are now we ourselves have caused. Whatever we're going to be in the future, it's up to us. It's ourselves who get ourselves in a mess or get ourselves out of it. But we seem to be in the world as a whole to be more in a mess than not in a mess, although there's a lot of great souls in the world."[22]

'The Lord Loves The One (That Loves The Lord)' was written to remind him and others to be humble. Writing in *I Me Mine*, he said: "Most of the world is fooling about, especially the people who *think* they control the world and the community. The presidents, the politicians, the military etc., are jerking about acting as if they are Lord over their domains. That's basically Problem One on the planet."[23] Unfortunately, most chose not to listen. The problems addressed in the song have, if anything, got worse. Our leaders continue to 'act like big girls', the gap between rich and poor has grown larger, society has become more secular and religious tolerance has diminished with horrific consequences.

Harrison's musical setting reflects his lyrics perfectly. Set to a down home, bluesy shuffle, 'The Lord Loves The One (That Loves The Lord)' is devoid of unnecessary ornamentation. Introduced with a simple two note motif borrowed from the blues back pages and followed by Nicky Hopkins' electric piano, the basic track is a model of simplicity. To this Harrison added a double-tracked vocal, overdubbed slide guitar, percussion and saxophone.

Be Here Now

George Harrison (vocals and guitars), Nicky Hopkins (piano), Gary Wright (organ), Klaus Voormann (upright bass), Jim Keltner (drums)

Lying in bed one night in his rented Nichols Canyon house in Los Angeles, Harrison was drifting into unconsciousness when a tune popped into his head. Picking up a guitar, he wrote a melody in open G tuning that became 'Be Here Now'. Harrison's bedtime reading provided the inspiration for his lyric. The book was called *Be Here Now* by Baba Ram Dass (born Richard Alpert). A kind of cosmic comic book guide to becoming a yogi, it has been described as in a study on daydreaming.

Harrison instinctively tapped into the book's astral theme. His semi-conscious state probably helped him compose this treacle slow and melodically conservative melody, while his lyric was directly inspired by Dass' cosmic ramblings. The song conveys both its author's bleary state and Dass' suggestion that one should focus on the here and now in order to become fully 'aware'. Pure awareness is, according to some, a way of manipulating consciousness to see the world as one, or the manifestation of the one. Dass suggests that: "When we're identified with Awareness, we're no longer living in a world of polarities. Everything is present at the same time."[24] As Dass says in his book, it's as simple as that. Only it isn't, few manage to achieve such a state of being.

When it came time to record the song, Harrison's band certainly seems to have been keenly aware of each other. Each is remarkably aware of what the others are playing and responds accordingly. There's a remarkable understanding between the musicians that usually takes years to develop. This is due in part to Harrison's arrangement and production skills. "His approach to a lot of things was extremely simple," recalled Wright. "He would strip things down to the bare bones and whatever parts you played he would want it to be really simple. I kind of intuitively knew what he was going to play and I knew what he wanted me to play."[25]

Nicky Hopkins followed Wright's example and played a beautifully simple, light and sparse piano part. All Wright had to do was fill in the spaces with drones akin to those used in Indian classical music. Both of the keyboard parts are infused with conventions borrowed from Indian classical music, but it's Wright's playing that is the sonic metaphor of the awareness that Harrison wanted to attain. It holds everyone and everything together, uniting the individual players and parts into a whole. A rough mix of the basic track with a guide vocal was issued on the bootleg *Living In The Alternative World*. Harrison later recorded a new vocal, added harmony vocals and what sounds like a Leslie effect guitar to the track.

Try Some, Buy Some

George Harrison (vocals, guitar), Carl Radle (bass), Jim Gordon (drums), Leon Russell (piano), Pete Ham (acoustic guitar, backing vocals)

Dusting off the song he'd given to Ronnie Spector, Harrison added his vocal to the multi-track tape and used it on his album. His reason for doing so was simple, he liked it. "The song itself, I think, is really good," he told the *Record Mirror*. "It's so simple and yet so complicated. It was the sort of thing I found myself playing over and over again and being amazed by the simplicity of the movement in the bass line."[26] Although Phil Spector's production makes it stand out like a sore thumb, placed in its new context the song that Ronnie Spector struggled to connect with makes perfect sense.

'Try Some, Buy Some' covers many of the spiritual themes explored on the album. Sung by Harrison it is transformed from a girl group pastiche into something all together more weighty and meaningful. The ambiguity of Harrison's lyric leads one to conclude that he's singing about spiritual rather than physical love and the salvation it brought him. Describing the effects and consequences of ignoring the spiritual realm in favour of cheap and easy thrills, it's an expression of belief made all the more powerful by the journey Harrison took to achieve it. Rejecting the temptations and passions that had previously enslaved him, he rejoices in the knowledge and love he found in divine grace.

'Try Some, Buy Some' has been criticized for its bombastic production. Harrison could have re-recorded the song and given it a leaner production that was more in keeping with the rest of the album. But he deliberately retained Spector's overblown production to make a point. As incongruous as it is, in its new setting it works perfectly. Placed between two austere Harrison productions, it highlights the perils of material excess. If anything Spector's production unwittingly reinforces the message and the sense of epiphany Harrison experienced on the road to rock 'n' roll damnation.

The Day The World Gets 'Round

George Harrison (vocals and 12-string acoustic guitar), Nicky Hopkins (piano), Gary Wright (harmonium), Klaus Voormann (bass), Jim Keltner (drums), Ringo Starr (drums), John Barham – string arrangements

When Harrison left the stage on the evening of 1 August 1971 he should have felt a sense of relief and accomplishment. With the Concert for Bangladesh he'd done something remarkable, something that no other musician had done before. He'd saved lives. But if anything he felt more frustrated, angry and disenchanted than ever. Rather than celebrating his recent achievement, Harrison started work on a song that expressed his anger, frustration and disgust at the establishment's stupidity and indifference.

The resulting song, 'The Day The World Gets 'Round', extends the theme explored in 'The Lord Loves The One (That Loves The Lord)' and once again finds Harrison railing against the status quo and proffering an alternative solution of his own. Recoiling with horror from a world poisoned by state sanctioned violence and corporate greed, his response extends calls for social and economic equality that date back to the 17th century. Like the Diggers, a group of agrarian communists that came to prominence in Oliver Cromwell's Commonwealth of England, Harrison argues for a radical redistribution of wealth. God created the world for all to share, but the wealth had ended up in the hands of a greedy, selfish plutocracy who used it to further their own destructive power games.

Harrison wanted nothing to do with the establishment's maniacal plans and calls upon us all to become more conscious of the all-pervading corruption that exists in a society ruled by greed, corruption and lies. He urges people to reject the established order and define their own position within society. He believed the way to achieve this was through a revolution of the head and the soul. However, by expressing his protest in spiritual rather than political terms he alienated some critics who preferred less cant in their pop than he was prepared to offer. What they failed to comprehend was Harrison's avowed religiosity; of course he was being pious, that's what he believed in.

An early version of the backing track has surfaced on bootleg recordings. For the most part it is without vocals. The only line Harrison sings is "bow before you, in silence they pray, oh how they pray for the day...". It's his religious beliefs as much as his anger that drive the song. Yes, the song has a political message, but Harrison suggests that it's spirituality not the body politic that will unite people and change the world for the better. Speaking to Annie Nightingale he said: "Each living being is entitled to be Christ-Conscious, and actually has to become Christ-Conscious in the end. And that is why we are all in these bodies. We are given senses, our experience becomes knowledge, and our knowledge liberates us from the tedium of just being boring, ignorant people."[27]

Harrison knew that simply promoting spiritually wasn't enough and formed the Material World Foundation to promote alternative life views and philosophies. Funding for the charity came from copyrights donated by Harrison; almost all the song writing royalties from the *Material World* album went to the foundation. It was good karma and a way to addressing the material/spiritual dialectic. "I wrote a song called 'Living In The Material World' and it was from that I decided to call the foundation the Material World Foundation. Most people would think of the material world as representing purely money and greed and take offense. But in my view, it means the physical world. It's the idea that if it is money and greed, then give the greedy money away in the material world," he explained.[28]

That Is All
George Harrison (vocals and electric guitar), Nicky Hopkins (piano), Gary Wright (electric piano and harpsichord), Klaus Voormann (bass), Jim Keltner (drums), John Barham – string arrangements

Living In The Material World closes with an achingly beautiful ballad that rates among Harrison's best, and which must surly place him in the pantheon of great songwriters. Its soaring melody and meticulously crafted arrangement transcend time and place and lend it a sense of intense passion and longing. The melody came to Harrison first, the lyrics came later. When he wrote the lyrics he left them deliberately ambiguous. In doing so he transforms the personal into something universal. 'That Is All' is a love song, but to whom? By leaving it open Harrison encourages us to think about what or who he's singing about, to call upon our own experiences and memories and to engage with the question itself. It's a technique that encourages the listener to develop their own interpretations and one that Harrison employed many times.

Harrison suggests that language alone cannot express what he wants to say. It has failed, it is too ambiguous, its meanings too cursory to convey the way he feels. Harrison loved playing with words and here he employs the ambiguity of language to explore the limitations it imposes on us all. Music, however, has power beyond words and often does what words alone can't. Harrison's melody has an intrinsic beauty that enhances the emotional impact of his lyrics. Add to this a sublime vocal performance, that adds further meaning and beauty to the song, and what you have is one of his most emotional and soulful performances ever.

Harrison's own religiosity contributes to the layers of meaning that can be attributed to the song. When Andy Williams and Harry Nilsson recorded 'That Is All' the context changed. Neither were as avowedly spiritual as Harrison, consequently in their hands 'That Is All' loses some of its weightiness. Although Williams and Nilsson were technically better singers, neither comes close to matching Harrison's glorious performance.

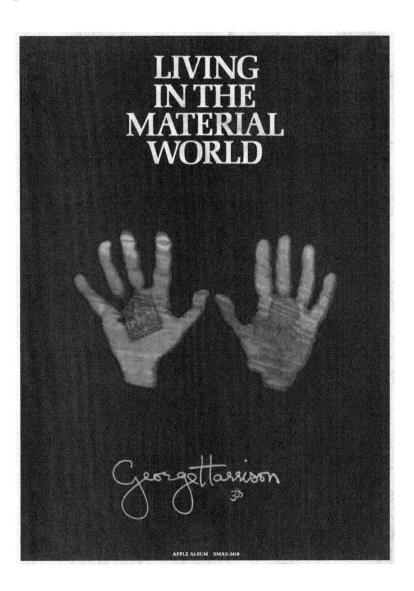

'Photograph' / 'Down And Out'*
RINGO STARR
Produced by Richard Perry / George Harrison & Richard Perry*
UK release: 19 October 1973 ; Apple R5992; chart high; number 8.
US release: 24 September 1973; Apple 1865; chart high; number 1.

Ringo Starr (vocals, drums), George Harrison (12-string acoustic guitar, backing vocals), Vini Poncia (acoustic guitar), Jimmy Calvert (acoustic guitar), Nicky Hopkins (piano), Klaus Voormann (bass), Bobby Keys (tenor saxophone), Lon & Derrek Van Eaton (percussion), Jim Keltner (drums), Jack Nitzsche (orchestral and choral arrangements).

The Harrison-Starkey hit making machine kept on rolling with this joint composition, 'Photograph', which powered up the charts on both sides of the Atlantic. The song's anthemic quality, Spectoresque production and theme of longing for a lost love, made it an instant pop classic. Such was its popularity that it topped the charts in America, Canada, New Zealand, Australia and France, and went top ten in many more.

Starr began the song while he was in Spain and asked Harrison to help him finish it. Although Harrison gets a song writing credit, Starr later claimed that he wrote most of the song himself and, as with 'Back Off Boogaloo', he'd asked Harrison to finish it. "'Photograph' is so well crafted. I wrote the song, I wrote the words, I wrote the melody, I wrote the chorus, and 3 verses. I never know how to end so George would end the song for me," he said.[29]

Besides helping to edit and hone the song, Harrison also helped record it. Recording took place in March 1973 in Los Angeles with Harrison contributing guitar and harmony vocals to a recording that employs many of the regular cohort of musicians he'd recently worked with himself.

Down and Out
Ringo Starr (vocals and drums), George Harrison (slide guitar), Gary Wright (piano), Klaus Voormann (bass)

'Down and Out', was written by Starr and initially produced by Harrison. Richard Perry added horns to the track which is why it's credited to George Harrison and Richard Perry.

219

PCTC 252
stereo
OC 066 ● 05492

RINGO

SIDE ONE

I. I'M THE GREATEST
(J. Lennon)
Drums: Ringo Starr
Piano and Harmony Vocal:
John Lennon
Guitars: George Harrison
Bass: Klaus Voormann
Organ: Billy Preston

II. HAVE YOU SEEN MY BABY
(R. Newman)
Drums: Ringo Starr, Jim Keltner
Guitar: Marc Bolan
Piano: James Booker
Bass: Klaus Voormann
Percussion: Milt Holland
Horns arranged and played by:
Tom Scott

III. PHOTOGRAPH
(R. Starkey-G. Harrison)
Drums: Ringo Starr, Jim Keltner
12 String Acoustic Guitar and
Harmony Vocal: George Harrison
Piano: Nicky Hopkins
Bass: Klaus Voormann
Acoustic Guitars: Vini Poncia,
Jimmy Calvert
Percussion: Lon and
Derrek Van Eaton
Tenor Sax Solo: Bobby Keyes
Orchestra and Chorus arranged by:
Jack Nitzche

IV. SUNSHINE LIFE FOR ME
(SAIL AWAY RAYMOND)
(G. Harrison)
Drums and Percussion: Ringo Starr
Guitars: George Harrison,
Robbie Robertson
Mandolin: Levon Helm
Fiddles: Rick Danko,
David Bromberg
Accordian: Garth Hudson
Upright Bass: Klaus Voormann
Banjo: David Bromberg
Backing Voocals: George Harrison,
Vini Poncia

V. YOU'RE SIXTEEN
(R. Sherman-R. Sherman)
Drums: Ringo Starr, Jim Keltner
Backing Voices: Harry Nilsson
Piano: Nicky Hopkins
Guitars: Jimmy Calvert, Vini Poncia
Bass: Klaus Voormann
Mouth Sax Solo: Paul McCartney

**PRODUCED BY
RICHARD PERRY**

ENGINEERED BY
Bill Schnee

℗ 1973 **EMI Records Ltd.**

Also available on cassette and cartridge

IV. DEVIL WOMAN
(R. Starkey-V. Poncia)
Drums: Ringo Starr, Jim Keltner
Bass: Klaus Voormann
Guitar: Jimmy Calvert
Piano: Tom Hensley
Percussion: Milt Holland
Horns arranged by: Tom Scott
Played by: Tom Scott, Chuck Finley
Backing Vocals: Richard Perry,
Klaus Voormann

V. YOU AND ME (BABE)
(G. Harrison-M. Evans)
Drums: Ringo Starr
Elec. Guitar: George Harrison
Acoustic Guitar: Vini Poncia
Bass: Klaus Voormann
Elec. Piano: Nicky Hopkins
Marimba: Milt Holland
Horns arranged by: Tom Scott
Strings arranged by: Jack Nitzche

SIDE TWO

I. OH MY MY
(V. Poncia-R. Starkey)
Drums: Ringo Starr, Jim Keltner
Piano and Organ: Billy Preston
Bass: Klaus Voormann
Guitar: Jimmy Calvert
Harmony Vocal: Vini Poncia
Sax Solo: Tom Scott
Horns arranged by: Tom Scott
Jim Horn
Backing Vocals: Martha Reeves,
Merry Clayton, and Friends

II. STEP LIGHTLY
(R. Starkey)
Drums: Ringo Starr
Elec. Guitar: Steve Cropper
Elec. Piano: Nicky Hopkins
Bass: Klaus Voormann
Acoustic Guitar: Jimmy Calvert
Clarinets arranged by: Tom Scott
Featuring the Dancing Feet of:
Richard Starkey, M.B.E.

III. SIX O'CLOCK
(P. McCartney-L. McCartney)
Drums: Ringo Starr
Piano and Synthesizer:
Paul McCartney
Bass: Klaus Voormann
Acoustic Guitar and percussion:
Vini Poncia
Backing Vocals: Paul and
Linda McCartney
Strings and flutes arranged by:
Paul McCartney

220

221

RINGO
RINGO STARR
Side one: I'm The Greatest / Have You Seen My Baby? / Photograph / Sunshine Life For Me (Sail Away Raymond) / You're Sixteen (You're Beautiful And You're Mine)
Side two: Oh My My / Step Lightly / Six O'clock / Devil Woman / You And Me (Babe)
UK release: 23 November 1973; Apple PCTC 252; chart high; number 7.
US release: 2 November 1973; Apple SWAL-3413; chart high; number 2.

'I'm The Greatest' (John Lennon)
Ringo Starr (vocals, drums), John Lennon (piano, harmony vocal), Billy Preston (organ), George Harrison (electric guitar), Klaus Voormann (bass).

'Photograph' (George Harrison–Richard Starkey)
Ringo Starr (vocals, drums), George Harrison (12-string acoustic guitar, backing vocals), Vini Poncia (acoustic guitar), Jimmy Calvert (acoustic guitar), Nicky Hopkins (piano), Klaus Voormann (bass), Bobby Keys (tenor saxophone), Lon & Derrek Van Eaton (percussion), Jim Keltner (drums), Jack Nitzsche (orchestral and choral arrangements).

'Sunshine Life For Me (Sail Away Raymond)' (Harrison)
Ringo Starr (vocals, drums, percussion), George Harrison (guitar, backing vocals), Robbie Robertson (guitar), Levon Helm (mandolin), Rick Danko (fiddle), David Bromberg (banjo, fiddle), Garth Hudson (accordion), Klaus Voormann (double bass).

'You and Me (Babe)' (George Harrison–Mal Evans)
Ringo Starr (vocals, drums), George Harrison (electric guitar), Vini Poncia (acoustic guitar), Nicky Hopkins (electric piano), Milt Holland (marimba), Tom Scott (horn arrangements), Jack Nitzsche (string arrangements).

   Having finished _Living In The Material World_, Harrison flew to Los Angeles for a series of business meetings and recording sessions. In early March, Harrison, Lennon and Starr held meetings with Capitol Records to try and stop the release of an unofficial Beatles compilation album, _Alpha Omega_, and to discuss plans for an official compilation of their own tentatively title _The Best Of The Beatles_. Harrison was also planning to launch his own record label, Dark Horse, and was in town to produce an album for Ravi Shankar. Sessions for what became _Shankar Family and Friends_ took place in April but prior to this he joined Ringo Starr to work on his new album being produced by Richard Perry.

According to Starr his new album came together by accident. "I worked with Harry Nilsson in London on his album (*Son Of Schmilsson*) with producer Richard Perry. So Harry and I were invited to do the Grammy awards, and Richard was saying, 'Remember you were talking to me in the club one night, you know... You'd like to do something? After the Grammys, why don't you come down to L.A. for a week?' And we went in. It worked so well, in ten days we had eight tracks, you see. Once we started we couldn't stop. And then I got John to write me something, and I got Paul, I got George. You know... dragged in all me friends, 'cuz I'm lucky – I got a lot of people who'll work for me. I'll work for them, but I always feel very lucky that people will come out for me."[30]

Richard Perry remembers it slightly differently and recalls calling Starr on the telephone to remind him about the plans they'd made to work together: "Ringo was a drummer who I had long admired. Then we got friendly, and one night we were sitting together in Tramp, the London club, semi-inebriated, and I told him how wonderful I thought it would be if he were to do a solo album. I felt that it would have a tremendous audience, although he was very skeptical about it, having had the experience of Beatle albums which apparently took a tremendous amount of time and obvious care, and he was assuming that the same sort of thing would be more of an ordeal than he wanted to go through. He appreciated my suggestion, but for the moment, decided to shelve it. [Later, I said] remember you talked about going in the studio? Let's go in and see what happens'. So without any lawyers knowing anything about it, we came back to L.A., and in five days had recorded five tracks, which included the three major singles from the album, 'Photograph', 'You're Sixteen' and 'Oh My My'."[31]

Recording had already started at Sunset Sound when Harrison dropped in to see how things were going. He liked what he heard and vowed to return a few days later to help record a couple of songs with his buddy. The first song they worked on was 'Photograph'. Harrison is alleged to have tried producing the song with Starr during sessions for *Living In The Material World*. But it would take Richard Perry to perfect it. The following week John Lennon heard what they'd recorded and was so excited he offered Starr a song he'd been working on since his *Imagine* album, 'I'm The Greatest'. Richard Perry: "It was on that session that John came down, and it was the first time that I had met John. To say that it was an exciting experience to work with him would be a gross understatement, because it was really quite unique and very special, and something I'll never forget, which goes without saying. The song wasn't quite complete, so we started to run it down, so there was also that very special thrill of experiencing a song being completed in the studio by John Lennon, and we all gathered round the piano and chipped in our ideas to help to complete it. Then the phone rang and it was George, who said, 'I hear there's a track going down. Is it OK if I come?', and I said, 'Hold on a minute, and I'll ask John if it's OK'. So here I am asking John if George can come down... And John said, 'Hell, yes, tell him to get down here and help me finish this bridge'. That was very much like John, and it was on that session that the three of them played for the first time, I believe, since the break-up of the Beatles."[32]

It was just like the old days. Lennon, Harrison and Starr played the track live in the studio with

Lennon issuing instructions and singing a guide vocal with each take. Most of the takes they recorded that day have found their way onto bootlegs. They offer a tantalizing glimpse into what it was like to be in a studio with the Fab Three as they worked on a new Lennon composition together.

The sessions continued with Harrison contributing a further two songs, 'Sunshine Life for Me (Sail Away Raymond)' and 'You and Me (Babe)'. 'Sunshine Life for Me (Sail Away Raymond)' dates from 1969. Harrison started the song while visiting Donovan in Ireland. As with several songs written during this period, it represents escape and looks to nature and the sun as restoratives. Harrison wasn't the only Beatle who looked to escaping his woes by heading to the country. McCartney did the exact same thing and wrote several songs that extol the virtues of a bucolic lifestyle. With contributions from Levon Helm, Robbie Robertson, Rick Danko and Garth Hudson of the Band, and multi-instrumentalist David Bromberg, the song was given a down-home feel that compliments its pastoral theme perfectly.

'You and me (Babe)' was co-written with Mal Evans. The Beatles old road manager had moved to Los Angeles in an attempt to re-build his life and would hang out with members of the group when they hit town. Harrison and Evans seem to have been reminiscing about the good old days when they penned his romantic remake of 'With A Little Help From My Friends'. Looking back through rose-tinted spectacles to a time before the mania made their lives unbearable, it's a lyrical and musical snapshot that refers back to the band's golden era. Harrison perfectly tailored the song to Starr's chummy persona, vocal style and range. Perry's master-stroke was to programme it as the closing song on the album. Having Starr thank everybody involved brought the album to a perfect end. (It was a trick Lennon would borrow for his *Rock 'n' Roll* album.)

1974 : Running On A Dark Racecourse

SIDE ONE
1. I Am Missing You (3.40)
   sung by Lakshmi Shankar

2. Kahān gayelavā Shyām saloné (3.15)
   sung by Lakshmi Shankar

3. Supané mé āyé preetam sainyā (4.44)
   sung by Lakshmi Shankar

4. I Am Missing You (reprise) (3.56)
   sung by Lakshmi Shankar

5. Jaya Jagadish Hare (4.50)
   sung by Jitendra Abhisheki & Chorus

All music composed and arranged by Ravi Shankar
except I Am Missing You (reprise)
arranged by George Harrison.
Lyrics (except 5) by Ravi Shankar.

SHANKAR
FAMILY
ॐ
FRIENDS

SIDE TWO
Dream, Nightmare & Dawn
Music for a Ballet by Ravi Shankar

Overture (2.28)
Part One. Dream
Festivity & Joy, (3.52)
Love – Dance Ecstasy (3.10)

Part Two. Nightmare
Lust (Rāga Chandrakauns) (3.12)
Dispute & Violence (3.05)
Disillusionment & Frustration (2.51)
Despair & Sorrow (Rāga Marwā) (3.07)

Part Three. Dawn
Awakening (3.07)
Peace & Hope (Rāga Bhattyār) (4.21)

All music composed and arranged by Ravi Shankar

Produced by George Harrison
Recording Engineer: Norman Kinney
Re-Mix Engineer: Gary Kellgran
Recorded at A&M Studios, Los Angeles
Re-Mixed at the Record Plant, Los Angeles

Art Direction: Fabio Nicoli
Design: Jack Katz, Nick Marshall
Front cover photo: Jan Steward
Back cover photo: Kumar Shankar

Licensed to and Distributed by A&M Records Ltd.
136-140, New Kings Road, London SW6 4LZ
Sleeve printed and made by Shorewood Packaging Co. Ltd., England
This stereo record can be played on mono reproducers provided either a compatible or stereo cartridge wired for mono is fitted.
Recent equipment may already be fitted with a suitable cartridge. If in doubt consult your dealer.

DARK HORSE
RECORDS
AMLH 22002

228

STEREO
AMLH 22002
℗ 1974 Ganga
Distributors B.V.
AMLH 22002-A
SIDE ONE

SHANKAR FAMILY & FRIENDS
SONGS ON LORD KRISHNA
✿1. I Am Missing You (R. Shankar) 3.40
2. Kahan Gayelava Shyam Salone (R. Shankar) 3.15
3. Supane Me Aye Preetam Sainya (R. Shankar) 4.44
4. I Am Missing You (Reprise) (R. Shankar) 3.56
5. Jaya Jagadish Hare (R. Shankar) 4.50
SHANKAR FAMILY & FRIENDS
Arr. by R. Shankar except ✿ Arr. by George
Harrison. Produced by George Harrison
'OOPS' PUBLISHING LTD. (1—5)

STEREO
AMLH 22002
℗ 1974 Ganga
Distributors B.V.
AMLH 22002-B
SIDE TWO

SHANKAR FAMILY & FRIENDS
DREAM, NIGHTMARE & DAWN   MUSIC FOR A BALLET
Overture 2.28
Part One: Dream   Festivity & Joy 3.52   Love — Dance Ecstasy 3.10
Part Two: Nightmare   Lust 3.12   Dispute & Violence 3.05
Disillusionment & Frustration 2.51   Despair & Sorrow 3.07
Part Three: Dawn   Awakening 3.07   Peace & Hope 4.21
SHANKAR FAMILY & FRIENDS
Composed & arranged by R. Shankar
Produced by George Harrison
'OOPS' PUBLISHING LTD.

AMS 7133-A
℗ 1974
Ganga
Distributors
B.V.
45 r.p.m.

Side 1
3.40

I AM MISSING YOU
(R. Shankar) (From the album "Shankar
Family & Friends" AMLH 22002)
SHANKAR FAMILY & FRIENDS
Vocals by Lakshmi Shankar
. Prod. by George Ha...
PUBLISHING...

AMS 7133-B
℗ 1974
Ganga
Distributors
B.V.
45 r.p.m.

Side 2
3.12

LUST
(R. Shankar) (From the album "Shankar
Family & Friends" AMLH 22002)
SHANKAR FAMILY & FRIENDS
by R. Shankar. Prod. by Geor...
...rison 'OOPS' PUB. LT...

231

SHANKAR FAMILY & FRIENDS
RAVI SHANKAR

Side one: I Am Missing You / Kahān Gayelavā Shyām Saloné / Supané Mé Āyé Preetam Sainyā / I Am Missing You (reprise) / Jaya Jagadish Haré
Side two: Dream, Nightmare & Dawn (Music For a Ballet) Overture Part One (Dream): Festivity & Joy : Love-Dance Ecstasy / Part Two (Nightmare): Lust (Rāga Chandrakauns) : Dispute & Violence : Disillusionment & Frustration : Despair & Sorrow (Rāga Marwā) / Part Three (Dawn): Awakening : Peace & Hope (Rāga Bhatiyār)
UK release: 20 September 1974; Dark Horse AMLH 220002; chart high; failed to chart.
US release: 7 October 1974; Dark Horse SP 220002; chart high; failed to chart.
Produced by George Harrison.

Ravi Shankar (direction, spoken voice, sitar, surbahar, Moog synthesiser, backing vocals), Lakshmi Shankar (vocals, swarmandal, backing vocals), Jitendra Abhisheki (vocals), Tom Scott (saxophones, flute, handclaps), George Harrison (electric and acoustic guitars, autoharp, arrangement on 'I Am Missing You'), Shivkumar Sharma (santoor, shaker, backing vocals), Shubho Shankar (sitar), Alla Rakha (tabla, pakavaj), Emil Richards (marimba), Hariprasad Chaurasia (bansuri, cowbell), Ashish Khan (sarod, swarmandal, backing vocals), Subramaniam (violin), Palghat Raghu (mridangam), Harihar Rao (spoken voice, dholak), Kamala Chakravarty (backing vocals), G.S. Sachdev (bansuri), Sharad Kumar (bansuri), Pranesh Khan (dholak), Fakir Mohammad (tamboura), Nodu Mullick (kartal, tamboura), Krishna Temple (kartal), Klaus Voormann (bass), Nicky Hopkins (piano), Jim Keltner (drums), Billy Preston (organ), Ringo Starr (drums), Fred Teague (organ), Ed Shaunessey (drums), (Dennis Budimir), (acoustic guitar), David Bromberg (electric guitar), Vini Poncia (tambourine), Paul Beaver (Moog synthesiser), Malcolm Cecil (Moog synthesiser), Robert Margouleff (Moog synthesiser), Ray Cramer (cello), Al Casey (mandolin), W. Webb (esraj), Ronald Cohen (sarangi), George Ruckert (sarod), Ray Pizzi (bassoon), Bobby Bruce (violin), Gordon Swift (violin), Gene Cipriano (oboe).

Harrison spent the spring of 1973 in Los Angeles dealing with business and making music with Ringo Starr and Ravi Shankar. The brace of albums he worked on were destined for Apple, however the company was starting to run down its record division with the consequence that the *Shankar Family & Friends* album was put on hold. Harrison's original vision for Apple Records was to follow the template established by Sue Records in the early '60s. "I wouldn't mind if we turned out something like Sue Records," he said, "they didn't often reach the hit parade with their records, but all the stuff they issued was great."[1] The Shankar album would have fitted neatly into Apple's eclectic catalogue, but it was never to be. Instead the album was issued by Harrison's new record label, Dark Horse.

Harrison had been thinking about starting his own record company for some time. One idea was to buy out Apple Records from The Beatles partnership and run it with Ringo Starr. However, it proved too difficult to untangle all the legal knots and the idea was quietly dropped. Instead, he decided to form a record label of his own. Talking to Anne Nightingale about the label's genesis he said: "Later down the line, someone needed a name for a company. Publishing, it was. So I said: 'I can't think of any names.' I was sick of thinking of company names. So they said: 'How about one of your songs?' So I said: 'Okay, Dark Horse.' Then I thought, well, this period when Apple was getting swept under the carpet, and I still had a lot of things that I was working on, which were intended for Apple. So I decided: 'hell, I'll have a label too, and I shall call it Dark Horse.'"[2]

Harrison's new label would reflect his tastes with releases encompassing Indian classical music, soul, funk and soft rock. It would, of course, also release his solo records once his contract with EMI expired on 26 January 1976. In the meantime, he booked A&M Studios, Los Angeles, and began work on the *Shankar Family and Friends* album. Recording began on 1 April 1973 and continued into May with a break towards the end of the first month.

Although he'd produced Shankar before this was the first time they had collaborated on a studio album together. The way Shankar worked was to improvise in the studio. "Ravi would tell everybody what their part was, and Indian musicians are very good at memorizing what they have to do," Harrison explained. "They would make some notation if they needed to remember something specific or especially difficult – and then he'd say, 'OK, ready?' He'd go to count them in, and I thought, 'This is going to be chaos.' But we'd start playing and it would be magic."[3]

Shankar had written a song about Krishna that Harrison thought was a potential hit. "I wrote one song called 'I Am Missing You'. One of the few that I have written in English, a simple lyric that gushed out of me when I was travelling on a plane,' explained Shankar.[4] The lyric could have easily flowed from Harrison's own pen, such was its air of devotion and desire for spiritual fulfillment. Harrison arranged 'I Am Missing You' for a pop band and recorded it with his regular cohort of musicians which included Ringo Starr, Billy Preston, Tom Scott, Emil Richards and Jim Keltner. Released as a single by Dark Horse 'I Am Missing You' wasn't the hit Harrison had hoped for. Neither was the album. Like the Sue Records of old, it was good, but didn't reach the hit parade on either side of the Atlantic.

234

SIDE ONE
GRAVY TRAIN (4.00)
Vocals: Bill Elliot and Bob Purvis
Bass: Klaus Voorman
Drums: Mike Kelly
Guitars: Hari Georgeson and Alvin Lee
Horn arrangements: Mel Collins
Electric piano: Billy Preston

'DRINK ALL DAY' (3.20)
(GOT TO FIND YOUR OWN WAY HOME)
Vocals: Bill Elliot and Bob Purvin
Acoustic bass: Klaus Voorman
Drums: Jim Keltner
Guitars/dobro: Hari Georgeson
Harmonium: P. Roducer
Percussion: Jai Raj Harisein

CHINA LIGHT (4.35)
Vocals: Bill Elliot and Bob Purvis
Bass: Willie Weeks
Drums: Mike Kelly
Electric and Acoustic guitar/
Mandolin: Hari Georgeson
Piano: Gary Wright
Organ: Billy Preston

SOMEBODY'S CITY (5.20)
Vocals: Bill Elliot and Bob Purvis
Bass: Klaus Voorman
Drums: Mike Kelly
Guitars: Hari Georgeson
Piano: Gary Wright
Horn arrangements: Mel Collins
Percussion: Jai Raj Harisein

SIDE TWO
COSTAFINE TOWN (3.10)*
Vocals: Bill Elliot and Bob Purvis
Bass and eight-string bass: Hari Georgeson
Drums: Mike Kelly
Harmonium: P. Roducer
Piano: Gary Wright
Accordian: Graham Maitland
Percussion: Jai Raj Harisein

THE PLACE I LOVE (4.25)
Vocals: Bill Elliot and Bob Purvis
Bass: Klaus Voorman
Drums: Mike Kelly
Guitars: Hari Georgeson
Electric Piano: Gary Wright
Percussion: Jai Raj Harisein

SITUATION VACANT (4.00)
Vocals: Bill Elliot and Bob Purvis
Bass: Willie Weeks
Drums: Jim Keltner
Guitars: Hari Georgeson
Piano: Gary Wright
Horn arrangements: Mel Collins

ELLY MAY (2.43)
Vocals: Bill Elliot and Bob Purvis
Acoustic Bass: Klaus Voorman
Drums: Mike Kelly
Acoustic guitar: Hari Georgeson
Moog synthesizer: P. Roducer
Piano: Gary Wright

HAVEN'T GOT TIME (3.55)
Vocals: Bill Elliot and Bob Purvis
Bass: Klaus Voorman
Drums: Mike Kelly
Guitars: Hari Georgeson and Alvin Lee
Horn arrangements: Mel Collins
Percussion: Jai Raj Harisein

Produced by George Harrison
Recording and remix engineer: Phil McDonald
Assistant engineer: Kumar Shankar
Special thanks to Mal, Ted & Joe
Alvin Lee appears courtesy of Chrysalis (U.K.)
& C.B.S. (U.S.A.)
Recorded at F.P.S.H.O.T.
All titles written and composed by R. J. Purvis
except * words: R. J. Purvis & W. Elliot.
Music R. J. Purvis

Art Direction: Fabio Nicoli
Design: Jack Katz/Nick Marshall
Photography: Terry O'Neill

Licensed to and distributed by A&M Records Ltd.
136/140 New Kings Road, London SW6 4LZ.

Sleeve printed and made in England by MacNeill Press Ltd, London, SE1

DARK HORSE
RECORDS
AMLH 22001

STEREO
AMLH 22001

℗ 1974 Ganga
Distributors B.V.
AMLH 22001-A
SIDE ONE

THE PLACE I LOVE

1. Gravy Train (R. J. Purvis) 4.00
2. Drink All Day (R. J. Purvis) 3.20
3. China Light (R. J. Purvis/W. Elliott) 4.35
4. Somebody's City (R. J. Purvis) 5.20

SPLINTER

Produced by George Harrison
'OOPS' PUBLISHING LTD. (1—4)

STEREO
AMLH 22001

℗ 1974 Ganga
Distributors B.V.
AMLH 22001-B
SIDE TWO

THE PLACE I LOVE

1. Costafine Town (R. J. Purvis/W. Elliott) 3.10
2. The Place I Love (R. J. Purvis) 4.25
3. Situation Vacant (R. J. Purvis) 4.00
4. Elly May (R. J. Purvis) 2.43
5. Haven't Got Time (R. J. Purvis) 3.55

SPLINTER

Produced by George Harrison
'OOPS' PUBLISHING LTD. (1—5)

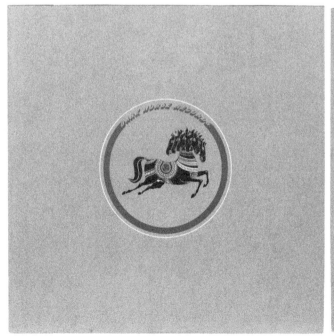

THE PLACE I LOVE
SPLINTER
Side one: Gravy Train / Drink All Day (Got to Find Your Own Way Home) / China Light / Somebody's City
Side two: Costafine Town / The Place I Love / Situation Vacant / Elly-May / Haven't Got Time
UK release: 20 September 1974; Dark Horse AMLH 220001; chart high; failed to chart.
US release: 20 September; Dark Horse SP 220001; chart high; failed to chart.
Produced by George Harrison.

Bill Elliott (vocals), Bobby Purvis (vocals), George Harrison (acoustic guitar (2, 3, 4, 6, 8), electric guitar (1, 4, 6, 7, 9), 12-string acoustic guitar (2, 4), dobro (2, 6), mandolin (3), bass (5), 6-string bass (5), harmonium (2, 6), percussion (2, 4, 5, 6, 9), jaw's harp (2), Moog synthesizer (8), backing vocals (7), Gary Wright (piano) (4, 5, 8), electric piano (6, 7), Klaus Voormann (bass (1, 4, 6, 9), upright bass (2, 8), Mike Kellie (drums) (1, 3, 4, 5, 6, 8, 9), Billy Preston (organ) (3), piano (1), Willie Weeks (bass) (3, 7), Jim Keltner (drums (2, 7), Alvin Lee (electric guitar (1, 9), Graham Maitland (accordion (5), Mel Collins (horn arrangement) (1, 7, 9).

The other major project occupying Harrison at this time was the film *Little Malcolm and His Struggle Against the Eunuchs*. Harrison had seen a stage production of David Halliwell's satirical play some eight years earlier. Approached by the actor John Hurt and writer Derek Woodward, he became the film's exclusive producer. "He was an absolute delight, totally committed to the project," recalled the film's director Stuart Cooper. "George was a kind of 'spiritual' leader. He had this lovely quality about him; very unpretentious, very passionate, and very genuine."[5]

Cooper asked Harrison to score the film but, because he had other commitments, he declined. Stanley Myers took his place with Harrison providing some incidental music that included the song 'Living In The Material World', which appeared, somewhat incongruously, playing on a pub jukebox. Harrison also produced a track by a group from Newcastle called Splinter.

The Beatles road manager and erstwhile talent scout, Mal Evans, had discovered Bobby Purvis and Bill Elliott playing in a band called Half Breed and for a while become Purvis' manager. Bill Elliott had already recorded for Apple Records, providing vocals for the Lennon composition 'God Save Us', issued to raise money for the Oz magazine obscenity trial. Between Elliot recording for Apple and *Little Malcolm* going into production, Purvis and Elliott had gone their separate ways. They were reunited by Rob Hill, who got them to reform as Splinter.

Apple thought Splinter was perfect for a scene in the film and wanted them to record a Cat

Stevens song called 'How Can I Tell You'. Harrison had other plans. He'd heard a song that Evans had co-written with Purvis called 'Another Chance That I Let Go', subsequently retitled 'Lonely Man', and booked the duo into Apple Studios to produce the song. "I thought, because the film is not the sought of film that's easy to sell, you know, I thought if I could make it a hit, then maybe the film people would be more interested in the movie," Harrison explained. "So I went to do the single with them, but then I heard the rest of the songs and they were so good I got involved in making the album."[6]

Work on the album continued at Apple Studios throughout '73 before relocating to F.P.S.H.O.T.. Basic tracks for 'The Place I Love', 'Gravy Train', 'Somebody's City', 'China Light' and 'Drink All Day (Got To Find Your Way Home)' were finished by late '73, at which point Harrison began looking for a distributor for his new label. Among those he approached was the head of Elektra/Asylum Records, David Geffen. In early '74 Harrison sent Geffen a tape of Splinter rough mixes but he declined the offer. Next Harrison turned to the president of A&M Records, Jerry Moss. According to *Billboard*, Moss flew to Paris to meet Harrison and conduct the negotiations. Moss liked what he heard and signed a partnership agreement with Harrison on 15 May 1974.

A&M would distribute Dark Horse Records, which Harrison would produce, and secure the rights to Harrison's future solo releases. Initially, everything looked rosy. Jerry Moss said: "This is a great moment for A&M Records. The stimulation of working with one of the world's most creative and unique personalities is heightened by our involvement in and support of his well know humanitarian activities. I know I speak for Lou Adler when I say that the addition of Dark Horse Records to the A&M/Ode family flatters us immensely and the possibilities for the future are dazzling."[7] However, fate intervened and the future was anything but dazzling.

Before signing with A&M, Harrison visited Ravi Shankar to attend the opening ceremony of his friend's new house in Benares, India. Returning to England he continued work on Splinter's début album and on another Shankar album, *Music Festival From India*. The Shankar album was recorded quickly at F.P.S.H.O.T., but work on the Splinter album continued to occupy him for months. Once again, he called upon his musical friends to assist. Alvin Lee contributed guitar to 'Gravy Train' and 'Haven't Got Time'. Klaus Voormann and Willie Weeks contributed bass, while Gary Wright and Billy Preston played keyboards. As producer, Harrison added guitar, dobro, mandolin, harmonium, bass, jaw's harp and percussion. However, because he was still under contract to EMI he was obliged to hide under the pseudonyms Hari Georgeson, Jai Raj Harisein and P. Roducer.

Harrison's meticulous production and melodic invention transformed Purvis and Elliott's simple folk-based songs into pop hits. When 'Costafine Town' was issued as a single in Britain it climbed steadily into the top twenty. It was a soft-rock sound that Harrison would perfect and employ for his own solo albums, eventually reaching its apogee with the *George Harrison* album. While he'd been producing sterling work for others, he'd unintentionally neglected his own. The result was that his next album was anything but well-crafted, smooth or particularly commercial.

From:
"The Place I Love"
a new single
"Costafine Town"
by Splinter.
Produced by George Harrison.
On Dark Horse Records.
Marketed by A&M Records.

AMS 7135

DARK HORSE/GEORGE HARRISON

You thought that you knew where I was and when
But it looks like you've been foolin you again,
You thought that you'd got me all staked out
But baby looks like I've been breaking out

I'm a dark horse
Running on a dark race course
I'm a blue moon
Since I stepped from out of the womb
I've been a cool jerk
Looking for the source
I'm a dark horse.

You thought you had got me in your grip
Baby looks like you was not so smart
And I became too slippery for you
But let me say that was nothing new.

I'm a dark horse
Running on a dark race course
I'm a blue moon
Since I picked up my first spoon
I've been a cool jerk
Looking for the source
I'm a dark horse

I thought you knew it all along
Until you started getting me not right
Seems as if you heard a little late
But I warned you when
We both were at the starting gate

I'm a dark horse
Running on a dark course
I'm a blue moon
Since I stepped from out of the womb
I've been a cool jerk
Cooking at the source

R6001

apple

An Apple record
An EMI recording
℗ 1974 EMI Records Limited

240

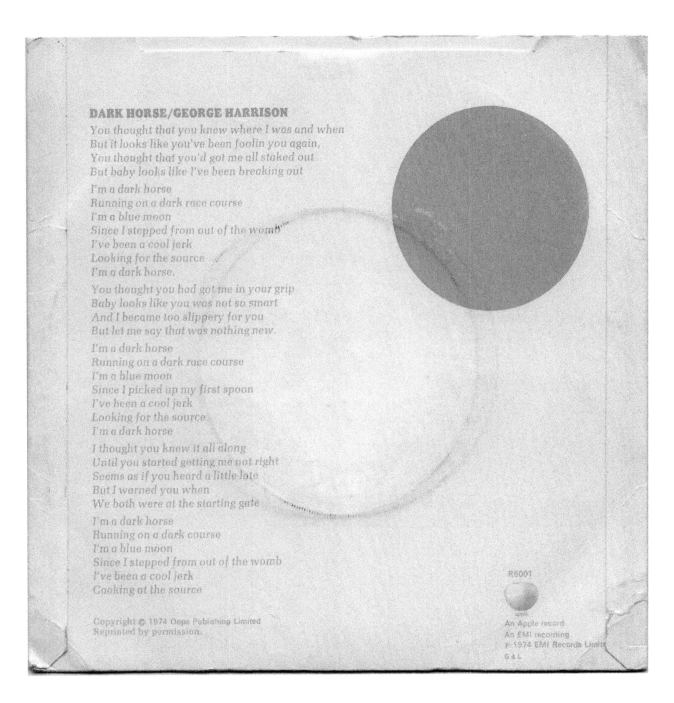

DARK HORSE/GEORGE HARRISON

You thought that you knew where I was and when
But it looks like you've been foolin you again,
You thought that you'd got me all staked out
But baby looks like I've been breaking out

I'm a dark horse
Running on a dark race course
I'm a blue moon
Since I stepped from out of the womb
I've been a cool jerk
Looking for the source
I'm a dark horse.

You thought you had got me in your grip
Baby looks like you was not so smart
And I became too slippery for you
But let me say that was nothing new.

I'm a dark horse
Running on a dark race course
I'm a blue moon
Since I picked up my first spoon
I've been a cool jerk
Looking for the source
I'm a dark horse

I thought you knew it all along
Until you started getting me not right
Seems as if you heard a little late
But I warned you when
We both were at the starting gate

I'm a dark horse
Running on a dark course
I'm a blue moon
Since I stepped from out of the womb
I've been a cool jerk
Cooking at the source

R6001

An Apple record
An EMI recording
℗ 1974 EMI Records Limited
G & L

STEREO
℗1974 EMI
Records Ltd.
From the Album
"Dark Horse"—
PAS 10008
Recorded
in England

DEMO RECORD
NOT FOR
SALE A (28.2.7?)

R 6001
An Apple
Record
An EMI
Recording
7YCE 21755
Oops Publishing
Ltd.

GEORGE HARRISON
DARK HORSE
(George Harrison)

Produced by
George Harrison

STEREO
℗1974 EMI
Records Ltd.
From the Album
"Dark Horse"—
PAS 10008
Recorded
in England

DEMO RECORD
NOT FOR
SALE (28.2.7?)

R 6001
An Apple
Record
An EMI
Recording
7YCE 21760
Oops Publishing
Ltd.

GEORGE HARRISON
HARI'S ON TOUR (EXPRESS)
(George Harrison)

Produced by
George Harrison

STEREO
℗1974 EMI
Records Ltd.
From the Album
"Dark Horse"—
PAS 10008
Recorded
in England

R 6001
An Apple
Record
An EMI
Recording
7YCE 21755
Oops Publishing
Ltd.

GEORGE HARRISON
DARK HORSE
(George Harrison)

Produced by
George Harrison

STEREO
℗1974 EMI
Records Ltd.
From the Album
"Dark Horse"—
PAS 10008
Recorded
in England

R 6001
An Apple
Record
An EMI
Recording
7YCE 21760
Oops Publishing
Ltd.

GEORGE HARRISON
HARI'S ON TOUR (EXPRESS)
(George Harrison)

Produced by
George Harrison

An Apple Record

DARK HORSE
(George Harrison)

★ NOT FOR SALE

STEREO

P-1877
(S45-X48945)

Ganga Publishing B.V.-BMI

Intro.-:05
3:52

Recorded in England

Produced by George Harrison

GEORGE HARRISON

℗1974 EMI Records Limited

MFD. BY APPLE RECORDS, INC.

An Apple Record

DARK HORSE
(George Harrison)

★ NOT FOR SALE

MONO

P-1877
(PRO-8009)

Ganga Publishing B.V.-BMI

Intro.-:05
3:52

Recorded in England

Produced by George Harrison

GEORGE HARRISON

℗1974 EMI Records Limited

MFD. BY APPLE RECORDS, INC.

DARK HORSE
(George Harrison)

STEREO

1877
(S45-X48945)

Ganga Publishing B.V.-BMI

Intro.-:05
3:52

Recorded in England

Produced by George Harrison

GEORGE HARRISON

℗1974 EMI Records Limited

An Apple Record

MFD. BY APPLE RECORDS, INC.

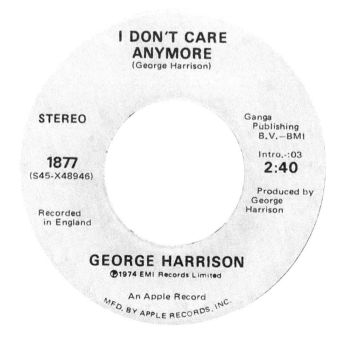

I DON'T CARE ANYMORE
(George Harrison)

STEREO

1877
(S45-X48946)

Ganga Publishing B.V.-BMI

Intro.-:03
2:40

Recorded in England

Produced by George Harrison

GEORGE HARRISON

℗1974 EMI Records Limited

An Apple Record

MFD. BY APPLE RECORDS, INC.

STEREO
1877

Intro — :05
Total — 3:52

℗ 1974 EMI
Records Limited

GEORGE HARRISON
DARK HORSE
(George Harrison)
Produced by
George Harrison
MFD. BY APPLE RECORDS, INC.

An Apple
Record
48945

Ganga
Publishing B.V.
BMI

STEREO
1877

Intro. — :03
Total — 2:40

℗ 1974 EMI
Records Limited

GEORGE HARRISON
I DON'T CARE ANYMORE
(George Harrison)
Produced by
George Harrison
MFD. BY APPLE RECORDS, INC.

An Apple
Record
48946

Ganga
Publishing B.V.
BMI

An Apple Record

DARK HORSE
(George Harrison)

NOT
FOR SALE

MONO

P-1877
(PRO-8037)

(from the LP
"DARK HORSE"
SMAS-3418)

GEORGE HARRISON

℗1974 EMI Records Limited
MFD. BY APPLE RECORDS, INC.

Ganga
Publishing
B.V.-BMI

Intro.—:04
2:48

Produced by
George
Harrison

An Apple Record

DARK HORSE
(George Harrison)

NOT
FOR SALE

STEREO

P-1877
'SPRO-8036)

(from the LP
"DARK HORSE"
SMAS-3418)

GEORGE HARRISON

℗1974 EMI Records Limited
MFD. BY APPLE RECORDS, INC.

Ganga
Publishing
B.V.-BMI

Intro.—:04
2:48

Produced by
George
Harrison

'Dark Horse' / 'I Don't Care Anymore'*
GEORGE HARRISON
Produced by George Harrison
US release: 18 November 1974; Apple 1877; chart high; number 15.

'Dark Horse' / 'Hari's on Tour (Express)'
GEORGE HARRISON
Produced by George Harrison
UK release: 28 February 1975; Apple R 6001; chart high; failed to chart.

George Harrison (vocals, acoustic guitar, jaws harp*), Robben Ford (acoustic guitar), Billy Preston (electric piano), Willie Weeks (bass), Tom Scott (flute), Jim Horn (flute), Chuck Findley (flute), Andy Newmark (drums), Jim Keltner (hi-hat), Emil Richards (percussion), Derrek Van Eaton (backing vocals), Lon Van Eaton (backing vocals).

Released in America one week into Harrison's trek across the country, 'Dark Horse' found the ex-Beatle confessing his sins and railing against a media that still labelled him Fab. Written in late 1973, it was inspired by a particularly British idiom that popped into his head early one winter morning. "Yeah, well, the song came to me just early one morning when I was sitting by the fire in Henley. I thought of dark horse in relation to Liverpool which was running through my mind at that moment. When I was a kid there, I always remember them saying: 'You'll never believe that Mrs Jones, she's running around with Mr Badger, you know she's a dark horse,'" he explained.[8]

With this phrase in mind he started searching for a rhyme with horse but almost dismissed his first thought for being too frivolous. "I thought, 'I'm a dark horse', then I thought, okay the next line, 'running on a dark race course'. That just cracked me up. I thought, 'no I can't use that'. It's silly. Then the next day it was still on my mind and I thought running on a dark race course, it may be silly, but it's so silly it's fantastic," he told Alan Freeman.[9] "Next day, I woke up and wrote all the lyrics having breakfast at tea-time which is always a good situation for writing a song, I find. Went straight from writing it to the studio and recorded it straight away."[10]

Popping upstairs to his home studio, Harrison cut a rough demo with a drummer, some suggest it's Ringo Starr, and a bassist, most probably Klaus Voormann. This stripped down take has a guide vocal that is almost as husky as the version he'd cut a year later. Harrison's rough draft features slightly different lyrics, which he perfected by adding subtle layers of meaning and intricate word play. As far as he was concerned the most significant line in the song was the one he'd almost dismissed. "The best line in the song, which is the most important, is 'running on a dark race course'. So, while the first line is very English, and might be taken as an admission to something, the second means the whole situation is pretty shady," he told Ray Coleman.[11]

The first verse restates a theme first explored with 'The Light That Has Lighted The World', a song that bemoans people's inability to accept change. While Harrison had grown, matured and moved on, the media hadn't. If anything, it had got worse, it couldn't let go of The Beatles or the past. And now that Harrison was getting divorced it wanted to dish the dirt on his private life as well. This irked him. "I'll admit my sins, or failings or whatever, as long as you all admit to all yours too. I don't need *Woman's Own* magazine, or *Rolling Stone*, or any of those other journalists, who think they've caught me doing this or that, or getting a divorce or being a looney or whatever. They can't catch me, cause I caught myself before they ever knew it," he said.[12]

Besides railing at the media, 'Dark Horse' is a very public confession. It's a personal manifesto and warning to others, family, friends and perhaps ex-lovers that he's a complex person who has spent most of his life being under-appreciated. As if to reinforce this he proclaims himself a rare talent – a blue moon – something that only happens every two to three years. He also admits to being a jerk, albeit a stylish one. It's a cutting indictment of himself and, by implication, the band he'd previously performed with – The Beatles.

His love of wordplay adds another layer of meaning to the song. Just exactly what is the 'source' he's looking for? Is it enlightenment? God? Or a more worldly source – alcohol? It's as if he's still standing at a crossroads, tempted by the material world whilst knowing that the spiritual world is infinitely more rewarding. He's trapped by the demands of the race he's running; a race he wants no part of.

I Don't Care Anymore
George Harrison (vocals, acoustic guitar, jaws harp)

Everything about 'I Don't Care Anymore' is a joke. From the mumbled introduction, the fluffed vocal delivery and the shaky production, it all adds up to the fact that Harrison had had enough. Although everything about the song conspires to make light of his feelings, he nevertheless manages to evoke a striking picture of desire, frustration and desolation.

A lazy, lusty Dylanesque folk blues, it finds Harrison physically exhausted and emotionally frustrated. Tired of the bizarre love triangles, the music business and what his life had become, he's at the end of his tether. Tempted by carnal thoughts, he simply gives in to his lustful desires, takes another sip from the bottle and tells it like it is. Speaking to Ray Coleman in the summer of 1975, he said that he didn't think of himself as being particularly virtuous: "Maybe compared to the average pop star, but compared to what I should be, I'm a heathen."[13]

Here is Harrison the heathen laid bare. Is this really the same guitarist who played with such finesse and style on earlier recordings? It is and he doesn't give a damn. Is this the same man who sang about spirituality with such monkish zeal? It is and if he now wants to lust after women he will. Is this the same musician who produced exquisite, finely-crated pop gems? It is and if he wants to make sloppy records he will.

Harrison wanted desperately to rid himself of his Fabness. This was one way of doing just that. If his audience wanted to live vicariously through pop stars and were stupid enough to follow false idols, let them follow somebody more willing to indulge their fantasies. He was certainly reluctant to give fans who came to see him in concert what they wanted – old Beatles songs. And once the tour ended any plans for future shows in Europe were quickly dropped. He wouldn't tour again until 1991, and then only in Japan.

Dark Horse data

Apple issued 'Dark Horse' / 'I Don't Care Anymore' in America on 18 November 1974 with white labels with black text that incorrectly state "Recorded in England" in a white sleeve that reproduced the lyrics for 'Dark Horse'. "Recorded in England" was removed from later pressings of the single issued with white labels. The single was also issued with customized labels featuring a photograph of Harrison's eyes. Promotional copies of the single (P-1877) were manufactured with white labels and black text with the addition of 'NOT FOR SALE' at 11 o'clock.

The British release was held back until 28 February 1975. It was also issued in a sleeve with printed lyrics, but with 'Hari's on Tour (Express)' as the b-side. The British edition was issued with customized labels, the A-side featured a photograph of Harrison's eyes while the B-side featured a photograph of the future Mrs. Harrison's eyes. Promotional copies have 'DEMO RECORD NOT FOR SALE' a large 'A' and the release date '28-2-75' directly below the spindle hole. Like the American release, the British pressings erroneously state that the record was "Recorded in England".

251

PAS 10008

SIDE ONE

HARI'S ON TOUR (EXPRESS)
(Instrumental)
Music by George Harrison
© 1974 Oops Publishing Ltd.

SIMPLY SHADY
Somebody brought the juices
I thought I'd take a sip
Came off the rails so crazy
My senses took a dip
Before the bottle hit the floor
And I'd had have to think
I was blinded by desire
The elephant turned pink

The rest is simply shady
It's all been done before
But it doesn't make life simple
That's for sure
You may think about a lady
Cause yourself a minor war
And your life won't be so easy anymore

No colour had I seen it
When I began to reap
I was torn from shallow water
And plunged into the deep
And I started drowning
I clung onto a straw
That somehow kept me floating
While my madness craved for more

The rest is simply shady
It's all been done before
But it doesn't make life simple
That's for sure
You may think of Sexy Sadie
Let joy in through your front door
Andyour life won't be so easy anymore

Words & Music by George Harrison
Copyright © 1974 Oops Publishing Ltd.
Used by permission. All rights reserved
International Copyright secured

SO SAD
Now the winter has come
To eclipse out the sun
That has lighted my love for sometime
And a cold wind now blows
Not much tenderness flows
From the heart of someone feeling so tired
And he feels so alone
With no love of his own
So sad, so bad, so sad, so bad

While his memory raced
With much speed and great haste
Through the problems of being there
In his heart at arms length
Held within its great strength
To ward off such great despair
And he feels so alone
With no love of his own
So sad, so bad, so sad, so bad

Take the dawn of the day
And give it away
To someone who can fill the part
Of the dream we once held

Now it's got to be shelved
It's too late to make a new start
And he feels so alone
With no love of his own
So sad, so bad, so sad, so bad

Words & Music by George Harrison
Copyright ©1974 Oops Publishing Ltd.
Used by permission. All rights reserved
International Copyright secured

BYE BYE, LOVE
Bye bye love
Bye bye happiness
Hello loneliness
I think I'm gonna cry

Bye bye love
Bye bye sweet caress
Hello emptiness
I know I'm gonna die
Goodbye my love bye bye bye

There goes our baby
With a "you know who"
I hope she's happy
And "old Clapper" too!
We had good rhythm
(and a little slide)
Then she stepped in
(what a favour)
I threw them both out.

(MMM) goodbye happiness
Hello loneliness
Bye bye my love bye bye
(MMM) bye bye love of doom
It's a gonna be a raining out of doors
(MMMM) hello happiness (MMM)
Goodbye my love goodbye

Now I'm into romance
I stay away from love
Got tired of ladies (ooh ooh)
That plat and shove me
And that's the reason
We all can (see) so clearly
They see that our lady
Is not on a 'green'

Bye bye love
Bye bye happiness
Hello loneliness
Think I'm gonna cry

Bye bye love
Bye bye happiness
Hello emptiness

Composed by F. Bryant & B. Bryant
Copyright © 1957 Acuff Rose Music Ltd.
Used by permission. All rights reserved
(Parody lyrics added by George Harrison and
permission to use given for this album only.)

MÀYA LOVE
Màya Love — Màya Love,
Màya Love is like the sea
Flowing in and out of me
Màya Love — Màya Love,
Màya Love is like the day
First it comes, then it rolls away
Màya Love — Màya Love,
Màya Love is like the wind
Blowing hard on everything
Màya Love — Màya Love,
Màya Love is like the rain
Beating on your window brain
Màya Love — Màya Love,
Màya Love is like a stream
Flowing through this cosmic dream

Words & Music by George Harrison
Copyright © 1974 Oops Publishing Ltd.
Used by permission. All rights reserved
International Copyright secured

SIDE TWO

DING DONG; DING DONG
Ring out the old
Ring in the new
Ring out the old
Ring in the new

Ring out the false
Ring in the true
Ring out the old
Ring in the new

Ding-dong, ding-dong
Ding-dong, ding-dong
Ding-dong, ding-dong
Ding-dong, ding-dong

Yesterday, today was tomorrow
And tomorrow, today will be yesterday
So ring out the old
Ring in the new
Ring out the old
Ring in the new

Ring out the false
Ring in the true
Ring out the old
Ring in the new

Ding-dong, ding-dong
Ding-dong, ding-dong
Ding-dong, ding-dong
Ding-dong, ding-dong

Words & Music by George Harrison
Copyright © 1974 Oops Publishing Ltd.
Used by permission. All rights reserved
International Copyright secured

DARK HORSE
You thought that you knew where I was
and when
But it looks like you've been foolin' you again.
You thought that you'd got me all stranded out
But baby looks like I've been breaking out

I'm a dark horse
Running on a dark race course
I'm a blue moon
Since I stepped from out of the womb
I've been a cool jock
Looking for the source
I'm a dark horse.

You thought you had got me in your grip
Baby looks like you was not so smart
And I became too slippery for you
But let me say that I was nothing new.

I'm a dark horse
Running on a dark race course
I'm a blue moon
Since I picked up my first spoon
I've been a used jock
Looking for the source
I'm a dark horse

I thought that you knew it all along
Until you started getting me not right
Seems as if you heard a little late
But I warned you when
We both were at the starting gate

I'm a dark horse
Running on a dark course
I'm a blue moon
Since I stepped from out of the womb
I've been a cool jock
Cooking at the source
I'm a dark horse.

Words & Music by George Harrison
Copyright © 1974 Oops Publishing Ltd.
Used by permission. All rights reserved
International Copyright secured

FAR EAST MAN
While the world wages war
it gets harder to see
Who your friends really are
I won't let him down
Got to do what I can
I won't let him drown
He's a far east man

All three ups and those downs
Makes me question what love is
Is it a fix or worthwhile
I won't let him down
Got to do what I can
I won't let him drown
He's a far east man

Sometime is so short
And in the long is losing
Wondering if it is
Or if I'm wrong
Even then my heart seems
To be the one to change
Can only do what it tells me

We can't let them down
We've got to do what we can
We can't let them drown
He's a far east man

Looks like right here on earth
God, it's hellish at times
But I feel that's heaven's in sight
And I can't let him down
Got to do what I can
I can't let him drown
He's a far east man

Words by George Harrison
Music by George Harrison & Ron Wood
Copyright © 1974 Oops Publishing Ltd.
Used by permission. All rights reserved
International Copyright secured

IT IS "HE" (JAI SRI KRISHNA)
Jai krishna jai krishna krishna
Jai krishna jai sri krishna
Jai radhe jai radhe radhe
Jai radhe jai sri radhe
Jai krishna jai krishna krishna
Jai krishna jai sri krishna
Jai radhe jai radhe radhe
Jai radhe jai sri radhe

He whose name have been
What our lives have been
And who we really are
It is 'HE'
Jai sri krishna

Jai krishna . . . . . (as above)
He whose sweetness flows
Yo be the one to change
That raves to look His way
See His smile
Jai sri radhe

Jai krishna . . . . . (as above)
He who is complete
Three worlds at His feet
Cause of every star
It is 'HE'
Jai sri krishna

Jai krishna . . . . . (as above)
Words & Music by George Harrison
Copyright © 1974 Oops Publishing Ltd.
Used by permission. All rights reserved
International Copyright secured

G & L

Above: Chile edition.
Below: USA edition
(left) and Venezuela
edition (right).

DARK HORSE
GEORGE HARRISON
Side one: Hari's on Tour (Express) / Simply Shady / So Sad / Bye Bye, Love (Felice Bryant, Boudleaux Bryant, George Harrison) / Mãya Love
Side two: Ding Dong; Ding Dong / Dark Horse / Far East Man (George Harrison, Ron Wood) / It Is 'He' (Jai Sri Krishna)
UK release: 20 December 1974; Apple PAS 10008; chart high; failed to chart.
US release: 9 December 1974; Apple SMAS 3418; chart high; number 4.
Produced by George Harrison.

George Harrison (vocals, electric and acoustic guitars, Moog synthesizer, electric piano, harmonium, bass, percussion, gubgubbi, drums, backing vocals), Tom Scott (saxophones, flute and horn arrangements), Billy Preston (electric piano, organ, piano), Willie Weeks (bass), Andy Newmark (drums, percussion), Jim Keltner (drums, percussion), Robben Ford (electric guitar, acoustic guitar), Jim Horn (flute), Chuck Findley (flute), Emil Richards (percussion), Ringo Starr (drums), Klaus Voormann (bass), Gary Wright (piano), Nicky Hopkins (piano), Roger Kellaway (piano, organ), Max Bennett (bass), John Guerin (drums), Ron Wood (electric guitar), Alvin Lee (electric guitar), Mick Jones (acoustic guitar), Derrek Van Eaton (backing vocals), Lon Van Eaton (backing vocals).

Visiting Shankar in early '74, Harrison suggested they tour Europe and America together. The shows would follow the format established with the Concert for Bangladesh but without the superstar guests. It would be a good way to promote his new label, his new acts and his new album. But it wasn't enough to simply promote Shankar and Dark Horse Records, EMI/Capitol wanted Beatle related product in the shops to coincide with the proposed tour. The only problem was that Harrison didn't have a new album ready to release. All he had was half an unfinished work in progress. He had no other option than to finish the album quickly, and that piled on the pressure. Now he had to juggle three albums (Splinter, Shankar and his own) and prepare for his first solo tour. The European leg of the tour with Shankar was quietly dropped. Shankar went out on his own and performed a short tour of Europe, which closed with a show at the Royal Albert Hall on 23 September.

While Shankar was on the road wowing audiences with his orchestra of classically trained Indian musicians, Harrison was sweating over a hot mixing desk desperately trying to pull his album together. *Dark Horse* was an album recorded on the run by a musician who spread himself too thin and was close to burning out. Tracking sessions began in November 1973 while Harrison was still fully immersed in producing Splinter's *The Place I Love* album. While he'd spent hours perfecting every note recorded for

Splinter's album, his own recordings appeared hurried and workmanlike. Calling upon the same rhythm section who'd played on *Living in the Material World*, Harrison the cut basic tracks for 'Ding Dong; Ding Dong', an early version of 'Dark Horse', and 'So Sad'.

Harrison gave 'So Sad' to Alvin Lee, who issued his version on Alvin Lee and Mylon Le Fevre *Road To Freedom* in November '73. Lee's version featured Harrison on guitar and backing vocals and Lee returned the favour by playing guitar on 'Ding Dong; Ding Dong'. This probably took place sometime after Harrison's return from India in early '74 because the version Harrison sent to David Geffen shortly before leaving for India doesn't feature any guitar overdubs. Ron Wood also played on the track and would co-write 'Far East Man' with Harrison.

In April, Harrison went to see Joni Mitchell at the New Victoria Theatre in London to check out her backing band L.A. Express. He'd already met the band's saxophone player, Tom Scott, whilst working on the *Shankar Family & Friends* album in Los Angeles. Harrison hung out with the band that night and invited them back to his house with a view to booking them for his forthcoming tour. "I was the first Western musician he'd approached about the possibility of going on tour this year," explained Scott. "I worked on several of the tracks that had already begun, most of which involved some of the guys – Weeks, Preston and Newmark – who also came on tour. I think the connections were made during the recording of Ron Wood's album. They wanted me to play on it, but I was with Joni then. Somehow we all connected. I'd played on 'Will It Go Round In Circles' on Billy's album, but I didn't know him that well. We've all come to be close friends now through our mutual association with George. Because of where he lives, he doesn't have the chance to get the best sidemen he can, so he has to fly guys in or bring them in one at a time. For the most part that's how the album was made – in pieces. All in all it turned out quite well," said Scott.[14]

L.A. Express arrived at Harrison's house in the early afternoon, but Harrison was still in bed. Having reverted to the recording routine favoured by The Beatles, he was working through the night and eventually appeared about teatime. But recording didn't start until much later. "We started recording about 1 in the morning," recalled Robben Ford, "until about 7am. You can imagine there were things to keep you up."[15] Harrison broke the ice and put the band through its paces by jamming on a half finished melody he'd been working on before moving on to record a song he had finished, 'Simply Shady'.

With a slack handful of half finished backing tracks in the can, Harrison took a break from recording to finish the Splinter and Shankar albums and to set up his new record label. In July, he guested on Ron Wood's album playing guitar and singing backing vocals on 'Far East Man'. During this session he met drummer Andy Newmark and bassist Willie Weeks, both of whom would feature in his touring band. Along with Billy Preston and Tom Scott they would start work on another batch of Harrisongs in late October. This line-up recorded 'Māya Love', 'Far East Man', 'It Is 'He' (Jai Sri Krishna)' and 'His Name Is Legs', which Harrison used to close his 1975 album *Extra Texture*. They also recorded a re-make of 'Dark Horse' that replaced the version recorded with Starr, Voormann et al. earlier in the year. While in Los Angeles, Harrison also cut solo versions of 'Bye Bye, Love' and 'I Don't Care Anymore'. The album was finished with a burst of activity that took place over 30 and 31 October. Harrison overdubbed vocals onto several tracks, Jim Horn and Chuck Findley overdubbed flutes and Emil Richards added wobble board to 'It Is 'He' (Jai Sri Krishna)'.

If the album disappoints musically; lyrically and thematically it's as revealing and personal as his two previous albums and then some. Documenting the breakdown of his marriage and a return to a more worldly lifestyle that he'd thought he'd left behind him; it's possibly one of the most poignant albums he made. Speaking at a pre-tour press conference, he said: "If you get my album, it's like *Peyton Place*. I mean, it will tell you exactly what I've been doing..."[16] *Dark Horse* is Harrison's *Plastic Ono Band* album. At times it's a heartbreaking, bewildering and demanding. It's not an easy album to listen to because Harrison's life wasn't pleasant when he wrote it. If *Living In The Material World* had found him caught in the horns of a spiritual dilemma, *Dark Horse* demonstrates just how human and fallible he was. There's no shying away from the ugly truth, this album is utterly challenging.

Having become the brightest star in The Beatles, outshining both Lennon and McCartney, he had become the victim of his own success. Tired of the limelight, all he wanted was to wander to the back of the stage and do what he did best – be a musician. Harrison never was a showman and *Dark Horse* was his attempt to smash that illusion in much the same way his friend and peer Bob Dylan did with *Self Portrait*. *Dark Horse* was the very antithesis of what people had come to expect from a Harrison album. It's deliberately understated, lacking in melodic invention, uncharacteristically worldly, sloppy and just a little grubby.

Only two years earlier, Harrison had appeared every inch the rock star god, dressed from head to toe in a white suit, slinging a white Fender guitar and surrounded by some of the biggest stars in the rock cosmos. Now he looked like the kind of down and out hippie you'd cross the street to avoid making eye contact with. Whether or not it was consciously designed to distance him from his public it worked. While *Dark Horse* sold well in America it did not chart in Britain.

Dark Horse data

Apple issued *Dark Horse* in a gatefold sleeve with printed inner sleeve and lyric sheet. The record labels were customized and based on photographs of Harrison's and the future Mrs. Harrison's eyes. Initial American pressings reproduced the labels in pale blue, which made reading the label text difficult. Later pressings reproduced the labels in black. Some copies of the American edition also featured a 3½ inch circular sticker adhered to the shrink wrap. The sticker has 'George Harrison' in red in the upper half and 'Dark Horse' also in red in the bottom half, the centre reads 'Includes the hits/Dark Horse/Ding Dong Ding Dong/Maya Love/Far East Man/And Other Hits'.

Hari's on Tour (Express)
George Harrison (electric guitar), Tom Scott (saxophones), Robben Ford (electric guitar), Roger Kellaway (piano), Max Bennett (bass), John Guerin (drums)

George Harrison was a big star when *Dark Horse* was issued in the winter of 1974. He was more than a star, he was a star maker. Whether he'd planned it or not, his career had gone supernova and in terms of success he'd very nearly out Beatled The Beatles. But you wouldn't know that if all you had to go on was 'Hari's on Tour (Express)'. His friend, Bob Dylan, had chosen to open his tenth album, *Self Portrait*, with a minimalist composition that didn't even feature him singing. Harrison chose to open his album in a similar manner. Like Dylan, Harrison was being provocative, if not bloody-minded. He wasn't going to give fans the very thing they wanted or expected. That would have been too much like playing the game, and he wasn't about to do that. Speaking after the tour, Tom Scott concluded: "They [the fans] have to try and understand that George is an ex-Beatle. He has other interests, other musical interests, other musicians he prefers to the Beatles for musical reasons. I don't think there's anything wrong with that. If he wanted to, I think that would be great. But he does not, so let the guy do what the heck he wants. He's a tremendous talent."[17]

According to Tom Scott, Harrison invited L.A. Express over to his house for a social visit. Never one to waste an opportunity, he put them to work in the studio. They were hardly going to say no. After all, he was a Beatle. Okay, an ex-Beatle. "He asked us to play – an instrumental tune. I made a lead sheet for the band, we went into the studio and a couple of hours later we had a track that's now called 'Hari's On Tour Express'," explained Scott.[18] It's the kind of instrumental that bands jam on at sound checks. Somebody comes up with a riff, in this case Harrison, and the rest of the band jump on it. As Max Bennett explained it was all very spontaneous, "He had an idea and we just latched onto it. There wasn't anything arranged, we just sort of ambled down the musical path until we came to some place where we felt it sounded good".[19]

Jamming with L.A. Express, Harrison took a step backwards to a time when he was content to lurk in the shadows with Delaney, Bonnie and Clapton and chop out some snappy rhythm guitar licks while those with bigger egos stood centre stage. 'Hari's on Tour (Express)' didn't even sound much like a Harrison record. Where were the beautifully arranged acoustic guitars? Where was the distinctive Harrison vocal? Where was the spirituality? The only thing that remained from the sonic signature of his recent past was his slide guitar, and even that didn't match his previous high standards. It's as if he decided to play sideman on his own album. He's just one of the boys and to make the point the track opens with his guitar sharing the same sonic space as Robben Ford's pithy rhythm stabs and Roger Kellaway's piano. He doesn't step into the limelight until 20 seconds into the track and even then he's introduced by a prominent pedal-steel inspired lick played by Ford.

Opening an album with something as musically unadventurous as this was an act of deliberate provocation. It was a strategy he shared with his old band mates and was his way of de-constructing the Beatle myth and his own superstar status. Some critics considered it an act as breathtaking egotism. The *NME*'s Bob Woffinden thought Harrison was: "someone whose universe is confined to himself. And his guru ..."[20] He was right, but for the wrong reasons. Woffinden had obviously chosen to forget that that's what artists do. They write about themselves and their experiences, and when they do it well they transcend the humdrum and point to something magical. That's what made Harrison a star. Unfortunately, 'Hari's on Tour (Express)' wasn't great art, nor was it transcendent, but it rocked, in parts, and it certainly helped disassemble the myth that was Beatle George.

Simply Shady
George Harrison (vocals, electric guitar), Tom Scott (saxophones), Robben Ford (electric guitar), Roger Kellaway (piano), Max Bennett (bass), John Guerin (drums)

Harrison's Roman Catholic roots surface in this dark confessional. It's a sorry but all too familiar tale of rock 'n' roll excess and contrition. In his biography, Harrison said: "'Simply Shady' is about what happens to naughty boys in the music business."[21] When he wrote the song, he was being a very naughty boy indeed. Like it or not, he was deeply embedded in one of the most hedonistic businesses on the planet. If you weren't that way inclined when you started, the business ensured that you were by the time it had finished with you.

1973 hadn't been a good year for Harrison, drink, drugs and infidelity had seen to that. If previously he had the other Fabs to turn to now he had only himself, and at times that wasn't enough. "I don't have control over nothing. I'd be a fool to think I had control over anything," he told Ben Fong-Torres on the 12 November 1974 for the *Rolling Stone News Service*.[22] He wasn't out of control but he was swerving between periods of piety and hedonism. "He would meditate for hour after hour," explained Pattie Boyd, "Then, as if the pleasures of the flesh were too hard to resist, he would stop meditating, snort coke, have fun, flirting and partying."[23]

It was no different when he hit the road. Talking about his time on tour with Harrison, Robben Ford said: "there was a tremendous amount of drugs around. And drugs don't do anyone any good [laughs]. But, as a person, he was very kind to me. I always use the word 'kind' because these people were older and more sophisticated than me. I was just really a bumpkin from a little Northern California town, kind of thrust into the world. So the whole thing was a bit overwhelming for me."[24]

Harrison was self-medicating to mask the pain brought about by the breakdown of his marriage, but he also turned to song writing to exorcise his demons. 'Simply Shady' was the result. Rather than keeping his weaknesses hidden in the dark corners of his life, Harrison came out of the closet to confess his sins to the world. He did so with a candid honestly that was largely overlooked at the time. He even went as far as to alert the media to his guilty secrets when quizzed by them at the November press conference that launched his tour and album. But they appeared to miss the clues he planted.

'Simply Shady' extends the metaphors he'd employed on his previous album to describe his relationship with the material and spiritual worlds. He may have wandered from the spiritual path, but he hadn't abandoned it completely. Andy Newmark remarked: "I'm sure that George's whole religious thing was, in a sense, his way of keeping himself grounded while having to be on his own."[25] As was noted earlier, Harrison had caught himself long before the press had caught onto his indiscretions. Recognising that he had a problem was the first step on the road to recovery.

So Sad

George Harrison (vocals, 12-string acoustic guitars, electric guitar, electric pianos, slide guitars, backing vocals), Nicky Hopkins (piano), Ringo Starr (drums), Jim Keltner (drums), Willie Weeks (bass)

'So Sad' was written by a man who'd gained the world but lost his soul. To the outside world, Harrison had it all. That was certainly what Eric Clapton thought. The god-like guitarist wanted what his friend had, and that included his wife. "I coveted Pattie because she belonged to a powerful man who seemed to have everything I wanted – amazing cars, an incredible career and a beautiful wife," he wrote in his biography.[26] But privately Harrison was a tired, stateless and lonely man. Sex and drugs and rock 'n' roll had taken its toll. "Friar Park was a madhouse," Pattie confessed, "We were all as drunk, stoned and single-minded as the other. Nobody seemed to have appointments, deadlines, or anything pressing in their lives, no structure and no responsibilities..."[27]

This bohemian attitude extended to their marriage. Both had affairs, and by the time Harrison wrote 'So Sad', Clapton had made his intentions clear. A constant presence at the Harrisons Henley-on-Thames home, he did little to hide his feelings for the future Mrs. Clapton. A year before Harrison penned 'So Sad', Clapton poured his feelings into a pained song of unrequited love, 'Layla'. While he attempted to mask his feelings by referring to a 12th-century poem by Nizami Ganjavi, only a fool would have failed to spot his message.

A year after Clapton made his feelings known, Harrison found himself in New York. Alone and lonely he put pen to paper and let his emotions run free. Harrison calls on the bleakness of winter as a metaphor for the death of something that once filled him with love. It's as dark and desolate a picture of sadness as has ever made its way onto record. As Harrison said: "It's depressing. It is so sad." But through this grey, swirling maelstrom of wretchedness he recalls a memory of what had been. As with 'Here Comes The Sun' the rising sun represents hope and a new beginning. But it offers little solace for Harrison. Instead, he offers it as a gift to his usurper in the hope that it will bring him what he once had.

Before recording the song Harrison gave it to Alvin Lee, who, in the summer of 1973, recorded the song with Mylon LeFevre. Lee was in the process of building a studio at Woodcote near Henley-on-Thames, and like Harrison liked to record at night. "We'd come in here [to record] about dark," recalled LeFevre. "We'd go on until about 4:pm the next afternoon, thinking it was still dark outside. We'd been up two days doing things in here and George Harrison would be asleep for two days and he'd come over. He'd be ready and raring to go, and we'd get into it again."[28] Harrison added dobro to their wistful interpretation of his desolate break-up song. Issued as a single, and on the album *On The Road To Freedom*, 'So Sad (No Love Of His Own)' received mixed reviews. Reviewed in *Circus* magazine it was described as a 'genuine country tearjerker'. However, the *New Musical Express* considered it 'disappointingly Harrisonesque'.

Harrison began recording his own version in November '73 with the usual crew of Ringo Starr, Klaus Voormann, Jim Keltner and Nicky Hopkins. (Voormann's bass part was replaced by Willie Weeks when Harrison moved to Los Angeles to finish the album.) Recorded in the relaxed settings of Friar Park it has all the hallmarks of a great Harrison song and production. The instrumentation is sparse, but exquisitely played, the arrangement gives Harrison's vocal and guitar acres of space while the dynamics provide drama. Harrison's double-tracked acoustic guitar plays a key role in establishing the mood of the song; it is as clear and cold as the icy wind blowing through his soul. His slide guitar licks complement the melody, taking it in new and unexpected directions that draw the listener deeper into the song. While his vocal sounds burdened with fatigue and anguish in the verses, the harmonic lift in the chorus does much to counterbalance the sense of despair established in the opening bars of the song. Harrison's reading isn't as contemplative as Lee and LeFevre's but it's not as depressing as he'd have you believe either.

Bye Bye, Love (Felice Bryant, Boudleaux Bryant, George Harrison)
George Harrison (vocals, 12-string acoustic guitars, electric guitars, electric piano, bass guitar, Moog synthesiser, drums, drum machine, bongos)

From despair to where? Well, revenge. When speaking to the media, Harrison made light of his recent marital break-up and the role Eric Clapton played in it. Asked if he'd delivered a musical rebuttal to 'Layla' on his album, he lied. "That's a bit nasty," he said. "I'd like to sort that one out. Eric Clapton has been a close friend for years. I'm very happy about it. Because he's great. I'd rather she was with him than some other dope."[29] In truth, he had included a musical rebuttal and a nasty one at that.

Harrison would later dismiss 'Bye Bye, Love' as a joke. But there can be little doubt that at the time this poison pen letter was designed to cause maximum hurt to Pattie and her new beau. His attempt to free himself of Pattie reeks of self-pity and was remarkably inconsistent in attitude and approach. Speaking to Alan Freeman on 18 October 1974, Harrison said: "People embrace happiness and the good, and un-happiness, they don't want to know about it. But the mere fact that you embrace good means you've laid yourself wide open to the bad because the bad and the good are just part of one whole. You have to discipline yourself not to go too up when good things happen in order that you don't go too down when it's bad."[30] If only he practiced what he preached.

'Bye Bye, Love' is the musical ramblings of a bitter, ill-disciplined rock star. Unfortunately for Pattie her ex-husband had access to the means of production to make this sorry song public. It had no place on *Dark Horse* and should have remained under lock and key far away from public scrutiny. Unfortunately Harrison's judgement was as shot as his voice and he was desperately short of material. In light of what he said elsewhere, there can be no reason for it making the final cut other than revenge.

Two years later he revisited the song while rehearsing for his appearance on *Saturday Night Live* with Paul Simon. Stripped of vitriol it retains the bitter-sweet character of the original. If only he'd remained true to the original when recording the song for *Dark Horse*, he would have made his point with more style and grace and saved himself a critical bashing to boot.

Māya Love

George Harrison (vocals, slide guitars, acoustic guitar, backing vocals), Billy Preston (electric piano), Tom Scott (saxophones, horn arrangement), Willie Weeks (bass), Andy Newmark (drums, shaker)

'Māya Love' began as a slide guitar piece to which Harrison added lyrics later. Reproduced in his biography *I Me Mine* are two sets of lyrics. In one the song is titled 'My Love', in the other 'Māya Love'. The change was subtle but significant. It turns something personal into something universal. It's no longer a song about his love, but a song about what love is. Attempting to explain the song Harrison said: "It's like, if you take a flower, it's made out of petals and it's made out of leaves and it's made out of the stem and all the little bits. But if you take the petals, it's made out of sap, and the leaves are made out of sap, it's all made out of sap. So the sap is the cause and the effect is the petals and the leaves. So then, love, which is like the day or night, or up and down, or in and out, or rich and poor, or black and white; love based upon duality, that is, I love you when you do this, or I love you when it's summer, or I love you if you smile at me, or I love you but... Māya is the illusion that it isn't all the one thing really."[31]

Once again Harrison employs naturally occurring phenomenon, water, wind and light as similes. Like the romantic poets and artists of the 19th century, he draws on the power, glory and beauty of the natural world to remind us that it is all God's work. Like them, he equated the natural world with the spiritual. Nature is a source of healthy emotions and ideas that oppose the polluted, industrialized material world that is the source of unhealthy emotions, morals, and thoughts. Speaking at the press conference called to launch the tour, he said: "We're all so conditioned, and our consciousness have been polluted with material energy that it's hard to pull it all away in order to reveal our true nature."[32] Warming to the subject, he continued: "Everyone of us has [...] the same qualities as God. Just like a drop of the ocean has the same qualities as the whole ocean, each one of us has the potential. Everybody is looking for something, but we are it. It's right there within ourselves. All we have to do is try and slow down the pollution of our senses and of our consciousness and try and unveil that which is already within us."[33]

Harrison's way of detoxing was to become a gardener, to work with and enjoy God's gift of nature. He'd often use his garden to instigate conversations about spirituality. Olivia Harrison recalled one such occasion: "I might have said, 'Oh, your bit of the garden looks great', to which he would reply, 'It's not my garden, Liv'. It was his way of reminding himself that we are pure Spirit, and that the Spirit is in every grain of sand, belonging to everyone and no one; that nothing is 'mine' and that the 'I' we all refer to must be recognized as the little 'i' in the larger scheme of the universe. George was tired of all the I Me Mines of this world, including his own."[34] 'Māya Love', then, is about seeing through the illusions that we've created to reveal the true nature of love – its spiritual nature. It's about recognizing our potential, our place within the cosmic scheme and about freeing ourselves of possessions, and that includes the ones we love.

Working with L.A. Express, Harrison laid down a funky groove as a bed for his slide guitar and vocals. There's not a lot going on melodically, like most funk tracks, it's the groove that's important. Harrison was increasingly drawn to the mellower side of funky soul. His Dark Horse record label was peppered with soul funk hybrids from the white boy funk of Jiva to the first family of soul The Stairsteps. Harrison would employ three quarters of the multi-racial funk band Attitudes to record his next album, *Extra Texture*, and eventually sign the band to Dark Horse. The reason for Harrison's move away from rock to mellower, more soulful music was simple, he liked it and was growing tired of constantly repeating himself. "There's a lot of music I listen to, which is popular music, which just makes me uptight," he told Dave Herman, "Even if I'm not listening too closely to it, it's just the sound of it, and the repetition, the boring repetition of how it's played."[35] Soul music had the opposite effect. That's why he liked it and played it.

Ding Dong; Ding Dong
George Harrison (vocals, 12-string acoustic guitar, slide guitars, electric piano, harmonium, percussion, backing vocals), Tom Scott (saxophones, horn arrangement), Gary Wright (piano), Klaus Voormann (bass), Jim Keltner (drums, percussion), Ringo Starr (drums), Ron Wood (electric guitar), Alvin Lee (electric guitar), Mick Jones (acoustic guitar), uncredited tubular bells, uncredited female choir

The walls of Friar Park did more than keep a roof over Harrison's head, they inspired him. The original owner and designer of the house, Sir Francis Crisp, had a quirky sense of humour that mirrored Harrison's. Crisp had a habit of adorning the walls of the house with quotations from his favourite poems or his own quirky aphorisms. Harrison found them intriguing, humorous and inspirational. "Sir Frank helped my awareness; whatever it was I felt became stronger or found more expression by moving into the house, because everything stepped up or was heightened. The thing about Sir Frank with his advice, like: 'scan not a friend with a microscopic glass...' I mean that helped me actively to ease up on whomsoever I thought I loved, gave me that consciousness not to hang onto the negative side of it, to be more forgiving," Harrison wrote in his biography.[36]

On one wall Crisp had inscribed a line from Alfred, Lord Tennyson's poem *Ring out, wild bells*. Harrison decided to use it in a song and combined it with another line of unknown origins that he found carved on the wall of a garden building. "'Ding Dong; Ding Dong' was the quickest song I ever wrote. It took me three minutes, except it took me four years of looking at the thing, which was written on the wall at my home, 'Ring out the old, ring in the new. Ring out the false, ring in the truth,' before I realized it was a hit song. It makes me laugh because it's so simple. That song evaded me for years," he explained.[37]

'Ding Dong; Ding Dong' would take considerably longer to record that it took to write. The basic track of drums, bass, guitars, piano and guide vocal was recorded in November 1973 and a 'quick mix' of the song sent to David Geffen in the early part of 1974. In the following months Harrison fleshed out the arrangement by adding several more guitar parts, saxophones, percussion and female backing singers. Speaking on the tape he sent to David Geffen, Harrison said of his vocal "some of it's going to be okay and I'll use it, but some of it I don't sing on". Close comparison of the early 'quick mix' with the finished mix reveals that Harrison used all of the guide vocal for the finished record. He didn't replace his guide vocal because by the time he got round to recording overdubs his voice was shot. Although he sounds a little husky in places, his vocal performance is nowhere as disappointing as some would have you believe.

If the vocals weren't up to scratch, the finished backing track was. It swings like Andy Stewarts's sporran at a Hogmanay hootenanny. While it didn't have the swagger or pomp of some contemporary hits, it certainly had all the bonhomie of a well lubricated New Year's Eve sing-along. The repeated 'Ding Dong' refrain and guitar stabs reel you in and once you've been hooked they stay with you long after the record has stopped playing. While the record buying public lapped it up, most critics overlooked its sense of seasonal whimsy. Inspired by an eccentric, recorded by a wisecracking gadfly, it was never intended as anything other than a bit of light-hearted fun.

Harrison was sure he had a hit on his hands, and he did. The single did very well in Europe, particularly in the Benelux states where it made the top ten. It didn't fair as well in the UK or the US, but still managed to crack the top forty in both countries. In the UK, Harrison's ode to the turning of the year was outperformed by Mud, The Wombles, The Goodies, Gilbert O'Sullivan and Showaddywaddy, all of whom had Christmas records in the top thirty. It's lack of success in the UK can be put down to a late release date and too much competition that monopolized airtime on national radio. With the charts and airwaves awash with Christmas songs, Harrison's seasonal effort got lost in the scramble to be top of the pops at Christmas and has subsequently been incorrectly labelled a flop.

Far East Man
George Harrison (vocals, electric guitar, slide guitar, backing vocals), Tom Scott (saxophones, horn arrangement), Billy Preston (electric piano), Willie Weeks (bass), Andy Newmark (drums, shaker, tambourine)

Ronnie Wood began recording his début album at his home in Richmond Hill in 1973. A constant flow of hangers on, actors and musicians passed through its doors, several of whom ended up playing on the album. Writing in his autobiography, Wood said: "Whoever came over would bring their instrument or they'd pick up whatever they could find lying around, and we'd play."[38] Harrison was a regular guest at the Wood's house and during one visit wrote the verse section of what became 'Far East Man' with his new friend. Wood wanted the song for his album and asked Harrison to finish it. Harrison added a middle-eight and finished the lyrics as he was driving to Wood's house to record the song. When he got there, Wood was wearing a tee-shirt with the wording 'Far East Man' – The Faces had recently completed a tour of the Far East – that became the title.

Wood recorded his version with Harrison contributing vocals and slide guitar. Remarkably similar to Harrison's later re-make, Wood's version has a busier slide guitar part which Harrison would refine for his own version. The song's minor seven chord changes and jazzy inversions suited Wood to a tee. A consummate sides-man with a knack of complementing a melody with tasteful licks, it was tailor made for him.

Harrison recorded his version with the same rhythm section that played on Wood's recording, but added Billy Preston on electric piano and Tom Scott on saxophone. Scott's saxophone replaces most of the slide guitar parts that Harrison employed for Wood's recording, but when Harrison does add some slide guitar, it's typically refined, tasteful and played with a feather-light touch. Although Harrison dedicated the song to Frank Sinatra, it would have suited Smokey Robinson better. At times Harrison imitates Robinson's falsetto vocal style with singular ease, proof, if any where needed, that he could sing his socks off when not incapacitated with laryngitis.

When asked by Alan Freeman if he had any downfalls in assessing friendships, Harrison answered by playing the first verse of 'Far East Man'. An acknowledgement of human frailties, both his own and others, it is a song shot through with stoic fortitude. As phlegmatic as his assessment is, it's hope and love that inspired Harrison. 'Far East Man' is a contemplation on friendship and Dharma – living life in harmony with the laws of the physical and spiritual worlds. In the preceding years Harrison had experienced dizzying highs and deep lows. It was time to re-establish order, harmony and re-build relationships.

'Far East Man' finds Harrison addressing these issues. The song begins with the world thrown into turmoil by war. Harrison extends the theme in the second verse with reference to his own anxiety. He paints a desolate picture of depression and inner turmoil which finds him struggling to overcome his doubts and deal with the vicissitudes of daily life. Each verse ends with a metaphor – drowning – that represents emotional and spiritual suffocation. Harrison finds the answer in his heart and declares; 'Got to do what I can. I won't let him drown'. It's not in his heart to surrender to negativity or to let his friend succumb to hopelessness. It's always darkest before the dawn, but Harrison's optimism shines bright. "What I'm trying to say is, we've all got faults, but don't accent the faults or look at the faults through a microscope and then start criticizing the faults. Take the good and try and emphasize that in the hope that they will overpower the faults rather than feed the faults," he explained.[39] By the end, he's concluded that while at times it might be miserable on earth with discipline, love and a strong moral compass eternal bliss awaits us all.

It Is 'He' (Jai Sri Krishna)

George Harrison (vocals, acoustic guitar, gubgubbi, Moog synthesizer, percussion, backing vocals), Billy Preston (piano, organ), Tom Scott (flute), Jim Horn (flute), Chuck Findley (flute), Willie Weeks (bass), Andy Newmark (drums), Emil Richards (wobbleboard)

The most significant song on the album, at least as far as Harrison was concerned, is 'It Is 'He' (Jai Sri Krishna)'. Before heading to Los Angeles in the spring of 1974, Harrison went to India to visit his friend Ravi Shankar and attend the opening ceremony for his new house in Benares. While there Shankar arranged for them to visit Vrindavan where Krishna had lived 4000 years previously. The city, one of the holiest in India, is full of ancient temples and spiritual masters. According to Harrison "the whole town is Krishna conscious". The experience was one of the most spiritual he ever had. "It's fantastic to be in a place where the whole town is [chanting]. And I also got the idea that they were knocked out at the idea of seeing some white person chanting on beads. Vrindavan is one of the holiest cities in India. Everyone, everywhere chants Hare Krishna. It was my most fantastic experience," he recalled.[40]

Inspired by Sripad Maharaj, the spiritual master who was his guide, Harrison took the devotional song he'd been singing at morning prayers, gave it a Western twist, added some words of his own and 'It Is 'He' (Jai Sri Krishna)' was born. He'd done something similar a few years earlier when he'd taken another Bhajan – a devotional song – and put it to his own music to create 'Gopala Krishna'. The twist, this time, was to incorporate Western lyrics. Harrison incorporated a tempo change to distinguish the two sets of lyrics. The up-tempo sections are particularly uplifting and swing with all the euphoria Harrison must have experienced while chanting in Vrindavan. The resulting song was a pop hybrid that married devotional lyrics with a Western pop melody. Unlike 'My Sweet Lord', where he'd surreptitiously slipped Hare Krishna into the song, this time the reference is explicit.

The basic track was recorded in August and September 1974 as F.P.S.H.O.T. with Preston, Weeks, Scott and Newmark. Harrison must have recorded his vocals during this period because unlike 'Dark Horse', for example, which was recorded entirely in L.A., his vocals show no sign of the hoarseness that marred other tracks on the album. The remaining musical elements were overdubbed at A&M Studios in L.A. in October, with Horn and Findley adding flutes and Richards wobbleboard. Harrison also overdubbed some Indian instruments including gubgubbi and finger cymbals to re-create the atmosphere of Vrindavan. The album *Shankar Family & Friends*, recorded in April 1973, featured the Shankar composition 'I Am Missing You'. "In the original Indian [version], sung mainly by Lakshmi Shankar, we attempted to convey the sounds and atmosphere of Vrindavan, the ancient holy city where Krishna grew up," Shankar explained.[41] The album also included an alternative version with a Western pop arrangement by Harrison that featured flutes and a saxophone part played by Tom Scott. When Harrison came to record 'It Is 'He' (Jai Sri Krishna)', he took a similar mix of instrumentation and styles to create a blend of music that took his original vision for the 'Hare Krishna Mantra' to its logical conclusion.

GEORGE HARRISON

Ding Dong; Ding Dong

Ring out the old 1879
Ring in the new
Ring out the false
Ring in the true

Yesterday, today was tomorrow
And tomorrow, today will be yesterday

So ring out the old
Ring in the new
Ring out the false
Ring in the true

b/w
HARI'S ON TOUR (EXPRESS)

PRINTED IN U.S.A.

Above: American edition with black and white labels. Below: Canadian edition with blue and white labels.

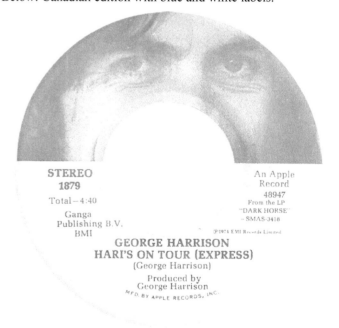

STEREO
R 6002
℗1974 EMI
Records Ltd.
Recorded
in England

An Apple
Record
An EMI
Recording
7YCE 21757
Oops
Publishing Ltd.

GEORGE HARRISON
DING DONG
(George Harrison)
Produced by
George Harrison

269

'Ding Dong; Ding Dong' / 'I Don't Care Anymore'*
GEORGE HARRISON
Produced by George Harrison
UK release: 6 December 1974; Apple R 6002; chart high; number 38.

'Ding Dong; Ding Dong' / 'Hari's on Tour (Express)'
GEORGE HARRISON
Produced by George Harrison
US release: 23 December 1974; Apple 1879; chart high; number 36.

George Harrison (vocals, 12-string acoustic guitar, slide guitars, electric piano, harmonium, percussion, backing vocals), Tom Scott (saxophones, horn arrangement), Gary Wright (piano), Klaus Voormann (bass), Jim Keltner (drums, percussion), Ringo Starr (drums), Ron Wood (electric guitar), Alvin Lee (electric guitar), Mick Jones (acoustic guitar), uncredited tubular bells, uncredited female choir

Issued in Britain on 6 December 1974 as the lead single from *Dark Horse*, 'Ding Dong; Ding Dong' was released with the non-album track 'I Don't Care Anymore' on the B-side. Issued with bespoke labels based on those used for the album, but in blue monochrome rather than black, the single was issued with either a pale blue or white paper sleeve. (The pale blue sleeve has become increasingly difficult to find in recent years.) Demo copies of the single were issued with 'DEMO RECORD NOT FOR SALE' on two lines below the spindle hole with a large 'A' and the release date below.

In America, Apple issued the single with similar labels to the British edition but in black monochrome rather than blue. The American edition flipped the labels with Olivia appearing on the A-side while Harrison appeared on the B-side. The American edition was issued in a picture sleeve with the song lyrics printed on an off-white background with Om symbols and the F.P.S.H.O.T. logo. Demo copies of the single were issued with white labels with black text with a 3:12 edit of the A-side in mono and stereo. In America, where 'I Don't Care Anymore' had already been issued as the B-side to 'Dark Horse', 'Ding Dong; Ding Dong' was backed with with the instrumental 'Hari's on Tour (Express)'.

Harrison compiled a colour promotional film for 'Ding Dong; Ding Dong', a first for him. Although it was screened at the time of release, it did little to promote the single and make it the hit he'd hoped for. 'Ding Dong; Ding Dong' was moderately successful, peaking at number 38 in Britain and number 36 in America. It was more successful in Europe, particularly in Holland and Belgium, where it achieved a chart high of number 10 and number 12 respectively.

THE NEW SINGLE

DING DONG/GEORGE HARRISON

Ring out the old, ring in the new,
Ring out the old, ring in the new
Ring out the false, ring in the true
Ring out the old, ring in the new.

Reprise:

Ding Dong, Ding Dong, Ding Dong, Ding Dong,
Ding Dong, Ding Dong, Ding Dong, Ding Dong,

Yesterday today was tomorrow
And Tomorrow today will be yesterday.
Ring out the old, ring in the new;
Ring out the old, ring in the new.
Ring out the false, ring in the true,
Ring out the old, ring in the new.

Ring out the old, ring in the new;
Ring out the old, ring in the new
Ring out the false, ring in the true
Ring out the old, ring in the new.

Reprise:

Ding Dong, Ding Dong, Ding Dong, Ding Dong
Ding Dong, Ding Dong, Ding Dong, Ding Dong
Dark Ding Horse Dong, Ding Dong, Ding Dong
Dark Ding Horse Dong, Ding Dong, Ding Dong, etc.

Copyright © 1974 Oops Publishing Limited
Reprinted by permission. All rights reserved.
International copyright secured

R6002
Marketed by
EMI Records Limited, 20, Manchester Square, London W1A 1ES

272

1975 : Never Mind The Quality Feel The Texture

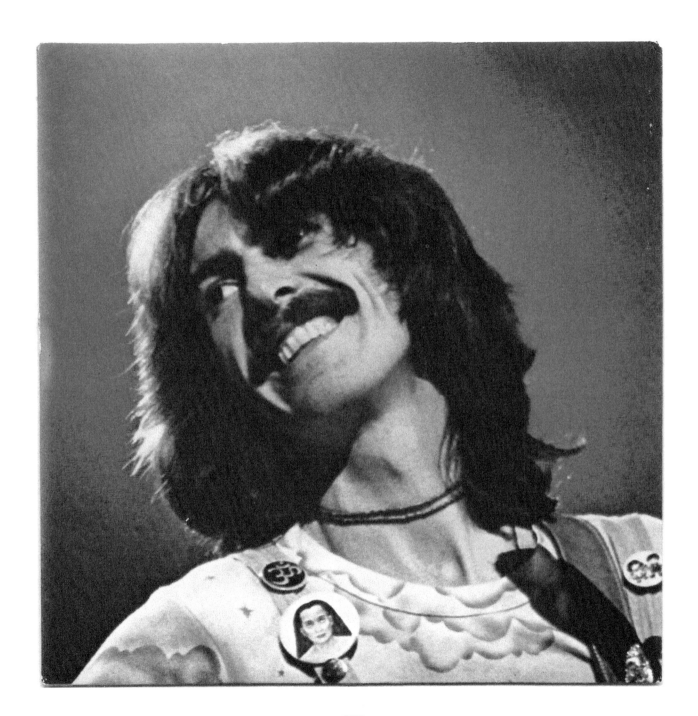

You

George Harrison

From The Album
PAS 10009

George Harrison
EXTRA TEXTURE

apple records
R 6007

'You'* / 'World Of Stone'
GEORGE HARRISON
Produced by George Harrison

UK release: 12 September 1975; Apple R 6007; chart high; number 38.
US release: 15 September 1975; Apple 1884; chart high; number 20.

George Harrison (vocals, electric guitars, backing vocals), Ronnie Spector* (backing vocals), Jim Horn* (saxophone), Leon Russell* (piano), Gary Wright (electric piano*, organ), Carl Radle* (bass), Klaus Voormann (bass), Jim Gordon* (drums, tambourine), David Foster (organ**, string synthesizer**, piano, ARP synthesizer), Jim Keltner (drums), Jesse Ed Davis (electric guitar)
**Overdubbed A&M Studios 31 May 1975

'You' was recorded in February 1971 during sessions for a proposed Ronnie Spector album (see 'Try Some, Buy Some'). Recorded live in the studio with a guide vocal by Harrison, the song was given a rough mix at the end of the session without Harrison's guide vocal. Ronnie Spector added her vocal to the track later, but the track was never finished. Four years later, Harrison decided to re-work the track and use it himself. "I wrote the song specifically for her, and what happened was at that time, Phil put down about six tracks and then finished one as a single and put that out and then never got round to doing the album for some reason. But that song I wrote particularly in the Ronettes sort of flavour, and what happened was I just suddenly remembered that I had this track and it was such a good backing track, so I decided that I'd resurrect it and finish it off because it was only just a basic track. And the song, actually, when I came to sing it, it was so high, my voice has been dropping over the years, but I couldn't believe how high it was, and I realized the key I wrote it in I'd put it up about three tones for Ronnie to sing and then suddenly found myself trying to sing it. It's really high," Harrison explained.[1]

When Harrison arrived in L.A. to record his new album, he dusted off the original backing track and overdubbed additional instrumentation including saxophone, keyboards and a new half-time drum track by Jim Ketlner. Despite having recorded the song in a key that didn't suit his vocal range, his voice had recovered sufficiently to allow him to deliver a soaring vocal with more than a hint of Ronnie Spector about it. An affectionate pastiche of the Brill building love songs that were the popular currency among girl groups like the Ronettes, 'You' captures the spirit and feel of pre-Beatles pop perfectly. It was a fresh, up-beat reincarnation that wiped away the bleak navel gazing of the previous year. Gone too are the spiritual and philosophical references that Harrison had thus far made his stock-in-trade. As trite a comeback as it was, there was nothing about it that even the harshest critic could find off-putting. Indeed, the single did respectable business making the top ten in Canada, the top twenty in America and the top 40 in Britain.

World Of Stone
George Harrison (vocals, electric guitars) Gary Wright (organ), Klaus Voormann (bass), David Foster (piano, ARP string synthesizer), Jim Keltner (drums), Jesse Ed Davis (electric guitar)

Harrison's Roman Catholic roots ran deep and their influence was strong. His brush with Catholicism irritated him to the extent that he attempted to rid himself of it in song on more than one occasion. Yet its papal pull was difficult to escape and songs like 'World Of Stone' walk a thin line between acquiesce and dissent. A confession in which he admits that he is far from perfect, nor the person we imagine him to be, it finds Harrison conceding that he was fallible.

Written in 1973 during a period of soul searching, 'World Of Stone' didn't make it on to *Dark Horse*, but was kept back for *Extra Texture (Read All About It)*. Speaking to Paul Gambaccini in 1975, he said: "I wrote that a couple of years ago, and only just got round to recording it."[2] If previous songs had alluded to his failings, this was the first time he'd actually outed himself in public. Here was a confession of human fallibility. His spirit was weak and worldly desires, which he liked to indulge in as much as the next rock star, had led him from light in to darkness. Klaus Voormann was so disgusted by his fall that he excused himself and never worked with him again.

If only Voormann had paid more attention to what his friend was saying, rather than what he was doing, he might have been more forgiving. Caught in a moment of self-doubt, Harrison asks what his quest for spiritual enlightenment had been for if it could be so quickly forsaken for a few grams of the devil's dandruff? His conclusion was that he was wiser, but no more enlightened. It may have come as a shock to him at the time, but it was something he grew to accept. As Shakespeare said: "We all are men, in our own natures frail, and capable of our flesh; few are angels." Harrison knew he was no angel, and the older he got the more he learnt to accept it.

Harrison began recording 'World Of Stone' on 2 May and completed it 2 June. He set his soul-searching to a soft rock shuffle that was fairly typical of the kind being made in California at the time. It shouldn't, however, be mistaken as merely the product of a coked up L.A. session scene or some bland, formulaic FM radio-friendly confection. Harrison's melody, vocal and production are infused with soul, the kind of soul that conveys pain rather than the tawdry hollowness of the L.A. experience. His singing expresses a depth of emotion that is absent from the Tin Pan Alley blandness that is too often mistaken for soul music. When Harrison sings the opening lines his voice is cracked with emotion that tells of a life that's been lived to the full; far from perfect, its fragility makes it all the more human, all the more soulful. The song closes with an equally soulful guitar solo. Abandoning his trademark bottleneck guitar, Harrison plays some beautiful, soaring phrases that extends the melody and takes the song to a higher, more intense emotional place. Rather than overextend the solo, as some others might, he lets it fade away, leaving us wanting more as it tails off into an empty silence.

You data

Apple issued 'You' with customized blue and tan labels and a picture sleeve featuring a photo of Harrison taken during his 1974 American tour. The labels feature the Om symbol and a symbolic apple core with the text 'From The Album EXTRA TEXTURE Read All About It PAS 10009' around the perimeter. Promotional copies of the single issued in Britain have a large 'A' beneath the artiste's name and 'DEMO RECORD NOT FOR SALE' below the song title. In America, Apple issued the single with identical labels and picture sleeve. It also issued mono/stereo promotional copies of the single (P-1884) to radio stations and the media.

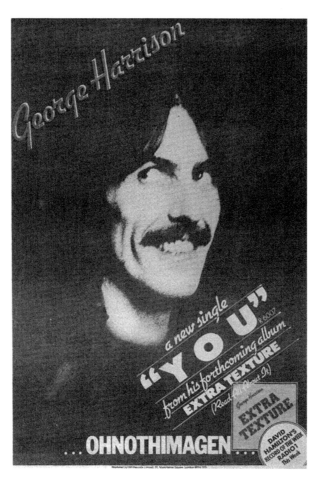

Read All About It

SIDE ONE

You (3:30)
Drums Jim Gordon/Jim Keltner · Bass Carl Radle · Piano Leon Russell · Electric Piano Gary Wright · Organ & Arp Strings David Foster · Sax Jim Horn · Guitar & Vocals George Harrison

The Answer's At The End (5:30)
Drums Jim Keltner · Bass Paul Stallworth · Piano David Foster · Organ Gary Wright · Guitar & Vocals George Harrison · Percussion Norm Kinney · String Arrangement David Foster

This Guitar (Can't Keep From Crying) (4:11)
Drums Jim Keltner · Piano David Foster · Guitar Jesse Ed Davis · Arp Strings Gary Wright · Acoustic & Electric Guitars/Arp Bass/Vocal George Harrison · String Arrangement David Foster

Ooh Baby (You Know That I Love You) (3:50)
Drums Jim Keltner · Bass Klaus Voormann · Electric Piano Gary Wright · Guitar Jesse Ed Davis · Horns Tom Scott/Chuck Findley · Guitar & Vocal George Harrison

World Of Stone (4:46)
Drums Jim Keltner · Bass Klaus Voormann · Piano/Arp Strings David Foster · Organ Gary Wright · Guitar Jesse Ed Davis · Guitar & Vocal George Harrison

Recorded and Remixed at A&M Studios—Los Angeles
Engineer—Norman Kinney
Machine Operator—Steve Katz
"His Name Is Legs" & "You"—Basic tracks recorded by Phil McDonald
(Mastered by George Peckham at The Master Room)

Photographs by Henry Grossman
Art Direction Roy Kohara
℗ 1975 EMI Records Limited

SIDE TWO

A Bit More Of You (:45)

Can't Stop Thinking About You (4:30)
Drums Jim Keltner · Bass Klaus Voormann · Piano Nicky Hopkins · Electric Piano David Foster · Arp Strings Gary Wright · Guitar Jesse Ed Davis · Guitar & Vocal George Harrison · Backing Vocals Paul Stallworth · String Arrangement David Foster

Tired Of Midnight Blue (4:50)
Drums & Percussion Jim Keltner · Bass Paul Stallworth · Piano Leon Russell · Guitars & Vocals George Harrison

Grey Cloudy Lies (3:41)
Drums Jim Keltner · Piano David Foster · Guitars Jesse Ed Davis/George Harrison · Arp/Bass Moog & Vocal George Harrison

His Name Is Legs (Ladies & Gentlemen) (5:45)
Drums Andy Newmark · Bass Willie Weeks · Electric Piano Billy Preston · Tack Piano David Foster · Horns Tom Scott/Chuck Findley · Acoustic Piano/Guitar & Vocal George Harrison · Guest Vocals Legs Larry "Smith"

Gary Wright appears courtesy of Warner Brothers Records
Leon Russell appears courtesy of Shelter Records
David Foster/Jim Keltner & Paul Stallworth appear courtesy of Dark Horse Records
Billy Preston by courtesy of A&M Records
Tom Scott appears courtesy of Ode Records
Legs Larry "Smith" appears courtesy of the Oxfordshire County Council
Danny Kootch doesn't appear on this record.
Also not appearing on this record: Derek Taylor, Peter Sellers, Chuck Trammell, Dino Airali, Eric Idle, Dennis Killeen and Emil Richards.
"Ooh Baby (You Know That I Love You)" is dedicated to Smokey Robinson

All songs written by George Harrison
and published by Ganga Publishing b.v.

Produced by George Harrison

PAS 10009

284

285

EXTRA TEXTURE (READ ALL ABOUT IT)
GEORGE HARRISON
Side one: You / The Answer's At The End / This Guitar (Can't Keep From Crying) / Ooh Baby (You Know That I Love You) / World of Stone
Side two: A Bit More of You / Can't Stop Thinking About You / Tired Of Midnight Blue / Grey Cloudy Lies / His Name Is Legs (Ladies and Gentlemen)
UK release: 3 October 1975; Apple PAS 10009; chart high; No. 16.
US release: 22 September 1975; Apple SW-3420; chart high No.8.
Produced by George Harrison.

George Harrison (vocals, electric and acoustic guitars, ARP synthesizer, Moog synthesizer, piano and backing vocals), David Foster (piano, organ, ARP synthesizer, electric piano and string arrangement, Gary Wright (organ, electric piano and ARP synthesizer), Jim Keltner (drums and percussion), Jesse Ed Davis (electric guitar), Klaus Voormann (bass), Paul Stallworth (bass and background vocals), Leon Russell (piano), Tom Scott (saxophone), Chuck Findley (trumpet and trombone), Nicky Hopkins (piano), Jim Horn (saxophone), Jim Gordon (drums and percussion), Carl Radle (bass), Billy Preston (electric piano), Willie Weeks (bass), Andy Newmark (drums), Legs Larry Smith (vocal), Ronnie Spector (vocal), Norm Kinney (percussion)

Four days before Christmas 1974, George Harrison brought his one and only tour of America to a close at Madison Square Garden, New York City. Despite the laryngitis, and despite having played over forty shows in thirty cities, Harrison and his voice had survived. Although he was still a little hoarse, he sounded better than could be reasonably expected. Dressed in a mustard yellow shirt, blue dungarees and slinging a sunburst Stratocaster, he seemed to actually enjoy being on stage. Freed of Beatle George, he appeared relaxed, good humoured and ready to rock. Four days before Harrison hit the stage in New York City, John Lennon attended his show at the Nassau Coliseum and enthused: "that night the band really cooked, the show I saw was a good show".[3]

The tour broke new ground by featuring Indian classical music alongside western pop and was a commercial if not critical success. "One reason I went on that tour with all those people was to do something which was not done every week," explained Harrison. "The whole idea [was] to have a different bunch of people, different attitudes and different types of music and a broader type of show because it's just boring just going on and on and on."[4] Apart from a particularly unsupportive review in *Rolling Stone*, the only negative as far as Harrison was concerned was the media circus that followed his every move. Speaking to KHJ Radio, he said: "When it [the tour] finally came, I thought what am I doing? It's mad, really mad."[5] It was all too much and too close to Beatlemania for comfort. Harrison never enjoyed the madness that surrounded touring and his 1974 American tour did little to convince him otherwise. Critical reaction to the tour soured what was an already fragile relationship with the media, and while his audience was happy to see him grow into a solo star, his critics couldn't accept the fact that he'd changed.

As well as attending Harrison's concert at Nassau Coliseum, Lennon joined his old buddy for an interview broadcast by KHJ radio on 21 December. The pair reminisced about the old days, the media's attitude to musical development and their problems with American immigration. Before returning to England, Harrison spent time unwinding in Hawaii. But he had projects old and new to finish and so left sunny Hawaii for another grey British winter.

In January he attended the première in London of the Apple film *Little Malcolm And His Struggle Against The Eunuchs*. Although the film was well received by the critics and won several awards, it was not a box office hit. Harrison's recent musical discovery, Splinter, was also struggling to stay afloat in the fickle pool of pop. Having scored a top twenty hit with 'Costafine Town', their follow up single 'Drink All Day (Got to Find Your Own Way Home)' was banned by the BBC and sank without trace. Not that airplay would have made much difference. Reviewed by Colin Irwin for the *Melody Maker*, it was described as a "mediocre song... lacking in all the essentials". Two weeks later Dark Horse issued 'China Light' as a single in the hope that would propel the band into the big time. It didn't. February also saw 'Dark Horse' released as a single in the UK. Remarkably, it too failed to chart.

Splinter never did become the money-spinners Harrison had hoped for, but that didn't mean he was about to give up on them. The duo was booked into A&M Studios, Los Angeles, to record their second album in April/May. However, ill-health and visa problems ensured they never made it. Although Harrison wasn't keen on the studio, which the previous year had played host to John Lennon and Phil Spector, the obvious answer was for him to record his new album there while Splinter stayed at home and recorded at F.S.H.O.T.. As usual, Harrison surrounded himself with stalwarts from the London session scene, Klaus Voormann, Gary Wright and Nicky Hopkins, but also employed some of Los Angeles seasoned session musicians including Jesse Ed Davis (Lennon's guitarist of choice), Tom Scott and Jim Keltner.

Unlike the *Dark Horse* sessions, which had dragged on for over a year, *Extra Texture (Read All About It)* was recorded relatively quickly. All the basic tracks were recorded over a two and a half week period from late April to early May. While he was in Los Angeles, Harrison continued to add to his Dark Horse stable of artists, which by early 1975 included ex-Wings guitarist Henry McCulloch, Chicago soul band The Stairsteps and two bands from California, Jiva and The Attitudes. Although the acts were musically diverse, they shared a similar slick, some would say bland, soft rock sound that was popular at the time. Writing in *Phonograph Record*, Greg Shaw said: "It's the George Harrison sound (or the Mantovani Sound updated) and while it works, just like the modern Nashville studio sound works, there's a lot missing".[6] The missing ingredient in most cases was charisma. There was no doubting the quality of musicianship, but the Dark Horse sound was musically sterile and unadventurous. It was rock 'n' roll with all the rough edges knocked off. The Dark Horse sound was slick, flawless, anodyne and, for the most part, the sonic equivalent of watching paint dry. The sound did, however, dovetail with the growing commercial radio format M.O.R.. But with the exception of Harrison none of the acts signed to Dark Horse were anywhere near as successful as Mantovani, let alone their boss.

Although he now had his own record label, Harrison showed little interest in becoming a vinyl mogul and signed acts either because they were friends or simply because he liked what they were doing. Jiva had toured with Fleetwood Mac, followed a controversial guru and played a brand of devotional soft rock that appealed to Harrison's musical and spiritual tastes. "They're like a little R&B/Rock band", Harrison explained, "very nice, very positive. That's the great thing about them, they know where they're going and are full of positive loving awareness. They're pretty funky too."[7] They were also hot property and had plenty of labels after their signature. According to the band's vocalist, Michael Lanning: "We had about fifteen labels interested in us at the time, as we were doing showcases around L.A.. Linda and her sister, Olivia Arias, who later became Mrs. George Harrison, were friends of ours and they turned our record on to George. George loved the record and he came to a place called the Topanga Corral to hear us perform. He said he loved our songs and loved our energy and he pretty much signed us on the spot."[8]

If Harrison had made pop stars of a bunch of Hare Krishna devotees then surely he could do the same for these clean cut boys from San Bernardino. Unfortunately, the fates and A&M were against them. Signed to Dark Horse they cut one album for the label that fell at the first fence. Lanning later claimed that despite national airplay "A&M would not promote the record".[9] Although the deal with A&M was to market and distribute Dark Horse records, it was clear that it was interested in one thing and one thing only—the prestige of having an ex-Beatle on its books. But even that was short lived and A&M fell out of love with Harrison almost as quickly as it had fallen for him.

Several of the L.A. session players who recorded *Extra Texture (Read All About It)* worked so well together in the studio that they decided to form a band. The Attitudes tended to lean towards funk rather than rock and on paper they too looked promising. However, the one thing they lacked was attitude. They weren't The Stooges, they certainly weren't the MC5, and if they had an attitude, it was to ride the groove and sing about their baby. Marginally more successful than Jiva, they managed to scrape into the top 100 US singles chart with 'Sweet Summer Music' in the summer of 1976. But by then it was too late. The times they were a-changing and on the other side of the Atlantic a storm was brewing that most definitely had an attitude and then some. But that was still some way off.

Extra Texture (Read All About It) data

Extra Texture (Read All About It) was issued by Apple in America and Britain on 22 September and 3 October. The album was issued with identical artwork on both sides of the Atlantic. However, the American edition had the title die cut into the front sleeve to reveal the inner picture sleeve. The inner sleeve featured two photographs of Harrison taken during the previous year's American tour and the original album title 'OHNOTHIMAGEN'. The records were pressed with bespoke labels with the Apple logo reduced to little more than a core. "The album marks the end of Apple as a label," Harrison explained, "unless somebody else forms a company called Apple. Paul's already done a deal for his future, which puts him on Capitol for the world. It doesn't look like Ringo or John will be doing another album this year, so I look like being the last one on Apple. Funny, the first Apple record was the music from *Wonderwall*, which I wrote."[10]

By March 1974, Apple Records had effectively stopped releasing records by artists other than Lennon, McCartney, Harrison and Starr. Badfinger's 'Apple Of My Eye' (APPLE 49) was the last non-Beatles related single issued by Apple, although the label limped on for another eighteen months until The Beatles' contract with EMI ended on 26 January 1976.

Harrison was due to deliver his next solo album to A&M Records by 26 July 1976. However, ill-health meant that he failed to complete the album on time with the consequence that A&M sued. According to Harrison, A&M used the non-delivery of his new album to back out of a contract it had discovered wasn't in its favour. "What happened was that they realized they had not made themselves such a good deal, and the only legal point they had.... Instead of telephoning me up and saying: 'Now look George, we have made ourselves a bad deal. Let's talk about it, and work it out.' Instead of doing that, they found the only legal grounds they had was that I had had hepatitis, so my album was two months delayed. We had, in the original contract, that I would give it to them around the twenty fifth of July. And so they picked on that legal point and said: 'Okay, we'll get him on that.'"[11]

On 26 September 1976, A&M Records filed a $10 million lawsuit to dissolve its partnership with Dark Horse and prevent Harrison from taking his new album to another record label. The dispute was settled by an out of court payment to A&M Records for $4 million. Harrison headed for Warner Brothers who distributed Dark Horse and released his next album, *Thirty Three And ⅓*, in November 1976.

The Answer's At The End
George Harrison (vocals, 12-string acoustic guitar, electric guitars, slide guitar, backing vocals), Gary Wright (organ), David Foster (piano, string arrangement), Paul Stallworth (bass), Jim Keltner (drums), Norm Kinney (tambourine)

Inspired by more of Sir Francis Crisp's Victorian graffiti, Harrison wrote 'The Answer's At The End'. "It's like a modern version of 'You Always Hurt the One You Love'," he told Paul Gambaccini. "It actually came from a Victorian thing written on the wall. That always stuck in my mind as a song and it ended up as one."[12] Harrison lifted the entire first verse from the writing on a wall in his home in Henley-on-Thames and finished his first draft while in Switzerland. The remainder of his lyric reworked Allan Roberts pop classic to the extent that he alludes to a line from 'You Always Hurt the

One You Love' in the second verse. His use of flowers as a metaphor for beauty being one of the more poetic references to Roberts' use of a rose to indicate the same quality.

'The Answer's At The End' is another plea for tolerance. It's an appeal for us to forgive him his foibles, but it's also an implicit acknowledgement by Harrison that he too should be more forgiving. While Harrison took solace from words left behind by Sir Francis' they didn't provide an answer, only guidance. Placed in a spiritual context, he had no way of knowing how his changed consciousness would affect the karmic laws. As far as he was concerned the answer would only be revealed at the moment his physical body ceased to exist and his spirit moved on. If he lived a balanced life then his soul had a better chance of attaining salvation. As personal as 'The Answer's At The End' is, its message is universal.

Recorded with three quarters of the latest Dark Horse signing, The Attitudes, augmented by stalwart Gary Wright, 'The Answer's At The End' navigates the listener away from the frothy pop of 'You' to a more adult listening experience. A sweeping, orchestrated melody introduces the song which proceeds at a stately pace until a descending motif announces the chorus and a change in mood. While recording the song Harrison was reminded of Nina Simone's version of 'Isn't It A Pity'. Simone's lengthy reworking of the song was taken at a similar pace to 'The Answer's At The End'. But it was the mood she captured that influenced the middle section of Harrison's new song.

While much has been made of the soul and gospel influences Harrison brings to the song, it's the mood of the piece that is central to understanding its meaning. It is neither dark nor sombre, but a blissful contemplation that conveys its author's personal and spiritual qualities and the importance he attached to them.

This Guitar (Can't Keep from Crying)
George Harrison (vocals, 12-string acoustic guitar, electric slide guitar, ARP bass), Jesse Ed Davis (electric guitar), David Foster (piano, string arrangement), Gary Wright (ARP strings), Jim Keltner (drums)

Most people who've made a career in showbiz will tell you that the best thing about becoming a star is the journey to the top. Once you've there and have looked down from its dizzying heights it can be a lonely place. The realization that only two options remain quickly hit home. You can either sustain your place in the pantheon of pop or enjoy the ride down. By the mid-70s Harrison had reached the top, not once but twice. Perhaps more than any other of the Beatles, he found it more difficult to cope with fame. His tour of America the previous year had brought this into sharp focus. Those few weeks on the road had delighted and disappointed in equal measure. Freed of his Beatles past, he found he could again enjoy the camaraderie of being in a band, delight in taking Indian classical music to the masses and revel in playing to adoring audiences. But he disliked being the eye of the hurricane, he detested the unthinking hedonistic circus that rock 'n' roll had become, but what irked him most was the criticism.

Speaking to Paul Gambaccini about 'This Guitar (Can't Keep from Crying)', Harrison said: "I decided to write that song because of the popularity of 'While My Guitar Gently Weeps'. It was really a cheap excuse to play guitar."[13] He was being more than a little disingenuous. While admitting that 'This Guitar' was the son of 'While My Guitar Gently Weeps', he neatly sidestepped his real reason for writing the song. Like 'The Answer's At The End', 'This Guitar (Can't Keep from Crying)' is a plea for tolerance, albeit one soaked in despair. Writing about the song in his biography, he said: "If people keep on at you long enough, the chances are you will become depressed. We must struggle even though we are all rats and valueless and try to become better human beings."[14]

Valueless rats! Had his world-view changed that much? Actually, no. He wasn't as misanthropic as his later remarks suggest. His anger wasn't so much directed at people as at the editor of a certain music magazine. Speaking to Dave Herman, Harrison said: "This is what kills me now. I see these people who a few years ago were supposed to love me, and I was supposed to love them, and I see them and they're just dropping apart at the seems with hate. I'm talking about *Rolling Stone* actually, Jann Wenner."[15]

In an attempt to distance himself from the vitriolic nature of the lyrics, Harrison employed his guitar as a surrogate self. It worked to an extent, but one didn't need the intellect of Albert Einstein to read between the lines. 'This Guitar (Can't Keep from Crying)' is a thinly veiled attack on sections of the music press that undermine the very people they'd helped become stars.

'This Guitar (Can't Keep from Crying)' articulates its author's feelings via some smooth blues licks that are, if anything, a little too controlled, too polished and too harmonious. But as far as Harrison was concerned the sweeter it sounded the more personal it was. "All I want is to sing the tunes I have and to do them as warm and simple as possible," he told Dave Herman. "It matters more to me that I can sing it better and play it better and with less orchestration if it gets over more feeling."[16] However, the feeling Harrison's playing evokes sits uncomfortably with his lyrics and doesn't convey the anger, pain and frustration he experienced of being betrayed by somebody he thought he could trust.

Ooh Baby (You Know That I Love You)

George Harrison (vocals, electric guitar), Jesse Ed Davis (electric guitar), Gary Wright (electric piano), Klaus Voormann (bass), Jim Keltner (drums), Tom Scott (saxophones, horn arrangement), Chuck Findley (trumpet, trombone)

If you want to know what George Harrison was listening to for pleasure in the mid-'70s you need look no further than Smokey Robinson. He'd been a fan for years and found the singer's sweet soul music relaxing. "I'm a big fan of Smokey Robinson just because musically he's so sweet, you know, he's so sweet he makes me feel nice, he makes me feel good," he told Dave Herman.[17] Harrison loved the smooth soul vibe so much it became the template applied to pretty much every act signed to his Dark

Horse label. If the Dark Horse label had a sound it was what radio programmers called the 'quiet storm'. Distinguished by its understated, mellow tones and relaxed grooves, it's utterly romantic and quintessentially laid-back.

That Harrison chose to record 'Ooh Baby (You Know That I Love You)' as a tribute to his hero speak volumes. "As a songwriter, he's been, for my taste, one of the most consistent. He's written so many fantastic tunes."[18] When Motown relocated from Detroit to Los Angeles, primarily to be closer to the film industry, Smokey Robinson moved with them. "George, for a time, was living in Los Angeles and I had the pleasure of being in his company a few times," Robinson explained. "We got to know one another kind of well and that was a wonderful thing for him to feel that and write ['Ooh Baby'] about it. So that the world could know that he felt like that."[19]

Harrison recorded the basic track for 'Ooh Baby' at A&M Studios in Hollywood on 25 April. Working with a band of all white musicians he managed to recreate Robinson's distinctive soft soul sound. Harrison's jazzy, Leslie-tone guitar sweeps over the track and does much to establish the mood of the song. It's complemented by some fine ensemble playing with each musician responding with considered embellishments to the others performances.

Compared with some of the vocal performances Harrison delivered for his previous album, 'Ooh Baby' proves that, while he was not the world's greatest singer, he could pull a sensitive, emotional and expressive vocal out of the bag when needed. He's not as sweet as Robinson but that's what gives it character. It's a voice that's lived and loved; it's a voice infused with passion and rapture. Anodyne and soulful, it complements the subject and mood of the song perfectly.

Can't Stop Thinking About You

George Harrison (vocals, electric guitar, backing vocals), Nicky Hopkins (piano), David Foster (electric piano, string arrangement), Jesse Ed Davis (electric guitar), Gary Wright (ARP synthesizer), Klaus Voormann (bass), Jim Keltner (drums), Paul Stallworth (backing vocals)

Side two of *Extra Texture (Read All About It)* opens with 'A Bit More Of You'. Coming, as it does, before 'Can't Stop Thinking About You' it's one of Harrison's little jokes. Often overlooked or dismissed as desperate attempts to enliven otherwise lacklustre work, the fact is that Harrison just couldn't resist a joke, no matter how good, bad or indifferent and thought it great fun to slip them into his songs and albums like a naughty schoolboy drawing rude pictures in his exercise book.

Harrison's infatuation with the smooth soul grooves of Los Angeles and Philadelphia continue with 'Can't Stop Thinking About You'. A simple soul-pop ballad, it was written in the winter of 1973 when its author was caught between two lovers and having a rough time of it. By the time he came to record the song in the late spring of 1975 he had a new lover, Olivia Trinidad Arias, that he couldn't stop thinking about.

The repetitive nature of the lyrics provided the song with a strong hook, which Harrison cleverly emphasized by employing a subtle opening crescendo that grows as his singing becomes more impassioned. Harrison then uses a quick decrescendo to introduce a more sombre mood for what he described as an 'interesting' melody for the verses. "I don't know what it is," he said, "I have this ability to write dramatic or melodramatic melodies, it makes me think it should be sung by Al Jolson or Mario Lanza."[20] Although he thought it the kind of melody that would suit somebody like Mario Lanza, when it came to recording his vocal Harrison drew inspiration instead from his friend and ex-bandmate John Lennon. "That was my impersonation of John Lennon," he said. "It was hard to sing that first chorus I tell you."[21]

Harrison recorded the basic track for 'Can't Stop Thinking About You' at A&M Studios in Hollywood on 1 May. The recording features three keyboard players – Nicky Hopkins (piano), David Foster (electric piano) and Gary Wright (ARP synthesizer). Overdubs were added on 7 May, the horn parts recorded on 2 or 3 June and the strings added on 6 June.

Tired of Midnight Blue

George Harrison (vocals, electric guitar, slide guitars, backing vocals), Leon Russell (piano), Paul Stallworth (bass), Jim Keltner (drums, cowbell, handclaps)

While Ringo Starr and John Lennon were making headlines for their alcohol and drug induced hell raising, Harrison managed to keep his name out of the papers. Perhaps it was because of the company he kept. Starr and Lennon certainly needed little encouragement, but their consumption of booze and pills wasn't helped by their choice of drinking companions – Keith Moon and Harry Nilsson. Deposited in Los Angeles to record his new album, Harrison fell back into his old habits and began painting the town red.

'Tired of Midnight Blue' was one of the few songs Harrison wrote from scratch while in Los Angeles. Speaking to Dave Herman he said: "I [hadn't written] a tune for about six months up until last Saturday. I sat down and decided I'd better get some tunes together. I just got into the mood of it and finished nine tunes and wrote a couple of new tunes."[22] He'd only been in the city for a few days before becoming disillusioned with the grubbier side of the rock 'n' roll dream. "I had been to a Los Angeles club – ended up in the back room with a lot of grey-haired naughty people and I was depressed by what I saw going on there," he recalled.[23]

Disillusioned by the music business and unsatisfied with the rock 'n' roll lifestyle, he knew just where to look for sustenance and warmth. If once he'd been lost, now, with his new love by his side, he was found. Only love provided the antidote to the worldly and transient temptations of the fickle music business.

Harrison recorded 'Tired of Midnight Blue' with a small four-piece band live in the studio. Overdubbing hand-claps and an exquisite slide guitar part, he produced a bright, uncluttered recording that focuses on musicianship rather than studio trickery for effect. "There's a lot of spaces, it doesn't have a lot of things going on," he said, "I deliberately just left spaces, because most people can imagine their own sax parts or guitar parts."[24] A master class in what to leave out, the arrangement, performance and production are meticulous. Leon Russell's playing is sparse and tasteful; adorned with elegant motifs, it adds just the right amount of decoration to the arrangement. This is the kind of record Harrison excelled at making. In other words, a return to form as both a songwriter and producer.

Grey Cloudy Lies
George Harrison (vocals, electric guitar, Moog synthesizer, ARP synthesizers, backing vocals), David Foster (piano), Jesse Ed Davis (electric guitar), Jim Keltner (drums)

If 'Grey Cloudy Lies' is a measure of just how depressed Harrison felt in the winter of '73/'74, it's off the scale. Written on the piano in the dead of night, its opening chords drag the listener deep into Harrison's bleak psyche with an unrelenting sense of gloom. There is no light at the end of the tunnel, no dawn to banish the darkness, no sun to warm the soul. It is the bleakest of songs, and yet it's predicated on a joke. "It's about a Red Indian Chief," he wrote in *I Me Mine*.[25] Admittedly, it's not a very good joke, but nevertheless it is a joke. Speaking to Paul Gambaccini, he said: "Sometimes I just think of titles and write them down on a piece of paper. And then I get round to writing a song about it."[26] This was undoubtedly one of those times.

'Grey Cloudy Lies' is possibly unique in as much as it's a song about depression that ends with a punchline. If there's any relief from the dark abyss of despair, it's in the form of dark gallows humour. A reflection on and response to hopelessness, it's an almost complete acceptance of defeat and rejection of conflict. There's a time to talk and a time to be silent, and while silence can signify deep sorrow it can also indicate inner strength and resolve. "After talking for a lot, sometimes it's nice to be quiet," Harrison explained.[27] Silence was Harrison's way of distancing himself from his troubles, of ignoring them and removing himself from them while maintaining his vision and will.

Harrison recorded the basic track at A&M Studios in Hollywood on 24 April 1975. Klaus Voormann is supposed to have played bass on the track, but Harrison was unhappy with his performance and replaced it with a bass part played on Moog synthesizer. This being the case, it's one of the few times Voormann's work was replaced by another musician. Harrison also overdubbed several ARP synthesizer parts onto the track at sometime between 31 May and 6 June.

294

His Name Is Legs (Ladies and Gentlemen)

George Harrison (vocals, piano, electric guitar, backing vocals), Legs Larry Smith (vocals), Billy Preston (electric piano), Tom Scott (saxophones, horn arrangement), Chuck Findley (trumpet, trombone), Willie Weeks (bass), Andy Newmark (drums, percussion), David Foster (tack piano)

The Bonzo Dog Doo Dah Band were the clown princes of pop. During their all too short career they played with everybody from Cream to Led Zeppelin and invariably blew them off stage. Other than the equally eccentric Ivor Cutler, they were the only musical act to appear in The Beatles' *Magical Mystery Tour*. It was only after the band split up that Harrison became friends with Legs Larry Smith and Neil Innes. Smith was part of the Henley music Mafia and became Harrison's very own court jester. "I had just met Larry. He just amazed me with the things he was saying, so I just decided to write a song about him," explained Harrison.[28]

Written around the same time as 'Grey Cloudy Lies', it was, perhaps, an attempt by Harrison to cheer himself up. It was, after all, described by Harrison as "a piece of personal indulgence", although no more indulgent than *Electronic Sound* and a good deal easier to listen to. Written on piano, its lyric consists of the kind of inventive word play Harrison adored and which he would return to again for songs like 'Gone Troppo'. It's a shame, then, that he placed both himself and Smith so low in what was already a flat mix that they are barely audible. "I decided to put them [Smith's vocals] both in and mix them down so people had to strain with headphones to hear what it is," Harrison told Paul Gambaccini.[29]

Recorded at F.P.S.H.O.T. during sessions for the *Dark Horse* album, it features Smith on vocals and stream of consciousness dialogue. "Larry sang the bridges on the record. It's pretty 'off the wall' both musically and lyrically; a piece of personal indulgence, like some other songs about things nobody else knows or cares about, except maybe two people," Harrison explained.[30] The song was overdubbed with a horn part by Tom Scott and Chuck Findley on 2 and 3 June 1975.

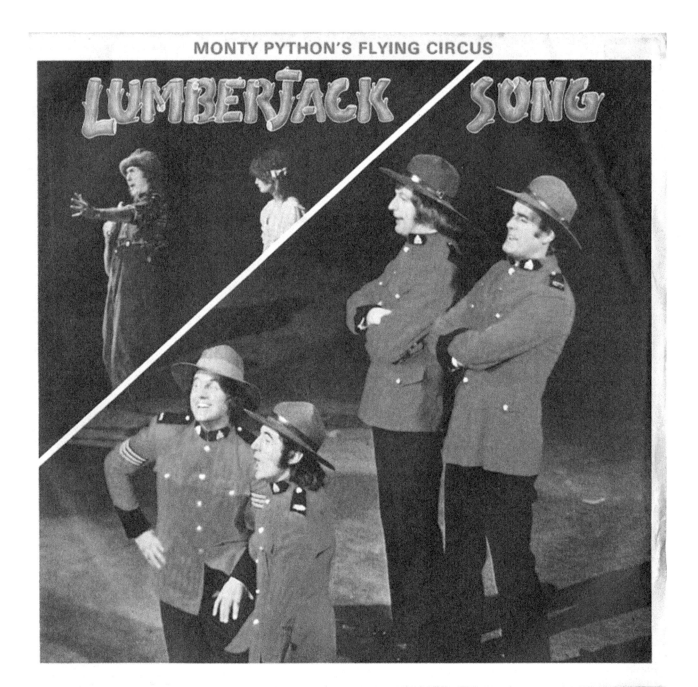

MONTY PYTHON'S FLYING CIRCUS

LUMBERJACK SONG

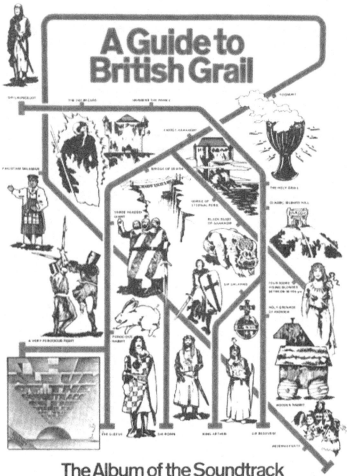

A Guide to British Grail

The Album of the Soundtrack
of the Trailer of the Film of
Monty Python & the Holy Grail

Manufactured & distributed by Phonogram Ltd, Phonodisc Ltd, Chadwell Heath, Essex
Marketed by Charisma Records, 35 Old Compton St, London W1
The Camberpack song and the Squire song recorded at the Workhouse
Re-mixed back at George's and by Andre Jacquemin
Sandwiches by Clive Davis

'Lumberjack Song'* / 'Spam Song'
MONTY PYTHON
Produced by George 'Ohnothimagen' Harrison*
UK release: 14 November 1975; Charisma CB 268; chart high; failed to chart.

To say that George Harrison was a fan of Monty Python would be an understatement. He could quote sketches verbatim, took to promoting the comic troupe whenever possible and paid for their films. "I've always liked comedy, back when I was a kid, I liked *The Goon Show*, I was a big fan of Peter Sellers, and later on I was a good friend of his. I liked Peter a lot. I loved Monty Python, I couldn't explain how much I liked it. The rut that television gets into, and people lives, Python just blew all that away by making fun of everything. Right down to the style of television we've been watching. The result is that I got to know some of them and we made *The Life of Brian* and *Time Bandits* and a couple of films with Michael Palin, so that kind of stuff makes me laugh," he recalled.[31]

'The Lumberjack Song' made its first appeared in the ninth episode of Monty Python's Flying Circus, "The Ant: An Introduction" on BBC1 on 14 December 1969. Harrison liked the song so much that it was played prior to him taking the stage throughout his American tour, much to the bemusement of his audience. It made perfect sense, then, for Harrison to produce the song for record.

Recorded at Workhouse Studios, London, with a small ensemble of drums, upright bass and brass, 'The Lumberjack Song' featured Michael Palin on vocals and the Pythons as chorus. The song was mixed at F.P.S.H.O.T.. 'The Spam Song' had been previously released as an A-side in 1972 and was produced by Monty Python. Issued by Charisma as a 7-inch single with a picture sleeve, the single did not chart.

300

'This Guitar (Can't Keep from Crying)' / 'Maya Love'
GEORGE HARRISON
Produced by George Harrison
UK release: 6 February 1976; Apple R 6012; chart high; failed to chart.
US release: 8 December 1975; Apple 1885; chart high; failed to chart.

'This Guitar (Can't Keep from Crying)' was the last single issued by Apple and marked the end of Harrison's contract with EMI. An edit of the song was prepared for release as a single and 'Maya Love' from the previous year's *Dark Horse* album was selected for the B-side. American promo copies of the single featured mono and stereo versions of the 3:49 edit. Two label variations of the American single were manufactured. Examples manufactured in Los Angeles have the text (from the LP "EXTRA TEXTURE (read all about it") SW-3420) at the top of the label above the spindle hole. Copies manufactured in Winchester have the text at 4 o'clock. The single was issued with generic Apple labels and black paper sleeve.

Promotional copies of the single issued in Britain are in stereo and have 'DEMO RECORD NOT FOR SALE' above the spindle hole and a large 'A' at 10 o'clock. The release date 6.2.76 appears under 'An E.M.I. Recording' at four o'clock. The single was issued with generic Apple labels and black paper sleeve.

'The Pirate Song' (Harrison–Idle)
George Harrison (vocals, acoustic guitar), Neil Innes (acoustic guitar), Billy Bremner (electric guitar), Roger Retting (pedal steel), Brian Hodgson (bass), John Halsey (drums)

More Pythonesque buffoonery from the pen of Harrison and Eric Idle came in the form of 'The Pirate Song', written for the BBC television programme *Rutland Weekend Television*. Post Monty Python, Eric Idle joined forces with ex-Bonzo Dog Doo Dah Band kingpin Neil Innes to write a comedy show about the world's smallest television station. The first series comprised six episodes broadcast by BBC2, with Harrison appearing as Pirate Bob in the Christmas special, broadcast on Boxing Day 1975.

Harrison appeared throughout the show dressed as a pirate, complete with a wooden leg, interrupting sketches and insisting that he'd been booked to "act, not sing". The running joke borrowed from the earlier Monty Python 'Lumberjack' sketch, only this time the conceit was that Mr. 'Arrison had become dissatisfied with his role as a pop star and wanted to be a pirate. (Harrison would often fly the Jolly Roger at Friar Park, and can be seen doing just that in the promo video for 'Ding Dong; Ding Dong' in which he also appears as a pirate.)

The show concluded with Idle introducing the star of the show with the words: "The moment you've all been waiting for, Mr. George 'Arrison sings". Dressed in a white suit, Harrison made his entrance to the opening chords of 'My Sweet Lord', played by Neil Innes' band Fatso, before breaking into 'The Pirate Song'.

Although an album featuring songs from the programme was issued by BBC Records (REB 233), it did not feature 'The Pirate Song'. The song appeared on several bootlegs, the best sounding of which is *Pirate Songs* issued by Vigotone (VIGO 146).

1976 : Thirty Three And ⅓

Side One/The Beatles

SOMETHING
(From the album Abbey Road) ℗1969
Produced by George Martin

IF I NEEDED SOMEONE
(From the album Rubber Soul) ℗1966
Produced by George Martin

HERE COMES THE SUN
(From the album Abbey Road) ℗1969
Produced by George Martin

TAXMAN
(From the album Revolver) ℗1966
Produced by George Martin

THINK FOR YOURSELF
(From the album Rubber Soul) ℗1966
Produced by George Martin

FOR YOU BLUE
(From the album Let It Be) ℗1970

WHILE MY GUITAR GENTLY WEEPS
(From the album The Beatles) ℗1968
Produced by George Martin

PAS 10011
stereo
0C 064-06 249
★

PAS 10011
stereo
0C 064-06 249
★

THE BEST OF GEORGE HARRISON

Side Two/George Harrison

MY SWEET LORD
(From the album All Things Must Pass) ℗1970
Produced by Harrison/Spector

GIVE ME LOVE
(Give Me Peace On Earth)
(From the album Living In The Material World) ℗1973
Produced by George Harrison

YOU
(From the album Extra Texture) ℗1975
Produced by Harrison/Spector

BANGLA DESH
(Single) ℗1971
Produced by Harrison/Spector

DARK HORSE
(From the album Dark Horse) ℗1974
Produced by George Harrison

WHAT IS LIFE
(From the album All Things Must Pass) ℗1970
Produced by Harrison/Spector

All songs written by George Harrison
Front Cover Photograph By Bob Cato
Inner Sleeve Photograph By Michael Putland
Design By Cream
℗ EMI RECORDS LTD

Available On Tape

7611 TM Garrod & Lofthouse Ltd

310

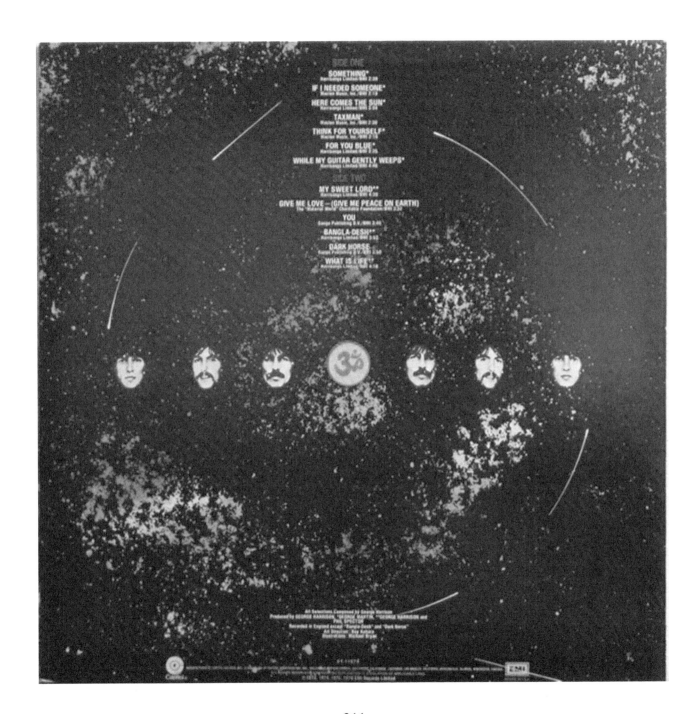

The Best Of
GEORGE HARRISON
Side one: Something / If I Needed Someone / Here Comes The Sun / Taxman / Think For Yourself / For You Blue / While My Guitar Gently Weeps
Side two: My Sweet Lord / Give Me Love (Give Me Peace On Earth) / You / Bangla Desh / Dark Horse / What Is Life
UK release: 20 November 1976; Parlophone PAS 10011; chart high; failed to chart.
US release: 8 November 1976; Capitol ST 11578; chart high No. 31.

Now that The Beatles' contract with Capitol/EMI had expired their back catalogue, both as a group and as individuals, was re-visited, re-packaged and re-issued. Capitol/EMI were so keen to exploit its assets that it couldn't even wait for its contract with The Beatles to expire. In October 1975, a good three months before the contract expired, Capitol/EMI issued a compilation of John Lennon's solo singles, *Shaved Fish*. It was followed in November by a Ringo Starr compilation, *Blast From Your Past*. Because Lennon and Starr were still under contract, Capitol/EMI was obliged to obtain clearance for both content and artwork before releasing the albums. Although Lennon wasn't happy, he later revealed that several of his masters had been misplaced and he'd been forced to dub several tracks from records, he nevertheless promoted the album which performed well in the charts.

In June 1976, Capitol/EMI released the first of many Beatles compilation albums, *Rock 'n' Roll Music*. Interest in The Beatles remained high, particularly as Paul McCartney, who'd re-signed with Capitol/EMI, was touring the world with his new group Wings. The Beatles weren't consulted about the *Rock 'n' Roll Music* album and this time it was Starr who voiced his disappointment. "All of us looked at the cover of *Rock 'n' Roll Music* and we could hardly bear to see it," he complained to the *Melody Maker*.[1] He told *Rolling Stone* magazine: "It made us look cheap and we never were cheap."[2]

To satisfy demand for Beatles related product, Capitol's next move was to cobble together a Harrison compilation which it released to coincide with his new Warner Bros./Dark Horse album. Although he was keen to assist with a track listing of his own devising, Harrison was not consulted about the album's running order which mixed songs by The Beatles with his own solo hits. "I did have a suggestion – which I made to Capitol earlier in the year – as to a title and format of songs," he explained. "What they've done is take a lot of songs which happen to be me singing lead on my songs which were Beatles songs, when there was really a lot of good songs they could have used of me separately. Solo songs. I don't see why they didn't do that. They did that with Ringo's *Blast From Your Past* and John's *Shaved Fish*. It wasn't digging into The Beatles records."[3]

Like Lennon, he wasn't impressed with either content or packaging: "It's tacky and the cover is tacky. We were with Capitol/EMI for so many years and they have the right, apparently, to do just what they like, but at the same time, you would think that after all those years and all that music that we did, they would at least have a bit of discretion," he complained.[4] Harrison had every right to be disappointed with the album. By including a side of material drawn from The Beatles' back pages, from which Harrison had done much to distance himself, it was almost as if Capitol/EMI had deliberately set out to lessen his standing as a solo performer. It did, however, remind people of just how good his contributions to The Beatles' oeuvre were. If he'd been overshadowed by Lennon and McCartney while he was with the group, at least now his songs were allowed to stand on their own and shine.

The simple fact is that *Best Of George Harrison* was put out to exploit material owned by Capitol/EMI that Harrison and The Beatles had little control over. Capitol had ruthlessly exploited The Beatles and their fans from the moment they signed the group. It held back songs from British Beatles albums and combined them with singles to cobble together 'product' not for artistic reasons but for financial gain. Capitol even went as far as to reduce the number of songs to eleven an album rather than the standard twelve for American long-players simply to save paying mechanical royalties and thereby making a considerable saving and additional profit. At the time nobody knew how long the group was going to last. The Beatles bubble could have burst at any time; Capitol's imperative was to make as much money as possible from the group before that happened. That attitude continued well into the 1970s and '80s. As far as Capitol was concerned, the only notes that mattered were the ones that came in wads.

Best Of George Harrison data

The American and British editions of the album were released with different artwork. The American sleeve was designed by Roy Kohara and featured a head and shoulders portrait of Harrison by Michael Bryan set against an image of the cosmos. It was, if possible, even worse than the cover used for The Beatles' *Rock 'n' Roll Music* album. The album was issued with bespoke record labels and a printed inner sleeve based on Bryan's illustrations. The British edition was designed by Cream designs and used a photograph by Bob Cato of Harrison sitting in front of a hot-rod car . The British edition also included an inner sleeve that used a photograph of Harrison by Michael Putland taken at Cannes in January 1976.

314

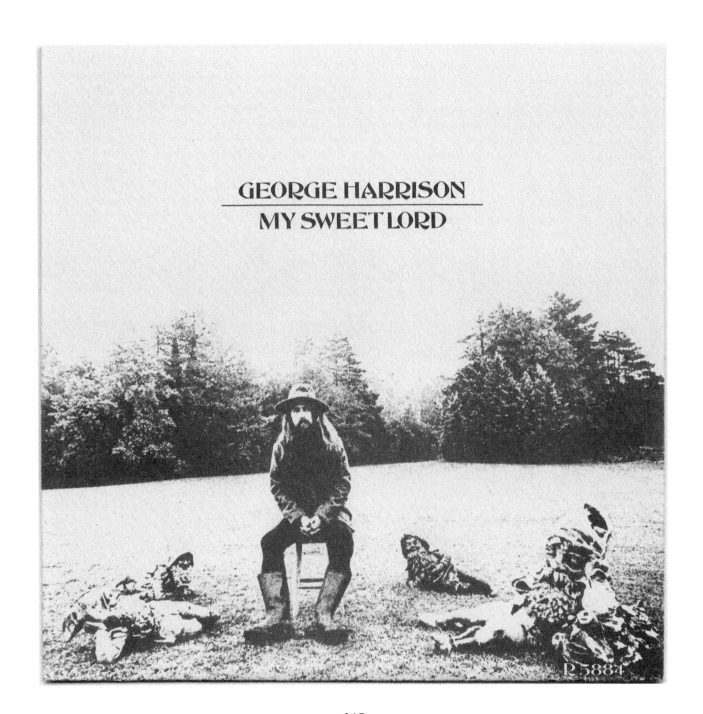

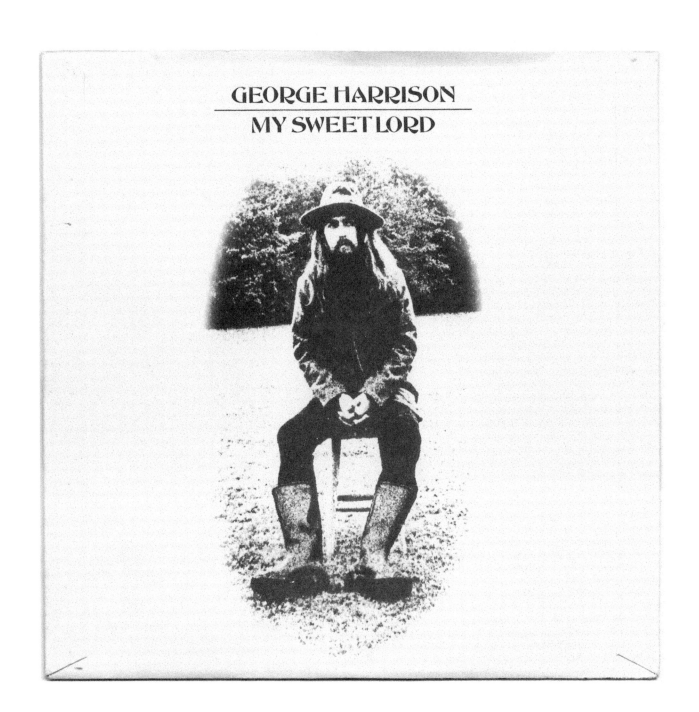

GEORGE HARRISON
MY SWEET LORD

(7YCE.2151)
R 5884
Harrisongs
℗ 1970
EMI Records
Ltd.
An EMI
Recording
DEMO
RECORD
NOT FOR SALE
Mfd. in U.K.
Produced
by:
HARRISON/
SPECTOR
A
MY SWEET LORD
(Harrison)
GEORGE HARRISON

(7YCE.21512)
R 5884
Harrisongs
℗ 1970
EMI Records
Ltd.
An EMI
Recording
DEMO
RECORD
NOT FOR SALE
Mfd. in U.K.
Produced
by:
HARRISON/
SPECTOR
WHAT IS LIFE
GEORGE HARRISON

(7YCE.21511)
R 5884
Harrisongs
℗ 1970
EMI
Records
Ltd.
Mfd. in U.K.
Produced
by:
HARRISON/
SPECTOR
An E.M.I.
Recording
45 r.p.m.
MY SWEET LORD
(Harrison)
GEORGE HARRISON

(7YCE.21512)
R 5884
Harrisongs
℗ 1970
EMI
Records
Ltd.
Mfd. in U.K.
Produced
by:
HARRISON/
SPECTOR
An E.M.I.
Recording
45 r.p.m.
WHAT IS LIFE
(Harrison)
GEORGE HARRISON

'My Sweet Lord' / 'What Is Life'
GEORGE HARRISON
Produced by George Harrison and Phil Spector
UK release: 19 November 1976; Apple R 5884; chart high; failed to chart.

Re-released to coincide with the *Best Of George Harrison* and *Thirty Three And ⅓* albums, 'My Sweet Lord' wasn't a hit second time round. A new master was cut for the A-side and the song publishing credits changed from 'Harrisongs, Essex Int MCPS Briteco NCB' to simply 'Harrisongs'. EMI produced a new picture sleeve for the single based on the *All Things Must Pass* album artwork. Demonstration copies of the single were produced with 'DEMO RECORD NOT FOR SALE' on three lines above the spindle hole and a large 'A' at three o'clock. Stock copies of the single have a different text layout with 'Produced by HARRISON/SPECTOR' at three o'clock and 'An E.M.I. Recording' below.

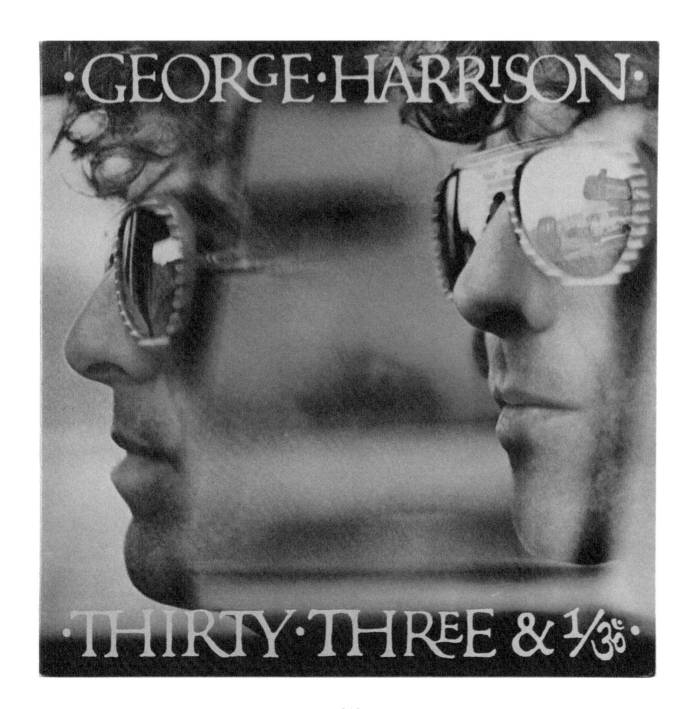

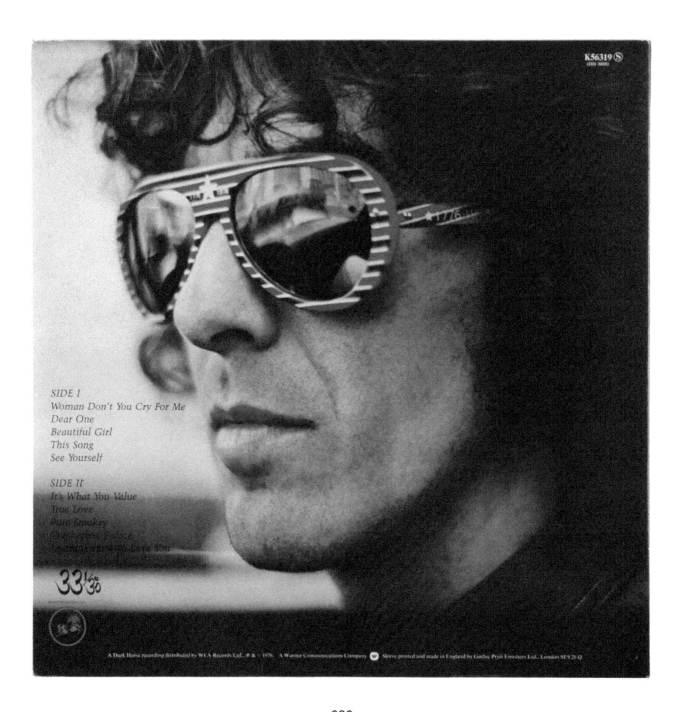

SIDE I
Woman Don't You Cry For Me
Dear One
Beautiful Girl
This Song
See Yourself

SIDE II
It's What You Value
True Love
Pure Smokey
Crackerbox Palace
Learning How To Love You

33⅓/30

K56319 Ⓢ
(DH 3005)

A Dark Horse recording distributed by WEA Records Ltd.. ℗ & © 1976. A Warner Communications Company Ⓦ Sleeve printed and made in England by Gothic Print Finishers Ltd., London SE9 2LQ

320

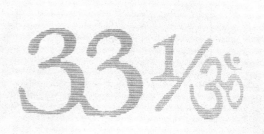

STEREO
K 56319
(DH 3005)
℗ & © 1976
K 56319 A
SIDE ONE

THIRTY THREE AND ⅓
1. WOMAN DON'T YOU CRY FOR ME 3.15
2. DEAR ONE 5.06
3. BEAUTIFUL GIRL 3.38
4. THIS SONG 4.11
5. SEE YOURSELF 2.48

GEORGE HARRISON
All titles written by George Harrison
Produced by George Harrison
Assisted by Tom Scott
GANGA PUBLISHING B.V. (1—5)

STEREO
K 56319
(DH 3005)
℗ & © 1976
K 56319 B
SIDE TWO

THIRTY THREE AND ⅓
1. IT'S WHAT YOU VALUE 5.05
2. TRUE LOVE (Cole Porter) 2.34
3. PURE SMOKEY 3.52
4. CRACKERBOX PALACE 3.52
5. LEARNING HOW TO LOVE YOU 4.15

GEORGE HARRISON
All titles written by George Harrison except as
indicated   Produced by George Harrison
Assisted by Tom Scott
GANGA PUBLISHING B.V. (1, 3—5)
CHAPPELL & CO. LTD. (2)

SIDE I
DH 3005

THIRTY THREE & ⅓
GEORGE HARRISON
Produced By George Harrison
Assisted by Tom Scott
1. WOMAN DON'T YOU CRY FOR ME   3:15
2. DEAR ONE   5:08
3. BEAUTIFUL GIRL   3:38
4. THIS SONG   4:11
5. SEE YOURSELF   2:48
All selections written by
George Harrison and published by
Ganga Publishing B.V.-BMI
℗1976 Ganga
Distributors, B.V.

SIDE II
DH 3005

THIRTY THREE & ⅓
GEORGE HARRISON
Produced By George Harrison
Assisted by Tom Scott
1. IT'S WHAT YOU VALUE   5:05
2. TRUE LOVE   2:34
   (Cole Porter) Chappell & Co., Inc.-ASCAP
3. PURE SMOKEY   3:52
4. CRACKERBOX PALACE   3:52
5. LEARNING HOW TO LOVE YOU   4:15
All selections written by George Harrison
and published by Ganga Publishing B.V.
BMI except as indicated
℗1976 Ganga
Distributors, B.V.

322

Thirty Three And ⅓
GEORGE HARRISON
Side one: Woman Don't You Cry for Me / Dear One / Beautiful Girl / This Song / See Yourself
Side two: It's What You Value / True Love / Pure Smokey / Crackerbox Palace / Learning How To Love You
UK release: 19 November 1976; Dark Horse K 56319; chart high; No. 35.
US release: 24 November 1976; Dark Horse DH 3005; chart high No.11.
Produced by George Harrison assisted by Tom Scott.

George Harrison (vocals, electric and acoustic guitars, synthesizers, percussion, backing vocals), Tom Scott (saxophones, flute, lyricon), Richard Tee (piano, organ, Fender Rhodes), Willie Weeks (bass), Alvin Taylor (drums), Billy Preston (piano, organ, synthesizer), David Foster (Fender Rhodes, clavinet), Gary Wright (keyboards), Emil Richards (marimba)

His contract with EMI having run its course, Harrison was free to release future solo albums on his Dark Horse label. While he'd been busy promoting his last album for Apple, *Extra Texture (Read All About It)*, Dark Horse had been quietly releasing albums by an eclectic roster of acts that ranged from the bluesy, laid back rock of ex-Wings guitarist Henry McCullough to the smooth pop of Splinter. Other than acting as label boss, Harrison had little to do with this second batch of Dark Horse releases. The exception being Splinter's second Dark Horse album *Harder To Live*, for which he co-produced 'Lonely Man' with Tom Scott. With or without Harrison at the controls, the label was developing its own sound. Smooth, laid back, harmonically rich and melodic, the Dark Horse sound dovetailed nicely with Harrison's musical tastes. But then it would. As label boss, he wasn't going to release anything he didn't like or that didn't make him feel 'nice'.

Nice wasn't a word Harrison would have used to describe the events that unfolded in late February 1976. The 'My Sweet Lord' plagiarism case finally came to court and Harrison was called to give evidence. It wasn't an enjoyable experience. If watching lawyers and experts de-construct his song wasn't bad enough, he was called to demonstrate how he wrote the song. "It was the worse experience of my life, taking my guitar to court, trying to explain how I write a song," he explained.[5] Harrison insisted that he'd drawn inspiration for 'My Sweet Lord' from 'Oh Happy Day' rather than 'He's So Fine' as was being alleged. It was difficult enough convincing his own lawyers, let alone a judge, and the only person to endorse his claim, an ethnomusicologist from New York, was all but ignored. After three days testimony the judge found in favour of Bright Tunes. Harrison was found guilty of subconscious plagiarism and despite an appeal by his lawyers a date was set in November to determine damages. Despite the unpleasantness, Harrison had the good grace to take it on the chin and used the experience to write the cathartic 'This Song' for his next album.

In March, A&M released its final batch of Dark Horse albums. As with the previous batch none of the albums made the charts, and very possibly lost A&M even more money. Albums by Stairsteps, Attitudes and Ravi Shankar slipped out without fanfare. Only Ravi Shankar's *Music Festival From India* was produced by Harrison, and this dated from the spring of 1974. A more traditional album than Shankar's previous record for the label, it was recorded in 'Ye Drawing Room' of Harrison's Friar Park estate. "Most of the music was played live in the drawing room of my house – we had mikes up to the studio," he recalled.[6] Despite the Harrison connection and the recent American tour, the album didn't enter the charts. Although its records sold only moderately well, Dark Horse didn't scrimp on packaging. Most came with printed inner sleeves or inserts and Ravi Shankar's *Music Festival From India* even had the inside of the record sleeve printed with a repeated pattern based on the Om symbol. All this cost money and without a hit in sight A&M began to think twice about its deal with the label.

While Dark Horse continued to plough its singular furrow through pop's hinterland, Harrison set about recording his follow up to *Extra Texture (Read All About It)*. Unlike his previous album his new collection of songs would be recorded at F.P.S.H.O.T.. Harrison had planned to co-produce the album with Tom Scott. "I tried to get Tom Scott to co-produce the album with me, but Tom is really busy. Tom is really good to work with. He's a very technical musician, whereas I'm more like a jungle musician," Harrison recalled.[7] Rather than co-produce with Harrison, Scott acted as production assistant. Harrison recruited some familiar faces to record with alongside some he'd be working with for the first time. Drummer Alvin Taylor came from the Dark Horse band Stairsteps, while jazz and funk session keyboardist Richard Tee was recommended by Scott. The proliferation of tasteful soul/funk musicians ensured that his new album, provisionally titled *Crackerbox Palace*, would be an upbeat affair with funky overtones.

Recording sessions were relaxed but focused affairs. Starting in May, the band worked steadily through the songs Harrison had chosen to record. "Most of the tracks were done in one, two or three takes," recalled Alvin Taylor. "We worked from 11 in the morning until four or five, recording basic keyboard, guitar and bass parts."[8] A few keyboard parts were also overdubbed at this time. "Billy Preston came over after The Rolling Stones' Earls Court show. He played on this one song, one take, and drunk out of his mind. He went straight into it. Billy came back [later] and put some synthesizer and piano on the album," Harrison recalled.[9] The Rolling Stones played five nights at Earls Court from 22 to 27 May before heading to The Hague for a gig on 29 May. That means Preston was free on 28 May to visit Harrison and overdub his keyboard part. The Rolling Stones tour ended on 26 June at which point Preston was free to return to F.P.S.H.O.T. to overdub keyboards.

Despite the promising start, work on the album ground to a halt when Harrison contracted hepatitis. "When I started cutting the new album, I felt really awful. I put in a lot of late nights and wasn't eating right and then there was that episode with the Bull's Blood," he explained. "The guy who played piano on the album kept bringing in this horrible red wine called Bull's Blood and I drank a lot of it. I think that's what really did me in. Then I got food poising and jaundice and liver trouble and I turned all yellow."[10] A few weeks bed rest and some herbal medication prescribed by Dr. Yu and he was soon back on his feet and feeling better than he had for years.

Work on the album resumed with Billy Preston and Gary Wright overdubbing more keyboard parts. "Gary Wright passed through one day and he played on a song called 'Beautiful Girl'," Harrison explained.[11] With everything recorded, all that was left was to mix the album and have it mastered. Harrison had missed his July deadline, but nevertheless headed to Los Angeles to deliver the album to A&M as promised. "I arrived in L.A. with my album under my arm, all happy and I was given this letter saying: 'Give us back the million dollars, which was an advance, and give us the album. And when you give us the album, you don't get the million back'," Harrison told Anne Nightingale.[12] A&M informed Harrison that it wanted to use income from his solo deal with the label to offset losses incurred by Dark Horse. But Harrison was having none of it, he paid-off A&M in an out of court settlement and took himself and Dark Horse to Warner Brothers.

Thirty Three And ⅓ was eventually released by Dark Horse via Warner Brothers in November. Its title seemed obvious, both Harrison's age while recording the album and the speed at which the LP played, but it hadn't been used before. "I thought somebody must have used it before," confessed Harrison, "but apparently they haven't."[13] A more balanced album than previous long-players, it nevertheless reflected Harrison's state of mind at that time. According to Harrison: "Some of the songs are closer to the songs and spirit of *All Things Must Pass*. This new one has a more focused production on it, and it's very positive, very up, and most of the songs are love songs or happy songs. It doesn't compare at all to the last album, *Extra Texture (Read All About It)*. That one caught me in a less than happy mood."[14] He wasn't wrong. *Thirty Three And ⅓* has sonic and stylistic consistency that's missing from *Dark Horse*, while joy and light banish the gloomy miasma of his previous album. Combined with some good natured humour the resulting album was an enjoyable return to form.

Warner Brothers and Harrison worked together to give the album a sizeable promotional push. Harrison undertook a short promotional tour of America to launch his new partnership with Warner Brothers during which he screened three specially made promotional videos. On 18 November he appeared with Paul Simon to record two songs, 'Here Comes The Sun' and 'Homeward Bound' which were broadcast along with the promotional videos for 'This Song' and 'Crackerbox Palace' on the US TV show *Saturday Night Live*. Harrison also gave interviews to Tony Wilson for Granada TV, broadcast on 18 November, and to the BBC's *Whistle Test*, broadcast on 30 November. The following year he appeared on the German television show *Disco 77* miming to 'This Song', broadcast by ZDF on 5 February. The quiet one was actually making quite a lot of noise about his new album, combined with a renewed interest in The Beatles and his appearances on key TV shows, *Thirty Three And ⅓* did reasonable business.

Dark Horse issued *Thirty Three And ⅓* with generic labels, printed inner sleeve and outer gatefold sleeve. The sleeve was photographed and designed by Bob Cato and Mike Manoogian did the hand lettering. To promote the album Dark Horse sent a promotional interview album *Dark Horse Records Presents A Personal Music Dialogue With George Harrison At Thirty Three And ⅓* (PRO 649) to radio stations. The album featured selected highlight from *Thirty Three And ⅓* and Harrison in conversation with *Radio & Records* editor Mike Harrison.

Woman Don't You Cry for Me
George Harrison (vocals, guitars), Willie Weeks (bass), Alvin Taylor (drums), David Foster (clavinet), Richard Tee (keyboards), Tom Scott (horns)

Thirty Three And ⅓ roars into life with the crack of Alvin Taylor's drums and the growl of Willie Weeks' bass. Their tight, dynamic rhythm section drives the track along with hip soul/funk sophistication and when it's joined by Harrison's trademark slide guitar it is, perhaps, the quintessence of Harrison's pop/funk template. He wasn't the only Beatle to dig funk, Lennon was a fan too. But Harrison did it best. He'd been honing his soul/pop/funk production style since producing Billy Preston and Doris Troy in the late '60s. Indeed, 'Woman Don't You Cry For Me' dates from 1969 when its author toured briefly with the oh so soulful Delaney & Bonnie and Friends. Asked by Delaney to replicate a slide guitar part Dave Mason had played on their *Coming Home* album, Harrison began experimenting with a bottleneck and wrote 'Woman Don't You Cry for Me'.

Composed using an open 'E' tuning it was, according to Harrison, "basically written for bottleneck guitar."[15] It was, however, influenced by the music of his youth. "'Woman Don't You Cry For Me' was really like one of my first influences as a kid, when I was about thirteen, fourteen, that period of time when I got my first guitar and the big craze in England at the time was skiffle. It was easy to play and there was a lot of bands, skiffle groups, and you only had to know two chords, which really got people off the ground playing," Harrison explained.[16] Sometime before recording the song for *Thirty Thirty Three And ⅓* he cut a solo acoustic demo played without a bottleneck. In its early incarnation it has more than a passing resemblance to 'I Don't Care Anymore', and stripped of a super slick backing its country-blues feel reveals the influence of skifflers like Lonnie Donegan. "It's only got a couple of chords," Harrison revealed, "but played more in the country rock sort of thing, with slide guitar from my old pal, Eric."[17]

While Clapton had encouraged Harrison to return to the guitar after his brief liaison with the sitar, it was Ry Cooder who helped shape his signature slide guitar sound. "George always loved Ry Cooder," recalled Jim Keltner. "Ry was a huge influence on him. It was the musical connection, I think, because he used to always talk about Ry and his music to me when we first met."[18] A fan of

Cooder's slide playing, Harrison met up with him sometime in the early '70s and quizzed him about his sound and guitar set up. "From a conversation with Ry Cooder, I realized it was better to jack the bridge [on the guitar] up high and put some heavy gauge strings on, and then I found it was a much better sound," he recalled.[19] While those technical changes helped improve Harrison's sound, his technique, choice of notes and lightness of touch give his playing its distinctive character. Mellifluous, melodic and inventive, his playing on 'Woman Don't You Cry For Me' is among some of his best.

Dear One
George Harrison (vocals, guitars, keyboards, hi-hat, percussion), Richard Tee (organ)

One of several new songs written while holidaying in the Virgin Islands immediately before recording *Thirty Three And ⅓* , 'Dear One' finds Harrison deep in contemplation and spiritual ecstasy. A song of love and thanks written for the teacher most responsible for his spiritual reawakening, it's an ethereal and beatific meditation on universal love. "I dedicate 'Dear One' to Paramahansa Yogananda, who is a swami from India who left his body in 1952, as opposed to dying, he left his body and he's been probably the greatest inspiration to me from all of the swamis and yogis I've met. I've met a lot of the really good swamis and yogis and I like their company whenever I get the chance to spend some time with them. Yogananda I never met personally in this body but he had such a terrific influence on me for some very subtle reason. I can't quite put my finger on it. I just dedicate this track to him because it's like a lot of my feelings are the result of what he taught and is teaching still in his subtle state and I wrote this. This song was one of the newer songs I'd written and it's like a prayer and again just a realization of that appreciation," Harrison explained.[20]

Harrison's message is presented in a way that avoids the tiresome neophyte proselytizing that had critics and fans denounce him as a bore. This time, he was anything but dull. The song is as much about love as it is a prayer. It's the idea of universal love that really excites Harrison. As he explained: "I think individual love is just a little of universal love. The ultimate love, the universal love or love of God, is a basic goal. Each one of us must manifest our individual love, manifest the divinity which is in us. All individual love between one person loving another, or loving this that or the other, is all small parts or small examples of that one universal love. It's all God, I mean if you can handle the word 'God'. Ultimately the love can become so big that we can love the whole of creation instead of 'I love this but I don't like that.' Singing to the Lord or an individual is, in way, the same. I've done that consciously in some songs."[21]

To record 'Dear One', Harrison dismissed most of his band and worked with Richard Tee who played the organ. He then overdubbed percussion and keyboards as he had on the previous year's 'Grey Cloudy Lies', but to better effect. The relative melodic tranquillity of the verse conveys a deep emotional state that is contrasted with a more mobile counterpoint employed for the chorus that celebrate God's creation. Harrison develops this with subtle shading of contrasting tones and textures to breathe life into what might otherwise have been yet another dirge-like composition. It unifies the song, brings depth and warmth to the darker passages and a bright clarity to the celebratory sections. The melodic tension and sonic chiaroscuro unifies the song in much the same way that Harrison hoped that love would unify the whole of creation.

Beautiful Girl

George Harrison (vocals, guitars), Willie Weeks (bass), Alvin Taylor (drums), Billy Preston (organ), Richard Tee (keyboards), Tom Scott (horns)

Digging deep into his reserve of unfinished songs, Harrison pulled out 'Beautiful Girl' and polished it off for *Thirty Three And ⅓*. Started in 1969, while working on an album with Doris Troy, it was written using a twelve-string guitar borrowed from Stephen Stills. A year later, it was performed, still unfinished, while auditioning songs for what would become *All Things Must Pass*. "I couldn't get past the first verse with the lyrics and so the song sank back into the distance," Harrison recalled. "But I remembered it during 1976 and finished the lyrics."[22]

Inspired by his new love, Harrison completed the lyrics and set about recording the song. "I related [the lyrics] to Olivia... I can see all around beautiful girls in one way, ones who look good, and sometimes you see ones who don't particularly look good but have such beauty within them. And when you get the combination of both, then it's fantastic. Beauty to me is something, which comes from within and is not limited to the physical body, although that is helpful."[23] Harrison's soon to be wife had helped turn his life around after his eighteen month depression. With Olivia at his side the darkness that had previously engulfed him was banished by love, light and stability. Although it wasn't inspired by her, it was a fitting token for the new love in his life.

Introduced by Billy Preston's swirling organ the song rises and falls with the grace and beauty of a bird playing on summer thermals. As the song lacked a distinct chorus Harrison employed some descending guitar lines as a turnaround to help resolve his melody. Using layers of electric guitars he created a sonorous musical bed over which his slide guitar solos soar. Despite it having no obvious chorus, Harrison's instinctive use of dynamics and production detail mask any shortcomings. The result is a song that reveals its charms slowly over repeated visits. Like many of Harrison's best songs instant gratification is eschewed in favour of a more lasting and rewarding listening experience; an experience that reaps greater rewards with each repeat visit.

This Song

George Harrison (vocals, guitars), Willie Weeks (bass), Alvin Taylor (drums), Richard Tee (piano), Tom Scott (saxophone), Billy Preston (organ)

As 1975 drifted in to 1976, Harrison found himself slipping back into another blue funk. The plagiarism case that had been dogging him for years finally came to court and it was time to bite the bullet. Harrison was obviously upset about being singled out because as far as he was concerned dozens of hit records 'borrowed' liberally from other songs with impunity. Speaking to Anne Nightingale he said: "There's a point where it's accepted, and most people's music is like that anyway. It's the result of their passive experience. And I think in that case anyway, we as individuals, and The Beatles, were the ones most ripped-off by everybody when it comes down to guitar lines, solos, harmony counterpoints, you know, and all that."[24]

Everything about the case irked him. The court appearance at which he was ordered to perform was a cruel and absurd extension of the media circus he abhorred. It was the music business at its ugliest and greediest; a headache he could well do without. It was almost as if he were being taken down a peg simply because he was no longer part of The Beatles. "They were suing me for three notes in effect," he bemoaned. "At first I got into it and I was a bit depressed and then, as it went on, I was thinking, 'It's a joke! What are they talking about? It's a record; it's nothing to do with those three notes. It's a song, it's just a record.' I was getting very depressed and I was getting a bit paranoid about writing songs. I didn't even want to touch a guitar or a piano."[25]

The way out of his depression and paranoia was to do the very thing he'd been avoiding; pick up a guitar and write a song about the experience. If previously he'd channelled his gloom into dark and despondent songs that made Leonard Cohen appear positively effervescent, on this occasion he took the opposite approach and wrote something upbeat and tongue in cheek. "If I were a lawyer or an accountant," Harrison said, "I could have been down about it, but a musician is what I'm supposed to be, so I decided to be up about it."[26] "I wrote 'This Song' as a bit of light comedy relief – and as a way to exorcize the paranoia about song writing that had started to build up in me."[27]

More than just an exercise to dispel his paranoia about song writing, Harrison used the song to tell his side of the story with as much wit as he could muster. If the song didn't make his message clear enough, to drive his point home he commissioned a satirical video that did. Directed by Eric Idle, it depicts a court room transformed into a circus sideshow populated with bloodsucking lawyers and an indifferent judge. The song's up-tempo, funky backing and playful melody help mask the cutting, sardonic lyric and give it a positive spin that might well have been lost had the track been treated differently.

Staying close to the soul/funk template he employed for much of the album, Harrison drew on his fascination with Mowtown to fashion a contemporary sounding, radio-friendly record that was as witty as it was funky. "It's got that Tamla sort of bass line," he said. "I also got Eric Idle, who is one of the Monty Pythons, to throw in the funny lines, 'Could be sugar pie, honey bunch,' and, 'Naaaoo, sounds more like 'Rescue Me'."[28] The result was an engaging, cheerful pop song packed full of witty word play and in jokes that brought some much needed light relief to Harrison's work.

See Yourself

George Harrison (vocals, acoustic guitar, keyboards, tambourine), Willie Weeks (bass), Alvin Taylor (drums), Gary Wright (keyboards), Billy Preston (piano)

Harrison had a huge backlog of songs that went unrecorded by The Beatles, so many in fact that he'd forgotten all about 'See Yourself'. Dating from 1967, it was inspired by Paul McCartney's confession that he'd taken LSD and the media reaction to it. "The original idea in the first verse came about in the '60s when this thing happened with Paul McCartney and the press (1967). There was a big story in the press where somewhere they had found out that Paul had taken the dreaded LSD and they came hounding him, saying, 'Okay, have you taken it? Have you taken LSD?' And he said, 'Well, look, whatever I say, I'm gonna tell the truth and whatever I say, I just want you to know that it's you, the media, are gonna be the people who spread out what I say,' and they were saying, 'Did you take it?' And he said, 'Yeah, I took it,' and then they put it all over the papers. 'Paul McCartney took LSD.' Then the press came after us saying, 'Have you had it? Have you had it?' And we said, 'Sure, we had it years ago.' And then there was an outcry saying, 'You should have said you didn't take it.' In effect, they were saying, 'You should have told a lie.' The press pushed the responsibility onto Paul, saying, 'You're going to influence other people to take it,' and he had said out front like, 'It's gonna be your responsibility whatever I say,' and so I just thought of that. It's easier to tell a lie than it is to tell the truth. It's easier to criticise somebody else than to see yourself because people won't accept responsibility for themselves and it's very often that we all, and I included, point our fingers at people and criticize or pass judgement on others when first what we should do is try and see ourselves."[29]

The song is littered with biblical references, or what could be mistaken for quotations from holy books. The first verse re-works the biblical parable 'he that is without sin among you, let him first cast a stone' and it shouldn't be forgotten that Harrison was as fond of quoting the *Bible* as he was the *Bhagavad Gita*. He would explore the theme again with 'The Answers At The End', which, like 'See Yourself', is a reminder to avoid judging others when there are faults in one's own life that need addressing. However, 'See Yourself' is more than simply about judgement and hypocrisy, it's about being true to oneself. It's about having the courage to stand outside of what Nietzsche called 'herd mentality' because the herd values what does not have value and that limits personal growth. It actually takes a great deal of fortitude to be different, to stand beyond the pale, and to take a stand for what you believe to be right.

As with several songs that went unrecorded at the time of writing, Harrison couldn't get passed his initial idea; consequently the song remained unfinished until revisited for *Thirty Three And ⅓*. While much has been made of its reliance on keyboards and the influence of Gary Wright, one shouldn't forget that musicians like Stevie Wonder and Pete Townshend had been experimenting with keyboards and sequencers for years. Harrison would have been well aware of their records and would have been as influenced by them as by anybody else. Although Wright's keyboards are placed high in the mix and play the melody, it's actually Billy Preston's piano that provides the foundation, and it's his vibrant playing that breathes life into what could have been an otherwise tired song.

It's What You Value
George Harrison (vocals, guitar), Willie Weeks (bass), Alvin Taylor (drums), Richard Tee (piano), Emil Richards (marimba), Tom Scott (saxophone)

Side two swings into life with an up-tempo number that features some particularly fine drumming and neat hi-hat work by Alvin Taylor. 'It's What You Value' was inspired by another of Harrison's drummer chums, Jim Keltner. Harrison had to work hard to persuade a particularly uncommitted Keltner to join him on his 1974 American tour. Keltner had backed out of the tour, but eventually acquiesced specifying that he didn't want to be paid in cash. Instead, he asked for a new car to replace his old VW camper van. "Everybody got paid really well on the tour and I was trying to get this friend to play and he wouldn't do it. But I really needed him to play and I was saying, 'Come on, come on, please play,' and he finally said, 'Okay.' I begged him to death until he agreed to play and he said, 'Okay, but look. I don't wanna be paid for the tour but I'm sick of driving that old Volkswagen bus,' and I said to him, 'Oh, well, okay. I'll get you a car.' So we got him a car. I bought him a Mercedes 450," Harrison explained.[30]

Sometime after the tour Harrison got to hear that there had been rumblings of discontent among other members of the band. Some of the band were complaining because instead of getting a car all they got was cash. "Some of the other people, I later heard, were saying, 'How come he got a motor car and I only got a...' You know, it was one of them. So I just thought that in song. To one person, it's a big deal, but to somebody else, it's just like a throwaway thing. One person can have an opinion about something and something can be very important to one person and it can be of no importance whatsoever to somebody else. It can be a big deal to one person and no deal at all to someone else. It's really a matter of values; it's what you value," Harrison explained.[31]

Harrison began work on the song while holidaying in the Virgin Islands. His original lyric was a somewhat clumsy attempt to contrast material possessions with spiritual values. This was rejected in favour of an extended metaphor based on cars and motoring that explored human nature, individualism and value systems. Typically, Harrison questions the nature of human drives and desires and relates it back to what he'd learnt from Hinduism. It's what you've done and where you're at that influences who you are and what you value, and that's fine with him. The theme of tolerance and acceptance isn't that different from 'See Yourself' or 'The Answer's At The End'; the suggestion being that we should think less about ourselves and be more forgiving of others.

Another keyboard based song with a strong saxophone solo from Tom Scott, 'It's What You Value' grooves along nicely thanks to Taylor's and Weeks' rhythm section. Locked in tight and funky the two provide the rhythmic heartbeat of the song and make it swing like an elephant's trunk. Harrison's guitar is placed low in the mix and provides a few low-key fills, but it's Richard Tee's piano that works hardest to keep the song moving along. Tee knew instinctively what to play and what not to play to get the best out of the song. He holds back on the verses playing only stabs and accents, then lifts the song in the chorus with fuller chords to give it a bigger sound.

True Love (Cole Porter)
George Harrison (vocals, guitar), Willie Weeks (bass), Alvin Taylor (drums), Richard Tee (piano), David Foster (electric piano)

Harrison was a sucker for a good tune and a clever lyric. "I'm a big fan of so many kinds of rock and popular music," he told Timothy White, "from Bob Marley to Cole Porter to Smokey Robinson to Hoagy Carmichael."[32] Harrison, like Lennon and McCartney, learnt a lot from listening to his parents' record collection and BBC radio shows that played well-crafted but anodyne popular music of the day. Anybody could write a three chord twelve-bar, it took skill and talent to write a truly melodic pop song. Unlike some teenagers who might have dismissed their parents' music out of hand, Lennon, McCartney and Harrison embraced it and featured some of their favourite 'oldies' in their repertoire. They also played songs like 'True Love' out of necessity. "We, The Beatles, used to play this in Hamburg, Germany. We had to play like eight hours a night, so we used to play every song we would ever imagine. We used to do whatever we heard and whatever we could come up with in order not to repeat ourselves. So, I think that somewhere down the line we might have done that song," Harrison explained.[33]

The song lodged itself in some dark corner of Harrison's mind and years later popped out while he was idly strumming his guitar. "I don't know why I did this this time, but it just stuck with me," he said. "This summer, I was just playing it one day and it sounded good and I put down the track and the track sounded even better and the track sounded comical. The song to me is a comedy. It depends on what way you want to take it. It has a very simple melody and simple words. There's only about four words in it. I liked the tune and I started fiddling with it, and then I heard that arrangement. But it could be done anyway, really."[34]

Harrison probably classified 'True Love' as a 'comedy' song because the thought it a piece of fluff without much in the way of substance. That was certainly the way he treated the video he made to promote it. Giving the song an up-tempo treatment that would have had Bing Crosby reaching for the Benzedrine, Harrison's arrangement with its layers of slide guitar, organ and keyboards, breathed new life into a timeworn song.

Pure Smokey

George Harrison (vocals, guitar), Willie Weeks (bass), Alvin Taylor (drums), Richard Tee (keyboards), David Foster (keyboards), Tom Scott (saxophone)

Written while recording *Extra Texture (Read All About It)* in Los Angeles, 'Pure Smokey' companions that album's tribute to the singer and songwriter Smokey Robinson – 'Ooh Baby (You Know That I Love You)'. A more obvious tribute than his earlier accolade; the song started to take shape when Harrison found some nice chord changes that reminded him of Robinson's song writing. "I always liked Smokey Robinson & The Miracles from that period [the Sixties]. I found myself playing a lot of his records and I dedicated a tune on my last album to Smokey but I had written this one at the same time as that song, which was 'Ooh Baby'. This song is called 'Pure Smokey' and that was the title of one of Smokey Robinson's albums and it was really just like an idea that I had," he explained.[35]

Although the song became an homage to Smokey Robinson, it might not have started like that. 'Pure Smokey' is more than just a tribute to a great musician; it's a song about letting go of one's inhibitions, of being in the moment and giving thanks for the beautiful things that God has provided. It's as much a prayer as it is a compliment. The real source of Harrison's pleasure is the Lord. It's the Lord who gives us each new day, the Lord who gave the world William 'Smokey' Robinson Jr. and it's the Lord who Harrison is ultimately praising with his song. By his own admission the song became something other than what he'd originally planned. "Sometimes you get an idea and write a specific song, but other times – often – it turns itself into whatever it's going to be – with the effort put into it – and this turned into 'Pure Smokey'," Harrison explained.[36]

The song also marked a change in Harrison's demeanour. If he liked something or somebody then he'd say so, there'd be no holding back from now on. "Sometimes when you like something, you never get to say to somebody that you appreciated it. So I thought I'd use this way of getting across a point. I didn't want to be late. I didn't want to die and realize that I hadn't told my dad that I like him or whatever. It's like that. So I try and make a point. If I really like something now, I want to tell the person I like it, rather than to find out that I should have done something and never did. I try and live like that now," he explained. "So the song just says, in the past I would hesitate. I would feel some joy but before I showed my thanks, it became too late and now, all the way, I want to find the time to stop to say, 'Thank you, Lord for giving us each new day,' so it's really just to say thanks for certain things. And then it gets into Smokey, because I get a lot of pleasure out of his records and so it's a big thank you."[37]

When Harrison took the song into the recording studio he created a mellow soul groove to compliment his lyrical tribute. It's typical of the 'quiet storm' sound that Dark Horse Records delighted in releasing. With its slinky electric piano and Scott's lush saxophones, it's just the right side of sweet. Harrison plays two pithy solos that complement the melody and lend some bite to the confection. These are no off the cuff improvised solos, they were considered and no doubt played many times until Harrison was positive they couldn't be improved.

Crackerbox Palace
George Harrison (vocals, guitar), Willie Weeks (bass), Alvin Taylor (drums), Richard Tee (keyboards), Emil Richards (marimba), Tom Scott (lyricon, saxophone)

A metaphor for the soul's journey from birth to death, 'Crackerbox Palace' is a wry look at the vicissitudes of life inspired, in part, by a chance encounter with the former manager of Harrison's favourite comedian Lord Buckley. "First of all, the idea of 'Crackerbox Palace' was, as in the third verse of the song, where it says, 'Some times are good, some are bad. That's all a part of life, standing in between them all, I met a Mr Grief.' Now Mr Grief isn't just to rhyme with life, as people will think. He was and is a real person. I met Mr Grief at MIDEM. He used to manage the singer, Barry White. I met this guy and I was talking to him and the way he was talking, I said to him, 'Hey, you really remind me of somebody. You remind me of, I don't know if this is an insult or a compliment, but you remind me of Lord Buckley, who is my favourite comedian. But this guy is now dead.' Lord Buckley was one of the first very hip comedians. When I said this, this guy nearly fell over, and he said, 'Hey, I managed him for eighteen years.' And so I was talking to this guy about all these Buckley things and he told me that he lived in a little old shack, which he called Crackerbox Palace and I thought, 'Wow, Crackerbox Palace.' It just sounded so good and I wrote it on my Gitane cigarette packet. I just loved it, the way that it sounded. Then, at a later date, it stuck in my mind and I thought I'd write a song called 'Crackerbox Palace', and there it is," Harrison explained.[38]

Crackerbox Palace represents the absurdity of the physical world. In a few simple couplets, Harrison addresses the existential crisis that we all experience as we try to make sense of the world we inhabit. "It [Crackerbox Palace] could be the place where you live but I turned it more into the world, the physical world," he explained.[39] He resolves the crisis by reminding us that the physical world is only the manifestation of our awareness of it. We shouldn't confuse the world we create in our own minds with the real world. He's telling us to beware of Maya. The only way to know the world is through the Lord, and Harrison reminds us that he lives within us all. It's the Harrison philosophy of old, but as Michael Gross noted: "He seems to know that audiences would rather hear his philosophy hidden in the words of songs like 'Crackerbox Palace' than being expounded in dirges or speeches from Madison Square Garden stage."[40]

'Crackerbox Palace' is no dirge, far from it. Harrison's glistening slide guitars and Scott's chunky saxophones announce the arrival of a verse swimming in double-tracked slide guitars placed high in the mix. Like the rest of the up-tempo songs on the album, it swings and has an infectious melody that once heard is difficult to shake off. Harrison employs keyboards throughout to give the guitars breathing space and produce subtle shifts in dynamics and tone. There's a dramatic change in tonality when he lets Scott take the pithy, well-defined lyricon solo that restates the melody and helps to take the edge off the persistent sound of Harrison's slurred guitar notes. An exquisitely arranged and produced pop song, there could be no mistaking 'Crackerbox Palace' for anything other than a Harrisong.

Learning How To Love You
George Harrison (vocals, guitar), Willie Weeks (bass), Alvin Taylor (drums), David Foster (keyboards), Richard Tee (keyboards), Tom Scott (saxophone)

Harrison closed the album in style with an exquisitely crafted love song, 'Learning How To Love You'. Herb Alpert – the 'A' in A&M – asked Harrison if he'd write him a song. Inspired by Alpert's reading of 'This Guy's In Love With You' he attempted to write something in a similar vain. However, being Harrison the resulting song is not so much a piece of pop fluff as a philosophical contemplation on the nature of love. "The main thing I felt from the result of the LSD thing and then later getting involved with meditation, was the realization that all the goodness and all the strength and things that can support life is all coming out of love and not just as simple as one guy saying to a chick, 'I love you', you know," Harrison explained. "So often we say, 'I love you if,' you know, or, 'I love you when,' 'I love you but,' and that's not real love. Love is 'I love you even if you kick me in the head and stab me in the back, I love you.' Or, 'I love you, unconditionally,' and that goes beyond everything, and that is a pretty far out love to try and conceive and when I realized a little bit of love, then I realized how shallow it was."[41]

As with 'All Things Must Pass', Harrison employs the shift from night to day, from darkness to light (enlightenment) as a metaphor for his own shifting perspective and knowledge. Harrison describes a process of becoming, a personal journey that required patience, fortitude and an acknowledgement of one's limitations. "It's like with everything, it's like saying, 'Okay, I'm a singer now,' and then you start thinking, 'How good, how many notes can I hit, where's my limitations?' And you realize, 'I wanna be the greatest singer in the world, but I'm not because I'm limited by something,' and with love, it's like that. Okay, 'I love you,' but how do you measure it? How do you live with it? How do you be it? And then you realize how limited you are and then it's a process of learning how to develop that. It's all right saying, 'I love you,' but let's see it manifest. I just don't wanna hear the word, I wanna feel it and see it and be it."[42]

Harrison recorded the basic track in May with a small ensemble of crack session musicians. Alvin Taylor's drumming is delicate and airy while Richard Tee's electric piano fills the spaces with flawless perfection. His performance is every bit as soulful and inventive as Harrison's own lyrical guitar solo. Harrison had plenty of time to think about what he was going to play. Having cut the track in May he was laid low with hepatitis and forced to abandon the recording. Returning to the project with renewed enthusiasm, he recorded an exquisite guitar solo. "When I got a bit better, I finished the album. It left me really weak. It was a sort of jaundice. I had a good rest, though. It was a good excuse to stay in bed and not answer the phones. But I actually got out of bed when I was still all yellow. In fact, that guitar solo on 'Learning How To Love You', I went and played that because it was boring lying in bed. So if you listen to that guitar solo, it's a yellow guitar solo," he joked.[43]

·GEORGE·HARRISON·

DARK HORSE RECORDS
presents
A PERSONAL MUSIC DIALOGUE
with
GEORGE HARRISON
at

33⅓

·THIRTY·THREE & 1/3·

A PERSONAL MUSIC DIALOGUE
with
GEORGE HARRISON

Recommended for : Radio Station Broadcast, Press Reviews,
and General Promotional Use

PROGRAM

The following cue-script has been provided as a convenient pro-
gramming guide for broadcast:

SIDE ONE

Time	Status	
0:00	Opening Cue, Mike:	"On the release of your brand new album…"
8:11	Closing Cue, George:	"…It was important that they be the same songs in the States."
	Three-Second Band	Station break
0:00	Opening Cue, Mike:	"Since we're also on the subject of titles…"
11:04	Closing Cue, George:	"This song is for you and your aunties."
	Three-Second Band	(cue "This Song" 4:11)
0:00	Opening Cue, George:	"Look, I'd be willing, if every time I write a song…"
4:00	Closing Cue, George:	"This way, you know, it's got a bit more life in it."
	Open-Band	(cue "True Love" 2:43)

END OF SIDE ONE

Program Director Note
All music selections are from the Dark Horse album. *George Harrison Thirty Three and 1/3* (DH 3005) for further information, contact:

Dark Horse Records, 3300 Warner Blvd., Burbank, Ca. 91510

SIDE TWO

Time	Status	
0:00	Opening Cue, Mike:	"I would imagine by now, many of the people…"
5:37	Closing Cue, George:	"I welcome you to 'Crackerbox Palace'. We've been expecting you."
	Three-Second Band	(cue "Crackerbox Palace" 3:52)
0:00	Opening Cue, George:	"The world is a very serious and, at times, a sad place."
2:51	Closing Cue, Mike:	"As opposed to your own personal feelings of living in the material world."
	Three-Second Band	(cue "It's What You Value" 5:05)
0:00	Opening Cue, Mike:	"Any difficulties in dealing with the long list of fine musicians…"
7:10	Closing Cue, George:	"…When first what we should do is try and see ourselves."
	Three-Second Band	(cue "See Yourself" 2:48)
0:00	Opening Cue, Mike:	"What role in your life, the important things you're mentioning, does the concept of love play?"
2:50	Closing Cue, George:	"I wanna feel it and see it and be it."
	Three-Second Band	(cue "Learning How To Love You" 4:15)
0:00	Opening Cue, Mike:	"Well, you wrote a song on this album, 'Beautiful Girl'…"
0:46	Closing Cue, George:	"It's really just something that's coming out of the heart, you know, beauty like that…"
	Three-Second Band	(cue "Beautiful Girl" 3:38)
0:00	Opening Cue, Mike:	"You always hear, in the flood of new music that comes out…"
3:01	Closing Cue, George:	"And so it's just a 'thank you'."
	Three-Second Band	(cue "Pure Smokey" 3:52)
0:00	Opening Cue, Mike:	"When you write a song, say, like 'Pure Smokey'…"
2:39	Closing Cue, George:	"But played more in the 'Country Rock' sort of thing for my old pal, 'Clapper'."
	Three-Second Band	(cue "Woman Don't You Cry For Me" 3:15)
0:00	Opening Cue, Mike:	"Can you tell us a little bit about what went into the inspiration and the creation of 'Dear One'?"
1:37	Closing Cue, George:	"You know, just a realization of that appreciation."
	Three-Second Band	(cue "Dear One" 5:08)
0:00	Opening Cue, Mike:	"I have a feeling that we'll be listening to '33-1/3' at the time you make your '53-1/3' album…"
0:38	Closing Cue, George:	"Well, it's actually going to be on, ah…"

END OF SIDE TWO

Interviewer—Radio & Records Editor Mike Harrison
Concept—Dark Horse Label Manager Dennis Morgan
Engineer—George Charoyhas

For Promotional Use Only —— Not for Sale

Dark Horse Records Presents A Personal Music Dialogue With George Harrison At Thirty Three And ⅓
George Harrison
Side one: Interview 8:11 / Interview 1:04 / Interview 4:00
Side two: Interview 5:37 / Interview 2:51 / Interview 7:10 / Interview 2:50 / Interview 0:46 / Interview 3:01 / Interview 2:39 / Interview 1:37 / Interview 0:38
US release: November 1976; Dark Horse Records – PRO 649
Interviewer: Mike Harrison

Dark Horse issued this interview album to radio stations in America to promote *Thirty Three And ⅓*. The interview, conducted by Mike Harrison, covers the making of the album, the recent 'My Sweet Lord' court case that inspired 'This Song' and naturally spiritual matters. The practice of distributing interview records to radio stations was long established and had been used by Capitol Records to promote The Beatles back in 1964; RCA had done the same thing with Elvis Presley in the '50s.

The Story Behind "This Song"

PRODUCED BY GEORGE HARRISON 1976

Five years ago, suit was filed against George Harrison and Harrisongs Music, Inc. by the estate of songwriter Ronald Mack and Bright Tunes publishing. The suit alleged that George Harrison's 1970 composition "My Sweet Lord" infringed on the copyright of Mack's "He's So Fine," recorded in 1963 by the Chiffons. In February of 1976, the case went to court before Federal Judge Richard Owen. Over three days of testimony and cross-examination, both sides attempted to prove the musical derivation of "My Sweet Lord." Both plaintiff and defendant solicited the opinions of musicologists and music experts from various fields. At one point in the proceedings, huge charts were introduced, on which were inscribed the 3-note pattern Harrison was alleged to have plagiarized. In the confused discussion which followed, differences arose as to whether or not the 3-note sequence constituted a "song." "That ain't no song," testified gospel music expert David Butler, "that's a riff!" On August 31, 1976, Judge Owen ruled against Harrison, finding "My Sweet Lord" and "He's So Fine" "virtually identical," but adding that Harrison had unknowingly lifted the riff, owing to an "unconscious" familiarity with the chord pattern in question.

"The whole thing made me sort of paranoid," Harrison explained. "I got to thinking, what if every time you sat down to write a song, you had to pass your music by some expert or into a computer, to make sure you weren't copying someone else's notes. It's all a joke, really. Basically, songs are written to entertain and that's all there is to it. That's where it's at."

340

This Song

by George Harrison

This song has nothing tricky about it
This song ain't black or white and as far as I know
Don't infringe on anyone's copyright, so…

This song we'll let be
This song is in E
This song is for you and…

This tune has nothing Bright about it
This tune ain't bad or good and come ever what may
My expert tells me it's okay

As this song came to me
Quite unknowingly
This song could be you could be…

This riff ain't trying to win gold medals
This riff ain't hip or square
Well done or rare
May end up one more weight to bear

But this song could well be
A reason to see — that
Without you there's no point to…this song

Dark Horse Records
DRC 8294

DARK HORSE RECORDS
KLOKA PRODUCTIONS S.A.
PROMOTION
NOT FOR SALE
GEORGE HARRISON
Produced by George Harrison
Assisted by Tom Scott
STEREO
DRC 8294
(UAA 7228)S
3:45
THIS SONG
(George Harrison)
Ganga Publishing B.V.-BMI
℗1976 Ganga Distributors, B.V.

DARK HORSE RECORDS
KLOKA PRODUCTIONS S.A.
PROMOTION
NOT FOR SALE
GEORGE HARRISON
Produced by George Harrison
Assisted by Tom Scott
MONO
DRC 8294
(UAA 7228)
3:45
THIS SONG
(George Harrison)
Ganga Publishing B.V.-BMI
℗1976 Ganga Distributors, B.V.

DARK HORSE RECORDS
KLOKA PRODUCTIONS S.A.
GEORGE HARRISON
Produced by George Harrison
Assisted by Tom Scott
DRC 8294
(UAA 7228)S
3:45
THIS SONG
(George Harrison)
Ganga Publishing B.V.-BMI
℗1976 Ganga Distributors, B.V.

DARK HORSE RECORDS
KLOKA PRODUCTIONS S.A.
GEORGE HARRISON
Produced by George Harrison
Assisted by Tom Scott
DRC 8294
(UAA 7224)S
4:15
LEARNING HOW TO LOVE YOU
(George Harrison)
Ganga Publishing B.V.-BMI
℗1976 Ganga Distributors, B.V.

342

GEORGE·HARRISON
"THIS SONG"

©LOKA PRODUCTIONS, S.A.

Dark Horse Records

DRC 8294

THIS SONG
by George Harrison

This song has nothing tricky about it
This song it might go white and as far as I know
Don't infringe on anyone's copyright, so...

This song we'll let be
This song is in E
This song is for you and...

This tune has nothing Bright about it
This tune ain't bad or good and come what may
My expert tells me it's okay

As this song came to me
Unknowingly
This song could be you could be...

This riff ain't trying to win gold medals
This riff ain't hip or square well done or rare
May end up one more weight to bear

But this song could well be
A reason to see - that
Without You there's no point to...this song

Produced by George Harrison
Assisted by Tom Scott

MANUFACTURED & DISTRIBUTED
BY WARNER BROS. RECORDS INC.

℗ 1976 Ganga Distributors B.V. Made in U.S.A.

Produced
by
George
Harrison
Assisted
by
Tom Scott
From The
Dark Horse
Album
DH-3005

DRC 8294
(UAA7228)S

3:45

Ganga
Publishing
B.V.-BMI

THIS SONG
(George Harrison)
GEORGE HARRISON
℗1976 Ganga
Distributors, B.V.

Produced
by
George
Harrison
Assisted
by
Tom Scott
From The
Dark Horse
Album
DH-3005

DRC 8294
(UAA7224)S

4:15

Ganga
Publishing
B.V.-BMI

LEARNING HOW TO LOVE YOU
(George Harrison)
GEORGE HARRISON
℗1976 Ganga
Distributors, B.V.

A WARNER
COMMUNICATIONS
COMPANY

A

K 16856
(DRC 8294)
Side 1
3.52
K 16856 A
℗ 1976
45 r.p.m.

THIS SONG   (G. Harrison)
(Edited from the album "33⅓" K 56319)
GEORGE HARRISON
Produced by George Harrison
Assisted by Tom Scott
GANGA PUB'G B.V.

A WARNER
COMMUNICATIONS
COMPANY

K 16856
(DRC 8294)
Side 2
4.15
K 16856 B
℗ 1976
45 r.p.m.

LEARNING HOW TO LOVE YOU (G. Harrison)
(From the LP "33⅓" K 56319)
GEORGE HARRISON
Produced by George Harrison
Assisted by Tom Scott
GANGA PUB'G B.V

'This Song' / 'Learning How To Love You'
GEORGE HARRISON
Produced by George Harrison assisted by Tom Scott
UK release: 19 November 1976; Dark Horse K 16856; chart high; failed to chart.
US release: 3 November 1976; Dark Horse DRC 8294; chart high; number 25.

Dark Horse issued 'This Song' b/w 'Learning How To Love You' as a single in November 1976. Harrison filmed a promotional video for the A-side which received its première on *Saturday Night Live* on 20 November 1976. The video for 'Crackerbox Palace' was also broadcast and Harrison joined Paul Simon to perform 'Here Comes The Sun' and Simon's 'Homeward Bound'.

In America, Dark Horse issued mono/stereo promotional copies of the single to radio stations. The promotional single has white labels with black text with the Dark Horse logo top centre with 'PROMOTION NOT FOR SALE' below. The single was issued in a picture sleeve that featured the story behind 'This Song' on one side and the lyrics on the other. Initial pressings of the commercial edition of 'This Song' also had white labels, without 'PROMOTION NOT FOR SALE', and a picture sleeve with GEORGE HARRISON "THIS SONG" top centre and the Dark Horse logo bottom centre. The sleeve also features the lyrics to 'This Song' on the back. Later pressings came with full colour generic Dark Horse labels.

In Britain, 'This Song' was issued with full colour generic Dark Horse labels with a large 'A' above the spindle hole on the A-side in generic Dark Horse paper sleeves. The single was issued in picture sleeves throughout Europe, most countries basing their designs on either a head and shoulders portrait of Harrison or the album cover.

'My Sweet Lord' / 'Isn't It A Pity'
GEORGE HARRISON
Produced by George Harrison and Phil Spector

'Bangla-Desh' / 'Deep Blue'
GEORGE HARRISON

Capitol Records' desire to milk every last drop from the cash cow that was The Beatles was done with indecent haste and little regard for the Fabs legacy. Several 'new' Beatles singles were issued to companion album length compilations and classic 'oldies' were revived and reinstated as demand for back catalogue remained strong. In America, Capitol re-pressed two of Harrison's biggest hits with generic orange labels. Both records sold well enough to remain part of Capitol's back catalogue for several years and were themselves re-pressed with purple Capitol labels in the 1980s.

'Crackerbox Palace' / 'Learning How To Love You'
GEORGE HARRISON
Produced by George Harrison assisted by Tom Scott
US release: 24 January 1977; Dark Horse DRC 8313; chart high; number 19.

Issued as a single in America and Europe, 'Crackerbox Palace' was not issued as a single in Britain which went with 'True Love'. In America, Dark Horse issued mono/stereo promotional copies of the single to radio stations. The promotional single has full colour generic Dark Horse labels with 'PROMOTION NOT FOR SALE' centre left. Commercial copies of the single were issued with full colour generic Dark Horse labels and paper sleeve. As with the previous American single, 'Learning How To Love You' was issued as the B-side. Copies of the single issued in Europe were issued in picture sleeves, unique to the country of origin.

350

'True Love' / 'Pure Smokey'
GEORGE HARRISON
Produced by George Harrison assisted by Tom Scott
UK release: 11 February 1977; Dark Horse K 16896; chart high; failed to chart.

Despite having a specially commissioned film to promote the single, 'True Love' failed to chart in Britain. This was hardly surprising considering that the Punk rock revolution was at its zenith. Harrison couldn't have been more out of touch with contemporary popular music had he tried. Dark Horse issued the single with full colour generic Dark Horse labels with a large 'A' above the spindle hole on the A-side in generic paper sleeves.

352

'It's What You Value' / 'Woman Don't You Cry For Me'
GEORGE HARRISON
Produced by George Harrison assisted by Tom Scott
UK release: 31 May 1977; Dark Horse K 16967; chart high; failed to chart.

'It's What You Value' was the third song lifted from the album and issued as a single in Britain. As with the previous British release, it failed to chart. With no promotional video and little in the way of promotional push from Dark Horse/Warner Bros., it was doomed to failure. Dark Horse issued the single with full colour generic Dark Horse labels with a large 'A' above the spindle hole on the A-side in generic paper sleeves.

1979 : Blow Away

357

K17327

George Harrison

Blow Away

C/W

Soft Touch

Produced by George Harrison and Russ Titelman
(From the Album K56562 GEORGE HARRISON)

DARK HORSE RECORDS

℗ Loka Productions S.A.

360

George Harrison
Blow Away

George Harrison

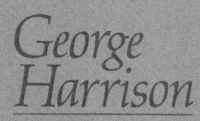

BLOW AWAY
SOFT-HEARTED HANA

Produced by George Harrison
& Russ Titelman

From the Dark Horse album
George Harrison (DHK 3255)

DRC 8763

DARK HORSE RECORDS
® Loka Productions S.A.

'Blow Away' / 'Soft Touch' [UK]
'Blow Away' / 'Soft-Hearted Hana' [US]
GEORGE HARRISON
Produced by George Harrison *and Russ Titelman*
UK release: 16 February 1979; Dark Horse K 17327; chart high; number 51.
US release: 14 February 1979; Dark Horse DRC 8763; chart high; number 16.

Blow Away
George Harrison (vocals, guitar), Willie Weeks (bass), Andy Newmark (drums), Steve Winwood (harmonium and Prophet synthesizer), Neil Larsen (electric piano), Ray Cooper (percussion)

Issued as a single a few weeks before the *George Harrison* album, 'Blow Away' is an up-beat pop song that packs a positive punch. Harrison began the song on a particularly wet winter's day in the grounds of his Friar Park estate. "I was sitting in the garden in a hut looking at the water as it was pouring with rain. We were having leaks in the house because some drain had blocked and I'd gone out in my hat and raincoat and was down there in the hut getting away from it all," he explained. Looking at the problem from a new perspective, he realized that it wasn't the leaking roof that troubled him, it was his thoughts about the leaky roof that were the source of his black mood. The solution was to realize that his thoughts were transitory and, like his malaise, would soon pass. 'Blow Away', he explained: "is [me] remembering again that that isn't me. Remember what the masters say 'I am basically a potentially divine, wonderful human being'; and all this rattiness or not feeling good is me attaching myself to the mind. The biggest thing that screws us up in life is the mind, it plays tricks on us and can trip you over. I thought 'I don't have to feel all this! I do love everybody', and that is really all you've got to do, manifest your love. The only thing we really have to work at in this life is how to manifest love."[1]

Russ Titelman suggests that 'Blow Away' was a metaphor for Harrison's life post-Beatles: "A lot of people don't realize that 'Blow Away' used the rebuilding of Friar Park, the broken-down nunnery that he restored as his family home, as a metaphor for how he had to rebuild his life after the Beatles broke up and his marriage to Patti Boyd ended."[2] It is, however, a more sophisticated metaphor than that. 'Blow Away' is about the power of positive thinking. Life can never happen the way your mind wants it to happen. If your life depends on the things around you being pleasant in order for your life to be pleasant you will always be disappointed. The mind is a lie and will always try and trick you into thinking falsehoods. Don't look to the physical world because if you do that you're looking in the wrong place. Everything that happens to you happens within you. That is where you should look.

The second verse is the most telling. It's here that Harrison embeds a subtle spiritual message within the song. The light that fills his head is not only physical light, it is the light of the world. It's the light of His Truth, the light of His Word, the light of eternal Life. It brings with it instant relief from the problems of the material world and reminds us that we are, in Harrison's words, 'potentially divine, wonderful human beings'. "George also brought both a very confident spiritual dimension and a knowledge of world music to pop music that it had never had previously," explained Titelman, "Things like that take guts and an inner will."[3] Harrison never lost the will to disseminate a spiritual message. He was as much a light as the light he believed in, reflecting the Lord's light through his music.

A demo recording of 'Blow Away' was issued on the re-mastered CD release of *George Harrison*. This multi-track recording features acoustic guitars, electric piano, bass and shaker, all, one assumes, played by Harrison. In light of his remark that once he passed away he'd rather people find a good finished master of his songs than a crummy old demo on a cassette, it's probably true to say that if he were still with us it would never have seen the light of day. As interesting as it is, the finished master knocks it into a cocked hat.

Soft Touch
George Harrison (vocals, guitar), Willie Weeks (bass), Andy Newmark (drums), Steve Winwood (backing vocals), Neil Larsen (electric piano), Ray Cooper (percussion)

Written while Harrison was holidaying in the Virgin Islands, 'Soft Touch' developed from a song he'd recorded at the beginning of the decade, 'Run Of The Mill'. Harrison found himself playing the descending horn part from the end of the song and used it to kick-start 'Soft Touch'. Inspired by his surroundings and, no doubt, by the new love in his life, he fashioned a pleasant song that draws on recurring imagery sun, moon, wind, rain, warmth, cold to paint a picture of both the island life he enjoyed and the new lady in his life.

Despite the fact that the song was inspired by the future Mrs. Harrison, its author dismissed it as 'nothing special'. Asked if there was one song that he was happiest with, or that meant more to him than the others, he admitted: "The two I least like are 'If You Believe' – I like the sentiment of that, but it's a bit obvious as a tune – and 'Soft Touch', which is just pleasant but there's nothing special about it, I feel."[4] That it was inspired by his future wife makes his remark all the more strange. Perhaps he thought the melody 'too obvious' and was a little embarrassed by its casual pop aesthetic. It is what it is, the sonic equivalent of those relaxing landscape photographs you see pinned to dentists' ceilings.

Soft-Hearted Hana

George Harrison (vocals, dobro, guitar), Willie Weeks (bass), Andy Newmark (drums), Steve Winwood (backing vocals), Neil Larsen (piano), Del Newman (brass arrangement)

An intoxicated sot of a song, 'Soft-Hearted Hana' reeks of Harrison's fascination with songwriters like Hoagy Carmichael, performers like George Formby and his delight in jokes and word play. You could argue that 'Soft-Hearted Hana' is itself little more than an extended joke. From Harrison's woozy dobro playing, which instantly evokes a sense of crapulence, made all the more intense by the use of varispeed tape effects as the song fades into a drunken stew, to the jokey rhyming slang and authentic audio verite recorded at his favourite boozer, it's as merry as Falstaff and as anarchic and playful as Vivian Stanshall on a boozy afternoon.

Harrison began writing the song while he was in Los Angeles soliciting advice from Warner Brothers about who should produce his new album. Ted Templeman told him he'd always liked 'Deep Blue', so Harrison took it upon himself to write something with similar chord changes. Writing the lyrics was more of a challenge and he only finished them a couple of months before work on the album began. When he did set pen to paper he drew on a recent trip to Maui for inspiration. The Hana is question isn't a woman but a small town on the east coast of Maui, and the hallucinogenic mumbo jumbo of the lyrics was intended to evoke a psychedelic experience brought on by consuming some magic mushrooms.

Blow Away data

'Blow Away' was issued by Dark Horse Records with generic labels and a picture sleeve. The British and American sleeves use different images of Harrison based on the album artwork. The British sleeve is based on the front cover of the album, while the American sleeve is based on the back cover of the album. In America, Dark Horse Records issued mono / stereo promotional copies of the A-side to radio stations as a single DRC 8763. The single was also issued with two label variations, one with large text the other with small text. 'Blow Away' reached number 51 on the UK charts and number 16 on the US charts. It peaked at number 2 on the US Adult Contemporary chart and at number 7 in Canada.

George Harrison

Faster

Chose a life in circuses
Jumped into the deepest end
Pushing himself to all extremes
Made it – people became his friend
Now they stood and noticed him
Wanted to be a part of it
Pulled out some poor machinery
So he worked, til the pieces fit
The people were intrigued
His wife held back her fears
The headlines gave acclaim
He'd realized their dreams
Faster than a bullet from a gun
He is faster than everyone
Quicker than the blinking of an eye
Like a flash you could miss him going by
No one knows quite how he does it but it's true
    they say
He's the master of going faster
Now he moved into the space
That the special people share
Right on the edge of do or die
Where there is nothing left to spare
Still the crowds came pouring in
Some had hoped to see him fail
Filling their hearts with jealousies
Crazy people with love so frail
The people were intrigued
His wife held back her fears
The headlines gave acclaim
He'd realized their dreams
Faster than a bullet from a gun
He is faster than everyone
Quicker than the blinking of an eye
Like a flash you could miss him going by
No one knows quite how he does it but it's true
    they say
He's the master of going faster
No need to wonder why
His wife held back her fears
So few have even tried
To realize their dreams
Faster than a bullet   (repeat chorus)

Words and Music by George Harrison © 1979. For
publishing details see label. All lyrics used by permission.
Reproduction prohibited. All rights reserved.

"Faster" is inspired by Jackie Stewart & Niki Lauda.
Dedicated to the Entire Formula One Circus.
Special thanks to Jody Scheckter. In memory of Ronnie Peterson.

Musicians

George Harrison
Guitars, Vocals & Backing Vocals. Bass on "Faster"
Andy Newmark Drums
Willie Weeks Bass
Neil Larsen Keyboards. Mini Moog
Ray Cooper Percussion
Steve Winwood Polymoog
Harmonium. Mini Moog & Backing Vocals
Emil Richards Marimba
Gayle Levant Harp
Eric Clapton Guitar Intro: "Love Comes To Everyone"
Gary Wright Oberheim. "If You Believe"
Del Newman String & Horn Arrangements

Lee Herschberg, Phil McDonald, Kumar Shankar
Engineers
Phil McDonald Remix Engineer
Recorded & Remixed at F.P.S.H.O.T.
Mastered at Strawberry, London.
Strings Recorded at A.I.R. Studios, London

Thanks To
Olivia Trinidad, Hailswood Gang, Baskerville Arms,
Cross Farm, Row Barge, Hook End Manor, Brands Hatch
Timekeepers, Barry & Steph, Eric & Tania, Ray Ray Cooper,
Derek & The Taylors, Walter Wolf, Maurice Milbourne, Molly
& Joan, Bernie Ecclestone, Mo & Ev, Steve Winwood, Russ
& Carol, Penny Ringwood, Lou & Zeke, Carl, Linda &
Prarthana, Denis O'Brien & Euro, Eddie Veale, Kumar,
Zion Yu and Old Uncle Cobbley.

"Soft-Hearted Hana" is for Bob Longhi
Porsches by Maltins
Hair by Peter Lawson
Tea by Louise de Ville Morel
Apprentice Millionaire Paul Lanzante

Mike Salisbury
Album Design & Cover Photographs

HARE KRSNA

Photographed by Jeff Burnham

368

Love Comes To Everyone

Go do it,
Got to go through that door,
There's no easy way out at all . . .
Still it only takes time
'Til love comes to everyone.

For you who it always seems blue
It all comes, it never rains
But it pours,
Still it only takes time . . .
'Til love comes to everyone.

There in your heart . . .
Something that's never changing;
Always a part of . . .
Something that's never ageing,
That's in your heart . . .

It's so true it can happen to you all; there,
Knock it and it will open wide,
And it only takes time
'Til love comes to everyone.

Not Guilty

Not guilty
For getting in your way
While you're trying to steal the day
Not guilty
And I'm not here for the rest
I'm not trying to steal your vest.
I am not trying to be smart
I only want what I can get
I'm really sorry for your ageing head
But like you heard me said
Not guilty.
Not guilty
For being on your street
Getting underneath your feet
Not guilty
No use handing me a writ
While I'm trying to do my bit.
I don't expect to take your heart . . .
I only want what I can get
I'm really sorry that you're underfed . . .
But like you heard me said . . .
Not guilty.
Not guilty
For looking like a freak
Making friends with every Sikh
Not guilty
For leading you astray
On the road to Mandalay.
I won't upset the apple cart
I only want what I can get
I'm really sorry that you've been misled . . .
But like you heard me said . . .
Not guilty.

Here Comes The Moon

Everybody's talking up a storm
Act like they don't noticed it
But here it is and here it comes . . .
Here comes the moon, the moon, the moon,
the moon, the moon.

Impulse always quickens when it's full
As it turns my head around me
Yes it does and here it comes
Here comes the moon, the moon, the moon,
the moon, the moon.

God's gift I see that's moving up there into the
night . . .
Though dark the mirror in the sky reflects us our
light:
Looks like a little brother to the sun
Or mother to the stars at night
And here it is and here it comes
Here comes the moon, the moon, the moon,
the moon, the moon.

Breath it always taken when it's new
Enhance upon the clouds around it
Yes it is and here it comes
Here comes the moon, the moon, the moon.

Soft-Hearted Hana

I ate it and at once my eyes could see you
No sooner had I ōōped it down
I felt so far off from the ground I stood on.
My legs they seemed to me like high-rise buildings
My head was high up in the sky
My skin the sun began to fry like bacon.
And then somebody old appeared and asked had I
come far . . .
And hadn't they just seen me up on Haleakala . . .
I kept on body surfing to pretend I hadn't heard
There was someone there beside me, swimming like
Richard III
And I'm still smiling.
Seven naked native girls swam seven sacred
pools . . .
Lone-ranger smoking doobies said you're breaking
all the rules . . .
You'd better get your clothes on or else there'll be a
row . . .
If it wasn't for my sunstroke I would take you on
right now . . .
And I'm still smiling.
I fell in love with my Soft-Hearted Hana
She entered right in through my heart
And now although we're miles apart
I still feel her.
She lives beneath the crater in the meadow
She moves among the fruit and grain
You can meet her after heavy rain has fallen.

Blow Away

Day turned black, sky ripped apart
Rained for a year 'til it dampened my heart
Cracks and leaks
The floorboards caught rot
About to go down
I had almost forgot.
All I got to do is to love you
All I got to be is, be happy
All it's got to take is some warmth to make it
Blow Away, Blow Away, Blow Away.
Sky cleared up, day turned to bright
Closing both eyes now the head filled with light
Hard to remember the state I was in
Instant amnesia
Yang to the Yin.
All I got to do is to love you
All I got to be is, be happy
All it's got to take is some warmth to make it
Blow Away, Blow Away, Blow Away.
Wind blew in, cloud was dispersed
Rainbows appearing, the pressures were burst
Breezes a-singing, now feeling good
The moment had passed
Like I knew that it should.
All I got to do is to love you
All I got to be is, be happy
All it's got to take is some warmth to make it
Blow Away, Blow Away, Blow Away.

Dark Sweet Lady

My dark sweet lady
You really got to me
You gave me everything
I've really fallen.
You came and helped me through
When I'd let go
You came from out the blue
Never have known what I'd done without you.
My dark sweet lady
Your heart so close to mine
You shine so heavenly . . . and
I love you dearly.

Your Love Is Forever

Sublime is the summertime, warm and lazy . . .
These are perfect days like Heaven's about here,
But unlike summer came and went—
Your love is forever,
I feel it and my heart knows

That we share it together.
Resigned to the wintertimes cold and dreary
Peering into fire flames, burning I know
That unlike winter came and went
Your love is forever
I feel it and my heart knows
That we share it together
I feel it and my heart knows you're the one
The guiding light in all your love shines on
The only lover worth it all
Your love is forever.

Soft Touch

You're a soft touch baby
Like a snowflake falling
My whole heart is melting.

As a warm son rises
Into joy I'm sailing
To your soft touch baby.

Eyes that shine from depths of your soul
Fixed by their charm, take my control
Love so sweet as the ocean is wide
Caught by your waves
Drawn to your side.

As a cool wind blows me
All the treetops whisper
To your soft touch baby.

As a new moon rises
Those ideas of heaven
Fall in your soft touch baby.

Eyes that shine from depths of your soul
Fixed by their charm, take my control
Love so sweet as the ocean is wide
Caught by your waves
Drawn to your side.

You're a soft touch baby
Like a snowflake falling
My whole heart is melting.

As a warm son rises
Into joy I'm sailing
To your soft touch baby.

If You Believe

You can worry your life away with
Not knowing what each new day may bring to you
Or take each day as it goes on
Wake up to the love that flows on, around you.
If you believe—if you believe in you
Everything you thought is possible, if you
believe . . .
If you believe in me . . .
All your love's reflected back to you
When you believe.
Too many troubles you can't control
To get you falling into the holes they dig for you
Get up—you have all your needs; Pray
Give up—and it all recedes away from you.
If you believe—if you believe in you
Everything you thought is possible if you believe . . .
If you believe in me . . .
All your love's reflected back to you
When you believe.

PRODUCED BY GEORGE HARRISON & RUSS TITELMAN

®Loka Productions S.A.

STEREO
K 56562
(DHK 3255)
© 1979 Ganga
Distributors B.V.
K 56562 A
SIDE ONE

GEORGE HARRISON
1. LOVE COMES TO EVERYONE
2. NOT GUILTY
3. HERE COMES THE MOON
4. SOFT-HEARTED HANA
5. BLOW AWAY

GEORGE HARRISON
All titles written by George Harrison
Produced by George Harrison
& Russ Titelman
GANGA PUBLISHING B.V. (1—5)

®Loka Productions S.A.

STEREO
K 56562
(DHK 3255)
© 1979 Ganga
Distributors B.V.
K 56562 B
SIDE TWO

GEORGE HARRISON
1. FASTER   2. DARK SWEET LADY
3. YOUR LOVE IS FOREVER   4. SOFT TOUCH
5. IF YOU BELIEVE (George Harrison/Gary Wright)

GEORGE HARRISON
All titles written by George Harrison
except where shown
Produced by George Harrison
& Russ Titelman

GANGA PUBLISHING B.V. (1—4)
GANGA PUBLISHING B.V.
WARNER BROS. MUSIC LTD. (5)

®Loka
Productions
S.A.

DHK 3255
SIDE 1

GEORGE HARRISON
Produced by George Harrison & Russ Titelman
1. LOVE COMES TO EVERYONE   4:33
2. NOT GUILTY   3:36
3. HERE COMES THE MOON   4:46
4. SOFT-HEARTED HANA   4:03
5. BLOW AWAY   3:59

All selections written by George Harrison
All selections published by
Ganga Publishing, B.V. - BMI

®1979 Ganga
Distributors, B.V.

®Loka
Productions
S.A.

DHK 3255
SIDE 2 RE-1

GEORGE HARRISON
Produced by George Harrison & Russ Titelman
1. FASTER   4:40
2. DARK SWEET LADY   3:20
3. YOUR LOVE IS FOREVER   3:45
4. SOFT TOUCH   4:00
5. IF YOU BELIEVE   2:53
(George Harrison, Gary Wright) Ganga Publishing, B.V. - BMI/High Wave Music - ASCAP
All selections written by George Harrison
except as indicated
All selections published by Ganga Publishing,
B.V. - BMI except as indicated
®1979 Ganga
Distributors, B.V.

George Harrison
GEORGE HARRISON
Side one: Love Comes To Everyone / Not Guilty / Here Comes The Moon / Soft-Hearted Hana /Blow Away
Side two: Faster / Dark Sweet Lady / Your Love Is Forever / Soft Touch / If You Believe (Harrison–Gary Wright)
UK release: 23 February 1979; Dark Horse K 56562; chart high; No. 39.
US release: 20 February 1979; Dark Horse DH 3255; chart high No.14.
Produced by George Harrison and Russ Titelman.

George Harrison (guitars, vocals, backing vocals, bass) / Andy Newmark (drums) / Willie Weeks (bass) / Neil Larsen (keyboards, mini-Moog) / Ray Cooper (percussion)/ Steve Winwood (polymoog, harmonium, mini-Moog, backing vocals) / Emil Richards (marimba) / Gayle Levant (harp) Eric Clapton (guitar intro 'Love Comes To Everyone') / Gary Wright (oberheim 'If You Believe') / Del Newman (string and horn arrangements)

Harrison began 1977 with a trip to Germany, Holland and France to promote his *Thirty Three And ⅓* album. The five day tour of Europe saw him give a number of interviews and make an appearance on the ZDR TV show *Disco 77*. His promotional duties over, he took a holiday to India to attend the wedding of Kumar Shankar before returning home via Los Angeles. Once home, he recorded his tribute to his new label boss, Mo Ostin. 'Mo' was played at Mr. Ostin's fiftieth birthday party, but remained unreleased until December 1994, when it was issued by Warner Bros. as part of a six CD promotional boxed set celebrating Mo Ostin's distinguished career. It remains commercially unavailable.

Despite his recent run of positive reviews and hit records, Harrison had grown tired of the music business and decided to take a year out. "Having been in this business now for so long – it was 1961 when we first made a record, I think, so it's eighteen years now – the novelty's worn off," he told Mick Brown. "Really, it comes down to ego. You have to have a big ego in order to keep plodding on being in the public eye. If you want to be popular and famous, you can do it; it's dead easy if you have that ego desire. But most of my ego desires as far as being famous and successful were fulfilled a long time ago."[5] While he still enjoyed making music, the process of promoting it, even the relatively small scale promotion that he was asked to undertake, had become tiresome. Instead, he decided to follow his favourite Formula One racing teams as they crisscrossed the globe.

As a boy, Harrison had spent hours watching motor racing at the Aintree Racecourse. Now he was as famous as the racing drivers he admired, he socialized with the people he'd previously idolized from afar. The exclusive world of Formula One racing was the next best thing to being a rock star. Indeed, it was better than being a rock star. He could hang out with glamorous celebrity peers without having to be Beatle George. However, even in the exclusive world of Formula One he couldn't escape his past. "I was getting embarrassed because I was going to all these motor races, and everybody was talking to me like George, the ex-Beatle, the musician, asking me if I was making a record and whether I was going to write some songs about racing, and yet musical thoughts were just a million miles away from my mind. Anyway, I talked to [Niki Lauda] once after he had won the world championship again, 1977 at Watkins Glen, and he was talking about all the bullshit in his business – the politics and the hassles – and he was saying how he just likes to go home and relax and play some nice music. And I thought, 'Shit, I'm going to go and write some tunes, because these people are all relating to me as a musician, and yet I'm here just skiving; maybe I can write a song that Niki on his day off may enjoy.' So that was it," he explained.[6]

As autumn rolled into winter, he made his way to Hawaii, where he began writing in earnest. Having already penned a brace of new songs inspired by his motor-racing buddies, he found that he couldn't stop the songs flowing out of him and he began making simple demo recordings for what would become his next album. Another reason for recording a new album was that he wanted to turn his demos into finished recordings. "Once you do write a tune, I don't know why, but there is that desire to have it made into a proper record. If I were to die, I'd rather people find a good finished master of my songs than a crummy old demo on a cassette. Maybe originally it was other people's expectations that prompted me, but once I got writing tunes I got my motor ticking over again and it's fun – you get in the studio, you get going and you can enjoy it all over again," he told Mick Brown.[7]

Before he began recording, Harrison decided that he needed to find somebody to co-produce the record with him. Heading back to Los Angeles, he found himself at Warner Bros. HQ soliciting advice about who he should work with. "I went to Warners in Burbank and spoke to the three staff producers there – Ted Templeman, Lenny Waronker and Russ Titelman. And I played them some demos of the tunes I'd written and said, 'Come on, you guys, give me a clue. Tell me what songs you've liked in the past, what songs you didn't like; give me a few ideas of what you think.' And they didn't know what to say. Templeman said he had liked 'Deep Blue', the B-side of the 'Bangla-Desh' single, which is a bit obscure – so I went home and wrote a song, with a similar sort of chord structure to that, 'Soft-Hearted Hana'. But in the end I decided I'd work with Russ Titelman. He did the first Little Feat album and, with Lenny Waronker, he's co-produced Randy Newman, James Taylor and Ry Cooder – he's Ry Cooder's brother-in-law, in fact. And he's a nice, easy person to get along with, which is more important than the person's musical taste, because you spend five months together – you've got to like each other a bit. He helped me decide what sort of tunes to use, encouraged me to actually finish certain songs, and helped actually lay the tracks down. It's hard for an artist to be in the booth and in the studio," Harrison revealed.[8]

Harrison had long admired Ry Cooder, so the chance to work with his producer, who also happened to be his brother-in-law, may well have influenced his decision. Titelman had an impressive track record, so Harrison knew what he was capable of. The records he'd produced dovetailed nicely with Harrison's taste and as it was his job to keep pace with current trends he could guide Harrison, who'd lost touch with what was happening in the charts. "At the time I felt I didn't really know what was going on out there in music, and I felt Russ, who was in music day by day, would give me a bit of direction," he explained.[9]

Although he'd worked with some big names, Titelman hadn't produced anybody as successful or famous as Harrison and later admitted to being somewhat star struck. "With George Harrison, there was a certain awe I had to get past, but I came to understand the specialness of what he brought to the Beatles and to popular music in his solo work. George's guitar style and sounds are incredibly unique, but it's important to realize that George was not that much of a jamming soloist, as Eric Clapton was and is. So all George's unforgettable Beatles solos were very deliberately thought out. He was a craftsman of the highest order and he remains that kind of player in his solo music. The fluid approach he got from India was in songs on *George Harrison*, like 'Dark Sweet Lady', 'Love Comes To Everyone' and 'Blow Away', which is a phenomenal pop single."[10]

Titelman gave Harrison's sound a subtle revamp. Punk and New Wave may have been a hit with the critics and kids, but in radioland Pop was still king to Disco's queen. Occasionally one of the more melodic New Wave acts like Elvis Costello or The Police would get daytime airplay, but as far as most radio producers and the general public were concerned a nice tune and a good beat was all that mattered. If you wanted to listen to more esoteric bands like The Pop Group, The Fall or The Damned, you had to wait until late into the evening when John Peel was allowed to broadcast pretty much what he wanted.

As a staff producer at Warner Bros., Titelman knew how to make commercial records that appealed to radio stations. He took Harrison's penchant for R&B and tailored it to match the fashion for soft rock with a disco-lite back beat. It was exactly the kind of laid back, middle-of-the-road sound that Harrison and his motor racing friends would relax to after a hard day at the studio or racing track. In fact, Harrison admitted to David 'Kid' Jensen that 'Here Comes The Moon' was such a peaceful song that when mixing it he kept drifting off. "By the time it gets to the end, it's put me in a dream world," he confessed.[11]

As with his previous album, Harrison recruited an American rhythm section to lay down the back beat. Andy Newmark, who'd played drums on the *Dark Horse* album, was recalled and Willie Weeks made a return trip to Henley-on-Thames to play bass. Emil Richards also returned to play the Marimba. The British were represented by his old friend Eric Clapton and new boy Steve Winwood, who played keyboards on the album, and made his first appearance on a Harrison record. Also appearing on a Harrison album for the first time was Elton John's percussionist Ray Cooper. The extrovert percussionist would develop a close friendship with his new employer and eventually take up a management position within Harrison's HandMade film company.

Work on the album began midway through April 1978 and finished in early October. Finished too late to catch the lucrative Christmas sales period, the eponymous album was held back until February 1979 and released in Britain on 23 February – two days before Harrison's 36th birthday. To promote the album in Britain, Harrison appeared on the BBC Radio 1 programme *Roundtable*. Joining Harrison to review that week's record releases was presenter David 'Kid' Jensen and Michael Jackson. Harrison also gave interviews to Nicky Horne for ITV's *Thames At Six* and Capitol Radio's *Your Mother Should Know* and was interviewed by Peter Clements for Beacon Radio.

George Harrison data

Dark Horse issued *George Harrison* with generic labels, printed inner sleeve and full colour cover in February 1979. In American the album was also issued by Columbia House Record Club. These editions, sold via mail order, can be distinguished by the text "Manufactured by Columbia House under License" on the back cover. The album was issued on CD by Warner Bros. in America (9 26613-2) and Japan (WPCP-4382) in 1991. A re-mastered edition with the 'bonus' track, 'Here Comes The Moon' (demo) was issued in 2004. When the album was issued as a download via iTunes an additional 'bonus' track, 'Blow Away' (demo), was included with the album.

Love Comes To Everyone
George Harrison (vocals, guitar), Eric Clapton (guitar), Willie Weeks (bass), Andy Newmark (drums), Steve Winwood (mini-Moog, backing vocals), Neil Larsen (keyboards), Ray Cooper (percussion)

The album opens with what was possibly the strongest song Harrison had written and recorded in some time, 'Love Comes To Everyone'. If ever a song passed the old grey whistle test, this was it. It's an infectious earworm that once heard is almost impossible to shake off. A near perfect pop song that flows seamlessly from one harmonically rich passage to the next, its easy, loose shuffle, a feature of many records from this period, compounded Harrison's desire to fashion an audio anodyne with a contemporary radio-friendly production.

Harrison began the song in the autumn of 1977. He'd bought a Roland effect unit that inspired him to write this and other melodies on the album. "It [the Roland effect] is slightly different to phasing or to the Leslie speaker which is a revolving speaker in a cabinet," he explained. "It gives a little added atmosphere to the sound, so when you even play one chord on electric guitar it sounds pretty."[12] Harrison liked pretty sounds, relaxing sounds, sounds that made him feel nice and were in harmony with his world. While others were cranking up the distortion to express the anger and angst of youth, Harrison's guitar chimed with good vibes and sunny optimism.

This is Harrison re-establishing his creative persona, both musically and lyrically. It may not have been obvious to the casual listener, but 'Love Comes To Everyone' was every bit as evangelical as 'My Sweet Lord'. As with previous songs, Harrison couched his message in deliberately ambiguous statements. However, it's not too difficult to uncover the real meaning beneath the worldly varnish he applies here. The love that comes to everyone is eternal, pure and untarnished, it's God's love.

'Love Comes To Everyone' alludes to Revelation 3:20: "Behold, I stand at the door and knock; if any man hear My voice, and open the door, I will come in to him, and will sup with him, and he with Me". A confirmed Hindu, Harrison was nevertheless fond of quoting the Bible. "He was a very, very avid reader and not just an avid reader of Eastern spirituality, but a very avid reader of the Gnostic gospels, the other versions of the historical Christ, the Gospel of Thomas," said his friend Deepak Chopra. "When he signed a letter he would always put an eastern symbol and also put a cross. He very much had a relationship with Christ as well."[13]

'Love Comes To Everyone' was chosen as the first single taken from the album, but was held back when it was decided to go with 'Blow Away'. It was eventually issued as a single, but despite its pop pedigree, it failed to catch the public ear and disappeared, leaving little trace of ever having been released at all.

Not Guilty

George Harrison (vocals, guitar), Willie Weeks (bass), Andy Newmark (drums), Steve Winwood (harmonium), Neil Larsen (electric piano), Ray Cooper (percussion)

As with previous albums, Harrison rifled through his back pages in search of suitable material and selected a song from a decade earlier. 'Not Guilty' was written during a burst of creativity that would see The Beatles fill a double album and more during 1968. "It was after we got back from Rishikesh in the Himalayas on the Maharishi trip, and it was for the *White Album* . We recorded it, but we didn't get it down right or something. Then I forgot all about it until a year ago, when I found this old demo I'd made in the Sixties," Harrison recalled.[14]

The Beatles had so much material to choose from that despite spending considerable time and effort, three nights and 99 takes, fashioning 'Not Guilty' it remained locked in EMI's tape archive until finally issued in 1996 when on The Beatles *Anthology 3*. The Beatles recording is full of the post-Summer of Love anger and frustration that spilled over into riots in London, Paris and Chicago. Distorted, disjointed and selfishly apologetic, its screaming guitars and jarring changes in time signature mark it the work of a group of angry young men irritated as much with each other as with the world around them.

The Beatles made an acoustic demo recording of 'Not Guilty' at Harrison's Esher home prior to taking it to the studio. It's not as aggressive or fractured as the group's later studio take, but still nowhere near as mellifluous as Harrison's solo remake which was based on The Beatles' demo. Like his solo version it lacks the clumsy 3/8 section that made The Beatles' studio version so problematical to record.

His new laid back remake is the antithesis of the Fabs studio prototype. Its shimmering electric piano and warm acoustic guitars are inviting and enveloping. The change was such that Harrison thought the song "would make a great tune for Peggy Lee or someone". It would be difficult to imagine Peggy Lee attempting The Beatles angry original, but this new recording was made by an older, wiser, more mature Harrison. The bitterness and anger haven't entirely disappeared, but it has been tempered by age and experience. If anything, Harrison's tart lyrics sit rather uncomfortably with the smoky jazz-pop backing. "The lyrics are a bit passée – all about upsetting 'Apple carts' and stuff – but it's a bit about what was happening at the time," he admitted.[15]

Here Comes The Moon

George Harrison (vocals, guitar, sitar drone), Willie Weeks (bass), Andy Newmark (drums), Steve Winwood (keyboard, backing vocals), Neil Larsen (electric piano)

Further references to Harrison's musical past surface with 'Here Comes The Moon'. A little brother to 'Here Comes The Sun', it was perhaps too obvious a reference, but one that Harrison acknowledged: "I thought I couldn't write a song called that, they'll kill me. But as it happened, I wrote the song and it turned out really nice, so it stands up in its own right."[16] He also argued that there were plenty of "other songwriters around, they have had ten years to write 'Here Comes The Moon' after 'Here Comes The Sun'. As nobody else wrote it I thought I might as well do it myself."[17]

Inspired by a particularly beautiful sunset he witnessed in Hawaii, 'Here Comes The Moon' shares more than just a similar title with its progenitor. Both songs employ a descending motif to link the chorus and verse. Harrison couldn't have been more self-referentially brazen if he'd tried. In keeping with its title, 'Here Comes The Moon' was possibly the most soporific song on the album. It certainly had desired effect on its composer who admitted that it sent him into a 'dream world'.

The bringer of hope and spiritual awakening, the moon nevertheless excited Harrison. It symbolized something very important to him. Besides being an example of one of the many wondrous things that God has bestowed upon us, it symbolizes new beginnings and the state of wholeness that human beings attain at full Self-realization. The moon reflecting the light of the sun as people reflect the Light of the Lord. Self-realization grows over time, from total darkness and non-existence to illuminated wholeness. It's only when we reflect His light that we can claim to be made in His image. Harrison was responding to more than the moon's appearance when he wrote the song, for him it was a powerful metaphor for the state of fully realized human beings.

Faster
George Harrison (vocals, acoustic guitar, electric slide guitar, bass), Andy Newmark (drums), Ray Cooper (percussion), Del Newman (string arrangement)

Some songs arrive as if by magic, others are crafted, honed and perfected over weeks, months and sometimes years. 'Faster' evolved over several months and was written as a challenge to see if he could write about something specific, Formula One racing. Harrison began by lifting the title from racing driver Jackie Stewart's biography for his own. While the original idea was to write about something specific, the song turned into something much more ambiguous. "The story can relate to me or you or anybody in any occupation who becomes successful and has pressure upon them caused by the usual jealousies, fears, hopes, etc. I have a lot of fun with many of the Formula One drivers and their crews and they have enabled me to see things from a very different angle than the music business I am normally involved with," he explained.[18]

Harrison used speed as a metaphor for the pressures that come with fame. If anything, the pressure Formula One drivers face is even more intense than that experienced by pop stars. Formula One racing can be a matter of life and death, being a pop star isn't. That is unless you're a Beatle. When The Beatles were at the height of their fame things got so dangerous that the only way they could get to their concerts was by armoured car or helicopter. Even after the fame had abated, Lennon, and later Harrison, became victims of their fame. 'Faster' is as much Harrison's condensed autobiography as it is Jackie Stewart's. Speaking to Mick Brown, he said: "I'm happy with the lyrics because it can be seen to be about one driver specifically or any of them, and if it didn't have the motor-racing noises, it could be about the Fab Four really – the jealousies and things like that."[19]

Harrison plays guitars and bass on the track, which is odd because he had one of the world's best bassists at his disposal. There can be little doubt that had Weeks played on the track he would have added some much needed Vroom Vroom to the recording. For a song inspired by motor racing, it's just a little too pedestrian. Coupled with an unadventurous melody and a workmanlike string arrangement, it fails to capture the heightened sense of awareness that Harrison was trying to convey.

Dark Sweet Lady
George Harrison (vocals, guitars, mandolin), Willie Weeks (bass), Steve Winwood (harmonium), Andy Newmark (drums), Ray Cooper (marimba, conga, maracas), Gayle Levant (harp)

'Dark Sweet Lady' was inspired by the new love in Harrison's life, Olivia Trinidad Arias. The soon to be Mrs. Harrison asked her future husband if he could write a song with a Spanish feel. Naturally, he obliged. A song cocooned in a rich, velvety glow of sonic textures, 'Dark Sweet Lady' conveys a sense of rootedness and contentment that had been missing until she arrived in his life.

The use of a harp adds definition and lifts the song with its subtle swirling glissandos. Ray Cooper's marimba serves a similar function by helping to describe the melody. While the harp and marimba work to reinforce the tune, Harrison's solo, played on a nylon strung guitar, develops the melody. Borrowing licks from the likes of Django Reinhardt, Harrison adds bewitching ornamentation that counterpoints the melody perfectly.

Your Love Is Forever

George Harrison (vocals, guitars), Willie Weeks (bass), Steve Winwood (synthesiser), Andy Newmark (drums)

Harrison wrote the melody for 'Your Love Is Forever' on guitar using open D tuning. Like most slide guitar players he frequently used open tunings, and sure enough the song features a trademark Harrison slide solo. But what he wrote was a country mile from a rustic folk-blues tune. Harrison fashioned an exquisite melody that even in its rough hewn demo state caught producer Russ Titelman's ear. The producer was so smitten with it that he asked Harrison to add some lyrics pronto, so it could be included on the album they were about the record.

Harrison had to admit that he found it easier to write words and music together, and that it was always difficult to put words to a tune he'd already composed. However, he preserved because he knew he had something good. "In this case because I felt the tune was good I wanted the lyric also to be good, and to mean something," he explained.[20] He wrote the lyrics whilst in Hana, Maui, and they did have a special meaning for him. His initial idea was to write a love song, perhaps for Olivia, but that was soon abandoned in favour of a more ambiguous lyric that took God's love as its theme.

Once he'd found a way into the song by returning to a favourite theme, the changing seasons, the idea of eternal spiritual love quickly established itself. The seasons may come and go, the beauty of God's creation may also change, but His love is constant. Wrapping his paean to the Lord in ambiguous phrases, Harrison continued to nourish his soul without alienating those who may not share his views.

Having expressed his delight with Harrison's melody, Titelman ensured his production emphasized its graceful beauty. The first fifty seconds of the track comprise solely of Harrison's double-tracked guitar and Weeks' understated bass. Once again, Harrison used a Roland effect and claimed: "I think the success of the melody was largely due to the Roland effect on the guitars."[21] Harrison's guitar and vocal, also double-tracked in places, are placed high in the mix to emphasize the power of his melody and lyric. Harrison turns in a confident vocal performance on this challenging melody and sings with conviction and passion. The final touch was the addition of Winwood's synthesiser which provides just the right amount of texture without contaminating the melody. The resulting production floats as warm and sublime as the scent of night-blooming Jasmine wafting across a Maui sunset.

If You Believe (Harrison–Wright)
George Harrison (vocals, guitars), Willie Weeks (bass), Steve Winwood (synthesiser), Neil Larson (organ), Andy Newmark (drums), Ray Cooper (conga)

Besides having played on several of Harrison's albums, Gary Wright was also a friend and fellow Hindu. Wright had been introduced to ISKCON by his friend who encouraged his spiritual journey for over thirty-five years. "George Harrison was actually my mentor; he got me interested and introduced me to all that," he explained.[22] Wright visited the Harrisons over Christmas / New Year 1978 and played his host a fragment of a song he was working on. The two spent the rest of New Year's day and most of the night working on the melody. The lyrics were finished by Harrison later. Having admitted that he preferred writing music and words together, it's odd that he didn't do precisely that when working on the song with Wright. Instead, they decided to leave the song unfinished with Harrison writing the lyrics several weeks later while on holiday in Hawaii.

Harrison knew his friend well and wrote a lyric that he knew he'd appreciate. "I would have to say that there's a spiritual side to my lyrics," Wright confirmed. "I like to have positive lyrical messages, because I believe music is an uplifting force, not a negative force. So I try to make my music that way, so when people listen to it, they'll be in some way uplifted.[23] Harrison's lyric was exactly that. An open letter to his friend, it's a condensed contemplation on friendship, positive projection and Eastern philosophy. Its message is positive and spiritual, and it dovetailed nicely with Wright's faith.

Harrison's lyric suggests that his friend should stop worrying about things beyond his control and put his faith in the Lord. There are many things, including spiritual longing, that create disturbances we find troubling. It's the thoughts, emotions and opinions that we have gathered that distort our perception and cause us anxiety. They have been created subconsciously and if you stop creating them, they no longer exist. This state of affairs will continue for as long as you associate yourself with your physical body. The way to break the cycle is by experiencing oneself beyond the limitations of the physical body and mind. The way to do that is through the spiritual – that which is not physical or mental. Harrison reminds us that during prayer one is with God, our mind will clear, we will experience bliss and our troubles will recede, but only if you believe.

An up-beat pop song that recalls the kind of work Harrison produced with Phil Spector at the beginning of the decade, its layers of slide guitar and banks of synthesizers gave it a big commercial sound. Had it been released a few years earlier it could have topped the charts. As it was, Harrison was having to compete in a fast changing market place where disco and New Wave made 'If You Believe' sound positively old hat.

DARK HORSE RECORDS

A

K 17284
(DHS 0056)
K 17284 A
℗ 1979 Ganga
Distributors B.V.
Side 1
45 r.p.m.
STEREO

Produced
by George
Harrison &
Russ Titleman

Manufactured
in the UK

LOVE COMES TO EVERYONE (George Harrison)
(Edited from the LP K 56562 George Harrison)
GEORGE HARRISON
GANGA PUB'G B.V.
©Loka Productions S.A.

ALL RIGHTS OF THE MANUFACTURER AND OF THE OWNER OF THE RECORDED WORK RESERVED · UNAUTHORISED PUBLIC PERFORMANCE BROADCASTING AND COPYING

380

'Love Comes To Everyone' / 'Soft-Hearted Hana' [UK]
'Love Comes To Everyone' / 'Soft Touch' [US]
GEORGE HARRISON
Produced by George Harrison and Russ Titelman.
UK release: 20 April 1979; Dark Horse K 17284; chart high; failed to chart.
US release: 11 May 1979; Dark Horse DRC 8844; chart high; failed to chart.

The hit that never was. Had 'Love Comes To Everyone' been released a few years earlier, it would surely have been a hit. But for some reason, probably apathy from radio programmers and lack of airplay, it failed to register with the record buying public and flopped.

As with the first single taken from the album, 'Love Comes To Everyone' was issued with different B-sides for the American and British markets. The American edition, backed with 'Soft Touch', was also briefly available in a picture sleeve. This has become very difficult to find and commands serious money from collectors. Such is its rarity that reproductions are available, you have been warned. Based on the album cover, the picture sleeve featured the photo of Harrison surrounded by shrubbery. A mono / stereo promotional single with the same catalogue number as the commercial pressing was issued to US radio stations. The single was also manufactured with two label variations, one with small type the other with larger type. In Britain the single was issued with generic labels in a white paper sleeve or generic WEA sleeve.

George Harrison's much in-demand new single comes to radio and retail just in time. On the heels of his hit "Blow Away." Off the same gold-and-growing album...

"Love Comes to Everyone" (DRC 8844) from
George Harrison

Produced by George Harrison and Russ Titelman
On Dark Horse Records & Tapes (DHK 3255)

All royalties due to George Harrison from the sale of this record are being donated to the Gunnar Nilsson Cancer Fund.
K 17423

K 17423
(DHS 0116)
K 17423 A
℗ 1979 Ganga
Distributors B.V.
Side 1
45 r.p.m.
STEREO

Produced
by George
Harrison &
Russ Titelman
Manufactured
in the UK

FASTER (George Harrison)
(Taken from the LP K 56562 George Harrison)
GEORGE HARRISON
GANGA PUB'G B.V.
℗ Loka Productions S.A.

384

DARK HORSE RECORDS

A

K 17423
(DHS 0116)
K 17423 A
Ⓟ 1979 Ganga
Distributors B.V.
Side 1
45 r.p.m.
STEREO

Produced
by George
Harrison
& Russ Titelman

Manufactured
in the UK

ALL RIGHTS OF THE MANUFACTURER AND OF THE OWNER OF THE RECORDED WORK RESERVED · UNAUTHORISED PUBLIC PERFORMANCE BROADCASTING AND COPYING OF THIS RECORD PROHIBITED

FASTER (George Harrison)
(Taken from the LP K 56562 George Harrison)
GEORGE HARRISON
GANGA PUB'G B.V.
ⓅLoka Productions S.A.

DARK HORSE RECORDS

K 17423
(DHS 0116)
K 17423 B
Ⓟ 1979 Ganga
Distributors B.V.
Side 2
45 r.p.m.
STEREO

Produced
by George
Harrison
& Russ Titelman

Manufactured
in the UK

ALL RIGHTS OF THE MANUFACTURER AND OF THE OWNER OF THE RECORDED WORK RESERVED · UNAUTHORISED PUBLIC PERFORMANCE BROADCASTING AND COPYING OF THIS RECORD PROHIBITED

YOUR LOVE IS FOREVER (George Harrison)
(Taken from the LP K 56562 George Harrison)
GEORGE HARRISON
GANGA PUB'G B.V.
ⓅLoka Productions S.A.

George Harrison *Faster*

Your Love Is Forever

Chose a life in circuses
Jumped into the deepest end
Pushing himself to all extremes
Made it— people became his friend.
Now they stood and noticed him
Wanted to be a part of it
Pulled out some poor machinery
So he worked 'til the pieces fit.
The people were intrigued
His wife held back her fears
The headlines gave acclaim
He'd realized their dreams.
Faster than a bullet from a gun
He is faster than everyone
Quicker than the blinking of an eye
Like a flash you could miss him going by
No one knows quite how he does it but it's true
they say
He's the master of going faster.
Now he moved into the space
That the special people share
Right on the edge of do or die
Where there is nothing left to spare.
Still the crowds came pouring in
Some had hoped to see him fail
Filling their hearts with jealousies
Crazy people with love so frail.
The people were intrigued
His wife held back her fears
The headlines gave acclaim
He'd realized their dreams.
Faster than a bullet from a gun
He is faster than everyone
Quicker than the blinking of an eye
Like a flash you could miss him going by
No one knows quite how he does it but it's true
they say
He's the master of going faster.
No need to wonder why
His wife held back her fears
So few have even tried
To realize their dreams.
Faster than a bullet ... (repeat chorus)

*Words and Music by George Harrison. All Lyrics used by
permission. Reproduction prohibited. All rights reserved.
Both titles © 1979 Ganga Publishing B.V. WEA Records Ltd.
A Warner Communications Company. Made in U.K.
Printed in England by Garrod and Lofthouse Ltd.*

"Faster" is inspired by Jackie Stewart & Niki Lauda.
Dedicated to the Entire Formula One Circus
Special thanks to Jody Scheckter. In memory of Ronnie Peterson.

K1423P

385

'Faster' / 'Your Love Is Forever'
GEORGE HARRISON
Produced by George Harrison and Russ Titelman.
UK release: 30 July 1979; Dark Horse K 17423 and K 17423P (picture disc); chart high; failed to chart.

The third single from the *George Harrison* album, 'Faster' was only issued in Britain. Although a video was made to promote the record, like his previous single, it flopped. Royalties from the sale of the record went to the "Gunnar Nilsson Cancer Fund", a fund started after the death of the Swedish driver Gunnar Nilsson in 1978.

Dark Horse released the single with generic labels and generic WEA sleeve with a sticker alerting punters to the fact that Harrison was donating his royalties to charity. The picture disc was issued in a clear PVC sleeve with a printed card insert. It too had a sticker attached to the sleeve.

FOOTNOTES

Chapter 1

1. http://www.elsewhere.co.nz/film/3852/joe-massot-interviewed-2001-and-after-all-youre-my-wonderwall
2. Wonderwall Music CD booklet
3. Mojo, July 2012, page 61
4. Interview, Australian television, 30th November 1984
5. Wonderwall Music CD booklet
6. http://www.ravishankar.org/indian_music.html
7. Those Were The Days, Stefan Granados, page 60
8. Wonderwall Music CD booklet
9. Those Were The Days, Stefan Granados, page 60
10. Beatles Anthology, page 280.
11. Wonderwall Music CD booklet
12. Mojo, July 2012, page 61
13. Interview with the author
14. www.classicbands.com/JackieLomaxInterview.html
15. Jackie Lomax/2004/Terry Staunton/Record Collector/Jackie Lomax: Is This What You Want?
16. Mojo, November 2011, page 80
17. Beatles Anthology, page 267
18. The Beatles Off The Record, Keith Badman, page 382
19. NME, 21 September 1968.
20. I Me Mine, George Harrisonpage 142
21. www.classicbands.com/JackieLomaxInterview.html
22. NME, 21 September 1968.
23. Melody Maker, 28 September 1968
24. Melody Maker, 28 September 1968
25. www.classicbands.com/JackieLomaxInterview.html
26. Crawdaddy, February 1977
27. www.beatlesireland.info/George%20Harrison/Interviews/georgeinterview05.html
28. Interview with David Wigg, London, 1969
29. Beatles Anthology
30. The Beatles: Ten Year That Shook The World, page 366
31. The Beatles Anthology, page 318
32. Apple Record biography, www.applerecords.com/#!/albums/Album_ThatsTheWayGodPlannedIt
33. Billy Preston/1979/John Abbey/Blues & Soul/Billy Preston: No Longer Going Round In Circles!
34. Apple Record biography www.applerecords.com/#!/albums/Album_ThatsTheWayGodPlannedIt
35. Billy Preston/1979/John Abbey/Blues & Soul/Billy Preston: No Longer Going Round In Circles!
36. NME, 21 September 1968.
37. Howard Smith WABC-FM 3 May 1970
38. http://beatlesnumber9.com/mantra.html
39. Interview with David Wigg, London, 1969
40. http://beatlesnumber9.com/mantra.html
41. http://beatlesnumber9.com/mantra.html
42. http://beatlesnumber9.com/mantra.html
43. Radha Krishna Temple CD sleeve notes
44. The Beatles Off The Record, Keith Badman, page 469
45. Eric Clapton, Delaney & Bonnie/1969/Chris Welch/Melody Maker/Delaney & Bonnie: Out Of The South Comes 'The Best Band In The World'
46. http://www.swampland.com/articles/view/title:bobby_whitlock
47. Delaney & Bonnie/1970/Lenny Kaye/Rolling Stone/Delaney & Bonnie Homecoming Knocks 'Em Dead
48. Q, 16 January 1988
49. Delaney & Bonnie/1970/Lenny Kaye/Rolling Stone/Delaney & Bonnie Homecoming Knocks 'Em Dead

50. http://www.applerecords.com/#!/albums/Doris_Troy
51. http://www.applerecords.com/#!/albums/Doris_Troy
52. http://www.applerecords.com/#!/albums/Doris_Troy
53. The Beatles Undercover p 494
54. Rockline radio interview 10 February 1988
55. Doris Troy/1974/David Nathan/Blues & Soul/Doris Troy: Stretchin' Out and Gettin' Ahead
56. Doris Troy/1971/Roger St. Pierre/West Indian World/Doris Troy: This Little Lady Is Miss Troy
57. While My Guitar Gently Weeps: The Music Of George Harrison, Simon Leng, page 41
58. The Beatles Undercover, Keith Badman, page 495
59. http://www.applerecords.com/#!/albums/Album_EncouragingWords
60. I Me Mine, George Harrisonpage 162
61. http://www.applerecords.com/#!/albums/Album_EncouragingWords
62. I Me Mine, George Harrisonpage 176
63. Billboard, 30 December 2000
64. Howard Smith WABC-FM 3 May 1970
65. George Harrison, Living In The Material World, Lionsgate Films
66. Howard Smith WABC-FM 3 May 1970
67. Timothy White, George Harrison Reconsidered, page 69
68. Howard Smith WABC-FM 3 May 1970
69. Clapton: The Biography, page 132
70. Crawdaddy Magazine, February 1977
71. Mojo, July 2001
72. http://www.swampland.com/articles/view/title:bobby_whitlock
73. While My Guitar Gently Weeps: The Music Of George Harrison, Simon Leng, page 57
74. The Beatles: Off The Record 2 -The Dream Is Over, Keith Badman
75. Mojo, July 2001
76. Mojo, July 2001
77. Letter from Phil Spector to George Harrison 19 August 1970
78. Letter from Phil Spector to George Harrison 19 August 1970
79. Crawdaddy Magazine, February 1977
80. NME, date unknown
81. Rolling Stone, 21 January 1971
82. The Beatles Off The Record, Keith Badman
83. The Beatles Off The Record, Keith Badman
84. The Beatles Off The Record, Keith Badman
85. The Beatles Off The Record, Keith Badman
86. Melody Maker, 6 September 1975
87. The Beatles: The Dream Is Over, , Keith Badman, page 30
88. beatlesnumber9.com/mantra.html
89. The Beatles: The Dream Is Over, , Keith Badman, page 30
90. Melody Maker, 6 September 1975
91. Melody Maker, 6 September 1975
92. Interview with Anne Nightingale BBC Radio 1977
93. Billboard, 30 December 2000
94. Melody Maker, 6 September 1975
95. www.swampland.com
96. I Me Mine, George Harrison, page 194
97. http://www.songfacts.com/blog/interviews/bobby_whitlock/
98. I Me Mine, George Harrison, page 170
99. Unknown
100. The Beatles: Off The Record 2 -The Dream Is Over, Keith Badman
101. http://www.bobdylanroots.com/daniels.html
102. I Me Mine, George Harrison, page 206
103. Bobby Whitlock: A Rock 'n' Roll Autobiography, page 80
104. Bobby Whitlock: A Rock 'n' Roll Autobiography, page 80

105. I Me Mine, George Harrison, page 188

106. The Beatles: Off The Record 2 -The Dream Is Over, Keith Badman

107. I Me Mine, George Harrisonpage 200

108. beatlesnumber9.com/mantra.html

109. beatlesnumber9.com/mantra.html

110. beatlesnumber9.com/mantra.html

111. Billboard, 30 December 2000

112. The Beatles Thirty Days bootleg recording

113. Billboard, 30 December 2000

114. The Beatles Thirty Days bootleg recording

115. Beatles, The, George Harrison/1967/ Miles/International Times/The Way Out is In: A George Harrison

116. I Me Mine, George Harrison, page 180

117. George Harrison/1979/Mick Brown/Rolling Stone/An Interview with George Harrison/03/09/2012

118. Howard Smith interview 3 May 1970

119. I Me Mine, George Harrison, page 180

120. George Harrison: Living In The Material World, Lionsgate Films

121. Billboard, 30 December 2000

122. Billboard, 30 December 2000

123. Billboard, 30 December 2000

Chapter 2

1. Ronnie Spector/1971/Phil Symes/Disc and Music Echo/Ronnie Spector: Ronnie Tries It Solo/03/09/2012

2. Ronnie Spector/1971/Phil Symes/Disc and Music Echo/Ronnie Spector: Ronnie Tries It Solo/03/09/2012

3. I Me Mine, George Harrison, page 218

4. Ronnie Spector/1971/Phil Symes/Disc and Music Echo/Ronnie Spector: Ronnie Tries It Solo/03/09/2012

5. Ronnie Spector, Be My Baby: How I Survived Mascara, Miniskirts, and Madness, p 184

6. I, Me, Mine page 214

7. The Music Of George Harrison, page 98

8. I Me Mine, George Harrison, page 214

9. http://www.beatlesbible.com/1969/08/28/apple-launch-party-radha-krsna-temple/

10. The Beatles Tapes from the David Wigg Interviews, Polydor Records, 1976

11. http://www.beatlesbible.com/1969/08/28/apple-launch-party-radha-krsna-temple/

12. Interview with Anne Nightingale, BBC Radio, 1977

13. swampland.com/articles/view/title:leon_russell_Michael Buffalo Smith

14. I Me Mine, George Harrison, page 220.

15. The Beatles The Dream Is Over, Keith Badman, page 60.

16. I Me Mine, George Harrison, page 220.

17. The Beatles The Dream Is Over, Keith Badman, page 60.

18. Yoga Journal, November-December 1996.

19. Yoga Journal, November-December 1996.

20. Dan Matovina, Without You: The Tragic Story of Badfinger, page 135

21. Dan Matovina, Without You: The Tragic Story of Badfinger, page 136

22. Dan Matovina, Without You: The Tragic Story of Badfinger, page 137

23. The Beatles After The Break-Up, Keith Badman, page 38

24. Badfinger/1972/Mark Leviton/Phonograph Record/Badfinger At The Crossroads/03/09/2012

25. Dan Matovina, Without You: The Tragic Story of Badfinger, page 158

26. Interview with Anne Nightingale, BBC Radio 1977

27. The Concert For Bangladesh DVD booklet

28. Interview with Anne Nightingale, BBC Radio 1977

29. Eric Clapton/1974/Steve Turner/Rolling Stone/The Rolling Stone Interview:

30. Jesse Ed Davis/1973/Steven Rosen/LA Free Press/Rock And Roll's First Indian Superstar: Jesse 'Ed' Davis

31. Interview with Anne Nightingale, BBC Radio 1977

32. Interview with Anne Nightingale, BBC Radio 1977

33. Interview with Anne Nightingale, BBC Radio 1977
34. Interview with Anne Nightingale, BBC Radio 1977
35. www.guardian.co.uk/music/2011/jul/28/concert-for-bangladesh-charity-pop
36. NME, 16 October 1971
37. NME, 16 October 1971
38. NME, 16 October 1971
39. Dick Cavett show 23 November 1971
40. While My Guitar Gently Weeps: The Music Of George Harrison, Simon Leng, page 78.
41. Paul Du Noyer Interview Mojo June 2001
42. Paul Du Noyer Interview Mojo June 2001
43. http://www.beatlelinks.net/forums/showthread.php?t=47627

Chapter 3

1. I Me Mine, George Harrison, page 246
2. I Me Mine, George Harrison, page 226
3. http://www.acousticguitar.com/issues/ag122/feature122.html
4. Interview with Anne Nightingale, BBC Radio 1977
5. http://www.acousticguitar.com/issues/ag122/feature122.html
6. Interview with Anne Nightingale, BBC Radio 1977
7. Nicky Hopkins/1971/Andrew Tyler/Disc and Music Echo
8. Nicky Hopkins/1973/Harold Bronson/Zoo World
9. http://www.youtube.com/watch?v=Rel3bq_GqPA&list=HL1367829502
10. Stephen Holden, "George Harrison, Living in the Material World" album review, Rolling Stone, 19 July 1973
11. Pattiee Boyd, Wonderful Tonight, page 170
12. http://www.youtube.com/watch?v=PeJ352EdZBE
13. I Me Mine, George Harrison, page 268
14. Disc, 19 April 1969.
15. Interview with Dave Herman for the King Biscuit Flower Hour 1975
16. I Me Mine, George Harrison, page 43
17. John Lennon Playboy interview David Sheff, September 1980
18. I Me Mine, George Harrison, page 238
19. I Me Mine, George Harrison, page 258
20. I Me Mine, George Harrison, page 258
21. I Me Mine, George Harrison, page 258
22. http://www.spiritualworld.org/hinduism/print.htm
23. George Harrison interview with Nicky Horne 1974.
24. I Me Mine, George Harrison, page 254
25. Daytrippin', autumn 2003 page 27
26. Record Mirror, 15 April 1972.
27. Interview with Annie Nightingale, BBC Radio, 1975
28. Living In The Material World CD re-issue booklet
29. Norwegian Wood festival http://wogew.blogspot.co.uk/2011/05/q-with-ringo.html
30. http://beatlesinterviews.blogspot.co.uk/2009/02/ringo-starr-interview-inner-view-1976.html
31. Stuart Grundy, John Tobler, The Record producers, BBC Books, 1982
32. Stuart Grundy, John Tobler, The Record producers, BBC Books, 1982

Chapter 4

1. Disc and Music Echo, August 3 1968
2. Interview with Anne Nightingale, BBC Radio, 1977
3. Raga Mala, Ravi Shankar, page 224

4. Raga Mala, Ravi Shankar, page 222

5. Little Malcolm and His Struggle Against the Eunuchs DVD booklet, page 12

6. http://badfinge.ipower.com/Splinter/AnotherChance.html

7. Billboard, 8 June 1974

8. Melody Maker ,6 September 1975

9. Interview with Alan Freeman BBC Radio 1975

10. Melody Maker, 6 September 1975

11. Melody Maker, 6 September 1975

12. Interview with Alan Freeman BBC Radio 1975

13. Melody Maker, 6 September 1975

14. Circus Raves, "George Harrison: How Dark Horse Whipped Up A Winning Tour", March 1975

15. http://www.youtube.com/watch?feature=player_embedded&v=SZuvMs6ppHo

16. Anne Moore, Valley Advocate, 13th November 1974

17. Circus Raves, "George Harrison: How Dark Horse Whipped Up A Winning Tour", March 1975

18. While My Guitar Gently Weeps: The Music Of George Harrison, Simon Leng, page 113

19. Bob Woffinden, "George Harrison: Dark Horse", NME, 21 December 1974

20. I Me Mine, George Harrison, page 282

21. Ben Fong-Torres, Rolling Stone News Service

22. http://theweek.com/article/index/219764/george-harrison-the-beatle-who-hated-fame

23. http://music-illuminati.com/interview-robben-ford/

24. J. Greene, Here Comes The Sun, page 216

25. Eric Clapton The Autobiography, page 113

26. Wonderful Tonight, Pattie Harrison, page 180

27. Geoff Brown, Melody Maker, 10th November 1973

28. Melody Maker, 2nd November 1974

29. Interview with Alan Freeman, 18th October 1974

30. KLOL-FM, Levi Booker's Overnight Shift, 25th November 1974

31. Press conference, 23rd November 1974

32. Press conference, 23rd November 1974

33. Unknown source

34. Interview with Dave Herman broadcast 27th March 1975

35. Me Mine, George Harrison, page 37

36. The Beatles: The Dream Is Over, Keith Badman, page 150

37. Ronnie Wood, Ronnie, page 98

38. Interview with Alan Freeman, 1974

39. Chant And Be Happy, page 50

40. Raga Mala, Ravi Shankar, page 222

Chapter 5

1. Interview with Paul Gambaccini 1975

2. Interview with Paul Gambaccini 1975

3. NME, 8th March 1975

4. Interview with Dave Herman

5. Radio KHJ interview December 1974

6. Greg Shaw, Phonograph Record, December 1974

7. Interview with Dave Herman

8. http://musicandartinterviews.blogspot.com.au/2013/03/michael-lanning.html

9. http://musicandartinterviews.blogspot.com.au/2013/03/michael-lanning.html

10. Interview with Paul Gambaccini 1975

11. Interview with Anne Nightingale 1977

12. Interview with Paul Gambaccini 1975

13. Interview with Paul Gambaccini 1975

14. I Me Mine, George Harrison, page 312

15. Interview with Dave Herman
16. Interview with Dave Herman
17. Interview with Dave Herman
18. Interview with Paul Gambaccini 1975
19. Interview with Smokey Robinson
20. Interview with Paul Gambaccini 1975
21. Interview with Paul Gambaccini 1975
22. Interview with Paul Gambaccini 1975
23. Interview with Dave Herman
24. I Me Mine, George Harrison, page 308
25. Interview with Paul Gambaccini 1975
26. I Me Mine, George Harrison, page 274
27. Interview with Paul Gambaccini 1975
28. Interview with Paul Gambaccini 1975
29. Interview with Paul Gambaccini 1975
30. I Me Mine, George Harrison, page 304
31. Interview with Paul Gambaccini 1975
32. Charles Bermant, unpublished, 17 September 1987

Chapter 6

1. The Beatles Forever, Nicholas Schaffner, page 188
2. The Beatles Forever, Nicholas Schaffner, page 188
3. The Beatles After The Break-Up 1970-2000, page 197
4. 20. I Me Mine, George Harrison, page 200
5. Behind That Locked Door, Graeme Thomson, page 298
6. Raga Mala, Ravi Shankar. page 224
7. The Beatles: The Dream Is Over, Keith Badman, page 202
8. Behind That Locked Door, Graeme Thompson, page 300
9. The Beatles: The Dream Is Over, Keith Badman, page 202
10. The Beatles: The Dream Is Over, Keith Badman, page 206
11. The Beatles: The Dream Is Over, Keith Badman, page 202
12. Interview with Anne Nightingale BBC Radio 1977
13. Michael Gross, Swank, 1977
14. The Beatles Book Magazine, January 1977, page 4
15. I Me Mine, George Harrison, page 172
16. The Beatles: The Dream Is Over, Keith Badman, page 202
17. The Beatles: The Dream Is Over, Keith Badman, page 202
18. Jim Keltner Talking About George Harrison Rolling Stone (2002) http://harrisonstories.tumblr.com/post/55720407260/jim-keltner-talking-about-george-in-an-interview-with
19. Curves, contours and body horns: A Celebration Of Forty Years Of The Fender Stratocaster https://www.youtube.com/watch?v=h6r25HyQSkE
20. The Beatles: The Dream Is Over, Keith Badman, page 202
21. Crawdaddy Magazine, February 1977
22. The Beatles: The Dream Is Over, Keith Badman, page 202
23. The Beatles: The Dream Is Over, Keith Badman, page 202
24. Interview with Anne Nightingale BBC Radio 1977
25. The Beatles: The Dream Is Over, page 202
26. Michael Gross, Swank, 1977
27. I Me Mine, George Harrison, page 340
28. The Beatles: The Dream Is Over, Keith Badman, page 202
29. The Beatles: The Dream Is Over, Keith Badman, page 203
30. The Beatles: The Dream Is Over, Keith Badman,page 204
31. The Beatles: The Dream Is Over, Keith Badman, page 204
32. George Harrison Reconsidered, Timothy White page

33. The Beatles: The Dream Is Over, Keith Badman, page 204
34. The Beatles: The Dream Is Over, Keith Badman,page 204
35. The Beatles: The Dream Is Over, Keith Badman,page 204
36. I Me Mine, George Harrison,page 320
37. The Beatles: The Dream Is Over, Keith Badman, 204
38. The Beatles: The Dream Is Over, Keith Badman, page 205
39. The Beatles: The Dream Is Over, Keith Badman, page 205
40. Michael Gross, Swank, George Harrison: The Zoned-Out Beatle Turns 33
41. The Beatles: The Dream Is Over, Keith Badman, page 205
42. The Beatles: The Dream Is Over, Keith Badman, page 205

Chapter 7

1. I Me Mine page 378
2. http://spectropop.com/RussTitelman/index.htm.
3. http://spectropop.com/RussTitelman/index.htm.
4. Mick Brown, Rolling Stone, 19 April 1979
5. Mick Brown, Rolling Stone, 19 April 1979
6. Mick Brown, Rolling Stone, 19 April 1979
7. Mick Brown, Rolling Stone, 19 April 1979
8. Mick Brown, Rolling Stone, 19 April 1979
9. George Harrison: Reconsidered, Timothy White
10. http://spectropop.com/RussTitelman/index.htm.
11. Roundtable BBC Radio 9th February 1979
12. I Me Mine, George Harrisonpage 362
13. http://www.beliefnet.com/Entertainment/Music/2001/12/Deepak-Chopra-On-His-Friend-George-Harrison.aspx
14. Mick Brown, Rolling Stone, 19 April 1979
15. Mick Brown, Rolling Stone, 19 April 1979
16. Roundtable, BBC Radio 9th February 1979
17. Roundtable, BBC Radio 9th February 1979
18. I Me Mine, George Harrison, page 370
19. Mick Brown, Rolling Stone, 19 April 1979
20. I Me Mine, George Harrison, page 362
21. I Me Mine, George Harrison, page 362
22. http://blog.musoscribe.com/?p=294
23. http://blog.musoscribe.com/?p=294

DISCOGRAPHY

Wonderwall Music
Side one: Microbes / Red Lady Too / Tabla and Pakavaj / In the Park / Drilling a Home / Guru Vandana / Greasy Legs / Ski-ing / Gat Kirwani / Dream Scene
Side two: Party Seacombe / Love Scene / Crying / Cowboy Music / Fantasy Sequins / On the Bed / Glass Box / Wonderwall to Be Here / Singing Om
UK release: 1 November 1968; Apple APCOR 1 / SAPCOR 1; failed to chart.
US release: 2 December 1968; Apple ST-3350; chart high; number 49.

Electronic Sound
Side one: Under The Mersey Wall
Side two: No Time Or Space
UK release: 9 May 1969; Zapple ZAPPLE 02; failed to chart.
US release: 26 May 1969; Zapple ST-3358; failed to chart.

'My Sweet Lord' / 'Isn't It a Pity' (US)
'My Sweet Lord' / 'What Is Life' (UK)
US release: 23 November 1970; Apple 2995; chart high; number 1.
UK release: 15 January 1971; Apple R5884; chart high; number 1.

All Things Must Pass
Side one: I'd Have You Anytime (Harrison—Dylan) / My Sweet Lord / Wah-Wah / Isn't It a Pity (Version One)
Side two: What Is Life / If Not for You (Dylan) / Behind That Locked Door / Let It Down / Run of the Mill
Side three: Beware of Darkness / Apple Scruffs / Ballad of Sir Frankie Crisp (Let It Roll) /Awaiting on You All / All Things Must Pass
Side four: I Dig Love / Art of Dying / Isn't It a Pity (Version Two) / Hear Me Lord
Side five: Out of the Blue / It's Johnny's Birthday (Bill Martin, Phil Coulter, Harrison) / Plug Me In
Side six: I Remember Jeep / Thanks for the Pepperoni
UK release: November 30 1970; STCH 639; chart high; number 1.
US release: November 27 1970; STCH 639; chart high; number 1.

'What Is Life' / 'Apple Scruffs'
US release: 27 February 1971; Apple 1821; chart high; number 10.

'Bangla-Desh' / 'Deep Blue'
UK release: 30 July 1971 ; Apple R5912; chart high; number 10.
US release: 28 July 1971; Apple 1836; chart high; number 23.

The Concert For Bangladesh
Various Artists
Side one: Introduction (Harrison and Shankar) / Bangla Dhun (Shankar)
Side two: Wah-Wah (Harrison) / My Sweet Lord (Harrison) / Awaiting On You All (Harrison) / That's The Way God Planned It (Billy Preston)
Side three: It Don't Come Easy (Ringo Starr) / Beware of Darkness (Harrison and Russell) / Band Introduction (Harrison) / While My Guitar Gently Weeps (Harrison)
Side four: Medley: Jumpin' Jack Flash/Youngblood (Russell and Don Preston) / Here Comes The Sun (Harrison)
Side five: A Hard Rain's A-Gonna Fall (Dylan) / It Takes A Lot To Laugh, It Takes A Train To Cry (Dylan) / Blowin' In The Wind (Dylan) / Mr. Tambourine Man (Dylan) / Just Like A Woman (Dylan)
Side six: Something (Harrison) / Bangla-Desh
UK release: 10 January 1972; Apple ; chart high; number 1.
US release: 20 December 1971, Apple ; chart high; number 2.

'Give Me Love (Give Me Peace On Earth)' / 'Miss O'Dell'
UK release: 25 May 1973; Apple R 5988; chart high; number 8.
US release: 7 May 1973; Apple 1862; chart high; number 1.

Living In The Material World
Side one: Give Me Love (Give Me Peace on Earth) / Sue Me, Sue You Blues / The Light That Has Lighted the World / Don't Let Me Wait Too Long / Who Can See It / Living in the Material World
Side two: The Lord Loves the One (That Loves the Lord) / Be Here Now / Try Some, Buy Some / The Day the World Gets 'Round / That Is All
UK release: 22 June 1973; Apple PAS 10006; chart high; number 2.
US release: 30 May 1973; Apple SMAS 3410; chart high; number 1.

'Dark Horse' / 'I Don't Care Anymore'
UK release: 28 February 1975; Apple R 6001; chart high; failed to chart.
US release: 18 November 1974; Apple 1877; chart high; number 15.

Dark Horse
Side one: Hari's on Tour (Express) / Simply Shady / So Sad / Bye Bye, Love (Felice Bryant, Boudleaux Bryant, George Harrison) / Māya Love
Side two: Ding Dong; Ding Dong / Dark Horse / Far East Man (George Harrison, Ron Wood) / It Is 'He' (Jai Sri Krishna)
UK release: 20 December 1974; Apple PAS 10008; chart high; failed to chart.
US release: 9 December 1974; Apple SMAS 3418; chart high; number 4.

'Ding Dong; Ding Dong' / 'Hari's on Tour (Express)' / 'I Don't Care Anymore'
UK release: 6 December 1974; Apple R 6002; chart high; number 38.
US release: 23 December 1974; Apple 1879; chart high; number 36.

'You' / 'World Of Stone'
UK release: 12 September 1975; Apple R 6007; chart high; number 38.
US release: 15 September 1975; Apple 1884; chart high; number 20.

Extra Texture (Read All About It)
Side one: You / The Answer's at the End / This Guitar (Can't Keep from Crying) / Ooh Baby (You Know That I Love You) / World of Stone
Side two: A Bit More of You / Can't Stop Thinking About You / Tired of Midnight Blue / Grey Cloudy Lies / His Name Is Legs (Ladies and Gentlemen)
UK release: 3 October 1975; Apple PAS 10009; chart high; No. 16.
US release: 22 September 1975; Apple SW-3420; chart high No.8.

'This Guitar (Can't Keep from Crying)' / 'Maya Love'
UK release: 6 February 1976; Apple R 6012; chart high; failed to chart.
US release: 8 December 1975; Apple 1885; chart high; failed to chart.

Best Of
Side one: Something / If I Needed Someone / Here Comes the Sun / Taxman / Think for Yourself / For You Blue / While My Guitar Gently Weeps
Side two: My Sweet Lord / Give Me Love (Give Me Peace on Earth) / You / Bangla Desh / Dark Horse / What Is Life
UK release: 20 November 1976; Parlophone PAS 10011; chart high; failed to chart.
US release: 8 November 1976; Capitol DT 11578; chart high No. 31.

'My Sweet Lord' / 'Isn't It A Pity'
UK release: 19 November 1976; Apple R 5884; chart high; failed to chart.

Thirty Three And ⅓
Side one: Woman Don't You Cry for Me / Dear One / Beautiful Girl / This Song / See Yourself
Side two: It's What You Value / True Love / Pure Smokey / Crackerbox Palace / Learning How to Love You
UK release: 19 November 1976; Dark Horse K 56319; chart high; No. 35.
US release: 24 November 1976; Dark Horse DH 3005; chart high No.11.

'This Song' / 'Learning How To Love You'
UK release: 19 November 1976; Dark Horse K 16856; chart high; failed to chart.
US release: 3 November 1976; Dark Horse DRC 8294; chart high; number 25.

'Crackerbox Palace' / 'Learning How To Love You'
US release: 24 January 1977; Dark Horse DRC 8313; chart high; number 19.

'True Love' / 'Pure Smokey'
UK release: 11 February 1977; Dark Horse K 16896; chart high; failed to chart.

'It's What You Value' / 'Woman Don't You Cry For Me'
UK release: 31 May 1977; Dark Horse K 16967; chart high; failed to chart.

'Blow Away' / 'Soft Touch' [UK]
'Blow Away' / 'Soft-Hearted Hana' [US]
UK release: 16 February 1979; Dark Horse K 17327; chart high; number 51.
US release: 14 February 1979; Dark Horse DRC 8763; chart high; number 16.

George Harrison
Side one: Love Comes to Everyone / Not Guilty / Here Comes The Moon / Soft-Hearted Hana /Blow Away
Side two: Faster / Dark Sweet Lady / Your Love Is Forever / Soft Touch / If You Believe (Harrison/Gary Wright)
UK release: 23 February 1979; Dark Horse K 56562; chart high; No. 39.
US release: 20 February 1979; Dark Horse DH 3255; chart high No.14.

'Love Comes To Everyone' / 'Soft-Hearted Hana' [UK]
'Love Comes To Everyone' / 'Soft Touch' [US]
UK release: 20 April 1979; Dark Horse K 17284; chart high; failed to chart.
US release: 11 May 1979; Dark Horse DRC 8844; chart high; failed to chart.

'Faster' / 'Your Love Is Forever'
UK release: 30 July 1979; Dark Horse K 17423 and K 17423P (picture disc); chart high; failed to chart.

PRODUCED BY GEORGE HARRISON

The Remo Four
'In The First Place'
Recorded 1967 at Abbey Road Studios during the *Wonderwall Music* sessions.
UK release: 15 March 1998; PILAR O2V; failed to chart.

'Sour Milk Sea' / 'The Eagle Laughs At You'
Jackie Lomax
UK release: 6 September 1968; Apple 3; failed to chart.
US release: 26 August 1968; Apple 1802; failed to chart.

Is This What You Want?
Jackie Lomax
UK release: 21 March 1969; Apple APCOR 6 / SAPCOR 6; failed to chart.
US release: 19 May 1969; Apple ST-3354; failed to chart.

'That's The Way God Planned It' / 'What About You?'
Billy Preston
UK release: 27 June 1969; Apple 12; chart high; number 11.
US release: 14 July 1969; Apple 1808; failed to chart.

That's The Way God Planned It
Billy Preston
Side one: Do What You Want / I Want To Thank You / Everything's Alright / She Belongs to Me / It Doesn't Matter / Morning Star
Side two: Hey Brother / What About You / Let Us All Get Together (Right Now) / This Is it / Keep It To Yourself / That's The Way God Planned It (Parts 1 & 2)
UK release 22 August 1969; SAPCOR 9; failed to chart.
US release 10 September 1969; ST-3359; failed to chart.

'Hare Krishna Mantra' / 'Prayer To The Spiritual Masters'
Radha Krsna Temple [London]
Produced by George Harrison
UK release: 29 August 1969; Apple 15; chart high; number 12.
US release: 22 August 1969; Apple 1810; failed to chart.

'All That I Got (I'm Going To Give It To You)' / 'As I Get Older'
Billy Preston
UK release: 30 January 1970; Apple 21; failed to chart.
US release: 2 March 1970; Apple 1817; failed to chart.

'Ain't That Cute' / 'Vaya Con Dios'
Doris Troy
UK release: 13 February 1970; Apple 24; failed to chart.
US release: 16 March 1970; Apple 1820; failed to chart.

'Govinda' / 'Govinda Jai Jai'
Radha Krsna Temple [London]
UK release: 6 March 1970; Apple 25; number 23.
US release: 24 March 1970; Apple 1821; failed to chart.

'Jacob's Ladder' / 'Get Back'
Doris Troy
UK release: 28 August 1970; Apple 28; failed to chart.
US release: 21 September 1970; Apple 1824; failed to chart.

Doris Troy
Doris Troy
Side one: Ain't That Cute / Special Care / Give Me Back My Dynamite / You Tore Me Up Inside / Games People Play /
Gonna Get My Baby Back / I've Got To Be Strong
Side two: Hurry / So Far / Exactly Like You / You Give Me Joy Joy / Don't Call Me No More / Jacob's Ladder
UK release: 4 September 1970, SAPCOR 13; failed to chart.
US release: 11 September 1970, ST-3371; failed to chart.

Encouraging Words
Billy Preston
Side one: Right Now / Little Girl / Use What You Got / My Sweet Lord (George Harrison) / Let the Music Play / The
Same Thing Again
Side two: I've Got a Feeling / Sing One for the Lord (Harrison—Preston) / When You Are Mine / I Don't Want You to
Pretend / Encouraging Words / All Things Must Pass (Harrison) / You've Been Acting Strange
UK release: 11 September 1970, SAPCOR 14; failed to chart.
US release: 1970, ST-3370; failed to chart.

'It Don't Come Easy' / 'Early 1970'
Ringo Starr
UK release: 9 April 1971 ; Apple R5898; chart high; number 4.
US release: 16 April 1971; Apple 1831; chart high; number 4.

Radha Krsna Temple
Radha Krsna Temple
Side one: Govinda / Sri Guruvastakam / Bhaja Bhakata-Arati / Hare Krishna Mantra
Side two: Sri Ishopanishad / Bhajahu Re Mana / Govinda Jai Jai
UK release: 21 May 1971; SAPCOR 18; chart high; failed to chart.
US release: 28 May 1971; ST3359; chart high; failed to chart.

'Joi Bangla' / 'Oh Bhaugowan' / 'Raga Mishra-Jhinjhoti'
Ravi Shankar
UK release: 27 August 1971; Apple 37; chart high; failed to chart.
US release: 28 August 1971; Apple 1838; chart high; failed to chart.

Raga
Ravi Shankar
Side one: Dawn To Dusk / Vedic Hymns / Baba Teaching / Birth To Death / Vinus House / Gurur Bramha / United Nations
Side two: Raga Parameshwari / Rangeswhari / Banaras Ghat / Bombay Studio / Kinnara School / Frenzy And Distortion / Raga Desh
US release: 7 December 1971, Apple SWAO 3384; chart high; failed to chart.

Straight Up
Badfinger
Side one: Take It All / Baby Blue / Money / Flying / I'd Die Babe* / Name of the Game*
Side two: Suitcase*? / Sweet Tuesday Morning** / Day After Day* / Sometimes / Perfection / It's Over
UK release: 13 December 1971; Apple SAPCOR 19; chart high; failed to chart.
US release: 11 February 1972, Apple ST3387; chart high; number 31.

'Back Off Boogaloo' / 'Blindman'
Ringo Starr
UK release: 17 March 1972 ; Apple R5944; chart high; number 2.
US release: 20 March 1972; Apple 1849; chart high; number 9.

Shankar Family & Friends
Ravi Shankar
Side one: I Am Missing You / Kahan Gayelava Shyam Saloné / Supané Mé Ayé Preetam Sainya / I Am Missing You (reprise) / Jaya Jagadish Haré
Side two: Dream, Nightmare & Dawn (Music For a Ballet) Overture Part One (Dream): Festivity & Joy : Love-Dance Ecstasy / Part Two (Nightmare): Lust (Raga Chandrakauns) : Dispute & Violence : Disillusionment & Frustration : Despair & Sorrow (Raga Marwa) / Part Three (Dawn):
Awakening : Peace & Hope (Raga Bhatiyar)
UK release: 20 September 1974; Dark Horse AMLH 220002; chart high; failed to chart.
US release: 7 October 1974; Dark Horse SP 220002; chart high; failed to chart.

Thye Place I Love
Splinter
Side one: Gravy Train / Drink All Day (Got to Find Your Own Way Home) / China Light / Somebody's City
Side two: Costafine Town / The Place I Love / Situation Vacant / Elly-May / Haven't Got Time
UK release: 20 September 1974; Dark Horse AMLH 220001; chart high; failed to chart.
US release: 20 September; Dark Horse SP 220001; chart high; failed to chart.

'Lumberjack Song' / 'Spam Song'
Monty Python
UK release: 14 November 1975; Charisma CB 268; chart high; failed to chart.

COLLABORATIONS

1968
Jackie Lomax
'Sour Milk Sea' b/w 'The Eagle Laughs At You'
Harrison produces and plays guitar

1969
Cream
'Badge'
George Harrison co-writes with Clapton and plays guitar,

Jackie Lomax
Is This What You Want? (album)
Harrison produces and plays guitar

Billy Preston
'That's The Way God Planned It' b/w 'What About You'
Harrison produces and plays guitar

Billy Preston
That's The Way God Planned (album)
Harrison produces and plays guitar

The Radha Krishna Temple
'Hare Krishna Mantra' b/w 'Prayer To The Spiritual Masters'
Harrison produces and plays various instruments

Jack Bruce
'Never Tell Your Mother Sings Out Of Tune' from the *Songs For A Tailor* album
Harrison plays guitar

Joe Cocker
'Something'
Harrison plays guitar

John & Yoko/Plastic Ono Band
'Cold Turkey' / 'Don't Worry Kyoko' recorded live at the Lyceum from the *Some Time In New York City* album
Harrison plays guitar

John Lennon with The Plastic Ono Band
'Instant Karma'
Harrison plays piano and guitar

Leon Russell
Leon Russell: 'Delta Lady' / 'Pisces Apple Lady' issued as single
Harrison plays guitar

Delaney And Bonnie
Delaney & Bonnie & Friends On Tour
Harrison plays guitar

Jackie Lomax
'How The Web Was Woven' b/w 'Thumbing A Ride'
Harrison produces A-side and plays guitar

Doris Troy
'Ain't That Cute' b/w 'Vaya Con Dios'
Harrison produces and plays guitar

Doris Troy
'Get Back' b/w 'Jacob's Ladder'
Harrison produces and plays guitar

Doris Troy
Doris Troy (album)
Harrison produces and plays guitar

Billy Preston
Encouraging Words (album)
Harrison produces and plays guitar

Derek & The Dominos
'Roll It Over'
Harrison plays guitar and sings backing vocals

Ashton, Gardner and Dyke
'I'm Your Spiritual Breadman' from *The Worst of Ashton, Gardner and Dyke* album
Harrison plays guitar and sings backing vocals

Bob Dylan
'If Not For You' from *The Bootleg Series Volumes 1-3* [rare & unreleased] 1961-1991
Harrison plays guitar

1971
Ringo Starr
'It Don't Come Easy' b/w 'Early 1970'
Harrison produces and plays guitar

Ronnie Spector
'Try Some, Buy Some' b/w 'Tandoori Chicken'
Harrison writes and plays guitar

The Radha Krishn Temple
'Govinda' b/w 'Govinda Jai Jai'
Harrison produces

The Radha Krishn Temple
The Radha Krishna Temple (album)
Harrison produces and plays various instruments

Gary Wright
Footprint: 'Stand For Our Rights' b/w 'I Can't See The Reason' issued as single
Harrison plays slide guitar

John Lennon/Plastic Ono Band with The Flux Fiddlers
Imagine (album)
Harrison plays electric and slide guitar on 'I Don't Wanna Be a Soldier', 'Gimme Some Truth', 'Oh My Love', and 'How Do You Sleep?'; dobro on 'Crippled Inside'

Billy Preston
'I Wrote A Simple Song' from the album *I Wrote A Simple Song*
Harrison plays guitar

1972
Badfinger
Straight Up (album)
Harrison produces tracks 5–7, 9 and plays slide guitar on 'Day After Day', guitar on 'I'd Die Babe'

Lon & Derrek Van Eaton
Brother (album)
Harrison produces 'Sweet Music'

Bobby Whitlock
Bobby Whitlock
Harrison plays on 'Where There's a Will' and 'Back in My Life Again'

Ringo Starr
'Back Off Boogaloo'
Harrison produces and plays guitar

Ravi Shankar
In Concert 1972
Harrison produces

Jesse 'Ed' Davis
'Sue Me, Sue You Blues' from the *Ululu* album
Harrison writes 'Sue Me, Sue You Blues'

David Bromberg
'The Hold Up'
Harrison co-writes with David Bromberg and plays guitar

Bobby Keys
Bobby Keys (album)
Harrison plays guitar

Harry Nilsson
Son Of Schmisson
Harrison plays slide guitar on 'You're Breaking My Heart'

1973
Dave Mason
'If You've Got Love' from the album *It's Like You Never Left*
Harrison plays slide guitar

Don Nix
'I Need You' and 'The Train Don't Stop Here No More'* from the album *Hobos, Heroes and Street Corner Clowns*
Harrison plays slide guitar and vocals "That's great Bob, come and hear it."*

Nicky Hopkins
The Tin Man Was A Dreamer
Harrison plays electric guitar, slide guitar (credited as George O'Hara)

Cheech And Chong
'Basket Ball Jones'
Harrison plays electric guitar

Ringo Starr
Ringo album
Harrison co-writes 'Photograph' and 'You and Me (Babe)', writes 'Sunshine Life for Me (Sail Away Raymond)', plays guitar on 'I'm The Greatest', 'Sunshine Life for Me (Sail Away Raymond)' and 'You and Me (Babe)'

Alvin Lee & Mylon Lefevre
'So Sad (No Love Of His Own)' from the album *On The Road To Freedom*
Harrison writes 'So Sad (No Love Of His Own)' plays guitar, slide guitar and bass

1974
Harry Nilson
'Day Break' from *Son Of Dracula* album
Harrison plays cow bell

Ravi Shankar
Shankar Family & Friends
Harrison produces and plays

Splinter
The Place I Love
Harrison produces and plays

Ron Wood
'Far East Man' from the album *I've Got My Own Album To Do*
Harrison co-writes 'Far East Man' and plays guitar

1975
Billy Preston
'That's Life' from the album *It's My Pleasure*
Harrison plays slide guitar

Peter Skellern
'Make Love Not War' from the album *Hard Times*
Harrison plays guitar

Splinter
'Lonely Man' from the album *Harder To Live*
Harrison plays slide guitar

1976
Ringo Starr
'I'll Still Love You' from the album *Ringo's Rotogravure*
Harrison writes 'I'll Still Love You'

Ravi Shankar
Ravi Shankar's Music Festival From India
Harrison produces

Monty Python
Lumberjack Song
Harrison produces

Tom Scott
'Aporonia (Foxtrata)' from the album *New York Connection*
Harrison plays slide guitar

Larry Hosford
'Direct Me' and 'Wishing I Could' from the album *Crossroads*
Harrison plays slide guitar and sings harmony vocals

1977
Splinter
'Round and Round', 'Motions Of Love', 'Love Is Enough' from the album *Two Man Band*
Harrison plays slide guitar

1978
Daryl Hall & John Oates
'The Last Time' from the album *Along The Red Ledge*
Harrison plays slide guitar

INDEX

CPSIA information can be obtained
at www.ICGtesting.com
Printed in the USA
LVOW06*1753020118
561540LV00018B/85/P